Lecture Notes in Computer Science 9369

Commenced Publication in 1973
Founding and Former Series Editors:
Gerhard Goos, Juris Hartmanis, and Jan van Leeuwen

More information about this series at http://www.springer.com/series/7411

Joachim Fischer · Markus Scheidgen
Ina Schieferdecker · Rick Reed (Eds.)

SDL 2015: Model-Driven Engineering for Smart Cities

17th International SDL Forum
Berlin, Germany, October 12–14, 2015
Proceedings

 Springer

Editors
Joachim Fischer
Humboldt-Universität zu Berlin
Berlin
Germany

Markus Scheidgen
Humboldt-Universität zu Berlin
Berlin
Germany

Ina Schieferdecker
Fraunhofer FOKUS
Berlin
Germany

Rick Reed
Telecommunications Software Engineering
Windermere
UK

ISSN 0302-9743   ISSN 1611-3349   (electronic)
Lecture Notes in Computer Science
ISBN 978-3-319-24911-7   ISBN 978-3-319-24912-4   (eBook)
DOI 10.1007/978-3-319-24912-4

Library of Congress Control Number: 2015950001

LNCS Sublibrary: SL5 – Computer Communication Networks and Telecommunications

Printed on acid-free paper

Springer International Publishing AG Switzerland is part of Springer Science+Business Media
(www.springer.com)

Preface

The System Design Languages Forum (SDL Forum), held every two years, is an international conference that provides an open arena for participants from academia and industry to present and discuss recent innovations, trends, experiences, and concerns in the field of system design languages and modeling technologies. Originally focussing on the Specification and Description Language — standardized and further developed by the International Telecommunications Union (ITU) over a period of nearly 40 years — the SDL Forum has broadened its topics in the course of time.

The SDL Forum conference series is run by the SDL Forum Society, a non-profit organization founded in 1995 by language users and tool providers to promote the ITU Specification and Description Language and related system design languages, including, for instance, Message Sequence Charts (MSC), Abstract Syntax Notation One (ASN.1), Testing and Test Control Notation (TTCN-3), User Requirements Notation (URN), Unified Modeling Language™ (UML), and Systems Modeling Language™ (SysML).

The local co-organizers of the 17th edition of the SDL Forum (SDL 2015) were the Humboldt-Universität zu Berlin and Fraunhofer FOKUS. A special focus of SDL 2015 was on model-driven engineering for smart cities: In the future, new information and communication technologies will be integrated in more and more buildings, streets, and institutions. The challenge will be to allow all citizens a seamless access to relevant information, to sustainably and economically use the available resources, to master the growing claims of networked mobility infrastructures, and to organize a modern, citizen-friendly administration. Modeling the structure and behavior of these kinds of complex systems of different domains requires adequate description, computation, testing, and general software techniques. Thus, the use of models serves no end in itself but should ideally allow for automatic derivation of complex software from models. In addition, practical problems of performance, scalability, robustness, and security of such systems come into the focus of interest.

This volume contains the papers presented at SDL 2015: 19 high-quality papers selected from 26 submissions. Each paper was peer reviewed by at least three Program Committee members and discussed during the online Program Committee meeting. The selected papers cover a wide spectrum of topics related to system design languages, ranging from the System Design Language usage and evolution to model transformations, and are grouped into six technical sessions as reflected in this volume. The first session is devoted to smart cities and distributed systems. The papers in the second session propose changes to the ITU-T Specification and Description Language. Domain-specific languages are proposed in the third session papers, followed by a number of papers tackling different issues related to goal modeling. The fifth session includes a set of papers on use-case modeling before concluding with contributions on model-based testing.

The SDL Forum has been made possible by the dedicated work and contributions of many people and organizations. We thank the authors of submitted papers, the members of the Program Committee, and the members of the SDL Forum Society Board. We thank the communications services, conference services, and instructional and information technology services of Fraunhofer FOKUS for their support. The submission and review process was run with easychair.org, and we thank the people behind the EasyChair conference system. We thank the sponsors of SDL 2015: Technische Universität Kaiserslautern, PragmaDev, Fraunhofer FOKUS, Humboldt-Universität zu Berlin, and SDL Forum Society.

October 2015   Joachim Fischer
                                                               Markus Scheidgen
                                                               Ina Schieferdecker
                                                               Rick Reed

SDL Forum Society

The SDL Forum Society is a not for profit organization that, in addition to running the System Design Languages Forum (SDL Forum) conference series of events (once every two years), also:

- Runs the System Analysis and Modelling (SAM) workshop series, every 2 years between SDL Forum years.
- Is a body recognized by ITU-T as co-developing System Design Languages in the Z.100 series (Specification and Description Language), Z.120 series (Message Sequence Chart), Z.150 series (User Requirements Notation) and other language standards.
- Promotes the ITU-T System Design Languages.

For more information on the SDL Forum Society, see http://www.sdl-forum.org.

Organization

Chairs

Joachim Fischer	Humboldt-Universität zu Berlin, Germany
Markus Scheidgen	Humboldt-Universität zu Berlin, Germany
Ina Schieferdecker	Fraunhofer FOKUS/Freie Universität Berlin, Germany
Holger Schlingloff	Fraunhofer FOKUS/Humboldt-Universität zu Berlin, Germany

Members

Reinhard Gotzhein	Chairman SDL Forum Society
Ferhat Khendek	Secretary SDL Forum Society
Joachim Thees	Treasurer SDL Forum Society
Rick Reed	Non-voting member of SDL Forum Society Board

Program Committee

Conference Chairs

Joachim Fischer	Humboldt-Universität zu Berlin, Germany
Markus Scheidgen	Humboldt-Universität zu Berlin, Germany
Ina Schieferdecker	Fraunhofer FOKUS/Freie Universität Berlin, Germany
Holger Schlingloff	Fraunhofer FOKUS/Humboldt-Universität zu Berlin, Germany
Reinhard Gotzhein	Chairman SDL Forum Society

Members

Daniel Amyot	University of Ottawa, Canada
Pau Fonseca i Casas	Universitat Politècnica de Catalunya, Spain
Gunter Mussbacher	McGill University, Canada
Shaukat Ali	Simula Research Laboratory, Norway
Rolv Bræk	NTNU Trondheim, Norway
Reinhard Brocks	HTW Saarland, Germany
Jean-Michel Bruel	University of Toulouse, France
Anders Ek	IBM Rational, Sweden
Stein Erik Ellevseth	ABB Corporate Research, Norway
Joachim Fischer	Humboldt-Universität zu Berlin, Germany
Markus Scheidgen	Humboldt-Universität zu Berlin, Germany
Emmanuel Gaudin	PragmaDev, France
Birgit Geppert	Avaya, USA

Abdelouahed Gherbi	École de technologie supérieure, Université du Québec, Canada
Reinhard Gotzhein	Technische Universität Kaiserslautern, Germany
Jens Grabowski	University of Göttingen, Germany
Øystein Haugen	SINTEF, Norway
Loïc Hélouët	Inria Rennes, France
Peter Herrmann	NTNU Trondheim, Norway
Andreas Hoffmann	Fraunhofer FOKUS, Germany
Dieter Hogrefe	University of Göttingen, Germany
Ferhat Khendek	Concordia University, Canada
Tae-Hyong Kim	Kumoh National Institute of Technology, Korea
Jacques Klein	University of Luxembourg, Luxembourg
Finn Kristoffersen	Cinderella, Denmark
Anna Medve	University of Pannonia, Hungary
Pedro Merino Gómez	University of Malaga, Spain
Birger Møller-Pedersen	University of Oslo, Norway
Patricio Moreno Montero	ACCIONA, Spain
Ileana Ober	University of Toulouse, France
Iulian Ober	University of Toulouse, France
Fei Peng	Siemens CT, China
Dorina Petriu	Carleton University, Canada
Andreas Prinz	Agder University College, Norway
Rick Reed	TSE, UK
Tom Ritter	Fraunhofer FOKUS, Germany
Manuel Rodriguez-Cayetano	Valladolid University, Spain
Richard Sanders	SINTEF, Norway
Amardeo Sarma	NEC Laboratories Europe, Germany
Ina Schieferdecker	Fraunhofer FOKUS/Freie Universität Berlin, Germany
Holger Schlingloff	Fraunhofer FOKUS/Humboldt-Universität zu Berlin, Germany
Edel Sherratt	University of Wales Aberystwyth, UK
Maria Toeroe	Ericsson, Canada
Peter Tröger	Potsdam University, Germany
Hans Vangheluwe	University of Antwerp, Belgium/McGill University, Canada
Martin von Löwis	Beuth-Hochschule für Technik Berlin, Germany
Thomas Weigert	Missouri University of Science and Technology and UniqueSoft, USA
Manuel Wimmer	Technische Universität Wien, Austria
Steffen Zschaler	King's College London, UK

Additional Reviewers

Ella Albrecht	Thomas Hartmann	Tanja Mayerhofer
El Kouhen Amine	Christopher Henard	Shuai Wang
Alexander Bergmayr	Hartmut Lackner	

Contents

Goal Modeling

Use-Case Modeling

Model-Based Testing

Smart Cities and Distributed Systems

Insertion Modeling and Symbolic Verification of Large Systems

Alexander Letichevsky[1], Oleksandr Letychevskyi[1], Volodymyr Peschanenko[2], and Thomas Weigert[3]([✉])

[1] Glushkov Institute of Cybernetics, Academy of Sciences of Ukraine, Kyiv, Ukraine
let@cyfra.net, lit@iss.org.ua
[2] Kherson State University, Kherson, Ukraine
vladimirius@gmail.com
[3] UniqueSoft LLC, Palatine, IL, USA
thomas.weigert@uniquesoft.com

Abstract. Insertion modeling has been developed over the last decade as an approach to a general theory of interaction between agents and an environment in complex distributed multiagent systems. The original work in this direction proposed a model of interaction between agents and environments based on an insertion function and the algebra of behaviors (similar to process algebra). Over the recent years, insertion modeling has been applied to the verification of requirement specifications of distributed interacting systems and to the generation of tests from such requirements. Our system, VRS (Verification of Requirements Specifications), has successfully verified specifications in the field of telecommunication systems, embedded systems, and real-time systems. Formal requirements in VRS are presented by means of local descriptions with a succession relation. Formalized requirements are represented in a formalism that combines logical specifications with control descriptions provided by the graphical syntax of UCM (Use Case Map) diagrams. This paper overviews the main concepts of insertion modeling, presents new algorithms developed for symbolic verification, especially a new predicate transformer for local descriptions, and provides a formal description of the method of generating traces from such specifications (which is the key technology used to verify requirements and derive test suites).

Keywords: Verification · Large system development · Symbolic techniques

1 Introduction

Insertion modeling has been developed as an approach to a general theory of describing the interaction between agents and their environments in complex distributed multiagent systems. The original presentation of insertion modeling, published in the mid-90s [12–14], relied on a model of interaction between agents and environments based on an insertion function and the algebra of

© Springer International Publishing Switzerland 2015
J. Fischer et al. (Eds.): SDL 2015, LNCS 9369, pp. 3–18, 2015.
DOI: 10.1007/978-3-319-24912-4_1

behaviors (similar to process algebra). Insertion modeling generalizes most of the traditional theories of interaction including CCS (Calculus of Communicated Processes) [24,25], the π-calculus [26], CSP (Communicating Sequential Processes) [7], ACP (Algebra of Communicated Processes) [2], the calculus of mobile ambients [3] and many variations of these basic approaches.

Each of these theories can be obtained by defining an insertion function as a parameter of a generalized insertion model. In such model we can leverage several insertion functions (to obtain multilevel environments). This makes it possible to combine different theories of interaction. Insertion modeling can represent abstract models of parallel computation, such as Petri nets [28] or the actor model of Hewitt [6], as well as automata network models and different abstractions of the object-oriented parallel programming paradigm.

Insertion modeling, as implemented by our system VRS, has been applied to the verification of requirement specifications of distributed interacting systems [1,9,16–18] and has successfully verified applications in the field of telecommunication systems, embedded systems, and real-time systems.

This paper reviews the main principles of insertion modeling, and describes formal models for requirements. It presents tools used for the verification of requirements and for generating tests from these requirements. The formal part of the paper presupposes familiarity with labeled transition system, bisimilarity, and basic notions of general process theory. The mathematical foundation of insertion modeling has been presented in [11].

2   The Elements of Insertion Modeling

Insertion modeling deals with the construction of models and studies the interaction of agents and environments in complex distributed multiagent systems. Informally, insertion modeling assumes the following basic principles:

1. The world comprises a hierarchy of environments with inserted agents.
2. Environments and agents evolve over time and have observable behaviors.
3. The insertion of an agent into an environment changes the behavior of the environment, producing a new environment into which other agents may be inserted in turn.
4. Environments can be considered as agents which may be inserted into higher level environments.
5. Agents and environments can model other agents and environments at different levels of abstraction.

These principles can be formalized in terms of transition systems, behavior algebras, insertion functions, and insertion machines: The first and the second principles are commonly used in information modeling of different kinds of systems. The third principle is intuitively clear, but has a special refinement in insertion modeling. We consider *agents* as transition systems with states considered up to bisimilarity or trace equivalence. The fourth and fifth principles establish multilevel environments. The sixth principle will be explicated in terms of an insertion machine that simulates the behavior of insertion models. Such machine can be considered as environment for models inserted into it.

A **transition system** (or labeled transition system) $< S, A, T >$ consists of a set of states S, a set A of actions (signals, events, instructions, statements, etc.), and a transition relation $T \subset S \times A \times S$ that relates states by actions.

Transition systems are evolving in time by changing their states, and perform actions which are observable symbolic structures used for communication. We use the notation $s \xrightarrow{a} s'$ to express the fact that a transition system can evolve from state s to state s' performing action a. Usually transition systems are nondeterministic and there can be several transitions leaving from a given state, even performing the same action.

Transition systems S can have three distinguished sets of states: the set $S^{(0)}$ of initial states, the set S_Δ of terminal states, and the set $S_\perp$ of divergent (or underdetermined) states.

Sometimes it is useful to enrich the structure of labeled transition system by adding a *state label function* $\varphi : S \to U$ which maps the set of states S to the set of state labels U. We call such systems *attributed* transition systems.

An **agent** is a transition system with states considered up to some notion of equivalence. Two main equivalence relations are of interest. The first is *bisimilarity* (first presented in [27]), the second is trace equivalence. In model checking, trace equivalence corresponds to linear time logic, while bisimilarity corresponds to branching time logic. Equivalence of agents characterizes their behaviors: two systems in a given states have the same behavior if these states are equivalent. To represent behaviors of transition systems we rely on **behavior algebras**. A behavior algebra is a two sorted (two typed) universal algebra. The first (main) sort is a set of *behaviors* (processes); the second is the sort of *actions*. The operations of a behavior algebra are *prefixing a.u* (where a is an action, and u is a behavior) and *nondeterministic choice* $u + v$ (an associative, commutative, and idempotent operation on the set of behaviors). Termination constants are the *successful termination* Δ, *deadlock 0* (the neutral element of nondeterministic choice), and *divergent behavior* $\perp$. The *approximation relation* $\sqsubseteq$ is a partial order on the set of behaviors with minimal element $\perp$, and is used for constructing a complete algebra by the fixed point theorem. A complete behavior algebra $F(A)$ over a set of behaviors A is a complete partial order with prefixing and nondeterministic choice as continuous functions. Completeness means that every directed set of behaviors has a minimal upper bound. Continuity means that

$$a.(\bigsqcup_{u \in U} u) = \bigsqcup_{u \in U} (a.u)$$

$$v + (\bigsqcup_{u \in U} u) = \bigsqcup_{u \in U} (v + u)$$

for any directed set U of behaviors. The construction of the algebra $F(A)$ for an infinite set of actions is described in detail in [11].

A basic behavior algebra, that is, an algebra generated by constants only, allows only finite behaviors. To define infinite behaviors we use equations over behavior algebras. These equations have the form of recursive definitions $u_i = F_i(u_1, u_2, \ldots), i = 1, 2, \ldots$ and define their left-hand side behaviors as the components of a minimal fixed point. The left-hand sides of these definitions can depend on parameters $u_i(x) = F_i(u, x)$ of different types. In a complete behavior algebra each behavior has a representation (normal form)

$$u = \sum_{i \in I} a_i.u_i + \varepsilon_u$$

which is defined uniquely (up to commutativity and associativity of nondeterministic choice) if all $a_i.u_i$ are different (ε_u is a termination constant). If all behaviors on the right-hand side are recursively represented in normal form, then u can be considered as an oriented tree, possibly infinite, with arcs labelled by actions and some nodes marked with symbols Δ and $\perp$. Any finite part of this tree (i.e. the part of the tree which is determined by a finite set of finite paths that start at the root and finish at a node labeled by $\perp$) is called a prefix of behavior u. Continuous functions of behaviors can be characterized by that their values depend only on finite prefixes of their arguments.

By definition, an **environment** is an agent that possesses an *insertion function*. More precisely, an environment is a tuple $< E, C, A, Ins >$ where E is the set of states of the environment, C is the set of environment actions, and A is the set of actions of agents which can be inserted into this environment, $Ins : E \times F(A) \to E$ is an insertion function. Thus, every environment E admits the insertion of any agent with the set of actions A. Since the states of transition systems are considered up to bisimilarity, they can be identified with their behaviors. The main requirement for the environment is the *continuity of the insertion function*. A number of useful consequences follow from this assumption. For example, the insertion function can be defined as the least fixed point of the system of functional equations in a behavior algebra.

The result $Ins(s, u)$ of the insertion of an agent in a state u into an environment in a state s is denoted as $s[u]$. The state $s[u]$ is a state of the environment and we can use the insertion function to insert a new agent v into the environment $s[u]$ such that $(s[u])[v] = s[u, v]$. Repeating this construction we can obtain the state of environment $s[u_1, u_2, \ldots]$ with several agents inserted into it. The insertion function can be considered as an operator over the states of the environment. If the states are identified with behaviors, then the insertion of a new agent changes the behavior of the environment.

An environment is an agent with an insertion function. Ignoring the insertion function, the environment can be inserted as an agent into a higher level environment. We can obtain a hierarchical structure such as

$$s[s_1[u_{11}, u_{12}, \ldots]_{E_1}, s_2[u_{21}, u_{22}, \ldots]_{E_2}, \ldots]_E$$

The notation $s[u_1, u_2, \ldots]_E$ explicitly shows the environment E to which the state s belongs (environment indexes are omitted if they are known from context).

Below we assume that the following identity holds: $e[u, \Delta] = e[u]$. The state e of the environment is called *indecomposable* if from $e = e'[u']$ it follows that $e' = e, u' = \Delta$. The set of indecomposable states of environment is called its *kernel*. Indecomposable state of the environment corresponds to the state before inserting any agent into it. If an environment has an empty kernel (that is, all states are decomposable), then there is an infinite number of agents that have originally been inserted into this environment. An environment is called *finitely decomposable*, if each of its state can be represented in the form $e[u_1, ..., u_m]$, where e is no decomposable. From now on, we will consider only finitely-decomposable environments unless otherwise stated.

Attributed environments are based on some *logical framework*. Such framework includes a set of types (integer, real, enumerated, symbolic, behavioral, etc.), interpreted in some data domains, it includes symbols to denote constants of these domains, and a set of typed functions and predicate symbols. Some of these symbols are interpreted (e.g., arithmetic operations and inequalities, equality for all types, etc.). Uninterpreted function and predicate symbols are called *attributes*. Uninterpreted function symbols of arity 0 are called *simple attributes*, the others are referred to as *functional attributes* (uninterpreted predicate symbols are considered as a functional attribute with the binary domain of values $0, 1$). Function symbols are used to define data structures such as arrays, lists, trees, and so on.

The *basic logical language* is built over an attributed environment. Usually, it is a first order language. If necessary, this language may include some of the modalities of temporal or fuzzy logic (e.g., if they simplify the reasoning in specific application domains). An *attribute expression* is a simple attribute or an expression of the form $f(t_1, ..., t_n)$, where f is a functional attribute of arity n, $t_1, ..., t_n$ (already constructed attribute expressions or constants of suitable types). If all expressions are constants, then the attribute expression is called a *constant expression*.

In general, the kernel of an attributed environment consists of the formulas of the basic language. Attributed environments are divided into two classes: the *concrete* environments and *symbolic* environments.

The indecomposable state of a concrete attributed environment is a formula of the form $t_1 = a_1 \wedge ... \wedge t_n = a_n$, where - $t_1, ..., t_n$ are different constant attribute expressions and $a_1, ..., a_n$ are constants. Typically, such a formula is represented as a partial mapping with domain $\{t_1, ..., t_n\}$ and a range equal to the set of all constants.

The states of a symbolic attributed environment are the formulas of the logic language. We consider the definition of transition functions for both types of environments.

Sometimes it is useful to consider an extended notion of concrete environment states with an infinite number of attribute expressions which have concrete values. This corresponds to an infinite conjunction or a function with an infinite domain. Such function is a mapping $\sigma : Attr \rightarrow D$ from the set $Attr$ of all constant attribute expressions to the set of their values D (taking into account types). The mapping σ is naturally extended to the set of all expressions of a given environment and to formulas of a given logical framework.

The states of a symbolic attributed environment are the formulas of the logic language. We consider the definition of a transition functions for both types of environments.

Concrete attributed environments are useful to formalize the operational semantics of programming or specification languages. An environment state is a memory state (data structures, objects, network structures, channels, etc.). Programs are agents inserted into this environment. For parallel programming languages, interaction is implemented via shared memory or message passing. When interacting via shared memory, the parallel composition of behaviors (asynchronous or synchronized) plays a major role. Message passing involves the use of special data structures in the environment for the organization of the interaction.

One of the first implementations of insertion modeling was the definition of the operational semantics of MSC [15] by means of attributed environments representing properties of evolving histories of a system described by MSC diagram.

3   Local Description Units

Local description units are used to specify the behavioral properties of transition systems. When a system is presented in the form of a composition of agents and environment, we consider the local properties of the insertion function.

We shall consider local properties of a system represented as a concrete or symbolic attributed environment. A local description unit of an attributed environment is a formula $\forall x(\alpha \to < P > \beta)$, where x is a list of (typed) parameters, α and β, formulas of the basic language, and P is a process (finite behavior of the specified system). The formula α is called the *precondition*, and the formula β the *postcondition* of the local description unit. Both the conditions and the behavior of a local description unit may depend on parameters. A local description unit can be considered as a temporal logic formula that expresses the fact that, if (for suitable values of parameters) the state of a system satisfies the precondition, the behavior P can be activated and after its successful termination, the new state will satisfy the postcondition. Local description units are analogous to Hoare triples (formulas of dynamic logic) as well as production rule systems (widely used in the description of the behavior of artificial intelligence and expert systems).

Postconditions may contain assignments $f(x) := y$ where $f(x)$ is an attribute expression and y is an algebraic expression. Such assignment is considered as a simple temporal logic statement which asserts that a new value of f at the point equal to the old value of attribute expression x is equal to the old value of algebraic expression y. Therefore the local description unit $\forall z(\alpha \to < P > (f(x) := y) \wedge \beta)$ is equivalent to $\forall(u, v, z)(\alpha \wedge (x = u) \wedge (y = v) \to < P > (f(u) = v) \wedge \beta)$.

Local description units used in the input language of the VRS system are called *basic protocols*. They are the main vehicles for expressing the formal requirements of multiagent and distributed systems. Basic protocols are expressed in the basic language of the VRS system; the processes are represented as

MSC diagrams. To study semantics underlying protocols several approaches were developed. These approaches are described in [18] and in [20].

We can formulate two kinds of semantics: *big step* semantics and *short step semantics*. Both define a transition system on the set of concrete or symbolic states of an attributed environment. The set of actions of a big step semantics are local description units, in a short step semantics the set of actions consists of actions used in processes of local description units. Local description units define operators on a set of state of environments which can be performed concurrently. In big step semantics this concurrency is hidden, while in short step semantics concurrency is defied explicitly. Below we shall consider only big step semantics.

To define the big step semantics of local descriptions we rely on the notion of a *predicate transformer*. A predicate transformer pr is a function that maps two formulas of the basic language to a new formula. This function is used to define a *big step transition system* for a symbolic attributed environment as follows. Let $B = \forall x (\alpha \to\, < P > \beta)$ be a local description unit, then

$$s \xrightarrow{B} s' \Leftrightarrow ((s \wedge \exists x \alpha) \neq 0) \wedge (s' = \exists x (pr(s \wedge \alpha, \beta)) \neq 0)$$

In $pr(s \wedge \alpha, \beta)$, the symbol x denotes a list of new simple attributes added to the environment, and after binding this formula by an existential quantifier it can be considered as a list of variables. If collisions appear, the symbols in the list x must be renamed.

The main requirement for the function pr is the relation $pr(s, \beta) \models \beta$. A big step transition system is deterministic which means that s' is a function of s, denoted by $s' = B(s)$. We also require that the predicate transformer is be monotone $(s \to s' \Rightarrow pr(s, \beta) \to pr(s', \beta))$ and distributive $(pr(s \vee s', \beta) = pr(s, \beta) \vee pr(s', \beta))$.

Example: The MESI protocol is used for the coherence control of shared memory in a multiprocessor system with local cache memories for processors. The higher level environment is a bus with shared main memory. The next level consists of processors with lines of cache memory. Each line (data unit) is synchronized separately. It is considered as an agent at the lowest level inserted into the environment of a processor. The states of the lines are M, E, S, and I: M means that the content of a line is modified. E means that the data on a line is exclusive and coincides with the corresponding data in the main memory. S means that this line may be stored in other lines. I means that the line is invalid. The actions of lines are Read and Write. The abstraction level of this model hides details as the content of the lines and the addresses for read and write actions. The behaviors of lines can be described by the following system of equations:

```
I = Read.(S+E+M) + Write.M, S = Read.S + Write.M
M = Read.M + Write.M, E = Read.E + Write.E
```

Local descriptions refer to a system with an undefined number of processors. Each processor contains one line. The statement $[i : q]$ means that line number i is in state q. It will be written as Mesi $= q$. No details about the structure of the environment will be specified except for identity $E[i : I, u] = E[u]$. In other words, the kernel of this environment is empty.

This environment is described by the following set of local descriptions:

```
R1:Forall i(Forall j (Mesi(j) = I) -> <Read i> (Mesi(i) = E));
R2:Forall(i,k)(Forall j (j!=k  -> (Mesi(j) = I)) & (Mesi(k) = E)
   & (i!=k) -> <Read(i)>(Mesi(k) = S  &  Mesi(i) = S));
R3: Forall (i,k) (Forall j ((j != i) -> Mesi(j) = S |/ Mesi(j) = I)
   & (i!=k) & Mesi(k) = S & Mesi(i) = I -> <Read(i)>(Mesi(i) = S));
R4: Forall(i,k)(Forall j (j!=k  -> (Mesi(j) = I)) & (Mesi(k) = M)
    & (i!=k) -> <Read(i)>(Mesi(k) = I  &  Mesi(i) = M));
R5: Forall i(~(Mesi(i) = I) -> <Read i>  1);
R6: Forall i(Mesi(i) = M -> <Write i>  1);
R7: Forall i(Mesi(i) = E  -> <Write i>  Mesi(i) = M);
R8: Forall i(Mesi(i) = S
    -> <Write i>Forall j (j!=i -> Mesi(j) = I) & Mesi(i) = M );
R9: Forall i(Forall j (Mesi(j) = I)
    -> <Write i> Forall j (j!=i -> Mesi(j) = I) & Mesi(i) = M );
R10: Forall i,k(Forall j (j != k  & j != i  -> Mesi(j) = I) &
    Mesi(i) = I & (Mesi(k) = E |/ Mesi(k) = S)
    -> <Write i> Forall j  (j!=i -> Mesi(j) = I) & Mesi(i) = M );
R11: Forall i,k(Forall j (j != k  & j != i  -> Mesi(j) = I) &
    Mesi(i) = I & Mesi(k) = M
    -> <Write i> Forall j (j!=i -> Mesi(j) = I) & Mesi(i) = M );
```

This example illustrates a method of describing an environment with an undefined number of agents. Real systems will consist of a finite number of agents, but there is no qualitative difference between a very large or an infinite number of agents. This example further illustrates the use of universal quantifiers. Below we will show how to define a predicate transformer with universal quantifiers.

There are many environments with similar structure at a higher level of abstraction (for example, telecommunication systems with an undefined number of subscribers or a smart city model with an undefined number of people or vehicles on the street). In such situations, we need to be able to reason about a system without assuming a specific number of subscribers, people, or vehicles.

4 Predicate Transformer

There are many functions pr that can serve as predicate transformer. The weakest such function is simply $pr(s, \beta) = \beta$. It is not a good choice, because we lost information about the state s. Following Dijkstra's methodology [5] we define the strongest predicate transformer similar to the strongest postcondition for a given precondition s after performing of postcondition β of a local description unit, considered as an operator over the formulas of the basic language.

To refine the notion of the strongest predicate transformer consider a transition system with states of a symbolic attributed environment and postconditions as actions: $s \xrightarrow{\beta} s' \Leftrightarrow s' = pt(s, \beta)$. Compare the execution of postcondition over a concrete and a symbolic attribute environment. Each state of a symbolic environment s simulates the set of states of a concrete environment. This set consists of the states σ such that $\sigma \models s$. The simulation condition can be formulated as

$$\sigma \xrightarrow{\beta} \sigma', s \xrightarrow{\beta} s', \sigma \models s \Rightarrow \sigma' \models s'$$

Now define a transition relation on the set of concrete states. The state of a concrete environment is a formula, so postconditions can be applied to concrete states as well, but the result in general is not concrete. The natural definition for a concrete environment is as follows:

$$\sigma \xrightarrow{\beta} \sigma' \Leftrightarrow (\sigma' \models \beta) \wedge Ch(\sigma, \sigma', \beta)$$

The condition $Ch(\sigma, \sigma', \beta)$ restricts the possible changes of the values of attribute expressions after transitioning from σ to σ' by means of the operator β. When β is an assignment the definition of Ch is clear: only the left hand side of an assignment can change its value. For the general case, assume that $\beta = R \wedge C$ where R is a conjunction of assignments, and C is a formula of the basic language. By definition, the following attribute expressions can change their values: (i) left hand sides of assignments, (ii) outermost occurrences of attribute expressions in C which do not contain variables, and (iii) the results of substituting arbitrary constants for variables in outermost occurrences of attribute expressions in C.

Assume that each postcondition is supplied with the set $Change(\beta)$ that includes the set of all attribute expressions obtained by the enumeration above. Predicate Ch can be defined as $Ch(\sigma, \sigma', \beta) \Leftrightarrow \forall (t \in Attr)(t \notin \sigma(Change(\beta)) \Rightarrow \sigma(t) = \sigma'(t))$.

We define $pt(s, \beta)$ as the strongest condition s' that satisfies the simulation condition. The inverse condition $\sigma' \models s' \Rightarrow \sigma \models s$ for some σ such that $\sigma \xrightarrow{\beta} \sigma'$ must be added. Finally, the strongest predicate transformer is defined as the condition satisfying the following two properties:

$$(\sigma \xrightarrow{\beta} \sigma', s \xrightarrow{\beta} s', \sigma \models s) \Rightarrow (\sigma' \models s')$$

$$(s \xrightarrow{\beta} s', \sigma' \models s') \Rightarrow (\exists \sigma (\sigma \xrightarrow{\beta} \sigma', \sigma \models s))$$

From this definition, the existence of the strongest predicate transformer and its uniqueness is obvious. We shall refer to the first property as *consistency* and to the second as *completeness* of the predicate transformer. Below we shall use the symbol pr for the strongest predicate transformer.

A **strongest predicate transformer** pt exists, but is is not obvious how it should be expressed leveraging a symbolic attributed environment. In [21], the formula $pt(s, \beta)$ was defined as a first order formula of the basic language when s contains only existential quantifiers and β is a quantifierless formula. Here we generalize this result to arbitrary first order formulas.

To compute $pt(s, \beta)$ for the state s of a symbolic attribute environment and postcondition $\beta = R \wedge C$, where s and C are first order formulas, and $R = (r_1 :=$

$t_1, r_2 := t_2, ...) = (r := t)$ is a parallel assignment the following four cases need to be considered: Case 1 corresponds to when only simple attributes are contained in the set $Change(\beta)$; case 2 restricts the set $Change(\beta)$ to attribute expressions without variables; case 3 allows variables bound by external universal quantifiers of C, and case 4 allows only variables bounded by external universal quantifiers of the formula s in $Change(\beta)$. Consider a set $Unch(s, \beta)$ along with $Change(\beta)$. This set consists of the outermost occurrences of attribute expressions in s which are not in $Change(\beta)$.

Represent the sets $Change(\beta)$ and $Unch(s, \beta)$ by lists $\mathbf{Q} = (q_1, q_2, ...)$ and $\mathbf{Z} = (z_1, z_2, ...)$. If an element of the list $\mathbf{Q}$ contains a variable, no substitution is needed. Mark the occurrence of a variable by the quantifier that binds it. Consider a list $\mathbf{X} = (x_1, x_2, ...)$ of variables and establish a one-to-one correspondence with the expressions from the list $\mathbf{Q}$.

Using the notation $\varphi = subs(v : s(v) := t(v)|P(v))$ for substitution, where v is a list of variables, the result $\varphi(E)$ of the application of a substitution φ to expression E is obtained by simultaneous replacement of all outermost occurrences of expressions of the form $s(v)$ such that v satisfies the condition $P(v)$ to $t(v)$. Substitution without matching is denoted by $subs(s_i := t_i|i \in I)$ and similarly refers to outermost occurrences.

Theorem 1. *If all attributes in the list $\mathbf{Q}$ have arity 0, and $\varphi = subs(q_i = x_i|i = 1, 2, ...)$, then*

$$pt(s, \beta) = \exists x(\varphi(s) \wedge (r = \varphi(t))) \wedge C.$$

Consistency. Let $\sigma \xrightarrow{\beta} \sigma', s \xrightarrow{\beta} s'$. We must prove $\sigma' \models s' = pt(s, \beta)$. From $\sigma' \models \beta \Rightarrow \sigma' \models C$. To prove $\exists x(\varphi(s) \wedge (r = \varphi(t)))$ it is sufficient to take the values of $Change(\beta)$ for x in σ and apply the semantics of assignments.

Completeness. Assume $s \xrightarrow{\beta} s'$ and $\sigma' \models pt(s, \beta)$. We must prove that there exists a concrete state σ such that $\sigma \xrightarrow{\beta} \sigma'$ and $\sigma \models s$. From $\sigma' \models pt(s, \beta)$ it follows that there exist constants $c_i, i = 1, 2, ...$ such that $\sigma' \models \mu\varphi(s) \wedge (r = \mu\varphi(t)) \wedge C$, where $\mu = subs(x_i = c_i|i = 1, 2, ...)$. Define σ so that $\sigma(q_i) = c_i, \sigma(r_i) = \mu\varphi(t_i)$ and $\sigma(g) = \sigma'(g), g \notin Change(\beta)$, Consequentially, $\sigma \xrightarrow{\beta} \sigma'$ and $\sigma \models s$.

Theorem 2. *If attribute expressions in the lists $\mathbf{Q}$ and $\mathbf{Z}$ do not contain variables, then pt can be expressed by a first order formula.*

When an attribute expression has an arity greater than 0, substitutionality of equality holds: if $u = v$ then $f(u) = f(v)$. It is obvious that if $f(u) \in Change(\beta), f(v) \in Unch(s, \beta)$ but $(u = v)$ then $f(v)$ can be changed and must be contained in $Change(\beta)$. Eventually, we consider all equalities and disequalities of arguments of such attributed expressions.

Let $M = \{(u,v)|f(u) \in \mathbf{Q}, f(v) \in \mathbf{Z}\}$. Enumerating all subsets of the set M as $(J_1, J_2, ...)$, we can obtain all combinations of equalities and disequalities:

$$E_i = \bigwedge_{(u,v)\in J_i} (u = v) \wedge \bigwedge_{(u,v)\in M\setminus J_i} (u \neq v)$$

Let $\varphi_i = \xi_i + \varphi$, where $\xi_i = subs(v : f(v) := x_j | f(v) \in \mathbf{Z}, (u,v) \in J_i, f(u) = q_j)$, and substitution φ is defined as above. The sum of two substitutions is a new substitution which applies one of them to the outermost occurrences of attribute expressions. It is obvious that only one of two substitutions can be applied to a given attribute expression.

The strongest predicate transformer is defined by the following formulas:

$$pt(s, \beta) = \exists x (p_1 \wedge p_2 \wedge ...)$$

$$p_i = (E'_i \to s_i \wedge R_i \wedge C)$$

$$E'_i = \varphi_i(E_i), s_i = \varphi_i(s), R_i = (r(\varphi_i(u)) := \varphi_i(t))$$

Some of the formulas $p_1, p_2, ...$ may be not satisfiable. In this case, transition $s \xrightarrow{\beta} s'$ is undefined, that is, the state s is deadlock state. Further, some of $p_1, p_2, ...$ may be identically true and can be deleted from the conjunction.

Theorem 2 for the definition of pt above is slightly more general than the result proven in [21].

Consistency. Let $\sigma \xrightarrow{\beta} \sigma', s \xrightarrow{\beta} s'$, and $\sigma \models s$. The conditions E'_i are mutually exclusive and their disjunction is identically true. We can select i such that E'_i is valid on σ'. Identified attribute expressions can be considered as simple attributes and the proof continues as in Theorem 1.

Completeness. $s \xrightarrow{\beta} s'$ and $\sigma' \models pt(s, \beta)$. Take the value of x such that all conditions $p_1, p_2, ...$ are valid on σ'. Select i such that $\sigma' \models E'_i$ is true. Therefore $\sigma' \models s_i \wedge R_i \wedge C$. Identifying attribute expressions according to E'_i we can consider them as simple attributes and the proof continues as in Theorem 1.

Theorem 3. *Let $C = \forall y C'$ in prenex normal form. Assume that no attribute expression from the list $\mathbf{Q}$ has variables other than variables from list y and assume attribute expressions from the list $\mathbf{Z}$ have no variables at all. Then*

$$pt(s, \beta) = \exists x \forall y (p_1 \wedge p_2 \wedge ...)$$

$$p_i = (E'_i \to s_i \wedge R_i \wedge C').$$

Consistency. Let $\sigma \xrightarrow{\beta} \sigma', s \xrightarrow{\beta} s'$, and $\sigma \models s$. We have $\sigma' \models \forall y C'$. Consider an arbitrary symbolic constant for y and continue as above.

Completeness. Take the value of x such that $\forall y (...)$ is true. Consider an arbitrary value for y, select i such that E'_i is true. Continue as in the previous Theorem, considering y as a symbolic constant.

Theorem 4. *Let* $s = \forall y s'$, $C = \forall z C'$, *both in prenex normal form. Let no attribute expression from the list* $\mathbf{Z}$ *have variables other than the variables from the list* y *and let no attribute expression from the list* $\mathbf{Q}$ *have variables other than the variables from the list* z. *Let* $s'_i = \varphi_i(s')$.

$$pt(s, \beta) = \exists x \forall y \forall z (p_1 \wedge p_2 \wedge ...)$$

$$p_i = (E'_i \rightarrow s'_i \wedge R_i \wedge C').$$

Consistency. Let $\sigma \xrightarrow{\beta} \sigma'$, $s \xrightarrow{\beta} s'$, and $\sigma \models s$. We have $\sigma' \models \forall y C'$. Take arbitrary symbolic constants for y. Continue as above.

Completeness. Take the value of x such that $\forall y \forall z (p_1 \wedge p_2 \wedge ...)$ is true. Take an arbitrary value for y and select i such that E'_i is true. Continue as in the previous theorem, considering y as a symbolic constant.

   Transitions of local descriptions are computed as follows: Reduce the conjunction $s \wedge \alpha$ of the state of the environment and the precondition of a local description $B = \forall x(\alpha \rightarrow < P > \beta)$ to prenex normal form. Let this normal form be $\exists z u$. Compute $v = pr(u, \beta)$ if u and β satisfy one of three conditions of Theorems 1–4. The variables of list z are considered as attributes. The result will be $B(s) = \exists x \exists z v$.

Example: Returning to the verification of the MESI protocol, the initial state of MESI is the symbolic state `Forall i(Mesi(i)=I)`. The application of local descriptions generates an infinite number of states. Proof the following safety property `Sf`:

```
Exist i((Mesi(i) = E) & Forall(j:int)(j!=i-> (Mesi(j) = I))) |/
Exist i((Mesi(i) = M) & Forall(j:int)(j!=i-> (Mesi(j) = I))) |/
Exist i((Mesi(i) = S) & Exist k((k!=i)&(Mesi(k)=S) &
                Forall j((Mesi(j) = I) |/ (Mesi(j) = S)))) |/
Forall i(Mesi(i)=I)
```

To apply the inductive method, one must prove that `Sf` is true in the initial state and is preserved by each local description. In VRS, this can be proven using static verification.

   To prove that a system, defined by means of a set of local descriptions, is free of dead locks, we use an abstraction to model the infinite state system by a finite state system. For MESI, this abstraction is introduced in the insertion function. Consider the following identity: $E[i : S, j : S, k : S] = E[i : S, j : S]$ where i, j, k are different. Usually i, j, k are bound by existential quantifiers, so it is not important which of them will be omitted. After this abstraction the system will be a finite state system and safety can be proven after generating all states.

5   Generic Trace Generator (GTG)

Local descriptions appear as the result of formalizing requirements. They can be applied to the environment states (concrete or symbolic) as operators. But it is not sufficient to use only local descriptions to completely specify a model. When constraints on the sequence of application of local descriptions are not defined, this may lead to the consideration of undesirable histories and traces. We define a succession relation on the set of local descriptions. This relation can be introduced by the definition of additional control attributes and conditions limiting the conditions of application of local descriptions on these attributes. An inconvenience of this description is the need for the partition of the basic attributes and auxiliary control attributes. Moreover, the local descriptions themselves become more complicated. The VRS system uses the graphical UCM notation [8] to specify this succession relation.

We combine the language of local descriptions with UCM. UCM is used for the definition of succession relation between the set of local descriptions and for the expressing the partial order of the evaluation of local descriptions.

Local descriptions give a specification of UCM responsibilities; the system of UCM maps is used as a multilevel environment for a system of local descriptions. A restricted set of UCM constructs is used in our models and includes start and end points, responsibilities, and-fork and and-join, or-fork and or-join, and stubs. The semantics of this combined specification language is described in [22].

The insertion function used is the following:

$$\frac{U \xrightarrow{B} U', S \xrightarrow{B} S'}{S[U] \xrightarrow{B} S'[U']} P$$

U is the state of the system, S is the state of UCM control part, B is a local description which can be applied in state $S[U]$, condition P defines the applicability of a local description B in the state of a model $S[U]$.

Verification and Testing. The VRS system considers two types of verification problems. The first one is the verification of requirements and programs; the second one is the generation of tests.

The language implemented in VRS supports attributes of numeric and symbolic types (free terms), arrays (functions with restricted arguments), lists, and functional data types. The deductive system supports the proof of the assertions in a first-order theory (an integration of theories of integer and real linear inequalities, enumerated data types, uninterpreted function symbols and queuing theory). As the deductive system can successfully prove or refute only some classes of formulas, during verification sometimes failures can be obtained on intermediate queries. In practice, such failures are quite rare and in most cases do not affect the final outcome. The MSC notation with insertion semantics [15] is used to model processes.

The main tools of VRS are concrete and symbolic trace generators, and static verification tools, which include checking the completeness and consistency of local descriptions and checking of safety properties.

The system has successfully been applied in a number of practical projects in the areas of telecommunications, embedded systems, telematics, etc. Projects with up to 10,000 requirements formulated as local descriptions were formalized, with up to 1000 attributes.

Strategies of Generic Trace Generator. A generic insertion machine has been developed and is adapted to proofing problems. This adaptation is controlled by a set of parameters defining the strategy of generating traces.

The main parameters are *reference points*, the algorithm of selection of the *next step, coverage criteria*, and conditions of *when to stop generation*.

Reference points are defined by standard rules or are selected by user. For example the set of all responsibilities can be chosen as the set of reference points. This set is sufficient when we solve the reachability problem. In this case, trace equivalence is used to define the equivalence of states. When generating traces for testing, bisimilarity must be used as equivalence criterion and the set of reference points must include also branching points (forks and joints).

The following UCM elements can be used as reference points: Start, end, forks, joins, responsibilities, and entry and exit to stubs. Reference points are used to abstract generated traces. Only the passing through reference points is observable, while transitioning through intermediate states is hidden.

The state of trace generation is data structure which contains all traces generated up to this point. Traces are represented by a tree with nodes corresponding to the choice points. The leafs of this tree are reference points which can be further extended. The next step generation algorithm selects one of the these points and tries to reach the next reference point. Criteria to choose the next step could be the shortest path or the path nearest to the end point.

The trace tree can be used derive test cases using various coverage criteria. An example of such a criterion is to cover all transitions between all pairs of reference points.

6   Conclusions

Tools for the verification and model-based testing have been presented; these tools are formally based on insertion modeling. The main reasoning mechanism is a predicate transformer for symbolic modeling of distributed multiagent systems. We have described and proven properties of the predicate transformer.

References

1. Baranov, S., Jervis, C., Kotlyarov, V.P., Letichevsky, A.A., Weigert, T.: Leveraging UML to deliver correct telecom applications in UML for real. In: Lavagno, L., Martin, G., Selic, B. (eds.) Design of Embedded Real-Time Systems, pp. 323–342. Springer, Heidelberg (2003)
2. Bergstra, J.A., Klop, J.W.: Process algebra for synchronous communications. Inf. Control **60**(1/3), 109–137 (1984). Elsevier

3. Cardelli, L., Gordon, A.D.: Mobile ambients. In: Nivat, M. (ed.) FOSSACS 1998. LNCS, vol. 1378, p. 140. Springer, Heidelberg (1998)
4. Cousot, P., Cousot, R.: Abstract interpretation frameworks. J. Logic Comput. **2**(4), 511–547 (1992)
5. Dijkstra, E.W.: Guarded commands, nondeterminacy and formal derivation of programs. CACM **18**(8), 453–457 (1992)
6. Hewitt, C., Bishop, P., Steiger, R.: A universal modular actor formalism for artificial intelligence. In: IJCA (1973)
7. Hoare, C.A.R.: Communicating Sequential Processes. Prentice Hall, London (1985)
8. International Telecommunication Union: Recommendation Z.151 - User Requirements Notation (2008)
9. Letichevsky, A.A., Weigert, T., Kapitonova, J.V., Volkov, V.A.: Systems validation. In: Zurawski, R. (ed.) Embedded Systems Handbook. CRC Press, Boca Raton (2005)
10. Letichevsky, A.A.: About one approach to program analysis. Cybernetics **6**, 1–8 (1979)
11. Letichevsky, A.A.: Algebra of behavior transformations and its applications. In: Kudryavtsev, V.B., Rosenberg, I.G. (eds.) Structural Theory of Automata, Semigroups, and Universal Algebra, NATO Science Series II, Mathematics, Physics and Chemistry, vol. 207, pp. 241–272. Springer, Heidelberg (2005)
12. Letichevsky, A.A., Gilbert, D.: A universal interpreter for nondeterministic concurrent programming languages. In: Fifth Compulog Network Area Meeting on Language Design and Semantic Analysis Methods (1996)
13. Letichevsky, A.A., Gilbert, D.: A general theory of action languages. Cybern. Syst. Anal. **34**(1), 1230 (1998)
14. Letichevsky, A.A., Gilbert, D.: A model for interaction of agents and environments. In: Bert, D., Choppy, C., Mosses, P.D. (eds.) WADT 1999. LNCS, vol. 1827, pp. 311–328. Springer, Heidelberg (2000)
15. Letichevsky, A.A., Kapitonova, J.V., Kotlyarov, V.P., Volkov, V.A., Letichevsky Jr., A.A., Weigert, T.: Semantics of message sequence charts. In: Prinz, A., Reed, R., Reed, J. (eds.) SDL 2005. LNCS, vol. 3530, pp. 117–132. Springer, Heidelberg (2005)
16. Letichevsky, A.A., Letichevsky Jr., A.A., Kapitonova, J.V., Volkov, V.A., Baranov, S., Kotlyarov, V.P., Weigert, T.: Basic protocols, message sequence charts, and the verification of requirements specifications. In: ISSRE (2004)
17. Letichevsky, A.A., Kapitonova, J.V., Letichevsky Jr., A.A., Volkov, V.A., Baranov, S., Kotlyarov, V.P., Weigert, T.: Basic protocols, message sequence charts, and the verification of requirements specifications. Comput. Netw. **47**, 662–675 (2005)
18. Letichevsky, A.A., Kapitonova, J.V., Volkov, V.A., Letichevsky Jr., A.A., Baranov, S., Kotlyarov, V.P., Weigert, T.: System specification by basic protocols. Cybern. Syst. Anal. **41**(4), 479493 (2005)
19. Letichevsky, A.A., Letychevskyi, O.A., Peschanenko, V.S.: Insertion modeling system. In: Clarke, E., Virbitskaite, I., Voronkov, A. (eds.) PSI 2011. LNCS, vol. 7162, pp. 262–273. Springer, Heidelberg (2012)
20. Letichevsky, A.A., Kapitonova, J.V., Kotlyarov, V.P., Letichevsky Jr., A.A., Nikitchenko, N.S., Volkov, V.A., Weigert, T.: Insertion modeling in distributed system design. Probl. Program. **4**, 13–38 (2008). Institute of Programming Systems
21. Letichevsky, A.A., Godlevsky, A.B., Letichevsky Jr., A.A., Potienko, S.V., Peschanenko, V.A.: The properties of predicate transformer of the VRS system. Cybern. Syst. Anal. **4**, 3–16 (2010)

22. Letichevsky, A.A., Letichevsky Jr., A.A., Peschanenko, V., Huba, A., Weigert, T.: Symbolic traces generation in the system of insertion modelling. Cybern. Syst. Anal. **1**, 3–19 (2015)
23. McCarthy, J.: Notes on formalizing context. In: IJCAI, pp. 555–562 (1993)
24. Milner, R. (ed.): A Calculus of Communicating Systems. LNCS, vol. 92. Springer, Heidelberg (1980)
25. Milner, R.: Communication and Concurrency. Prentice Hall, Upper Saddle River (1989)
26. Milner, R.: The polyadic π-calculus: a tutorial. Technical report, ECS-LFCS-91-180. Laboratory for Foundations of Computer Science, Department of Computer Science. University of Edinburgh (1991)
27. Park, D.: Concurrency and automata on infinite sequences. In: Deussen, P. (ed.) GI-TCS 1981. LNCS, vol. 104. Springer, Heidelberg (1981)
28. Petri, C.A.: Kommunikation mit Automaten. Bonn: Institut fur Instrumentelle Mathematik, Schriften des IIM Nr. 2 (1962)

A Model-Based Framework for SLA Management and Dynamic Reconfiguration

Mahin Abbasipour[1](✉), Ferhat Khendek[1], and Maria Toeroe[2]

[1] ECE, Concordia University, Montréal, Canada
{mah_abb,khendek}@encs.concordia.ca
[2] Ericsson Inc., Montréal, Canada
maria.toeroe@ericsson.com

Abstract. A Service Level Agreement (SLA) is a contract between a service provider and a customer that defines the expected quality of the provided services, the responsibilities of each party, and the penalties in case of violations. In the cloud environment where elasticity is an inherent characteristic, a service provider can cater for workload changes and adapt its service provisioning capacity dynamically. Using this feature one may provide only as many resources as required to satisfy the current workload and SLAs, the system can shrink and expand as the workload changes. In this paper, we introduce a model-based SLA monitoring framework, which aims at avoiding SLA violations from the service provider side while using only the necessary resources. We use UML models to describe all the artifacts in the monitoring framework. The UML models not only increase the level of abstraction but they are also reused from the system design/generation phase. For this purpose, we develop metamodels for SLAs and for monitoring. In the monitoring framework, all abstract SLA models are transformed into an SLA compliance model which is used for checking the compliance to SLAs. To avoid SLA violations as well as resource wasting, dynamic reconfigurations are triggered as appropriate based on the predefined Object Constraint Language (OCL) constraints using thresholds.

Keywords: Monitoring · Elasticity · SLA violation avoidance · Model driven engineering · OCL constraints

1 Introduction

A Service Level Agreement (SLA) is a contract between a customer and a service provider that aims at describing the level of service quality and the obligations of each party in the agreement. An SLA violation occurs when any of the parties fails to meet their obligations [14]. A violation may be associated with a penalty.

During the operation of a system its workload changes dynamically, which results in variable resource usage. To increase revenue, instead of allocating a fixed amount of resources, providers try to allocate only as much as required to satisfy the current customer needs and adapt subsequently to the workload

© Springer International Publishing Switzerland 2015
J. Fischer et al. (Eds.): SDL 2015, LNCS 9369, pp. 19–26, 2015.
DOI: 10.1007/978-3-319-24912-4_2

changes. This could be challenging as one would like to provision resources not too early or too much to avoid the waste of resources, and not too late or inadequately to avoid SLA violations. To accurately adapt the system at runtime, the system should be monitored: The metrics or events of interest are collected and after evaluation actions are triggered to modify the managed system accordingly.

Figure 1 gives an overall view of our SLA management framework. In this framework, the system is scaled according to the workload variations while avoiding SLA violations. For this, the system configuration and the related elasticity rules are generated offline during the design phase and determine the configuration changes needed to scale up/down (adding/removing resources of a node) and in/out (removing/adding a node). In this framework, all the SLAs, their corresponding measurements and the thresholds are combined into an SLA compliance model. The validation of the SLA compliance model may generate triggers for scaling down and/or in the system to save resources when the workload decreases or for increasing the resources when workload goes up to avoid SLA violations. The monitoring system feeds the framework with the measured data. The thresholds are related to the maximum and the minimum capacity of the current system configuration and are used to check if the system needs reconfiguration. Accordingly, the values for the thresholds are re-evaluated with each reconfiguration of the system. To map the measured data to SLA parameters and to generate the triggers for the reconfiguration OCL [10] constraints have been defined. When a trigger is generated the appropriate elasticity rules are invoked to reconfigure the system with the minimum required resources. In this short paper we target primarily, but not limited to, component based systems deployed on a number of virtual machines typical for cloud computing. Furthermore, we focus on the modeling aspects and the use of OCL constraints to trigger dynamic reconfiguration.

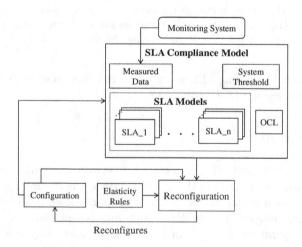

Fig. 1. SLA compliance management and dynamic reconfiguration

In this short paper, we introduce the principles of our approach for SLA compliance monitoring and dynamic reconfiguration. The rest of the paper is organized as follows. In Sect. 2, the metamodels for SLA and SLA compliance are presented. Section 3 explains how OCL constraints are used to generate dynamic reconfiguration triggers. We discuss the related work in Sect. 4 and conclude in Sect. 5.

2   Modeling for SLA Compliance Management

To manage the compliance to SLAs, the running system needs to be monitored, data has to be collected and the SLAs checked periodically. We adopt a model driven approach not only to facilitate the understanding, design and maintenance of the system [9], but also to reuse the models generated during the system design phase such as the system configuration, and to build on existing tools. We define our metamodels using Papyrus [5]. The Atlas Transformation Language (ATL) [6] is used to combine all SLA models into an SLA compliance model. In this section, we introduce the metamodels for SLA and for SLA compliance.

2.1   SLA Metamodel

The SLA metamodel is shown in Fig. 2. Each SLA has an ID and is an agreement between a provider and a customer. A third party may also participate to verify the agreed Service Level Objectives (SLO) and play the monitoring role [7]. An SLA is applicable for a specific time duration and has a cost. This cost can be a constant value or it can be a function based on the usage of the services. An SLA includes some service functionalities that the provider agrees to provide with specific Quality of Service (QoS). An abstract stereotype *SlaParameter* captures the different types of QoS the customer and the provider agree on. The agreed values are represented by *maxAgreedValue* and *minAgreedValue* in the figure. For example, the *maxAgreedValue* in the SLA parameter *DataRate* represents the maximum number of requests per second the customer may send for the specific service.

The monitoring system measures each metric (*MeasuredMetric*) at a predefined frequency. Customers may also want to specify how often the SLA parameters are monitored and checked. This customization is represented by *SlaMetric* stereotype. However, it should be compatible with the capability of the monitoring system. In other words, the frequency agreed on in the SLA must be less or equal to the frequency of measurements of the monitoring system.

2.2   SLA Compliance Metamodel

An SLA compliance model is the combination of all SLA models, part of the configuration model and the measurements obtained from the monitoring system. The main reason for merging all SLA models into one model is that we

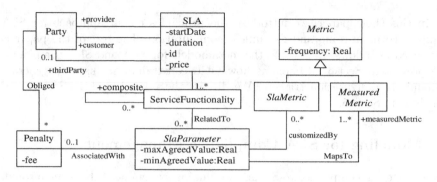

Fig. 2. SLA metamodel

want to be able not only to avoid violations in each individual SLA but also to trigger elasticity rules which are related to all customers resource usage.

The SLA compliance metamodel is shown in Fig. 3. The same service with the same or different SLA parameters is generally offered to multiple customers. The *MeasuredMetric* stereotype represents the value the monitoring system measures per service for each customer or per node of the system. When an SLA parameter related to a service is not respected, the *BelongsTo* relation indicates which SLA has been violated.

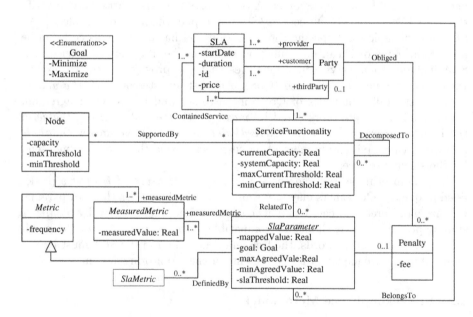

Fig. 3. SLA compliance metamodel

The monitoring system collects raw metrics. Some of these metrics (e.g. service up/down time) and the SLA parameters perceived by the customers (e.g. availability of service) are not at the same level. To bridge the gap between the measured values and SLA parameters, OCL constraints have been defined as mapping rules. The attribute *mappedValue* represents the value of such mapped measurements. A service may be a composition of different service functionalities, which may be mapped similarly or measured at the composite level.

The attribute *goal* of an SLA parameter specifies the parameters optimization goal. For some SLA parameters, like availability, the optimization goal is maximization while for others like response time, the goal is minimization. We categorize our OCL constraints for SLA violation avoidance based on these optimization goals. When a new SLA parameter is introduced and taken into consideration, there is no need for new OCL constraints as long as its optimization goal fits into one of the aforementioned categories.

3   Dynamic Reconfiguration

In the proposed framework, OCL constraints are used to trigger dynamic reconfiguration. The OCL constraints are defined on a number of attributes: The attribute *currentCapacity* in the *ServiceFunctionality* stereotype specifies the maximum workload (e.g. requests/second) the system in its current configuration can handle for a specific service. The attribute *systemCapacity* is defined at the design phase as the maximum system capacity for the service. This is the maximum capacity the system can be expanded to without major changes (e.g. upgrade/re-design). As mentioned earlier to avoid SLA violations and trigger reconfiguration, we use thresholds. Some of the thresholds are related to all customers (aggregate) resource usage while others are related to individual SLAs.

- *maxCurrentThreshold* and *minCurrentThreshold*: For each service, the system is dimensioned dynamically with a *currentCapacity* to handle a certain workload. In order to avoid SLA violations, i.e. workload exceeding *currentCapacity*, we define a *maxCurrentThreshold* point (with *maxCurrentThreshold* < *currentCapacity*) at which the system capacity is increased by scaling it up/out to a new *currentCapacity* and for which a new *maxCurrentThreshold* is defined. Therefore, the relation *workload* < *maxCurrentThreshold* must be respected. Not to waste resources we also define a *minCurrentThreshold* where we scale down/in the capacity of the system to a lower capacity (i.e. the relation *workload* > *minCurrentThreshold* must be respected). We use OCL constraints to define these restrictions. As a result the violation of the defined OCL constraints triggers the scaling of the system. In this paper, we assume that the service workload is distributed evenly in the system.
- *slaThreshold*: Some SLA parameters like service availability are set on a per customer basis. Therefore, to avoid SLA violations, we need to watch the SLAs separately using a *slaThreshold* for each SLA. These parameters behave similarly with respect to violation. Some of them like availability and throughput

for which a higher value is preferable (i.e. the attribute goal is equal to Maximize) will be violated by a service provider when in the SLA compliance model, the experienced quality is less than the *slaThreshold* (i.e. the relation *mappedValue > slaThreshold* must be respected all the time if *goal=Maximize*); while for others like response time, the violation happens from the service provider side when the measured response time is greater than the *slaThreshold* (i.e. the relation *mappedValue < slaThreshold* must be respected if *goal=Minimize*). Again, we use OCL constraints to define these restrictions. By violation of these OCL constraints, triggers will be generated to avoid SLA violations.

The following thresholds are related to the node resource utilization:

– *maxThreshold* and *minThreshold*: To avoid SLA violations because of node limitations, e.g. the load on a node exceeding its capacity, we define the *maxThreshold* point at which we allocate more resources to the node (e.g. virtual machine, hyper scale system) or add more nodes to the system (i.e. the relation *load < maxThreshold* should be respected). To avoid the wasting of resources, the *minThreshold* is used to reduce the node resources, for example, by removing a node or decreasing the virtual resources of a virtual machine. The addition/removal of resources to/from the node increases/reduces the capacity of the node and therefore new thresholds are defined. The *maxThreshold* and *minThreshold* are vectors where different types of node resources (e.g. CPU, RAM, etc.) are taken into account.

To obtain the SLA compliance model from the individual SLA models, we use model transformation. As the number of SLA models varies over time, SLAs may be added or removed, we use different model transformations. For the addition, the initial SLA compliance model is obtained directly from the first SLA model by transformation that creates all the model elements. Subsequent SLA models are added incrementally using another transformation which takes into account the already existing elements of the SLA compliance model. Similarly, when an SLA is removed, the elements related to only this SLA should be removed from the SLA compliance model together with their measurements. This is achieved with a different transformation that takes the SLA to be removed and the SLA compliance model as input and generates a new SLA compliance model. In the current prototype implementation the addition and removal of SLAs are done offline.

4   Related Work

There are a number of works that define languages for modeling SLAs. Most of the languages are for a specific domain. For example in [14,15], the authors define SLAng suitable for network services. Others like [7,12] focus on web services. QML [4] allows customers to define the SLA parameters to be measured for monitoring purposes. Since a customer defined parameter may not be observable for a specific system and an agreement needs a common understanding of parameters between parties, this can result in inconsistency with the monitoring systems capability. In our proposal, not only do we allow customers to customize their SLAs but we also make sure that this customization is compatible with the capabilities of the monitoring system.

In [2], a metamodel for SLA description and monitoring is proposed but it is not clear how the compliance to SLAs is checked. In [11], a timed automata is used to detect violations with respect to response time. The work in [14] is closely related to this paper. In [14], to detect SLA violations, different OCL constraints for different SLA parameters have been defined. However, to add a new parameter to an SLA a new OCL constraint for the violation detection has to be added as well, which is not the case in our framework. In [14], SLA compliance is the only goal, while in our case we want to achieve this goal with the minimum amount of resources needed for the workload at any given time and to grow/shrink the system according to the workload variations.

Monitoring and scaling of cloud systems based on the demand has been extensively investigated. However, only a few works have looked into SLA compliance at an abstract level. In [3], a framework for monitoring SLAs is proposed. It consists of three components: a monitoring system for providing measurements, LoM2HiS for mapping monitored data to parameters in the SLAs, and a knowledge database which uses past experience to solve current SLA related issues. This framework is suitable for the infrastructure layer of the cloud. Similarly, [1] focuses on the infrastructure level only but nothing is done at the other layers to respond to application level workload variations. In our framework both, infrastructure and application, levels are handled. On the other hand, [8,13] for instance do not take SLAs into account.

5   Conclusion and Future Work

Service providers aim at increasing their revenue by operating a system with the minimum amount of resources necessary to avoid SLA violation penalties. For this purpose, there is a need for an SLA management and dynamic reconfiguration framework that scales the system (up/down and in/out) according to the workload changes while avoiding SLA violations. In this paper, we proposed such a framework. It is model driven, it is at the right level of abstraction. OCL constraints are written for categories of parameters and are not specific for each parameter, which eases future extension. More important, the proposed framework reuses models developed at the system design stage. This work is at an early stage, more investigations are required, for instance, to generate the elasticity rules automatically and to handle the correlation of the generated triggers. We also need to investigate the challenging issue of SLA compliance model evolution at run time, i.e. addition and removal of SLA models while the system is in operation. The performance of such a model based framework needs to be assessed as well.

Acknowledgments. This work has been partially supported by Natural Sciences and Engineering Research Council of Canada (NSERC) and Ericsson.

References

1. Ali-Eldin, A., Tordsson, J., Elmroth, E.: An adaptive hybrid elasticity controller for cloud infrastructures. In: Network Operations and Management Symposium (NOMS), pp. 204–212. IEEE (2012)
2. Debusmann, M., Kroger, R., Geihs, K.: Unifying service level management using an MDA-based approach. In: Network Operations and Management Symposium (NOMS), IEEE/IFIP, Vol. 1, pp. 801–814. IEEE (2004)
3. Emeakaroha, V.C., et al.: Towards autonomic detection of SLA violations in cloud infrastructures. Future Gener. Comput. Syst. **28**(7), 1017–1029 (2012). Elsevier
4. Frolund, S., Koistinen, J.,: Qml: a language for quality of service specification. Hewlett-Packard Laboratories (1998)
5. Gérard, S., Dumoulin, C., Tessier, P., Selic, B.: 19 Papyrus: a UML2 tool for domain-specific language modeling. In: Giese, H., Karsai, G., Lee, E., Rumpe, B., Schätz, B. (eds.) Model-Based Engineering of Embedded Real-Time Systems. LNCS, vol. 6100, pp. 361–368. Springer, Heidelberg (2010)
6. Jouault, F., Kurtev, I.: Transforming models with ATL. In: Bruel, J.-M. (ed.) MoDELS 2005. LNCS, vol. 3844, pp. 128–138. Springer, Heidelberg (2006)
7. Keller, A., Ludwig, H.: The WSLA framework: specifying and monitoring service level agreements for web services. J. Netw. Syst. Manag. **11**(1), 57–81 (2003). Springer
8. Konig, B., Calero, J.A., Kirschnick, J.: Elastic monitoring framework for cloud infrastructures. IET Commun, **6**(10), 1306–1315 (2012)
9. MDA User Guide, version 1.0.0, OMG (2003)
10. OMG Object Constraint Language (OCL), version 2.3.1, OMG, January 2012
11. Raimondi, F. et al.: A Methodology for on-line monitoring non-functional specifications of web-services. In: First International Workshop on Property Verification for Software Components and Services (PROVECS), pp. 50–59 (2007)
12. Sahai, A., Machiraju, V., Sayal, M., van Moorsel, A., Casati, F.: Automated SLA monitoring for web services. In: Feridun, M., Kropf, P.G., Babin, G. (eds.) DSOM 2002. LNCS, vol. 2506, pp. 28–41. Springer, Heidelberg (2002)
13. Sedaghat, M., Hernandez-Rodriguez, F., Elmroth, E.: A virtual machine re-packing approach to the horizontal vs. vertical elasticity trade-off for cloud autoscaling. In: 2013 ACM Cloud and Autonomic Computing Conference (2013)
14. Skene, J., Emmerich, W.: Generating a contract checker for an SLA language (2004). https://www.researchgate.net/publication/32885283_Generating_a_contract_checker_for_an_SLA_language
15. Skene, J., Lamanna, D.D., Emmerich, W.: Precise service level agreements. In: 26th International Conference on Software Engineering, pp. 179–188. IEEE Computer Society (2004)

SDL - The IoT Language

Edel Sherratt[1]([⊠]), Ileana Ober[2], Emmanuel Gaudin[3],
Pau Fonseca i Casas[4], and Finn Kristoffersen[5]

[1] Aberystwyth University, Aberystwyth, Wales, UK
eds@aber.ac.uk
[2] IRIT, Université Paul Sabatier, Toulouse, France
ileana.ober@irit.fr
[3] PragmaDev SARL, Paris, France
emmanuel.gaudin@pragmadev.com
[4] Universitat Politècnica de Catalunya, Barcelona, Spain
pau@fib.upc.edu
[5] Cinderella ApS, Hvidovre, Denmark
finn@cinderella.dk

Abstract. Interconnected smart devices constitute a large and rapidly growing element of the contemporary Internet. A smart thing can be as simple as a web-enabled device that collects and transmits sensor data to a repository for analysis, or as complex as a web-enabled system to monitor and manage a smart home. Smart things present marvellous opportunities, but when they participate in complex systems, they challenge our ability to manage risk and ensure reliability.

SDL, the ITU Standard Specification and Description Language, provides many advantages for modelling and simulating communicating agents – such as smart things – before they are deployed. The potential for SDL to enhance reliability and safety is explored with respect to existing smart things below.

But SDL must advance if it is to become the language of choice for developing the next generation of smart things. In particular, it must target emerging IoT platforms, it must support simulation of interactions between pre-existing smart things and new smart things, and it must facilitate deployment of large numbers of similar things. Moreover, awareness of the potential benefits of SDL must be raised if those benefits are to be realized in the current and future Internet of Things.

Keywords: Internet of things · Modelling · Simulation · Testing · Safety · Reliability · Engineering practice

1 Introduction

Smart things are everywhere, and new smart things are being created and deployed all the time. Together, they form the Internet of Things (IoT), defined by Atzori and others as *'a collection of things that are able to interact with each other and co-operate with their neighbours to reach common goals'* [1]. Smart

© Springer International Publishing Switzerland 2015
J. Fischer et al. (Eds.): SDL 2015, LNCS 9369, pp. 27–41, 2015.
DOI: 10.1007/978-3-319-24912-4_3

things present wonderful opportunities, but when they participate in the complex system that is the Internet of Things, they challenge our ability to manage risk and ensure reliability.

Some smart things from the contemporary Internet of Things are described below. The potential for SDL to improve processes for developing things like these is explored, and recommendations are made for more closely aligning SDL [10] with the professional engineering practices and processes that will ensure the quality of the next generation of smart things. This is likely to be of interest both to those seeking a viable technology that will serve as a backbone for communication within the IoT, and also to the established SDL community to raise awareness and stimulate discussion about future evolution of SDL to meet the needs of the people who are already bringing the IoT into being.

2   SDL and the IoT

The Internet of Things is real, current and vulnerable. Novelty and complexity are essential characteristics of the IoT, but novelty and complexity also present direct challenges to reliability and security [18]. However, although the IoT is complex, individual smart things need not be complex, and are often developed by hobbyists or children. That is, even if a new smart thing or network of smart things is not very complex in itself, complexity explodes when new things are deployed amongst all the other things that populate the IoT. Moreover, the behaviour of a new thing in the IoT might well be affected by the pre-existing IoT population, which is likely to include smart things whose behaviour is unpredictable or hostile or both.

Although the challenges of novelty and complexity are difficult, they are not insurmountable. According to the Royal Academy of Engineering and The British Computer Society, the global communications backbone has very high availability – approximately two hours total system downtime in 40 years availability [18]. Much of that success can be attributed to mature engineering processes for adding new devices, protocols etc. to the telecommunications network. Modelling and simulation are central to those processes, as is adherence to standards such as the ITU Z.100 family of standards [10].

A few of the many smart things to be found in the contemporary IoT are briefly considered below, and the potential for SDL to enhance their benefits and limit their vulnerabilities is considered.

2.1   National Plant Phenomics Centre

EPPN, the European Plant Phenotyping Network, is an EU project that offers access to 23 different plant phenotyping facilities at seven different institutions in five countries. One of these seven institutions is the National Plant Phenomics centre in Aberystwyth[1], which provides access to phenotyping platforms

---

[1] http://www.plant-phenomics.ac.uk/en/.

that support research involving computer scientists, engineers and biologists to address how genetics and environment bring about the physical characteristics that constitute plant phenotypes. Current projects supported at the centre include predicting responses of food and fuel crops to future climates and development of robust standards for phenotyping experiments and environmental modelling.

At the heart of the National Plant Phenomics centre is a robotic greenhouse that enables controlled temperature, watering and nutrient regimes. Plants are automatically transported through the greenhouse on a conveyor system comprising over 800 individually RFID tagged carriages, and through five imaging chambers that allow different kinds of images – normal digital photographs, infrared images and fluorescence – to be obtained for further analysis.

This environment collects data that can be accessed via the Internet, but as most of its communications are internal, its vulnerability is limited.

SDL could have been used to good effect to model communications within the robotic greenhouse, thus limiting the potential for error within the system. It could also be used to model how data is made available for external processing, and to simulate – and prevent – situations that might lead to data loss or corruption.

2.2 Walls Have Ears

Internet enabled television sets are a common consumer device, providing access to more content than was available with the previous generation of TV sets. However, with greater interactivity comes greater vulnerability.

For example, concern was raised in *The Daily Beast*[2] regarding privacy of data captured by the voice control facilities available on some Samsung smart TV sets.

In a similar vein, *My friend Cayla*[3] is a doll that provides enhanced interaction by connecting with the public Internet. No data captured by Cayla is currently retained, and no analytics carried out, but nonetheless, the potential to capture and analyse such data is present.

Had SDL been used in the development of these smart things, the potential for data leakage could have been made explicit by simulation and could then have been controlled.

2.3 Field Robotics

In the realm of Field Robotics, sensors are mounted on an autonomous robot that can navigate and survive in an unconstrained environment – sea, land, air, extra-terrestrial – where data is collected and transmitted to a base for further

---

[2] http://www.thedailybeast.com/articles/2015/02/05/your-samsung-smarttv-is-spying-on-you-basically.html.

[3] http://myfriendcayla.co.uk/.

analysis. In other words, it is a typical smart thing that collects and uploads data for analysis and combination with other data to provide useful information.

Challenges include power management, securing the robot and its sensors against potentially hostile physical environments, and ensuring that both hardware and embedded software function reliably and correctly, as illustrated, for example by a glacier-surveying remote-controlled sailing robot [14].

SDL could have supported the development of communications for controlling the boat, and for collecting the sensor data. The effects of physical problems on communications could also have been modelled and simulated using SDL.

Similar applications of SDL include the communications infrastructure of smart cities described in the keynote address [5], and a smart bicycle, for use in training, that was developed using SDL [13]. These applications illustrate the benefits of simulation and automated code generation in the development of reliable smart things, as well as the versatility and usefulness of SDL.

SDL has also been used to model and interact with a factory in a virtual reality scenario. This virtual representation is particularly interesting since the IoT will use Virtual Reality to interact with all the smart devices [7].

However, SDL does not directly support the physical engineering processes that result in physical devices, and a complete process involving design and fabrication of physical things as well as programming their behaviour would require fusion of SDL with appropriate support for computer aided design and manufacturing.

2.4   Smart Living

Smart homes promise many things, from intelligent control of lighting and heating, through smart appliances to ambient support for people with disabilities, including age-related disabilities. But this promise is not without corresponding threats. Smart appliances and power management systems threaten privacy, and their failure or unexpected behaviour could lead to the kind of dystopian vision presented by Hecht [8].

In this section we review the Smart Home concept and how SDL can help to provide a holistic solution that encompasses the many different facets and components of the problem.

When we think about a Smart Home, we envisage a house where we can control almost everything, from the windows, to the doors, to the bathroom; or perhaps we think of the various cameras that allow us to see what happens inside or outside our home, with all the legal issues this implies. However, a Smart Home cannot be understood in isolation from the question of sustainability. Usually sustainability is limited to immediate environmental considerations, but, with present-day availability of information, a broader view of sustainability becomes possible. For example, we can take into consideration the origin of the different materials and the environmental and social implications of different construction solutions when we develop a building (or an urban area). This helps us to address not only the environmental aspect of sustainability, but also the social and the economic impacts. Moreover, interconnection of different smart devices enhances the possibility to observe the social effects of urban design with a view to improving future designs.

Since sustainability is one of the main challenges for legislators, ever more clear and specific rules are being applied to new architectural designs. For example, 2010/31/EU European Directive on the Energy Performance of Buildings (EPBD)[4] aims to speed up energy saving policies in the building sector in order to achieve a 20 % reduction of energy consumption in the European Union. Among many other measures, Article 9 of the directive stipulates that from December 31, 2020 new buildings must be nearly zero in energy consumption, and from December 31, 2018 for occupied buildings and/or public property buildings. In relation to this measure, the board recommends that Member States establish intermediate objectives in 2015 and gradually adopt the goals until 2020 to ensure compliance with the objectives set.

Regulation also applies to renovation and refurbishment of buildings, where all methods must be based on a cost benefit analysis, in order to achieve optimal levels of profitability and sustainability.

The energy that we can use in a building, the origins of this energy and the impacts on the society must all be considered in a Smart Home. In order to obtain this information, a Smart Home includes many devices that enable gathering of a huge amount of information. Differences between devices, methods and protocols make reuse of the devices, protocols and even information difficult. But since reuse is one of the key aspects of sustainability, and sustainability is a key aspect of a Smart Home, this is an issue that must be addressed.

Monitoring the Building. On one hand, from the point of view of the use of the building, or on the other, from the point of view of the design or refurbishment of the house, the interconnection of different hardware and software makes it difficult to extend and reuse the solutions. Now many different alternatives currently exist; some of the current alternatives that exist of the communication protocols used in this area are:

1. KNX [11], standardized on EN 50090, ISO/IEC 14543. KNX is an OSI-based network communications protocol mainly intended for the continuous monitoring of buildings. KNX was created from the convergence of three previous standards: the European Home Systems Protocol (EHS), BatiBUS, and the European Installation Bus (EIB or Instabus).
2. BACnet [9] is a communications protocol for building automation and control networks. It is an ASHRAE, ANSI, and ISO 16484-5 standard protocol.
3. Modbus [16] is a serial communications protocol originally published by Modicon (now Schneider Electric) in 1979 for use with its programmable logic controllers (PLCs). Simple and robust, it has since become a de facto standard communication protocol, and it is now a commonly available means of connecting industrial electronic devices

---

[4] http://eur-lex.europa.eu/legal-content/EN/TXT/?qid=1434227774810\&uri= CELEX:32010L0031.

4. There are many other alternatives such as LonWorks, Home Automation, BACnet, DOLLx8, EnOcean INSTEON, Z-Wave, Intelligent building, Lighting control system, OpenTherm, Room automation, Smart Environments, Touch panel.

These protocols are used on monitoring devices provided by various different manufacturers; for example, Schneider Electric, elvaco, Carlo Gava, Panasonic, among many others. This represents a huge disparity of elements that must be considered in the needed integration of information on a Smart Home. Also, and due to the huge opportunities that the Smart Home concept offers to the companies, big corporations are now able to offer complete development platforms to integrate several devices, offering a complete solution for the IoT.

SDL for the Smart Home. Because Smart Home technology makes use of different communication protocols, different devices and different development platforms, it is absolutely essential to create an abstraction layer that supports the definition and formalization of the multiple processes that must be taken into account in a smart home, or as an extension of this, in a smart city.

SDL can be used not only to define the communication mechanism between the different actors involved in the Smart Home processes, but also the modelling processes that help in the planning and refurbishment of the house. The Abstract State Machine semantics of SDL means that it can define both the communication architecture of the current Smart house elements, and also the complete behaviour and life cycle assessment (LCA) [15] between all the actors and elements that participate in the life of the building [6]. As a specification language targeted to the description of distributed systems, SDL is very suitable for defining communication elements at many levels of abstraction. This combination makes SDL a perfect language to define, in a holistic way, the main processes that govern the behaviour (both current and future) of a building or residential area.

While it is true that SDL does not directly address security in the sense of attacks on a system of communicating agents, it is perfectly possible to model malicious as well as desired agents in a system, and to simulate the behaviour of desired agents in the presence of malign agents. SDL models involving multiple environmental agents could be used to model threats without cluttering the model of the desired system.

Moreover, the unambiguous nature of the language, its graphical syntax and the clear semantics, make SDL a strong candidate to work in heterogeneous environments, with multidisciplinary teams that want to define a holistic view of a Smart Home.

3   Three Challenges

3.1   Making a Smart Thing Is Easy - Ensuring It Behaves Reliably in the Wild Is Not

As a whole, the Internet of Things is characterised by novelty and complexity – factors well known to challenge physical as well as software engineering [18].

However, individual smart things can be created relatively easily by children or young teenagers who are familiar with Minecraft[5], if they have access to a consumer-grade 3-d printer and some basic components. Even without 3-d printing, smart wearables based on Adafruit or Lilypad components are fun to make and use.

But this means that making safety- or business-critical smart things entails taking account of the other smart things that occupy the environment into which the new things must fit. In other words, the emergence of additive manufacturing and its domestic 3-d printing counterpart, together with the ready availabilty of microcontrollers, single-board computers and other components, has made it possible for any individual or organization to design, fabricate and program new kinds of smart thing, leading to an environment of interconnected smart devices some of which are likely to be badly-constructed or even malicious.

For these reasons, new communicating smart devices are threatened not only by inherent flaws in their own design, but also by flaws in the design of all the other devices that inhabit the Internet of Things. Modelling and simulation with SDL would help expose vulnerabilities before new devices are deployed and so improve security as well as reliability.

So, as we come to depend on ambient interconnected devices, better engineering processes and practices will be essential. SDL supports excellent engineering practices and processes by providing a precise way to specify communications, by enabling automated testing of distributed systems, and by supporting simulation before deployment.

3.2   New IoT Platforms

One of the major events that occurred recently in the IoT world, was the announcement of Brillo and Weave at the 2015 Google I/O conference [17]. Brillo[6], an Android derivate that covers just the lower levels, aims to become the underlying operating system for the Internet of Things, with a developer preview coming in the third quarter of this year.

Brillo represents an alternative to Microsoft's Windows 10, an OS that can be executed virtually on any device (from servers to RaspberryPi devices[7]. Windows 10, viewed as an IoT OS, offers the possibility to connect many different kinds of device such as may be found in a Smart Home.

---

[5] https://minecraft.net/.

[6] https://developers.google.com/brillo/.

[7] https://www.raspberrypi.org/windows-10-for-iot/.

It is clear that these will not be the only platforms to develop infrastructures for IoT. Canonical is taking a direction similar to that of Microsoft, announcing that in 2016 Unity8 will be integrated in Ubuntu desktop[8].

This brings into focus a trend in IoT platforms war, where two major kinds of IoT related technology are crystallizing.

One side there are IoT platforms supported by large industrial players such as the emerging Brillo-Weave platform supported by Google and the Intel® IoT. These platforms are addressed to third parties, yet their underlying technology is controlled by a single industrial actor.

On the other side, there are open IoT platforms. The emergence of such platforms is supported by public funding (see H2020 - ICT 30) and facilitated by the existence of standardised technologies, such as Machine-to-Machine communications (M2M) and Network Functions Virtualisation (NFV) standardised by the European Telecommunications Standards Institute.

Given the opaque nature of the industrial offerings and their projected dissemination, we suggest that efforts towards building open IoT platforms should be supported. Let us consider how SDL fits with respect to the above mentioned standards.

The main M2M assets are

- Unified access to data from any application domain.
- Management of Privacy (Access Rights) adapted to the Application needs.
- Management of security levels adapted to the Application needs.
- Suited for IP networks, yet agnostic to underlying communication technologies.

Although not primarily targeted to the IoT, Network Functions Virtualisation (NFV) is a standard relevant to the IoT. Among its principles the more pertinent with regard to the IoT seem to be

- The need for Inter-Domain Interfaces
- Generic functional blocks
- Multiplicity, Composition, and Decomposition

Originally designed to model telecom systems, SDL has also proved successful in addressing the needs of other application domains [5]. SDL can already support most of the concepts listed above; for example, SDL can deal with data management and with interfaces. However, it would need extensions for dealing with security and it would need adjustments to improve handling of multiplicity and dynamism.

The following section looks in more detail at the challenges of deployment, in particular the challenge of multiplicity, and describes how SDL rises to those challenges.

---

[8] http://news.softpedia.com/news/Canonical-Details-Plans-for-Unity-8-Integration-in-Ubuntu-Desktop-462117.shtml.

3.3   Deployment Issues

One of the main characteristics of IoT systems is that one of the sub-systems is usually instantiated a huge number of times. For example in a Smart Grid system the meters are sub-systems that are instantiated many times. Literally millions of them are deployed and any problem discovered on site is extremely costly for the operator to solve. Even though it is not always exactly the same sub-system that is instantiated, most of the main characteristics of the meters are the same. In the Smart Grid example, it could be that all meters will transmit the electrical consumption, some meters might do it every day, where some others might do it every month. Another characteristic is that the different sub-systems are physically separated entities that need to communicate with each other. The means of communication between the different sub-system are numerous but they all have the characteristics of a telecommunication protocol.

SDL has from its inception enabled precise description of telecommunication protocols. Static interface description is covered by ASN.1 data types with encoding and decoding rules, and dynamic aspects by the behaviour description of each protocol layer. These static and dynamic elements of an SDL specification are perfectly adapted to the description of exchanges between the different sub-systems in an IoT system. By extension, the application on top of the telecommunication protocols can also be described from a functional point of view. Because SDL is an executable language it is possible to verify the behaviour of the overall IoT system with an SDL simulator independently of any type of implementation. Functional variants of the IoT sub-system can be dealt with using object orientation in SDL. The common behaviour is described in a super-class, and the possible variants are described in different sub-classes.

Building up a system combining a mix of the different variants or several instances of the same sub-system is then very straight forward. Based on this concept, Humboldt University zu Berlin [3] has developed a deployment simulator of an SDL-RT[9] system based on the ns3 network simulator. This work was initially done to simulate an early warning earthquake detection system. The system is composed of hundreds of sensors deployed geographically and the information from the sensors is gathered and analyzed in one hub. PragmaDev has integrated and extended this work to automatically simulate the deployment of SDL or SDL-RT systems on numerous nodes.

The generic SDL architecture is used to define the different sub-systems (Fig. 1), an SDL-RT deployment diagram is used to define how many and where the nodes are deployed, and a csv file describes the scenario of events on each distributed node (Fig. 2).

Load Testing. The deployment simulator described above and illustrated in Fig. 3 is perfect from a functional point of view. But one of the most common IoT issues is limitation of the load that can be carried by the means of communication. If too many messages are sent at the same time it is quite possible that

---

[9] http://www.sdl-rt.org.

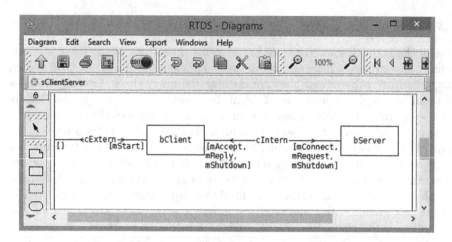

Fig. 1. The SDL architecture describes the different sub-systems: bClient and bServer

some or all of them get lost. These limitations can be described in the underlying network simulator but do not appear directly in the SDL model. It would be interesting and useful to be able to describe in the model a set of characteristics that integrate these limitations and to have the validation tools explore all the possible problems that might occur due to large numbers of deployed instances.

Interleaved Test Cases. The deployment simulator is a very powerful tool that is perfect for the early warning earthquake application. But from a functional point this simulator uses a csv file that describes only one scenario for all the possible nodes. Only a unique sequence among the different nodes is described that way. Usually, before the deployment, a set of test cases is written to test a single node of one of the sub-systems. The issue is to verify that having several instances of this node does not imply alteration of its functionalities. Each test case should be able to pass on one node independently of the execution of another test case on another node. In theory this leads to verification of any combination of the different test cases work on the deployed system and that creates a combinatoric explosion due to the number of possible interleaving combinations.

Work is currently on-going to identify blocks of messages that create interactions between the instances and to run a reduced number of relevant interleaved combination of the test cases.

4   What Is Needed to Make SDL the Language of Choice for IoT Systems?

The examples presented in previous sections highlight typical aspects of IoT systems development, validation and deployment, and illustrate the benefits of

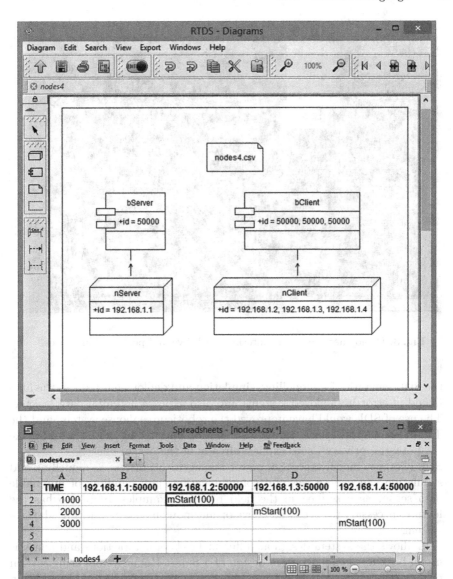

Fig. 2. The deployment diagram describes how many instances of each sub-system is deployed. One instance of bServer and three of bClient.

SDL. The SDL model of communicating agents fits the IoT systems model, and the formal semantics of SDL, with its associated data modelling capabilities, enables comprehensive validation of IoT sub-systems functionality by simulation and testing. Deployment of IoT systems designed in SDL is also currently well supported.

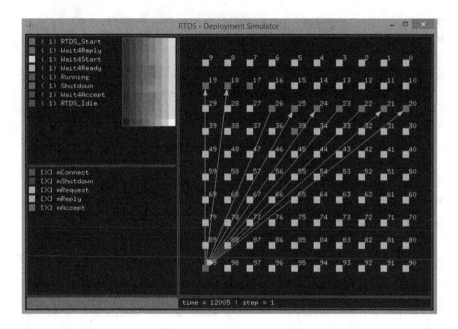

Fig. 3. Deployment simulator interface with live and post-mortem traces.

- the SDL semantics for modelling, simulation and deployment reduces the likelihood of error in deployed systems and also exposes potential data leakage. The use of SDL would have improved the robotic greenhouse system, and the TV and doll applications, through simulation and testing, which would make the potential privacy issues explicit already in the design phase.
- SDL allows to model aspects of power management, insofar as modelling and simulation can expose wasteful communications and handling of unreliable data sensor as described in the field robotics examples. SDL also has the features necessary to specify and develop autonomous self-monitoring adaptive systems.
- SDL allows the system design at different levels of abstractions and hence is useful both for detailed system design of a Smart Home system using several protocols as well as a building maintenance management system. In addition SDL also supports design of IoT systems using more protocols to implement the overall functionality of the system.
- SDL supports development targeting emerging platforms and new devices. It has proved its worth in protocol development and is sufficiently flexible to allow targeting of new devices.
- SDL offers support for well-established good engineering practices, including model simulation, automated testing and deployment. This increases reliability and reduces vulnerability of deployed systems.
- SDL allows simulations that involve large numbers of smart devices, and so addresses the need for scalability.

However, the IoT systems considered above also serve to identify areas where SDL needs improvement in order to fully support the design and development of such systems

- SDL tools are unlikely to compete with the small environments used by hobbyists with arduinos etc., not because these environments provide simulation and modelling, but rather because safety and reliability are not high-priority requirements amongs these developers. So instead of expecting all creators of smart things to use SDL and to follow sound engineering práctice, creators of secure, reliable smart things should use SDL to reduce inherent vulnerability in the things they produce and to increase their resilience to external agents that pose a threat whether because of poor design or malicious intent.
- While SDL supports development targeting emerging platforms, new IoT platforms mean that if SDL is to be used successfully for IoT system development, tools must be developed that map SDL models to these platforms. In particular, SDL should be mapped to open and freely-available platforms.
- The impact of deployment of an IoT system in contexts with numerous of other systems making use of the same communication resources causing potential delays and loss of messages is supported in SDL only to a limited degree. SDL may be extended with features to specify possible loss and delay of signals based on the load on a communication path.
- SDL semantics enables modelling of an environment populated by multiple agents. This provision should be explored and developed to facilitate development of secure networks of smart things, both with respect to privacy of data communicated between parts of an IoT system and protection against attacks to access data or to affect the system functionality.
- An emerging trend in the IoT is to design and 'print' a new device using additive manufacturing (3-d printing) techniques with suitable CAD software. SDL does not interface directly with CAD systems. For the future, it would be good to extract models of the implied SDL agent from designs of new devices. SDL would allow such models could be replicated, simulated and studied in a Virtual Reality populated by other smart devices.

Apart from these technical considerations, there is also an urgent need to raise awareness of the potential benefits of SDL for IoT systems development. For example, SDL is not mentioned in the 2011 survey [2], though this does include ns-2, which was used in conjunction with SDL [12]. Also there is no mention of SDL in [4]. Unless this situation is changed, it is highly likely that much that is already well established SDL will be re-invented, delaying development of the professional practices that will form the core of any effort to create a safe, reliable IoT.

5 Conclusion

We have looked at a variety of elements of the emerging Internet of Things and identified the role of SDL in supporting the engineering practices that will enable creation and deployment of safety and business critical smart things. We have also identified the need to improve SDL's capacity to model the behaviour of smart things when communications channels are heavily loaded, either because many instances of things are deployed in a smart system, or because different systems must co-exist in a crowded IoT environment. Security and privacy are also not adequately expressible in SDL as it stands.

But perhaps the greatest challenge lies in raising awareness of SDL amongst the people who will create and deploy the next generation of smart things.

References

1. Atzori, L., Iera, A., Morabito, G.: The internet of things: a survey. Comput. Netw. **54**, 2787–2805 (2010). Elsevier
2. Baumgartner, T., Chatzigiannakis, I., Fekete, S.P., Fischer, S., Koninis, C., Kröller, A., Krger, D., Mylonas, G., Pfisterer, D.: Distributed algorithm engineering for networks of tiny artifacts. Comput. Sci. Rev **5**(1), 85–102 (2011). Elsevier (Science Direct)
3. Brumbulli, M., Fischer, J.: Simulation configuration modeling of distributed communication systems. In: Haugen, Ø., Reed, R., Gotzhein, R. (eds.) SAM 2012. LNCS, vol. 7744, pp. 198–211. Springer, Heidelberg (2013)
4. Chatzigiannakis, I., Mylonas, G., Vitaletti, A.: Urban pervasive applications: challenges, scenarios and case studies. Comput. Sci. Rev. **5**(1), 103–118 (2011). Elsevier (SciVerse ScienceDirect Journals)
5. Fischer, J., Redlich, J.-P., Scheuermann, B., Schiller, J., Günes, M., Nagel, K., Wagner, P., Scheidgen, M., Zubow, A., Eveslage, I., Sombrutzki, R., Juraschek, F.: From earthquake detection to traffic surveillance – about information and communication infrastructures for smart cities. In: Haugen, Ø., Reed, R., Gotzhein, R. (eds.) SAM 2012. LNCS, vol. 7744, pp. 121–141. Springer, Heidelberg (2013)
6. Fonseca i Casas, P., Fonseca i Casas, A., Garrido-Soriano, N., Casanovas. J.: Formal Simulation Model to Optimize Building Sustainability. Adv. Eng. Softw. **69**, 62–74 (2014). doi:10.1016/j.advengsoft.2013.12.009
7. Fonseca i Casas, P., Pi, X., Casanovas, J., Jové, J.: Definition of virtual reality simulation models using specification and description language diagrams. In: Khendek, F., Toeroe, M., Gherbi, A., Reed, R. (eds.) SDL 2013. LNCS, vol. 7916, pp. 258–274. Springer, Heidelberg (2013). doi:10.1007/978-3-642-38911-5
8. Hecht, J.: The internet of **** things. Nat. Phys. **10**(7), 538–538 (2014)
9. ISO 16484–1:2010: Building Automation and Control Systems (BACS) - Part 1: Project Specification and Implementation, ISO 2010
10. ITU-T: Z.100 Series for SDL 2010, International Telecommunications Union 2011–2015
11. KNX Association: System Specifications (2014). http://www.knx.org/en-us/knx/technology/specifications/index.php
12. Kuhn, T., Geraldy, A., Gotzhein, R., Rothländer, F.: ns+SDL – the network simulator for SDL systems. In: Prinz, A., Reed, R., Reed, J. (eds.) SDL 2005. LNCS, vol. 3530, pp. 103–116. Springer, Heidelberg (2005)
13. Kuhn, T., Gotzhein, R., Webel, C.: Model-driven development with SDL – process, tools, and experiences. In: Nierstrasz, O., Whittle, J., Harel, D., Reggio, G. (eds.) MoDELS 2006. LNCS, vol. 4199, pp. 83–97. Springer, Heidelberg (2006)

14. Neal, M., Blanchard, T., Hubbard, A., Chauché, N., Bates, R., Woodward, J.: A hardware proof of concept for a remote-controlled glacier-surveying boat. J. Field Robot. **29**(6), 880–890 (2012). Wiley Periodicals

15. Ortiz, O., Castells, F., Sonnemann, G.: Sustainability in the construction industry: a review of recent developments based on LCA. Constr. Build. Mater. **23**(1), 28–39 (2009)

16. Pefhany, S.: Modbus Protocol, vol. 5. Penthon Media Inc. (2000)

17. Reaper, D.: Google IO 2015 Live Conference Keynote - Brillo & Weave. YouTube Video, 11:08 minutes, May 2015. https://www.youtube.com/watch?v=-BSRSCPxiPg. Accessed 4 Jun 2015

18. The Royal Academy of Engineering and The British Computer Society: The Challenges of Complex IT Projects. The Report of a Working Group from The Royal Academy of Engineering and The British Computer Society, The Royal Academy of Engineering (2004). http://bcs.org/upload/pdf/complexity.pdf. Accessed 4 Jun 2015

Event Pattern Mining for Smart Environments

Lars George[(✉)]

Humboldt-Universität zu Berlin, Unter den Linden 6, 10099 Berlin, Germany
lars.george@informatik.hu-berlin.de

Abstract. Complex Event Processing (CEP) systems find matches of a pattern in a stream of events. Patterns specify constraints on matching events and therefore describe situations of interest. Formulating patterns is not always trivial, especially in smart environments where a large amount of events are continuously created. For example, a smart home with sensors that can tell us if someone is flipping on a light switch to indicate how he would like his breakfast in the morning. Our work deals with the problem of mining patterns from historical traces of events.

Keywords: Complex event processing · Data Mining · Smart environments

1 Introduction

Our environment is already equipped with a lot of sensors delivering information, and it keeps on growing. Smartphones are detecting our positions, the current temperature is measured at multiple locations and sensor nodes detect movement using accelerometers. The sum of those events can describe more complex situations. For example a passing car can be described by combining the accelerometer values of sensor nodes near a road. Lots of cars on one road can lead to a traffic jam. With the information that it is a sunny and warm Friday afternoon the roads leading to swimming pools and recreation areas can be prioritized by smart traffic lights and navigation systems.

Formulating patterns that describe situations of interest is not always trivial. Even domain experts may not be able to precisely describe all causalities that lead to it. For example, how does the pattern for a car detection from accelerometer values look like? Our work deals with the problem of automatically mining event patterns from historical traces of events.

2 Related Work

Cook and Wolf [3] showed three methods for discovering models of software processes from event-based data. One uses neural networks, the second one uses an algorithmic approach and the third one uses a Markovian approach. All mined models only rely on the timestamp and the type of the involved events. Other attributes of events are not considered.

© Springer International Publishing Switzerland 2015
J. Fischer et al. (Eds.): SDL 2015, LNCS 9369, pp. 42–45, 2015.
DOI: 10.1007/978-3-319-24912-4_4

"The goal of process mining is to extract information about processes from transaction logs."[5] The transaction logs consist of events having a timestamp and some given attributes like the reference to an activity. The result is an ordering of activities for example expressed in terms of a Petri net. There exists work that extends this mining approach but the detection of trends in the data, like an increase of a numerical value in the events, is not handled.

Margara et al. address the same research goal of mining event patterns from historical traces. [6] Although they also allow for events having attributes and constraints on attributes, the mined constraints are only associated to event types. Different constraint combinations for events of the same type in a pattern are not handled. Their work does not support this due to the fact that they do not mine an order. The result only includes information about certain event types that are followed by other event types. This is not sufficient to for example mine trends from the data.

3 Background

We define an event e as a tuple $e = (E, t, A_1 = a_1, ..., A_n = a_n)$, where E is the event type, $A_1 = a_1, ..., A_n = a_n$ are the attributes of the event with A_i being the attribute names and a_i the attribute values, and t represents the occurrence time of the event. For t we assume a totally ordered and discrete time domain. The type of an event specifies the attributes of an event and their types.

An *event pattern* for event pattern matching is defined as a triple $P = (V, \Theta, \tau)$ where $V =< v_1, ..., v_k >, k \geq 1$, is a sequence of event variables, $\Theta = \{\theta_1, ..., \theta_c\}, c \geq 0$, is a set of constraints over the variables in V, and τ is the duration of the pattern.

Each *event variable* $v_e \in V$ binds an event and is used to state the order of the incoming events. Θ is a set of conditions over the event variables that express constraints on the values of event attributes which must be satisfied by the matching events. They can further be distinguished into property constraints and relationship constraints. *Property constraints* have the form $v_e.A \phi C$, where $v_e.A$ refers to an attribute of a matching event, C is a constant, and $\phi \in \{=, <, \leq, >, \geq\}$ is a comparison operator. *Relationship constraints* have the form $v_e.A_i \phi v_f.A_j$ and therefore are used to describe relationships between two attributes of matching events. τ is the maximal allowed time span between the first and last matching event.

The following example demonstrates an event pattern: $P_1 = (< a, b >, \Theta, 1h)$. The sequence of event variable states that two events are contained in this pattern. The maximal time span is 1 hour. The constrains are $\Theta = \{a.Type = "Ev"$, $b.Type = "Ev", a.Value > 21, a.Value < b.Value\}$. The event variable a is used for three constraints, the event type needs to be "Ev", its attribute *Value* needs to be greater than 21 and its attribute *Value* needs to be less than the attribute *Value* of b. The event type of event variable b also needs to be "Ev".

Our work concentrates on the problem of event pattern mining from historical traces. A historical trace is a sequence $T =< e_1, ..., e_h >$ where $< e_1, ..., e_h >$,

Table 1. Two example historical traces

Traces	Events
h1	("Ev", 10, Val=21.7), ("Ev", 15, Val=23.3), ("Ev", 25, Val=26.1)
h2	("Ev", 11, Val=21.7), ("Ev", 37, Val=27.4)

$h \geq 1$, is a sequence of events. The events are ordered by their occurrence time t. We only use historical traces where the situation of interest occurs. The situation of interest could for example be a dangerous situation like a fire outbreak where the temperature increases rapidly in a room. Table 1 shows two fictional example historical traces h1 and h2.

4   Event Pattern Mining

The problem of event pattern mining can be described as finding an event pattern from a given set of traces, that detects all situations of interest in a stream of events as matches. This involves finding an order of event variables, constraints, and a pattern duration.

We mine parts of a pattern by extracting them from each historical trace and only keep those that appear in every historical trace. For example the event types that occur in every historical trace of Fig. 1 is the set {"Ev"}. One trace having a second event type would not change the result. Instead of extracting the event types we introduce the concept of an event instance in the mining process as a core component. An *event instance* is an event with a selection of its attributes set to a constant value. We define it as $I = (E, E.A_i = c_i, ..., E.A_j = c_j)$, $\{A_i, ..., A_j\} \subseteq \{A_1, ..., A_n\}$, where E is the event type, $E.A_i$ is the name of an attribute of E and c_i is a constant value. Using event instances instead of event types allows to distinguish orders of incoming events of the same type.

Figure 1 shows the high level architecture of the proposed event pattern mining system. The first step involves mining all relevant event instances. Relevant here means that it occurs in all historical traces. For the example in Table 1 these are $i_1 = ("Ev", Ev.Val = 21.7)$ and $i_2 = ("Ev")$.

With a given set of relevant event instances the event instance order stating the sequence of event variables of the event pattern can be mined. Based upon the relevant event instances a transformation from the historical traces to the input format of sequential pattern mining algorithms introduced in [1] is performed. The output of the sequential pattern mining algorithm is a list of all possible orders occurring in all traces. For the example in Table 1 this is the sequence $< i_1, i_2 >$. Each mined sequence is handled separately for the next steps and results in a new pattern as output for the whole system.

The third step is an event instance matching. Each event instance in the mined order gets references to the events in the traces it can be applied to. An event instance applies to an event if all attribute values of the event instance are equal to the attribute values of the event. We also require all previous event

Fig. 1. High level architecture for mining event patterns

instances in the order to already have at least one applying event in the trace. The resulting data structure is used by the next step to mine the constraints Θ of the pattern. One relationship constraint for the example in Table 1 is $i_1.Val < i_2.Val$.

The output of the system is one or more patterns. Using all example results described above the following pattern can be mined: $P_1 = (< a, b >, \Theta, \tau)$ with $\Theta = \{a.Type = "Ev", a.Val = 21.7, b.Type = "Ev", a.Val < b.Val\}$.

Model to text transformations are used on the mined patterns. The targeted formats are existing event pattern matching languages such as Esper [4] and SES [2]. The learned patterns can then be evaluated and used in CEP systems.

5   Conclusion

In our work we develop an algorithmic approach that mines event patterns from historical traces of events. All attributes of the events are considered and can be part of the resulting pattern. Orders of events as well as trends in the data are mined. These are key differences to existing methods in this research area.

Future work includes a detailed evaluation of this approach and also considering historical traces where the situation of interest does not occur. Existing event pattern matching languages differ in their expressiveness and offer different operators for the patterns. We plan to mine for example aggregation operators, like the sum of attribute values over multiple events.

References

1. Agrawal, R., Srikant, R.: Mining sequential patterns. In: Eleventh International Conference on Data Engineering, pp. 3–14. IEEE (1995)
2. Cadonna, B., Gamper, J., Böhlen, M.H.: Efficient event pattern matching with match windows. In: 18th ACM SIGKDD International Conference on Knowledge Discovery and Data Mining, pp. 471–479. ACM (2012)
3. Cook, J.E., Wolf, A.L.: Discovering models of software processes from event-based data. ACM Trans. Softw. Eng. Methodol. (TOSEM) **7**(3), 215–249 (1998)
4. Esper - see http://www.espertech.com/
5. van Dongen, B.F., de Medeiros, A.K.A., Verbeek, H.M.W.E., Weijters, A.J.M.M.T., van der Aalst, W.M.P.: The ProM framework: a new era in process mining tool support. In: Ciardo, G., Darondeau, P. (eds.) ICATPN 2005. LNCS, vol. 3536, pp. 444–454. Springer, Heidelberg (2005)
6. Margara, A., Cugola, G., Tamburrelli, G.: Learning from the past: automated rule generation for complex event processing. In: 8th International Conference on Distributed Event-Based Systems, pp. 47–58. ACM (2014)

Specification and Description Language

Simulating Distributed Systems with SDL and Hardware-in-the-Loop

Tobias Braun and Dennis Christmann[✉]

Networked Systems Group, University of Kaiserslautern, Kaiserslautern, Germany
{tbraun,christma}@cs.uni-kl.de

Abstract. The Specification and Description Language (SDL) is a widespread language for the development of distributed real-time systems. One of its major advantages is its tool support, which enables the automatic generation of SDL implementations and the simulative evaluation of SDL systems in early development phases. However, SDL simulations often suffer from low accuracy, since they can not consider relevant non-functional aspects like execution delays of the target platform. In this paper, we present a novel approach improving the accuracy of simulations with SDL. It is based on the simulator framework FERAL and the simulation of SDL implementations on Hardware-in-the-Loop (HiL), thereby enabling both pure functional and performance evaluations of SDL systems. Besides providing a survey of SDL simulations with FERAL, this paper proposes a development process based on virtual prototyping, supporting step-wise system integration and tests of SDL systems by reducing the abstraction level of simulations gradually. To demonstrate this process and the significance of accurate simulations, results of a case study with an inverted pendulum are presented.

Keywords: SDL · Simulation · FERAL · Virtual prototyping · Hardware-in-the-Loop · Distributed systems · Networked control systems · Inverted pendulum

1 Introduction

The Specification and Description Language (SDL) [17] is a standardized language for the development of distributed systems, such as found in the domains of real-time systems and networked control systems. It is often applied in conjunction with model-driven development processes and also suitable for complex systems due to support for reuse and modularity. Due to extensive tool support, implementations for various software and hardware platforms can be generated from one SDL specification. Thereby, consistency between specification and implementation is ensured, and development effort is reduced significantly.

To evaluate SDL specifications, SDL tools like PragmaDev RTDS [22] or IBM Rational SDL Suite [14] come along with simulators enabling a step-wise inspection of an SDL system's behavior. If SDL is applied for reactive systems or in systems controlling a physical entity, this type of simulation is not sufficient

© Springer International Publishing Switzerland 2015
J. Fischer et al. (Eds.): SDL 2015, LNCS 9369, pp. 49–64, 2015.
DOI: 10.1007/978-3-319-24912-4_5

and more advanced methods are required to consider the environment of the systems, for instance, by means of a physical model of the controlled object. In our previous work [7,8], we introduced a modular simulator framework called *FERAL* (Framework for the Efficient simulator coupling on Requirements and Architecture Level), which supports virtual prototyping of SDL systems. Since FERAL incorporates several general and domain-specific simulators with different levels of abstraction like ns-3 or Matlab Simulink, the integration of SDL into FERAL enables the functional evaluation of SDL specifications in complex scenarios with simulated physical environments and communication media. Classical co-simulation approaches, such as Modelisar [3], are often limited to time-triggered simulation models. In comparison, FERAL provides generic concepts and interfaces to couple simulators with different models of computation and communication (e.g., time-triggered, event-triggered, and data flow).

Though with FERAL's support of simulator coupling and virtual prototyping, testing becomes possible in early development phases and in conjunction with specialized simulators, non-functional aspects like execution delays are still neglected. However, they may have a major impact on the behavior of a deployed system and may hence jeopardize time constraints. In particular with SDL, the early and accurate assessment of non-functional aspects needs specific attention due to the non-deterministic resolution of SDL's concurrent runtime model in SDL implementations and the related serialization of transition executions [6]. Since this non-determinism makes the behavior of an SDL system highly dependent from the runtime environment of the SDL implementation on the target platform, it is reasonable to test SDL systems with the same runtime environment and on the same platform as the final release.

In this paper, we present an approach to improve the significance of SDL simulations concerning performance and compliance with real-time properties by considering non-functional aspects of SDL implementations. It is based on the simulator framework FERAL and newly devised extensions to support Hardware-in-the-Loop (HiL) simulations, which are generally defined as closed-loop simulations, in which some of the subsystems are realized by physical replicas [11]. In our approach, the physical replicas – also called DUTs (*Devices Under Tests*) – are target platforms, on which SDL implementations are executed, whereas other components like communication media are simulated virtually. Unlike simulations with specialized platform simulators (e.g., Avrora for AVR microcontrollers), simulations with HiL do not require detailed hardware models, which are usually costly w.r.t. simulation effort and, particularly, a challenging task for modern platforms due to their complexity.

Besides providing a survey of HiL simulations with FERAL, this paper presents guidelines regarding virtual prototyping and the step-wise reduction of the level of abstraction in simulations. These guidelines are applied in a scenario with an inverted pendulum, in which controller, sensors, and actuators are interconnected by a simulated wireless communication medium. By increasing the fidelity gradually – and, finally, executing the controller node on HiL – we illustrate not only the importance of accurate simulations, but also show the advantages of *imprecise* simulations that state an adequate measure regarding first functional evaluations with decreased complexity and costs.

The remainder of this paper is structured as follows: In Sect. 2, the simulator framework FERAL is introduced together with the potential of simulating SDL systems on HiL, virtual prototyping, and the step-wise reduction of the abstraction level in simulations. Afterwards, Sect. 3 presents a case study with an inverted pendulum and simulation results. Section 4 provides a survey on related work. Finally, Sect. 5 draws conclusions.

2 The Simulator Framework FERAL

In this section, we introduce the simulator framework FERAL (Sect. 2.1) and extensions to support SDL (Sect. 2.2). Furthermore, guidelines to simulate networked systems with different levels of abstraction are outlined (Sect. 2.3).

2.1 Outline

FERAL is a modular, Java-based, and platform-independent framework [7,8] and incorporates several general and domain-specific simulators. One of its objectives is virtual prototyping for the early evaluation of design alternatives. By supporting various simulators and models with different abstraction levels, FERAL supports continuous testing of networked systems during different development phases and enables the functional and non-functional evaluation of various communication technologies.

In FERAL, two types of simulation components are distinguished: *Functional Simulation Components* (FSCs) modeling the behavior of (networked) nodes (e.g., a controller) and *Communication-based Simulation Components* (CSCs) simulating communication between FSCs (e.g., a CAN bus). In addition, FERAL supports *bridges* and *gateways* to interconnect different FSCs and CSCs and to simplify their exchange. FSCs can, for instance, be native components written in Java or Matlab Simulink models. CSCs can be simulated by a simulator for abstract Point-to-Point (PtP) media (short PtP CSC), by specialized bus simulators for CAN and FlexRay, or by ns-3 – thereby supporting various communication technologies like IEEE 802.3 (Ethernet) and IEEE 802.11 (WLAN). Data transfer between FSCs, CSCs, bridges, and gateways is realized by simulator messages, which are sent via ports of the simulation components. They represent the endpoints of links, enabling an arbitrary interconnection between simulation components. An example simulation topology from a previous adaptive cruise control scenario is given in Fig. 1 for illustrative purpose. The execution of simulation components is controlled by directors of FERAL, where both time- and event-triggered execution semantics are supported and can even be nested.

2.2 Simulation of SDL Models

To integrate SDL systems into FERAL and to support SDL FSCs, an existing SDL tool chain consisting of IBM's Rational SDL Suite [14], the SDL-to-C++

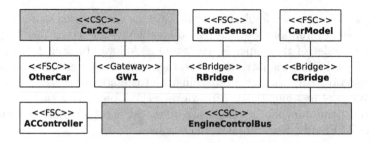

Fig. 1. Example simulation scenario with FERAL.

code generator ConTraST, the SDL runtime environment SdlRE [23], and the
SDL environment implementation SEnF has been extended. With these exten-
sions, SDL specifications can automatically be transformed to SDL implementa-
tions, which are able to run under control of FERAL and to interact with other
FSCs and CSCs. In total, two variants of SDL-based FSCs have been realized:
Library-based SDL FSCs and *HiL SDL FSCs.*

Library-based SDL FSCs incorporate SDL models by loading their implementations in the form of shared libraries. Since FERAL is written in Java but
generated SDL implementations are in C++, an additional wrapper with the
Java Native Interface (JNI) has been introduced to bridge the language bar-
rier. Though execution times of transitions and the SDL runtime environment
are not considered in this integration variant since FERAL has full control over
time progress, library-based FSCs are sufficient for functional evaluations of the
SDL system's behavior in early development phases and quantitative assessments
of simulated communication technologies.

The second integration variant (HiL SDL FSCs) executes the automatically
derived implementation of the SDL model on a physically independent device,
which is in our specific case a platform called Imote2 [19]. The Imote2 is a sensor node that is equipped with an ARM-based CPU running up to 416 MHz,
256 KB SRAM, 32 MB SDRAM, and 32 MB flash. With HiL simulations, execution delays and platform-specific timings are taken into account and performance
evaluations of the SDL system become possible.

The interplay between the simulator core of FERAL and the SDL model
running on an Imote2 is illustrated in Fig. 2. On the side of the FERAL core,
the SDL FSC is represented by a *proxy*, which is responsible for transmitting
commands and simulator messages to and from the SDL system on the HiL. In
a similar way, a *stub* is introduced in the implementation of the SDL environment (SEnF) on the HiL side that (de-)serializes messages and commands and
interfaces the SDL model.

The communication between proxy and stub is via a hardware gateway, which
communicates with the proxy by TCP/IP and with the stub by a serial line. By
introducing dedicated gateways, the node interconnecting the Imote2 can be
physically different from the node running the simulator core, thereby enabling
a spatial separation of simulator and HiL, simplifying the simultaneous simula-

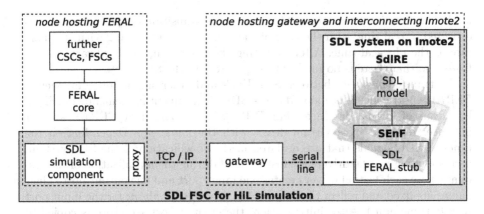

Fig. 2. Interrelation between FERAL and SDL FSCs running on HiL.

tion of multiple SDL FSCs, and improving scalability. Messages and commands between proxy and stub are encoded with ASN.1 [16] and suffixed with check-sums. To handle message losses, acknowledgments and timeouts are incorporated additionally. An overview of the most important types of messages is provided by Table 1. In this regard, the first listed message type (`RebootNode`) has been introduced to reset the hardware platform and to enable multiple independent simulation runs in series.

The biggest difference between library-based and HiL SDL FSCs is regarding time progress in the SDL system. While transition executions are instantaneous and time progress is fully controlled by the simulator with library-based SDL FSCs, time increases linearly during an SDL system's execution with HiL simulations, depending on the speed of the hardware and the workload of the system. In more detail, the time of the SDL system is managed as follows: Before executing the system, the simulation time of FERAL and the hardware clock of the Imote2 node get synchronized, thereby setting the system time of the SDL model

Table 1. Message types for the communication between proxy and stub.

Message type	Direction	Description
`RebootNode`	FERAL → HiL	Request to restart the Imote2
`InputPortNames`	FERAL ← HiL	List of names of reception ports
`OutputPortNames`	FERAL ← HiL	List of names of transmission ports
`SetSignals`	FERAL → HiL	Delivery of signals destined for the SDL FSC
`Run`	FERAL → HiL	Request to execute an SDL transition
`Terminated`	FERAL ← HiL	Information about the end of execution
`GetSignals`	FERAL ← HiL	Delivery of signals sent by the SDL FSC
`ACK`	FERAL ↔ HiL	Confirmation of a correct message reception

to the current simulation time. Afterwards, one transition of the SDL system is executed in real time with the time of the SDL system increasing with the same rate as the physical time. After executing the transition, the hardware clock is frozen, so that there is no further time progress in the SDL system.

To transfer messages between SDL FSCs and other simulation components, FERAL's port concept is adopted in the SDL environment implementation SEnF by means of virtual device drivers. PtP CSCs supported by FERAL are, for instance, reflected by a virtual driver with the name *ptp*. Depending on the types of SDL signals that are declared in the specification of the SDL system, corresponding virtual drivers are instantiated during the initialization of the system, where each virtual driver creates one input port and one output port. Their names are fixed and reflect the name of the driver (e.g., *ptp_rx* for the input port to a PtP medium). After initialization, the created port structure is copied to the proxy of the SDL FSC (cf. messages `InputPortNames` and `OutputPortNames` in Table 1). As result, all ports created in the SDL implementation are also provided by the proxy of the SDL FSC and can be used to connect the SDL system executed on the Imote 2 with other simulation components by means of their names.

To convert simulator signals into SDL signals (and vice versa), correspondent functions are introduced in the implementation of the SDL environment. Simulator signals sent by other simulation components to the SDL system are immediately delivered by FERAL to the SDL system, converted into SDL signals, and buffered in the SDL environment until the system is executed next. In a similar way, SDL signals generated by transitions of the SDL system and sent to the SDL system's environment are buffered until the end of execution of the system, when they are converted into simulator signals and forwarded to interconnected simulation components.

After executing an HiL SDL FSC, the time of the SDL system generally precedes the simulation time, since in our SDL implementation, SDL transitions are executed in a non-preemptive way and usually last considerably longer than the duration of a simulation step. To get semantically correct results despite this mismatch, SDL's integration into FERAL utilizes the simulator framework's support of directors with differing time granularity [9]. In particular, following measures are applied: First, after execution is complete, the simulator is informed about the time of the SDL system (cf. message `Terminated` in Table 1). Second, the SDL system is not again executed until the simulation time catches up to the time of the SDL system. Third, signals sent by the SDL system to another component are not available immediately but delayed until the destination's simulation time is up to the SDL time to avoid signals from the future.

2.3 Developing Distributed Systems with Virtual Prototyping

For complex distributed systems, it is reasonable to build up a system step-wise with increasing complexity. Our approach is the application of virtual prototyping, where system development starts with the definition of an abstract simulation system, consisting of a set of interacting FSCs and CSCs. In the next step, the abstract simulation system is instantiated by assigning behavior models (e.g., SDL systems) and by choosing concrete simulators for the FSCs and CSCs. This results in a concrete simulation system, which is executable by FERAL.

In early development phases, the simulated behavior models are abstract functional models with reduced complexity. In later phases, they are refined and extended step-wise until they are functionally complete and ready to be deployed to their target platform. Each refinement step of a behavior model can be seen as the definition of a new concrete simulation system. Since FERAL enables the interaction of FSCs (with behavior models) on different abstraction levels, each concrete simulation system remains executable and can, therefore, be used for functional evaluations. Hence, errors in the behavior of the models can be identified early and gradually, and also regression tests become possible.

When developing systems by step-wise reducing the level of abstraction, the last step of integration – i.e., switching from simulation to target platform – usually is most difficult and tedious. We identified two main reasons for this, which are not necessarily independent: First, by switching to the target platform, a real physical environment and no longer a simulated model of the physical world has to be handled. Hence, reproducibility of test runs is not guaranteed because of disturbances. Furthermore, debugging becomes harder, since it is usually not possible to pause and resume a physical process. Second, platform-specific execution delays occur, which may influence the behavior of the system and the timings. This non-functional aspect has not been covered in earlier development phases, yet its effects may sum up, since every node is affected (possibly in a different way). To better support the last integration phase, we developed extensions for FERAL to enable an SDL system's execution on HiL, thereby combining realistic timing behavior with a simulated (physical) environment.

Though the incremental development approach seems not to be viable regarding the problems of the integration phase, it has several advantages compared to direct development and testing on the (embedded) target platform, which is very time-consuming and troublesome. In particular, it enables a step-wise decrease of the abstraction level of behavior models and the simulated environment, for instance, by applying one integration step in which only communication delays are introduced. Additionally, this approach allows to first focus on functional aspects, before considering platform-specific performance aspects. Since each step leaves an executable simulation system, tests and functional/performance evaluations can be performed early and even automatic tests are realizable, which is hard to achieve when dealing with a real physical environment. Therefore, chances with a virtual prototyping-driven development process are good to detect errors and even conceptional defects early during development, when solutions are comparatively cheap. However, we do not deny that some functional aspects may suffer from performance issues detected in later development steps and HiL simulations, and need adjustments, e.g., control parameters.

Reasonable abstraction levels must be defined individually and depend on the complexity of the scenario and influencing factors, such as communication and execution delays. In the next section, we present appropriate abstraction levels for a distributed control system in our case study with an inverted pendulum.

3   Case Study – the Inverted Pendulum

In this section, results of a case study are presented to demonstrate the power of step-wise system refinement and the importance of accurate simulations. The scenario comprises an inverted pendulum, which is a standard example of a control system commonly found in control theory and realized in the form of a distributed networked system. After describing the setup of the scenario and the applied refinement steps in Sects. 3.1 and 3.2 presents results of several simulation runs, which have been performed with FERAL and the different levels of abstraction.

3.1   Scenario Description

The target of the inverted pendulum system is to balance the rod of the pendulum vertically with its mass pointing upwards and to preclude it from toppling by moving a cart on which the rod is mounted with a pivot point. In our scenario, the physics and behavior of the pendulum are given by a Simulink model[1], whereas sensor, actuator, and controller nodes are specified with SDL and allow executions with different abstraction levels. The conducted topologies are presented in Fig. 3 and contain a simulated communication medium, which interconnects all nodes and is refined during the development of the system. In order to obtain sensor values and to influence the movement of the cart, the sensor and actuator nodes are connected to the model of the pendulum. They provide the input and sink, respectively, for the controller node, which hosts a PID controller computing new manipulated variables periodically based on the sensor values of the pendulum's actual deflection and the actual speed and position of the cart.

Figure 4 shows an overview of the SDL system of the controller, which follows a classical layer architecture. Except for the application layer, the SDL systems of sensor and actuator nodes are similar. On the controller node, the application layer (block instance app) is realized by the block type PIDController, implementing the PID control algorithm for the inverted pendulum. To abstract from the communication on lower layers, the application communicates via the middleware NCS-CoM [12], which offers service-based interfaces to provide and access distributed functionalities in the network. NCS-CoM has also been developed in SDL and allows to abstract from the concrete location of services, i.e., from the nodes where data or functionalities are hosted. Thus, NCS-CoM provides transparent access to all services, whether they are executed remotely or

---

[1] First, we designed a mathematical model of the physics and behavior of the inverted pendulum based on differential equations. To enable simulations, this mathematical model has been transformed into a Simulink model. We have chosen Simulink, since its semantics is particularly suited to represent such kind of models.

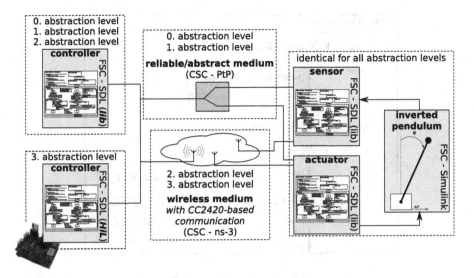

Fig. 3. Simulated network topology of the inverted pendulum scenario.

locally on the same node. In this regard, a service registry is introduced in NCS-CoM to find available services, to register new ones, and to subscribe to existing ones. In the inverted pendulum scenario, this registry stores corresponding services of the sensor and actuator nodes, which are accessed by the controller via the NCS-CoM middleware.

On the MAC layer, the SDL system provides two alternatives, which are realized as block types and implement the same interface (see also Fig. 4): A simple event-triggered MAC protocol (EVENT_MAC) and an advanced TDMA-based protocol (TDMA_MAC). They can be exchanged easily by just modifying the block instantiation. For first functional tests, the development of the inverted pendulum system starts with the simple event-triggered MAC layer. This MAC layer will be replaced later by the final TDMA-based MAC layer, which ensures deterministic guarantees and collision-free transmissions via exclusive slot reservations. Figure 5 shows the corresponding configuration of the message schedule for this protocol, where time is divided into macro slots, which are further subdivided into synchronization and reserved transmission slots. In this scenario, each macro slot has a duration of about one second and starts with a synchronization (*synch slot*). Afterwards, periodical transmission slots with a duration of 10 ms and an interval of 30 ms are reserved for each node (sensor, controller, and actuator).

Applying virtual prototyping, the inverted pendulum system has been developed and evaluated with a total of four abstraction levels:

– Level 0: This level performs functional evaluations of the control algorithm and the middleware NCS-CoM. It executes all nodes by library-based SDL FSCs, thereby neglecting execution delays, which would accumulate on real hard-

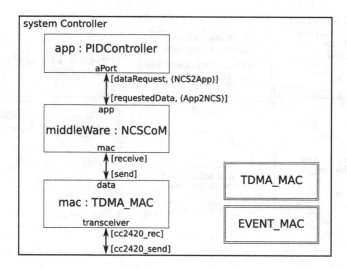

Fig. 4. SDL system of the controller node.

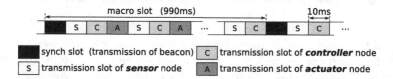

Fig. 5. Message schedule of controller, sensor, and actuator node.

ware. Communication is via the event-triggered MAC layer (cf. SDL block type
EVENT_MAC) and a reliable PtP communication medium of FERAL, enabling
simultaneous transmissions without propagation delays and collisions. With
this high level of abstraction, the designer can focus on the functionality of
the middleware, such as registration, subscription, and provision of services.
Furthermore, results of simulations can serve as a basis to select a suited
controller type and to derive a first set of control parameters.

– Level 1: This level replaces the event-triggered MAC layer by the TDMA-
based MAC layer (cf. SDL block type TDMA_MAC). With this abstraction level,
developers can concentrate on functional tests of the MAC protocol and its
interaction with NCS-CoM by using scenario-specific message characteristics as test input. Though the communication medium is still the simulated
PtP medium, first communication delays introduced due to the TDMA-based
message scheme are considered now, thereby enabling first estimates w.r.t.
their influence on the quality of control and the stability of the pendulum.

– Level 2: On this level, the simulated PtP communication medium is replaced
by the model of a wireless communication channel, which is provided by ns-3
in the form of a CSC of FERAL. In this regard, ns-3 has been extended in
previous works with a simulation model of the CC2420 transceiver [15], which

corresponds to the transceiver of the Imote 2. Thereby, this abstraction level enables accurate simulations of the communication, considering transceiver-specific delays (e.g., switching delays or transmission delays), propagation delays, and limitations (e.g., communication range or destructive interferences). Hence, the impact of theses factors on the quality of control can be evaluated.

– Level 3: This abstraction level executes the SDL system of the controller node no longer as library-based SDL FSC but on an Imote2 as HiL. Thereby, execution delays introduced by the real target platform and their influence on quality of control are assessed. In particular, execution times of the SDL run-time environment and the selection of transitions and their execution on the specific platform are considered now, thereby providing accurate simulation results and realistic statements about the behavior of the deployed system.

3.2   Results

Simulation runs were performed for each of the four aforementioned abstraction levels. In each simulation run, the same start conditions hold, consisting of a four degree deflection of the inverted pendulum from the unstable equilibrium, a non-moving cart, and a rotation speed of the rod of zero. Furthermore, the actual manipulated variable controlling the motor of the cart was set to zero.

Figure 6 shows the results of the respective simulation runs. The deflections of the inverted pendulum from the unstable equilibrium, as measured by the simulated sensor, are plotted as dashed lines, whereas the solid lines show the manipulated variables (voltage) used to operate the actuator of the cart. These variables are calculated by the controller in order to stabilize the pendulum, i.e., to minimize the deflection. The discrete steps in their progression reflect the control cycle of 60 ms, which is used by the PID controller to update the manipulated variables.

Figure 6(a) plots the simulation results with abstraction level 0. Although, the control algorithm causes some overshoots, the deflection of the pendulum is reduced to nearly zero fast. From that point on, the controller keeps the pendulum near its unstable equilibrium by applying minimal but continuous corrections. The generated curve progression of the manipulated variable is very smooth, thus avoiding fitful changes of load. Though, the parameters of the PID controller are not perfect (overshoots, not using the full range of the manipulated variable), they seem to be sufficient to stabilize the pendulum. Therefore, the same parameters are applied during all refinement steps and the impact of reduced abstraction levels on quality of control is evaluated in the concrete case.

The simulation results with abstraction level 1, where the event-triggered MAC protocol is replaced by the final TDMA-based MAC protocol, are plotted in Fig. 6(b). Compared with abstraction level 0, the amplitudes of the overshoots during the control process are higher and the decay of oscillation caused by the overshoots is slower. Thus, the control quality is obviously decreased due to the accruing communication delays. However, the applied control parameters still work, since the deflection slowly decreases over time and does not build up.

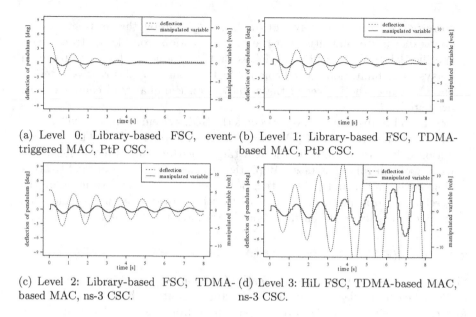

(a) Level 0: Library-based FSC, event-triggered MAC, PtP CSC.

(b) Level 1: Library-based FSC, TDMA-based MAC, PtP CSC.

(c) Level 2: Library-based FSC, TDMA-based MAC, ns-3 CSC.

(d) Level 3: HiL FSC, TDMA-based MAC, ns-3 CSC.

Fig. 6. Deflection of the pendulum with different levels of abstraction.

On abstraction level 2, the abstract PtP communication medium is replaced by the model of a real communication medium provided by ns-3, which simulates wireless communication with CC2420 transceivers with realistic delays. Since the TDMA-based MAC protocol prevents collisions, all nodes are in communication range, and there is no interference on the simulated wireless channel, the simulated communication remains reliable. As shown in Fig. 6(c), the overshoots during the control process are increased (amplitude and duration) by the additional delays, thereby demonstrating a decrease of the quality of control compared to abstraction level 1. However, the controller still is capable to slowly reduce the oscillation and to stabilize the pendulum, which is indicated by the decreasing amplitude of the overshoots.

On abstraction level 3, the controller is executed on the target platform Imote 2, whereas all other FSCs (sensor, actuator, physical model of the inverted pendulum) and CSCs are still simulated by FERAL. The arising impact on control quality caused by platform-specific execution delays are illustrated by Fig. 6(d) and shows an extensive deterioration. Here, the overshoots build up to an oscillation with increasing amplitude causing the pendulum to tilt significantly and to topple in the end. This shows that the chosen control parameters are not suitable to stabilize the pendulum when running on the target platform.

This example illustrates that simple functional simulations (such as in abstraction level 0) are not sufficient for complex real-time systems, since they may abstract from aspects having a relevant impact on the overall behavior. Here, the additional functional and non-functional delays finally lead to a functional failure of the developed networked control system. Although, the last abstraction level reveals a defect, the step-wise reduction of the abstraction level turned out to be useful in this case study, since the refinement allowed to focus on different aspects during system development and facilitated the detection and repair of errors. In the case study, abstraction level 0 was introduced to inspect, improve, and test the functionalities of the middleware and the control algorithm. Abstraction level 1, on the other hand, helped to evaluate the TDMA-based MAC protocol and its interaction with the middleware, whereas we could concentrate on timing errors caused by transceiver-specific delays in combination with the configuration of the MAC protocol with abstraction level 2. Finally, abstraction level 3 enabled to review the speed of the target platform and the efficiency of the SDL implementation, and to identify the bottleneck in our scenario.

4   Related Work

Since simulations in general and simulations of SDL system for the purpose of functional evaluations are a very broad topic, the following survey of related work is limited to performance simulations of SDL, incorporations of SDL into simulator frameworks, and HiL simulations.

In [18], a profiling tool for SDL is presented, whose dynamic analyses evaluate the computational effort of an SDL system by simulating the system and counting the number of executions of particular constructs. These executions are weighted with platform-specific execution times. With the objective to make SDL simulations more implementation-related, [5] removes the gap between SDL's concurrent execution semantics and serialized executions on real hardware platforms. For this purpose, SDL processes are mapped to nodes representing operating system processes with priorities and executed under control of newly devised observers of ObjectGEODE [24]. Though both approaches improve the confidence in an SDL system's execution, they still suffer from inaccurateness, since not all relevant delays (e.g., caused by scheduling overhead) are considered.

W.r.t. the incorporation of SDL into simulator and development frameworks, there are two related works: The first one is the simulator framework PartsSim [2], a component-based simulator, which incorporates several specialized simulators like ns-2. By supporting the simulator Avrora, PartsSim enables performance evaluations of SDL systems running on AVR platforms. A second framework with SDL support is TASTE [21], which combines domain-specific modeling techniques like SDL, Simulink, and SCADE. To validate the behavior and performance of generated systems, several tools are provided to monitor performance aspects, to generate message traces, and to perform schedulability analyses. Though, TASTE also supports the inclusion of real hardware to access sensors or actuators, the execution of SDL systems on HiL is not supported.

The roots of HiL simulations are found in military and civil avionics. Buford et al. report in [10] that the U.S. Army Aviation and Missile Command started developing HiL simulation and test capabilities for their missile defense and tactical missile program around 1960. Compared to tests within the real physical environment, HiL simulations, whether in missile or plane development, provide a non-destructive, less cost intensive, and threat-free option for testing. With the growing complexity of embedded systems and their safety criticality, HiL simulations became an enabling technology for developing and testing embedded devices [11]. Today, HiL simulations are common in an extensive range of industries, such as aerospace, avionics, automotive, and nuclear industries [20].

In the automotive domain, HiL simulations are often used to test ECUs (Electronic Control Units) in complex simulated environments such as engine management [4] and brake control systems [13]. In both mentioned references, the environment – like the engine and brake system – is modeled in Simulink. The second approach additionally relies on a commercial car model. Most commercial solutions – such as the HiL tools provided by MathWorks, dSpace, OPAL-RT, or Vector – only support a limited number of CASE-tools (usually Simulink or SCADE) to model the environment. The exchange of inputs and outputs with the DUT is either realized by special hardware, interpreting and providing analog as well as digital signals [13], or uses the XCP [1] protocol for calibration. This solution requires a special runtime environment on the DUT, memory maps of the software, and hardware support for the chosen transport protocol.

To our knowledge, there is no previous work about HiL simulations with SDL. Different to the discussed works, FERAL can in addition to physical models also simulate distributed systems consisting of many and dissimilar FSCs and CSCs as environment for the DUT. Thus, not only Simulink is supported to model the environment but all integrated simulators and techniques of FERAL. Since FERAL and the DUTs exchange data and control messages via a simple serial connection, no special hardware is needed. Because all functions required by HiL simulations with SDL have been integrated into a complete SDL tool chain, no manual effort is required to interconnect a DUT with the simulator core.

5   Conclusions

In this paper, we present an approach to increase the significance of SDL simulations and to enable the use of SDL in conjunction with virtual prototyping. The approach is based on the integration of SDL models into FERAL, a simulator framework for complex networked systems, and the execution of SDL systems in simulations with HiL. In total, the integration of SDL into FERAL renders possible both pure functional and reproducible performance evaluations of SDL specifications within the context of large networked systems and in combination with simulated physical environments. Besides providing an outline of necessary extensions of FERAL, this paper presents guidelines regarding the development of complex systems with virtual prototyping and the step-wise reduction of the level of abstraction. The application of these guidelines is illustrated in a case study with an inverted pendulum system.

In the case study, we demonstrate the advantages of step-wise system refinement, which enables to direct the focus on particular aspects during system development. By means of simulation runs with different levels of abstraction, newly developed functionalities can be tested early and faults can be removed cost-efficiently. Results of the simulation runs in the case study disclose the importance of accurate performance evaluations and the impact of non-functional influencing variables (e.g., communication and execution delays). In this regard, simulations with HiL revealed that pure functional evaluations of SDL systems are not sufficient due to the significant overhead of the runtime environment and non-negligible execution times, which demand evaluations of SDL systems on their target platform and with the real runtime environment. In summary, the case study demonstrates that simulations with HiL state a practical alternative to tests with the full system build-up and that they represent an adequate trade-off between costs and accuracy of results.

Our future work includes extensions of FERAL to support further simulators and hardware platforms to be utilized in simulations with HiL. Furthermore, improvements of the SDL integration into FERAL are planned to reduce the step size between different abstraction levels. Thereby, sources of overhead in SDL implementations and bottlenecks can be identified more precisely.

References

1. ASAM e.V: ASAM MCD-1 XCP V1.1.3 (2015)
2. Becker, P., Gotzhein, R., Kuhn, T.: Model-driven performance simulation of self-organizing systems with PartsSim. PIK - Praxis der Informationsverarbeitung und Kommunikation **31**(1), 45–50 (2008)
3. Blochwitz, T., et al.: The functional mockup interface for tool independent exchange of simulation models. In: 8th International Modelica Conference (2011)
4. Boot, R., et al.: Automated test of ECUs in a Hardware-in-the-Loop simulation environment. In: 1999 IEEE International Symposium on Computer Aided Control System Design, pp. 587–594 (1999)
5. Boutet, F., et al.: Scheduling in SDL simulation. Application to future air navigation systems. In: SAM, pp. 320–332. VERIMAG, IRISA, SDL Forum (2000)
6. Bræk, R., Haugen, Ø.: Engineering Real Time Systems. Prentice Hall, Englewood Cliffs (1993)
7. Braun, T., et al.: Virtual prototyping with feral - adaptation and application of a simulator framework. In: 24th IASTED International Conference on Modelling and Simulation (2013)
8. Braun, T., et al.: Virtual prototyping of distributed embedded systems with FERAL. Int. J. Model. Simul. **2**(34), 91–101 (2014)
9. Braun, T., et al.: FERAL - framework for simulator coupling on requirements and architecture level. In: 11th ACM-IEEE International Conference on Formal Methods and Models for Codesign, pp. 11–22 (2013)
10. Buford, Jr., et al.: HWIL weapon system simulations in the U.S. army aviation and missile command (USAAMCOM). In: SPIE 4366 (2001)
11. Fathy, H.K., et al.: Review of Hardware-in-the-Loop simulation and its prospects in the automotive area. In: SPIE 6228 (2006)

12. Gotzhein, R., Krämer, M., Litz, L., Chamaken, A.: Energy-aware system design with SDL. In: Reed, R., Bilgic, A., Gotzhein, R. (eds.) SDL 2009. LNCS, vol. 5719, pp. 19–33. Springer, Heidelberg (2009)
13. Hwang, T., et al.: Development of HILS systems for active brake control systems. In: SICE-ICASE, pp. 4404–4408, International Joint Conference, October 2006
14. IBM Corp.: Rational SDL suite (2015). http://www-03.ibm.com/software/products/en/ratisdlsuit
15. Igel, A., Gotzhein, R.: A CC2420 transceiver simulation module for ns-3 and its integration into the FERAL simulator framework. In: The Fifth International Conference on Advances in System Simulation, pp. 156–164 (2013)
16. International Telecommunication Union (ITU): Abstract syntax notation one (ASN.1) recommendations (Overview) (2008). http://www.itu.int/ITU-T/studygroups/com17/languages/
17. International Telecommunication Union (ITU): ITU-T recommendation Z.100 (12/11) - specification and description language - overview of SDL-2010 (2012). http://www.itu.int/rec/T-REC-Z.100/en
18. Langendörfer, P., Lehmann, M.: Implementation independent profiling of SDL specifications. In: Liggesmeyer, P., Pohl, K., Goedicke, M. (eds.) Software Engineering. LNI, vol. 64, pp. 155–166. GI, Bonn (2005)
19. MEMSIC Inc.: Imote2 datasheet (2015). http://vs.cs.uni-kl.de/dl/Imote2.pdf
20. Patil, P., Bhosale, S.: Review on Hardware-in-Loop simulation used to advance design efficiency and test competency. Int. J. Sci. Res. (IJSR) **4**(3), 2466–2468 (2015)
21. Perrotin, M., Conquet, E., Delange, J., Schiele, A., Tsiodras, T.: TASTE: a real-time software engineering tool-chain overview, status, and future. In: Ober, I., Ober, I. (eds.) SDL 2011. LNCS, vol. 7083, pp. 26–37. Springer, Heidelberg (2011)
22. PragmaDev SARL: Real Time Developer Studio (2015). http://www.pragmadev.com
23. Fliege, I., Grammes, R., Weber, C.: ConTraST – a configurable SDL transpiler and runtime environment. In: Gotzhein, R., Reed, R. (eds.) SAM 2006. LNCS, vol. 4320, pp. 216–228. Springer, Heidelberg (2006)
24. Telelogic Technologies: Object Geode 4–2 reference manual (2000)

Name Resolution of SDL Revisited: Drawbacks and Possible Enhancements

Alexander Kraas[(⊠)]

Poppenreuther Str. 45, 90419 Nürnberg, Germany
alexander.kraas@gmx.de

Abstract. The Specification and Description Language (SDL) is a formal specified and standardized modeling language, which is mainly used to specify protocols as well as distributed systems. The two algorithms 'Resolution by Container' and 'Resolution by Context' are specified for name resolution of identifiers in SDL specifications. In this paper, problems that were identified during an implementation of the 'Resolution by Context' algorithm are discussed. In addition, possible enhancements to remedy the identified problems are presented.

Keywords: SDL-2010 · Name resolution · Concrete syntax

1 Introduction

The Specification and Description Language (SDL) is a formal specified and standardized modeling language, which is mainly used in the telecommunication sector to specify protocols as well as distributed systems. A new version of the SDL standard series was published (under the acronym SDL-2010) in 2011 as ITU-T Recommendations Z.100–Z.107. The standard series for SDL is complemented by the ITU-Td Rec. Z.109 [3] that defines a profile for the Unified Modeling Language (UML) making it possible to specify an SDL specification in terms of a UML model. In addition to Z.100 [1], revised versions of the formal specifications were published in 2015 as Annex F1–F3 [4–6].

The SDL-UML Modeling and Validation (SU-MoVal) framework [7] is a prototypical implementation of the SDL-UML profile as specified in Z.109. The framework provides an editor for a textual notation, which supports SDL statements and expressions. Among other features, the editor supports syntax highlighting, syntax completion, syntax analysis etc. After the textual notation is entered into the editor, it is transformed to corresponding SDL-UML model elements. Before this transformation, identifier names for SDL entities have to be resolved in an appropriate manner. However, name resolution is also required for advanced editor services, such as syntax analysis etc. These services need to have a high-performance, because results shall be displayed to the user immediately.

During the implementation of the 'Resolution by Context' algorithm a few drawbacks concerning its specification in Z.101 [2] and also its formal specification in Z.100 Annex F2 [5] were identified.

© Springer International Publishing Switzerland 2015
J. Fischer et al. (Eds.): SDL 2015, LNCS 9369, pp. 65–80, 2015.
DOI: 10.1007/978-3-319-24912-4_6

The first identified drawback concerns the formally specified algorithm that returns invalid results in particular cases. In consequence, identifier names can be resolved to wrong entity definitions.

The second drawback concerns a combinatorial explosion of the specified algorithm that is also inherited by its formal specification. In consequence, a first standard compliant implementation of this algorithm had a poor performance (processing takes up to 30 s) so that editor services, e.g. syntax analysis, could not be used efficiently. Even if this problem has a negative impact on the required processing time for name resolution, it does not affect the correctness and completeness of the algorithm. However, when considering an automatic generation of editors resting on formal language specifications, the performance issue of algorithms should become more important, otherwise corresponding code had to be implemented manually.

In this paper, both before mentioned problems are analysed and possible solutions are proposed. The rest of this paper is structured as follows. Related work is discussed in Sect. 2. In Sect. 3, a short introduction to the formalisms of SDL is given. Afterwards, in Sect. 4 the drawbacks are analyzed in detail and possible solutions are proposed in Sect. 5. Finally, a conclusion is given in Sect. 6.

2   Related Work

The formal semantics of SDL-2000 and data type related aspects are treated in [8,9,13], but these works do not cover the identified drawbacks of the 'Resolution by Context' algorithm, which are the topic of the present paper. In another paper [12], the challenges and problems concerning the implementation of a parser for the concrete syntax of SDL-2000 are discussed. But this work does not address the validation of the static semantics and therefore also the problems treated in the present paper are not discussed. Furthermore, the generation of a compiler for SDL resting on the formal language definition of SDL-2000 is discussed in [10]. The different steps and requirements to generate a compiler are analyzed and discussed in detail, but the topic of a combinatorial explosion and the problem with no valid results of the 'Resolution by Container' algorithm are not mentioned in this work.

Apart from the already mentioned work, also a few more recent works addressing a meta-model or an UML profile based formalization of SDL exists, e.g. [7,11]. Even if the concrete syntax and semantics are covered by these works, the potential problems with name resolution on concrete syntax level are not treated.

The two works mentioned above, address issues concerning the implementation of parsers or compilers for the concrete notation of SDL, but they have not identified problems with the standardized algorithm for name resolution by context. In addition, also the other works have not covered this topic. In contrast, the present paper identifies two existing problems for the 'Resolution by Context' algorithm and proposes possible solutions for them.

3   Formalisms of the Specification and Description Language

A brief introduction to the formal syntax specification of SDL is given in the first part of this section. Details concerning both algorithms for name resolution are discussed in the second part.

3.1   Formal Syntax Specification

In the recommendations Z.101–Z.107, the concrete syntax of the textual and graphical notation of SDL is specified in terms of an extended Bakus-Nauer-Form (BNF). The syntax production rules contained in these documents are also used in a modified variant in Z.101 Annex F2 [5], which defines the static semantics of SDL on concrete and abstract syntax level. For this purpose, a set of constraints and transformations rules are defined, which are specified by using a first-order predicate logic. The formalisms for this predicate logic are defined in Z.101 Annex F1 [4].

Even if the formal specifications of both algorithms for name resolution are specified by using these formalisms, due to space restrictions no detailed introduction can be given here. Hence, interested readers should consult the Annex F1 document.

3.2   Algorithms for Name Resolution at Concrete Syntax Level

In general, an SDL specification can be considered as a hierarchical tree structure consisting of different kinds of nested entity definitions, e.g. agent type definitions, and behavior specifications. In total, 24 different kinds of entities are defined for SDL [2]. As in the case of other programming languages, an identifier is used in an SDL specification to refer to a particular entity definition in that tree structure. Therefore, an identifier consists of an optional qualifier and a name part. The qualifier defines the path from the root node (a system agent or package) of the tree to the context where an entity is defined. Definition contexts of entities are also referred to as scope units, which are particular kinds of SDL entities. In total, 15 different kinds of scope units are specified, which means that not every entity kind can own other entity definitions. However, an identifier can only refer to an entity that is visible according to the visibility rules of SDL [2]. Furthermore, entities that are defined in the same scope unit must be unique so that they can only have the same name, when they differ in their entity kinds or signatures, which are only present for operations and literals. A literal signature consists of the literal name and the data type that owns this signature, whereas an operation signature consists of the operation name, its parameter types and its result type. Usually, in SDL specifications only the name parts of identifiers are specified so that associated qualifiers have to be resolved by an appropriate algorithm. For this purpose, the two algorithms 'Resolution by Container' and 'Resolution by Context' are defined.

Resolution by Container. This algorithm is used for the resolution of identifiers that refer to entities that do not represent an operation or a literal. If the optional qualifier of an identifier is present, the name resolution starts in the scope unit that is identified by the qualifier. Otherwise, the next enclosing scope unit of an identifier is used as entry point for the name resolution. After the starting scope unit was identified, the resolution by container algorithm tries to bind an identifier to an entity definition in a particular order. Therefore, a matching entity definition is searched within different parts of the current scope unit. If no matching entity definition could be found, the name resolution proceeds with the next enclosing scope unit.

Resolution by Context. For the resolution of identifiers that refer to entities of kind operator, method or literal, the 'Resolution by Context' algorithm is used. In contrast to 'Resolution by Container', scope units are not taken into account by this algorithm. Instead, the 'context' in which an identifier occurs is used for the name resolution. Therefore, the following kinds of context are defined:

- Assignment statement
- Decision area/statement
- An SDL expression that is not part of any other expression.

In the formal definition of the static semantics for SDL [5], the 'context' is defined as follows:

$$Context_0 =_{def} < assignment > \cup < decision > \cup < expression > \quad (1)$$

Since identified problems of the 'Resolution by Context' algorithm are discussed in the subsequent sections, the detailed processing steps of the algorithm as specified in Z.101 [2] are cited here:

1. *For each <name> occurring in the context, find the set of <identifier>s, such that the <name> part is visible, having the same <name> and partial <qualifier> and a valid entity type for the context taking renaming into account.*
2. *Construct the product of the sets of <identifier>s associated with each <name>.*
3. *Consider only those elements in the product, which do not violate any static sort constraints taking into account also those sorts in packages that are not made visible in a <packageuseclause>. Each remaining element represents a possible, statically correct binding of the <name>s in the <expression> to entities.*
4. *When polymorphism is present in <assignment> (for example, in the support of object-oriented data), the static sort of an <expression> is not always the same as the static sort of the <variable> on the left hand side of the assignment, and similarly for the implicit assignments in parameters. The number of such mismatches is counted for each element.*

5. *Compare the elements in pairs, dropping those with more mismatches.*
6. *If there is more than one remaining element, all non-unique <identifier>s shall represent the same operation signature; otherwise in the context it is not possible to bind the <name>s to a definition.*

In the subsequent paragraphs, a few essential definitions and operations that are specified in the formal definition of the static semantics for SDL [5] are introduced. That is because especially for processing steps (1)–(3) this information is required for a detailed discussion of identified problems.

In general, all above cited processing steps of the algorithm are implemented by the operation $\texttt{resolutionByContext}_0()$ in the formal language definition. The result of processing step (1) is represented as a set of so called $\texttt{Binding}$ items for each operator, method or literal name occurring in a resolution context. Furthermore, each $\texttt{Binding}$ item in the result set is defined as a tuple consisting of the identifier name and one of the associated (visible) entity definitions. All required computations are performed by the $\texttt{possibleDefinitionSet}_0()$ operation.

$$Binding_0 =_{def} < name > \times < EntityDefinition > \qquad (2)$$

The set of all possible combinations of (identifier) names and associated entity definitions is computed in step (2) of the algorithm. This is implemented by the $\texttt{possibleBindingListSet}_0()$ operation in the formal language definition. The result of this operation is represented as a set of $\texttt{BindingList}$ items. Each of these items is a sequence of $\texttt{Binding}$ items and represents possible entity definitions for the operator, method and literal identifiers of a resolution context.

$$BindingList_0 =_{def} Binding_0* \qquad (3)$$

4   Problems of the Resolution by Context Algorithm

As already mentioned in the introduction of the present paper, some problems concerning the 'Resolution by context' algorithm where identified during the implementation of the textual notation editor for the SU-MoVal [7] framework. The problems can be divided into two groups. The first group concerns problems of the algorithm specified in Z.101 [2], whereas the second group concerns the formal specification of the algorithm [5].

4.1   Problems of the Specified Algorithm

For the 'Resolution by Context' algorithm as specified in Z.101 a major drawback concerning a combinatorial explosion exists. The drawback can be classified into a general problem and a problem that occurs in the context of decision statements.

General Combinatorial Explosion Problem. In step (2) of the algorithm, a set of possible binding lists for all combinations of (identifier) names and associated entity definitions is computed. Thereafter, all those binding lists that violate static sort constraints are removed in step (3). After these computations, a set of possible result binding lists is available, which is used for the remaining computations of the Resolution by Context algorithm. The total number of possible binding lists can be calculated as the product of the number of visible entity definitions `EntityDefs` for each identifier (i) in a resolution context. The following formula is used for this purpose:

$$NumOfPossibleBL = \prod_{i=1}^{n} EntityDefs_i \tag{4}$$

Since the number of possible binding lists is computed as a product, identifier names with a great number of associated entity definitions have a significant impact to the total number of possible binding lists. Especially, particular infix-operators (e.g. "<=") that are implicitly defined for all literal data types are present in large numbers. But also large numbers of operation and literal identifiers in a resolution context increase the total number of binding list enormously. The most important disadvantage of large numbers of possible binding lists is an negative impact to the required processing time for the validation of static constraints in step (3) of the algorithm. That is because the processing time is directly proportional to the number of binding lists to be processed. In order to make the discussed problem of a combinatorial explosion more descriptive, consider the subsequent code example that is an assignment to a `Boolean` variable. The expression on the right-hand side includes 5 literal and operation identifiers that have to be resolved by the algorithm.

```
boolVar = intVar <= 10 and intVar >= 0
```

In Table 1, the total number of possible binding lists is calculated for different numbers of visible literal data types, which includes the predefined data types of SDL and different numbers of user-defined literal data types. As shown in Table 1, an increasing number of literal data types induces an increasing number

Table 1. Possible binding lists for different numbers of user defined data types

User def. types	"<="	10	"and"	">="	0	Binding lists
0	7	5	4	7	5	4900
1	8	5	4	8	5	6400
2	9	5	4	9	5	8100
3	10	5	4	10	5	10000
4	11	5	4	11	5	12100
5	12	5	4	12	5	14400

of visible ''<='' and ''>='' infix-operators (see columns 2 and 5), whereas the numbers of the remaining identifiers is kept constant.

Combinatorial Explosion for Decision Statements. Apart from the general combinatorial explosion as discussed before, a similar issue exists for the 'Resolution by Context' for a <decision area> in the graphical notation or its corresponding textual notation, which is a <decision statement>. For simplicity, the term 'decision statement' is used for both notation kinds in the following discussion. The combinatorial explosion for a decision statement can occur, because all operation and literal identifiers that are contained in its <question> and all its answers (<range condition>) have to be taken into account during the resolution process. Before discussing the problem in more detail, consider the subsequent code example that is a decision statement in textual notation:

```
decision (intVar) //The <question>
{
   (=1): statement_1 // 1.Answer part
   (=2): statement_2 // 2.Answer part
   ...
   else: else_statement
}
```

As shown by the given example, a decision statement can consist of an arbitrary number of answer parts and an optional else part. A range condition can be specified in terms of a closed range or an open range. Without going into details, both kinds of range conditions contain <constant expression>s, which are very often literal identifiers. Only these parts are taken into account for the name resolution.

The total number of possible binding lists for a resolution context that is a decision statement can also be calculated with the already introduced formula. Based on the given code example, the total number of binding lists is calculated for a different number of present answer parts and the results are shown in Table 2. Since the decision question of the given example consists of an Integer variable, it has not taken into account for the calculation. In consequence, the total number of binding lists depends only on the number of literals that are present in the range conditions. Furthermore, it is supposed that each literal could be resolved to one of five predefined literal data types, which are: Integer, Real, Time, Duration or Natural. As shown in Table 2, the number of answer parts increases linear while the number of binding lists increases exponentially.

Table 2. Possible bindings lists in dependency of decision answers

Answer parts	1	2	3	4	5	6
Binding lists	5	25	125	625	3125	15625

4.2   Problems of the Formal Specification

Since the formal specification [5] of the algorithm for 'Resolution by Context' rests on the textual specification in Z.101 [2], the problem concerning a combinatorial explosion is also inherited. Hence, this issue is not discussed here once again. But apart from this, a further problem of the formal algorithm specification was identified during the implementation of the SU-MoVal [7] framework.

Identified Problem. As discussed in Sect. 3.2, for 'Resolution by Context' three different context kinds are defined. However, the problem discussed in this section only occurs for a resolution context that is of kind <expression>. That is because the formal specification of the resolution algorithm does not properly take into account the rules that are defined for processing step (3). In particular, the violation of static sort constraints for binding lists cannot be verified in an appropriate manner. In consequence, invalid results are returned for identifiers occurring in expressions that specify a default initialization or that represent actual context parameters of statements.

An Example. In order to discuss the identified problem and its impact more pragmatically, consider the following signal definition and an output statement that makes use of it:

```
signal SigA (Integer);
output SigA (varA + 1);
```

The given signal SigA owns one formal parameter that is of kind Integer. Apart from other constraints defined in [2], the corresponding actual context parameter (the expression varA + 1) of the given output statement must be sort compatible to the Integer sort. When 'Resolution by Context' is applied to this actual context parameter, the resolution context is of kind <expression>. Furthermore, the infix-operator ''+'' and the literal '1' have to be resolved by the algorithm.

Affected Operations in the Formal Definition. The identified problem of the formal specification is caused by the isSatisfyStaticCondition$_0$() operation and associated operations that are invoked in the body of this operation. These operations implement the main part of step (3) of the resolution algorithm. In particular, they are used in order to verify if a possible binding list (bl) violates any static sort constraints for a given resolution context (c).

```
isSatisfyStaticCondition₀(bl:BINDINGLIST₀, c:CONTEXT₀): BOOLEAN=def
  case c of
    |<assignment>=>isSatisfyAssignmentCondition₀(bl, c)
    |<decision>=>isSatisfyDecisionCondition₀(bl, c)
    |<expression>=>isSatisfyExpressionCondition₀(bl, c)
  otherwise False endcase
```

As shown in the code snipped above, in the case of an `<expression>` context, the $isSatisfyExpressionCondition_0()$ operation is invoked in order to validate static sort constraints that are related to expressions. Depending on the expression kind, a further operation is invoked or corresponding constraint validations are directly computed in the body of this operation. A code fragment of the operation that depicts this circumstance is shown below.

```
isSatisfyExpressionCondition₀(bl:BINDINGLIST₀, exp: <expression>)
  :BOOLEAN =def
 case exp of
|<create expression>=>isSatisfyCreateCondition₀(bl, exp)
...
|<binary expression>=>
  let opDef = getDefinitionInBindingList₀(exp.s-implicit, bl) in
  let fpl = opDef.operationParameterSortList₀ in
    fpl.length = 2∧
    isSortCompatible₀(getStaticSort₀
        (exp.s-<expression>, bl), fpl[1])∧
    isSortCompatible₀(getStaticSort₀
        (exp.s2-<expression>, bl), fpl[2])∧
    isSatisfyExpressionCondition₀(bl, exp.s-<expression>)∧
    isSatisfyExpressionCondition₀(bl, exp.s2-<expression>)
  endlet
 endcase
```

If the actual context parameter `varA + 1` (a binary expression) of the given example is passed to the $isSatisfyExpressionCondition_0()$ operation, corresponding static sort constraints are directly validated by this operation. In particular, the sort compatibility of the two operators `varA` and `'1'` of the binary expression will be verified, but the required sort compatibility of the return result of the expression is not validated. In consequence, not only the ``+''infix-operator name of the `Integer` data type is accepted as a valid operator name, but also any other operator with an equal name regardless its sort compatibility. Due to the discussed behavior, the formal specification of the 'Resolution by Context' algorithm considers each possible binding list as a valid binding list. Hence, wrong resolved identifiers for operator, method and literal entities can be returned by the algorithm. This problem does not only exist for the discussed example, but also for any other kind of expression. That is because also for these expressions any existing sort compatibility constraints of surrounding statements are disregarded.

5 Proposed Solution

Possible solutions for the drawbacks identified in Sect. 4 are proposed in this section. All proposed solutions rest on the reworked algorithm for 'Resolution by Context' that is implemented by the textual notation editor of the SU-MoVal framework [7].

5.1   Elimination of the Combinatorial Explosion Problem

A solution for eliminating the discussed problems concerning a combinatorial explosion of the algorithm for 'Resolution by Context' that is specified in Z.101 [2] is discussed in this section.

General Combinatorial Explosion. As stated in Sect. 4.1, the root of the problem with a general combinatorial explosion rests in steps (2) and (3) of the algorithm. Since the required computation time for validating static sort constraints in step (3) depends on the total number of possible binding lists, a possible solution for the identified drawback should reduce the total number of binding lists that have to be taken into account. That is because it is presumed that the static sort constraints that are validated in step (3) cannot be reworked or optimized. However, in step (1) of the current algorithm only the identifier name and the entity kind are considered for collecting possible entity definitions. In consequence, also invalid entity definitions are taken into account for calculating the set of possible binding lists. Since for all expressions and statements of SDL a static sort compatibility or equality of sorts is required [2], this circumstance could be regarded in step (1) to reduce the amount of possible entity definitions for a particular identifier name. Hence, the number of possible binding lists computed in step (2) would be decreased and in consequence also the required computation time for step (3).

Proposed Enhancement. In order to avoid a combinatorial explosion, it is proposed to extend the definition of processing step (1) for the 'Resolution by Context' algorithm with an additional rule taking sort compatibility into account. The definition could be reworked as follows (the additional rule is bold printed):

For each <name> occurring in the context, find the set of <identifier>s, such that the <name> part is visible, **sort compatibility to surrounding expressions or statements is taken into account,** *having the same <name> and partial <qualifier>* and a valid entity type for the context taking renaming into account.

When implementing the proposed enhancement for step (1) of the algorithm, the set of expected static sorts must be carried forward to directly enclosed sub-terms of a statement or expression during the collection of possible entity definitions for an identifier.

Result Evaluation. In order to evaluate that the proposed enhancement for the 'Resolution by Context' algorithm is able to avoid a combinatorial explosion, the already introduced code example of Sect. 4.1 is used for this purpose. The number of possible binding lists for different numbers of user-defined data types by applying the proposed enhancement is shown in Table 3. A comparison between the numbers of possible binding lists obtained by the standardized

Table 3. Number of possible binding lists for the enhanced resolution algorithm

User def. types	"<="	10	"and"	">="	0	Binding lists
0	4	5	4	4	5	1600
1	4	5	4	4	5	1600
...	...	...	...	...	...	1600

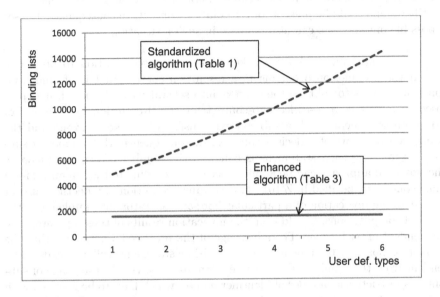

Fig. 1. Possible binding lists for the enhanced and the standardized algorithm

algorithm (dashed line) and those obtained by the enhanced version (solid line) is shown in Fig. 1.

As it can be determined from the results, the number of binding lists will keep constant even if the number of user-defined data types increases. That is because when taking type compatibility into account, not only the number of literals will keep constant, but also the number of operators. This is obtained by carrying forward the set of expected static sorts during the collection of possible entity definitions for an identifier.

Combinatorial Explosion for Decision Statements. The already proposed enhancement for a general combinatorial explosion cannot prevent all kinds of combinatorial explosions that can occur for a resolution context that is of kind decision statement. In particular, the proposed enhancement has only an effect for cases where the `<question>` of a decision statement does not contain an identifier that has to be resolved by 'Resolution by Context'. For instance, this is the case for the decision question `intVar` of the given example in Sect. 4.1, because it is a variable access with only one possible static sort, which is the predefined `Integer` sort. In such a case, the static sort of the decision question can be unambiguously determined by applying the 'Resolution by Container' algorithm, whereas this is not possible for a decision question consisting of an operator application or a method application or a literal value. For these kind of decision questions, instead of only one possible static sort, potentially a set of different static sorts has to be taken into account during the resolution process. That is because more than one visible operator or method with a matching identifier name could be present for a resolution context. In consequence, the set of possible binding lists can also increase in such a situation.

Proposed Enhancement. A success key of the proposed solution to prevent a combinatorial explosion occurring in a resolution context that is of kind decision statement is to split up the context into several parts. In detail, it is proposed to introduce a so-called sub-context for the 'Resolution by Context' of a decision statement. Such a sub-context consists of the `<question>` and the `<range condition>` of a decision answer. In consequence, the number of sub-contexts for a decision statement is equal to the number of decision answers. The proposed approach can be applied, because according to the semantics for a range condition specified in Z.101 [2], each range condition of a decision answer represents the invocation of a particular `Boolean` operator that implements the required computations. In addition, the invocation results of these operators are independent of each other. The advantage of the proposed approach is that the number of possible binding lists for a decision statement will be made independent from the number of present decision answers. Hence, the usage of sub-contexts restricts the number of identifier names, which have to be resolved with 'Resolution by Context' at one time, to an absolute minimum. In addition to the already proposed extension, it is proposed to rework the definition for step (1) of the 'Resolution by Context' algorithm as follows (proposed extensions are bold printed):

*For each <name> occurring in the context or in the **sub-context of a decision statement**, find the set of <identifier>s, such that the <name> part is visible, **sort compatibility to surrounding expressions or statements is taken into account,** having the same <name> and partial <qualifier> and a valid entity type for the context taking renaming into account.*

Result Evaluation. For the evaluation of the proposed enhancement of the algorithm for 'Resolution by Context' a slightly modified variant of the example given in Sect. 4.1 is used here. Hence, consider the following code snippet representing an SDL decision statement.

```
decision (intVar + 1)
{
  (=1): statement_1 // 1.Answer part
  ...
}
```

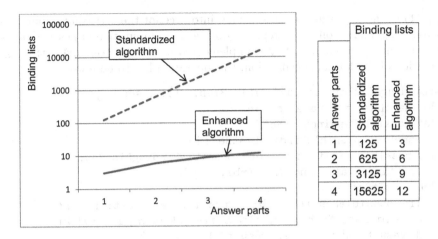

Fig. 2. Possible binding lists for the proposed and the standardized algorithm

In contrast, to the already introduced example, the decision question of the example used here consists of an operator application for the "+" infix-operator. In consequence, within the decision question two identifiers (an operator and a literal) have to be resolved. Furthermore, one additional literal identifier is present for each additional decision answer. The numbers of possible binding lists obtained by the currently standardized algorithm (dashed line) and the numbers obtained by the proposed version (solid line) are shown in Fig. 2. As evident, the numbers of binding lists obtained by the proposed algorithm are increasing linear. That is caused by splitting up the resolution context for a decision statement into different sub-contexts that are independent from each other. Hence, the number of possible binding lists can be calculated as a sum, whereas the number of binding lists for the standardized algorithm is calculated in terms of a product.

5.2 Rework of the Formal Specification

A possible rework of the formal definition of the 'Resolution by Context' algorithm [5] is proposed in this section. The proposal addresses all issues identified in Sect. 4.

Solution to Avoid Combinatorial Explosion. As discussed in Sect. 4.2, the problems of the algorithm for 'Resolution by Context' identified in Sect. 4.1 are also inherited by its formal specification [5]. Hence, a possible rework of the corresponding functions of the formal specification is proposed subsequently. Due to space restrictions and the complexity of necessary reworks, this can only be described informally here. In order to rework the formal specification in an appropriate manner, the solutions for avoiding a combinatorial explosion proposed in Sect. 5.1 have to be taken into account here. In general, the new definition for step (1) of the algorithm requires taking into account the sort compatibility to surrounding expressions or statements during the computation of possible binding lists. Since this computation is implemented by the $\texttt{getBindingListSet}_0()$ operation of the formal specification, this operation has to be reworked.

```
getBindingListSet₀(c: CONTEXT₀): BINDINGLIST₀-set =def
  let nameList = c.nameList₀ in
  let possibleBindingListSet =
    nameList.possibleBindingListSet₀ in
  let possibleResultSet = {pbl∈ possibleBindingListSet:
    isSatisfyStaticCondition₀(pbl, c)} in
  let resultSet =
    {r∈ possibleResultSet: ∀r'∈ possibleResultSet: r ¬ r'
      ⇒ mismatchNumber₀(r, c)≤ mismatchNumber₀(r', c)} in
    if |resultSet| = 1  then resultSet
    elseif |resultSet| = ∅  then ⊘
    else ⊘
    endif
  endlet
```

In order to take sort compatibility into account, the collection of relevant identifier names and the computation of the possible binding lists shall be combined. Therefore, the beginning of the $\texttt{getBindingListSet}_0()$ function body has to be reworked as follows:

```
getBindingListSet₀(c: CONTEXT₀): BINDINGLIST₀-SET =def
  let possibleBindingListSet =
    c.possibleBindingListSet₀ in ...
```

As shown by the code snippet above, instead of passing a name list to the $\texttt{getBindingListSet}_0()$ operation, the current resolution context (c) shall be passed. That is because this operation shall be reworked in such a way so that the initial static sort is determined from the resolution context. In detail, the initial static sort for the three different resolution context kinds shall be determined as follows:

– **Assignment statement:** The static sort that serves as starting point for computing possible binding lists shall be derived from the variable, which is the target of the assignment.
– **Decision area/statement:** In the case of an decision statement resolution context, the initial static sort for computing possible binding lists shall be derived from the <question> of a decision.
– *SDL expression (not part of any other expression):* If an expression specifies an actual parameter of a statement (e.g. output statement), the required initial static sort has to be derived from a corresponding formal parameter. Apart from this, if an expression specifies the default initialization for a data type definition, the enclosing data type definition has to be used as the initial static sort.

When the initial static sort is determined, the possible binding lists could be derived by a new recursive operation that traverses an expression in a top-down manner. For the first invocation of this operation, the already determined initial static sort is passed as argument to this operation. Afterwards, during a recursive call of this operation, the expected static sorts shall be propagated to nested expressions. Then this information is used to refuse all visible entity definitions that are not sort compatible to the propagated static sorts.

Solution to Avoid Incorrect Results for Expression Contexts. A problem directly concerning the formal specification of the 'Resolution by Context' algorithm is discussed in Sect. 4.2. The identified problem concerns invalid results that can occur for a resolution context that is of kind expression. In particular, this is caused by the isSatisfyStaticCondition$_0$() operation that implements step (3) of the algorithm. That is because the required static sort for expressions is not validated by this operation. However, no rework of the isSatisfyStaticCondition$_0$() operation is required when the solution for a combinatorial explosion as proposed above is implemented. That is because only sort compatible entity definitions are taken into account for computing possible binding lists, which are used as input for this operation. In consequence, the missing static sort constraints are already validated before invoking the isSatisfyStaticCondition$_0$() operation and therefore no invalid results can occur.

6   Conclusion

Even if the initial standardization activities concerning the formalization of SDL goes back to the beginning of the last decade, the problems discussed in this paper are also inherited by the revised version of SDL. Since the formal specification of the 'Resolution by Context' algorithm can return invalid results in the case of resolution contexts that are of kind expression (see Sect. 4.2), the impact of this problem is classified as high. Hence, the author of this paper suggests to fix the formal specification [5] as proposed in the second part of Sect. 5.2.

The problem of a combinatorial explosion mainly affects SDL tool vendors, because this problem does not have an impact to the soundness and completeness of the standardized algorithm. However, also for this problem it should be considered to rework the related parts of Z.101 [2] as well as of the formal specification [5] as proposed in Sect. 5.1. That is because if a tool vendor uses a model-driven development (MDD) approach for the generation of an SDL editor, the generated code would not be fixed manually.

References

1. International Telecommunication Union: ITU-T Recommendation Z.100 (12/11), Specification and Description Language - Overview of SDL-2010. http://www.itu. int/rec/T-REC-Z.100-201112-I/en

2. International Telecommunication Union: ITU-T Recommendation Z.101 (12/11), Specification and Description Language - Basic SDL-2010. http://www.itu.int/rec/T-REC-Z.101/en

3. International Telecommunication Union: ITU-T Recommendation Z.109 (10/13), Specification and Description Language - Unified Modeling Language Profile for SDL-2010. http://www.itu.int/rec/T-REC-Z.109/en

4. International Telecommunication Union: ITU-T Recommendation Z.100 Annex F1 (01/15), Specification and Description Language - Overview of SDL-2010 - SDL Formal Definition: General Overview. http://www.itu.int/rec/T-REC-Z.100/en

5. International Telecommunication Union: ITU-T Recommendation Z.100 Annex F2 (01/15), Specification and Description Language - Overview of SDL-2010 - SDL Formal Definition: Static Semantics. http://www.itu.int/rec/T-REC-Z.100/en

6. International Telecommunication Union: ITU-T Recommendation Z.100 Annex F3 (01/15), Specification and Description Language - Overview of SDL-2010 - SDL Formal Definition: Dynamic Semantics. http://www.itu.int/rec/T-REC-Z.100/en

7. Kraas, A.: Towards an extensible modeling and validation framework for SDL-UML. In: Amyot, D., Fonseca i Casas, P., Mussbacher, G. (eds.) SAM 2014. LNCS, vol. 8769, pp. 255–270. Springer, Heidelberg (2014)

8. Löwis, M.V.: Formale Semantik des Datentypmodells von SDL-2000. Humboldt-Universität zu Berlin, Berlin (2003)

9. Prinz, A.: Formal Semantics for SDL - Definition and Implementation. Humboldt-Universität zu Berlin, Berlin (2001)

10. Prinz, A., Löwis, M.V.: Generating a compiler for SDL from the formal language definition. In: Reed, R., Reed, J. (eds.) SDL 2003. LNCS, vol. 2708, pp. 150–165. Springer, Heidelberg (2003)

11. Prinz, A., Scheidgen, M., Tveit, M.S.: A model-based standard for SDL. In: Gaudin, E., Najm, E., Reed, R. (eds.) SDL 2007. LNCS, vol. 4745, pp. 1–18. Springer, Heidelberg (2007)

12. Schmitt, M.: The development of a parser for SDL-2000. In: Tenth GI/ITG Technical Meeting on Formal Description Techniques for Distributed Systems, pp. 131–142. Shaker Verlag (2009)

13. Schröder, R.: SDL-Datenkonzepte - Analyse und Verbesserungen. Humboldt-Universität zu Berlin, Berlin (2003)

An Experiment to Introduce Interrupts in SDL

Emmanuel Gaudin[1][✉] and Alain Clouard[2]

[1] PragmaDev, Paris, France
emmanuel.gaudin@pragmadev.com
[2] STMicroelectronics, Grenoble, France
alain.clouard@st.com

Abstract. Specific modelling technologies for digital hardware design are typically the synthesizable, cycle-accurate register-transfer level descriptions (VHDL or Verilog RTL) or bit-accurate transaction level models (SystemC TLM). Given nowadays complexity of circuits such as System-on-a-Chip (SoC) for multimedia embedded systems, and of the embedded software interacting with the SoC, there is a need for a higher abstraction level that would ease mastering the interaction, starting from initial conceptual stages of a product development. The Specification and Description Language (SDL) modelling technology allows to describe functional models independently from their implementation. This paper describes a work done by STMicroelectronics and PragmaDev to experiment the use of SDL high level functional description in a typical simple hardware/ software interaction scenario involving interrupts handling.

Keywords: Interrupts · Modelling · Hardware · Functional

1 Introduction

RTL (VHDL or Verilog) is the abstraction level for describing hardware for synthesis, TLM for fast simulation of hardware, and C is the typical programming language for coding interrupts routine. Since it is possible to simulate RTL or TLM, and as C is portable on many different platforms, a usual approach is to co-simulate the hardware and the software. In [1] the authors can test the final C code together with the hardware at a relatively early stage provided the models exist. But the abstraction level is very low and it is actually executing the real implementation, rather than a description, of both the hardware and of the software. TLM as presented in [8] makes models available earlier than RTL and do simulate orders of magnitude faster, but still is usually modelled using interfaces (ports, registers) with a bit-true description (typically from IP-Xact XML), which is often not available in the very early stages of a new SOC architecture study, when the system architect is performing what-if analysis.

The UML Profile for MARTE [2] has introduced the InterruptResource stereotype. As often seen with UML, a number of notations, usually stereotypes which are basically comments on elements, are available but there are no

© Springer International Publishing Switzerland 2015
J. Fischer et al. (Eds.): SDL 2015, LNCS 9369, pp. 81–88, 2015.
DOI: 10.1007/978-3-319-24912-4_7

execution semantics nor action language. Therefore, a MARTE diagram is basically a documentation of the organisation of an interrupt. Some UML extension for representing interrupts exists, however modelling simulatable UML does lead to complex graphical representation compared to our goal; work is still ongoing towards some simplification.

In [4] a way to represent interrupts in SystemC is currently proposed for standardisation in Accellera, but its intent is bit-true modelling, with similar concepts as RTL (level or edge interrupt, active high or low, etc.) hence is too detailed for earlier phases of architecture study.

In [9] the authors use the general concept of transfer event as a generalization of an interrupt behaviour in order to facilitate testing on the final hardware of pre-emption and nesting side effects.

In all the previous literature, no way is proposed to model an interrupt easily and at early, what-if system definition stage, that is before bit-true modelling stage of an SoC (or digital processing system) project; and with simulation capability.

Also note that a solution for interrupts should also address more generally the case of an event that is occurring in an asynchronous manner compared to the planned or protocol-driven scheduling of the behaviour of the system.

2   Hardware Modelling Requirements

Today there are established languages for hardware modelling and simulation: SystemC (C++ based) for modelling at transaction-level (TLM), and VHDL or Verilog for register-transfer level (RTL) at level of signals and clocks which are needed as input to hardware synthesis to gates and then silicon. The positioning of some hardware modelling languages is shown in Fig. 1.

Architects nowadays need to model complex digital processing systems, such as SoC's, and simulate these models to perform what-if analysis for functionality and performance studies, before and after hardware-software partitioning. Models need to be easy to modify within a couple of hours, for quick loops in the architecture study. Requirements for an architect-level modelling language do include:

- the ability to represent the various aspects of a system functionality;
- the possibility to simulate, and the existence of related tools to control the execution and analyse the trace during or after simulation;
- the simplicity for architects to represent their system and have it understood or even reused by customers, designers, developers;
- the need for the language to be standardised, to ensure interoperability of models across tools used by partners, customers, suppliers and also mid/long-term secure investment in modelling efforts.

SystemC/TLM is more suited to bit-true validation, and RTL for signal and clock-level verification, both in later phases of a product development.

For architects various system description languages exist; some of them are overviewed in the introduction.

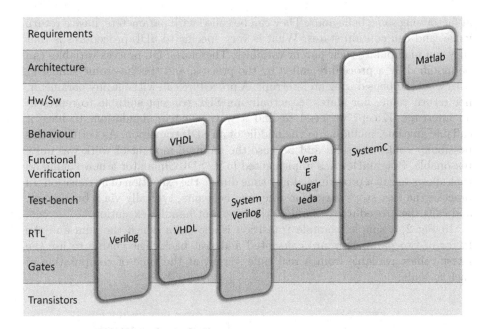

Fig. 1. ESA system level modelling in SystemC [3]

3 SDL

ITU-T Specification and Description Language [6] models are based on an asynchronous semantic of execution. Messages are exchanged between agents in the model through implicit message queues. Even synchronous mechanisms such as shared variables are actually based on an exchange of messages. The main benefit of an SDL model is that it is executable and therefore verifiable using a dynamic approach. This is particularly useful in asynchronous systems in which a lot of parallelism generates a huge number of possible execution paths.

Hardware description at RTL level is naturally synchronous for clock-based designs. The flow of information from one component to the next is synchronized by a hardware clock. Above RTL, at TLM and SDL levels, behaviour descriptions are not based on clocks. Rather, system level synchronizations need to be described and in particular asynchronous events such as interrupts. Therefore it is interesting to investigate how an SDL model can describe an interrupt, and how tools can simulate its behaviour.

4 A Pragmatic Approach

The SDL architecture is made of Agents called from top to bottom System, Blocks, Processes, and Procedures. A process is basically a state machine and a number of state machines describe the behaviour of a block. SDL procedures aim at factorizing some behaviour. They can be called with parameters, have a return value, and can contain states. What is very specific to SDL procedures is that they can manipulate their parent variables. Therefore SDL process variables can be modified by a procedure called by the process, and this has some similarity with what happens during an interrupt. A procedure call without any parameter, nor return value, nor states, is actually an SDL concept suitable to represent an interrupt. Except we need to find a way, when in simulation, to have it callable anytime, including in the middle of an SDL transition. As verifying this possibility could be useful and because the required amount of work was quite reasonable, PragmaDev has implemented in its SDL Simulator a new command that allows to call a procedure at any time during the execution of a transition. In practice the user stops execution wherever he wants, typically via a breakpoint, and calls the procedure to simulate the interrupt handler execution.

In Fig. 2, a simple example transition is shown in which the sum and the factor of two parameters are calculated and sent back. The goal is to use the latest values available from a real time sensor, at the time of computation of each formula.

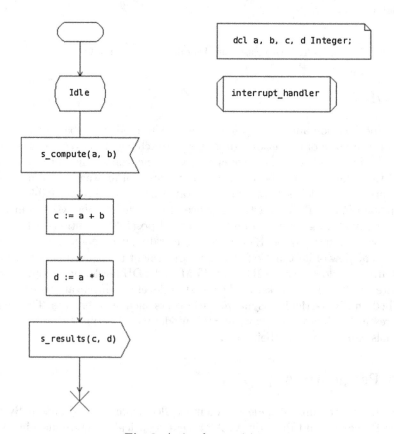

Fig. 2. A simple transition

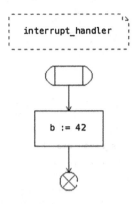

Fig. 3. The interrupt handler procedure

A procedure called interrupt_handler is defined in the process and its behaviour is described in Fig. 3.

The only thing the procedure does is to modify the value of b. As explained previously the b actually refers to the parent's b, therefore the procedure will modify the b manipulated in the process transition.

The default behaviour of the transition is displayed as an MSC trace [5] in Fig. 4.

During simulation the user steps in the transition and decides when to trigger the transition [7]. In Fig. 5, the selected symbol is the next one to be executed.

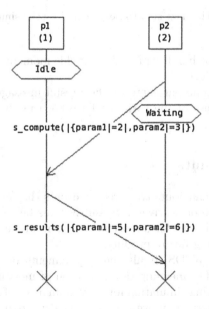

Fig. 4. Default behaviour of the example in Fig. 2

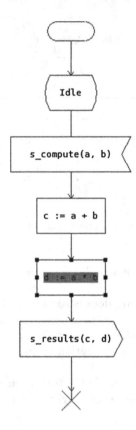

Fig. 5. The next step to be executed by the simulator

Calling the interrupt_handler procedure at this moment of the execution will produce the trace in Fig. 6.

The value of the second parameter of the s_result message has been modified, demonstrating the values of the variables have been modified in the middle of the transition.

5   Expected Results

The ability to model behaviours triggered by events that are occurring anytime during the planned, protocol-driven inter-subsystems behaviours of a system, is one of mandatory conditions for adoption by system architects of a new way of modelling and simulating future products.

SDL supported by RTDS, fulfils the requirements of a higher level modelling than TLM or RTL, meaning rapid creation of models, with fairly simple schematics, while enabling simulation for what-if analysis of system architecture.

The experiment described above does provide a way to extend SDL and make it suited for modelling a wider range of system types. It will be worth testing

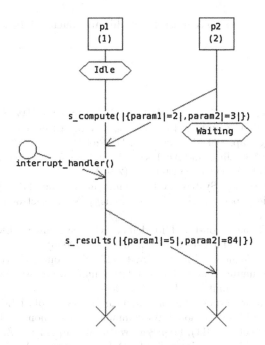

Fig. 6. Interrupted behaviour of the transition shown in Fig. 2

the scalability of the approach by working with system architects on full-scale system model.

Another next step is to allow an increase of the coverage of system simulation execution paths, by providing a way to script the occurrence of the asynchronous event (e.g. interrupt) at various places in the system behaviour. This would make such models useful to system validation engineers, by providing a range of architect-valid expected simulation executions, which can be used as reference for TLM or RTL simulation traces (execution branches, state variable values) in later stages of the product development.

Upon the adoption of the modelling methodology by architects and validation engineers, one should consider refining this concept and proposing standardisation of such an extension to SDL, as a standard-based modelling paradigm is better for interoperability and portability than a tool-specific feature.

6   Conclusion

This paper has shown how SDL could be used to describe interrupts from a functional point of view. Based on the original SDL execution semantics, a very pragmatic and simple solution has been developed in an industrial tool (RTDS V4.6) to support the concept. User acceptance includes ease of modelling by architects, and re-usability of traces by design engineers. Depending on the feedback from more users on real use cases, this approach will be further improved and developed.

References

1. Bauer, M., Ecker, W., Zinn, A.: Modeling interrupts for HW/SW co-simulation based on a VHDL/C coupling. In: Mermet, J. (ed.) Electronic Chips & Systems Design Languages, pp. 169–178. Springer, US (2001)
2. Bran Selic, S.G.: Modelling and Analysis of Real-Time and Embedded Systems with UML and MARTE. Elsevier, Amsterdam (2014)
3. European Space Agency: System level modelling in systemc (2015). http://www.esa.int/Our_Activities/Space_Engineering_Technology/Microelectronics/System-Level_Modeling_in_SystemC
4. Ghenassia, F.: Transaction-Level Modelling with SystemC: TLM Concepts and Applications for Embedded Systems. Springer, US (2006)
5. ITU-T: Message Sequence Chart (MSC): ITU-T recommendation Z.120, International Telecommunication Union - Telecommunication Standardization Sector (2002). http://www.itu.int/rec/T-REC-Z.120/en
6. ITU-T: Specification and description language - overview of SDL-2010. ITU-T recommendation Z.100, International Telecommunication Union - Telecommunication Standardization Sector (2011). http://www.itu.int/rec/T-REC-Z.100/en
7. PragmaDev: Real Time Developer Studio Reference manual V4.6 (2015)
8. STMicroelectronics, ARM and Cadence: Proposed interfaces for interrupt modelling, register introspection and modelling of memory maps (2013). http://forums.accellera.org/files/file/102-proposed-interfaces-for-interrupt-modelling-register-introspection-and-modelling-of-memory-maps-from-stmicroelectronics-arm-and-cadence/
9. Xu, X., Liu, C.C.: Modeling interrupts for software-based system-on-chip verification. Trans. Comput. Aided Des. Integr. Circ. Syst. 29(6), 993–997 (2010)

Domain Specific Languages

LanguageLab - A Meta-modelling Environment

Terje Gjøsæter[✉] and Andreas Prinz

University of Agder, Faculty of Engineering and Science, Postboks 422, 4604
Kristiansand, Norway
{terje.gjosater,andreas.prinz}@uia.no

Abstract. In the LanguageLab language workbench, we build on a
component-based approach to language specification that facilitates the
specification of all aspects of a computer language in a consistent manner, taking into account best practices in meta-modelling and language
design. The workbench allows operation on a suitable abstraction level,
and also focuses on user-friendliness and a low threshold to getting
started, in order to make it useful for teaching of meta-modelling and
language design and specification. The platform is open for third party
language modules and facilitates rapid prototyping of DSLs, re-use of language modules, and experiments with multiple concrete syntaxes. The
platform also allows interested parties to develop LanguageLab modules
that can further add to the features and capabilities of the LanguageLab
platform.

Keywords: Meta-modelling · Language workbenches · DSL Development Environments

1 Introduction

The rising abstraction level of modern general-purpose computer languages and
the introduction of model-driven development contribute to the efficiency of
software development. However, limitations in the current state of the art in
language specification, restrict the application of model-driven development for
language development.

The problem handled in this article, concerns lowering the threshold for
beginners and students in meta-model-based language specification as well as
making the job easier for language developers, primarily by making it possible
for the language modeller to operate on a higher level of abstraction. A major
concern is following and supporting best practices in meta-modelling and language design.

In meta-model-based language design, a major challenge is to be able to
operate on an adequate level of abstraction when designing a complete computer
language. If the abstraction level is too low, the language developer will spend
too much time on unnecessary details. There are several different technologies,
meta-languages and tools in use for defining different aspects of a language, that
may or may not satisfy the needs of a DSL developer.

© Springer International Publishing Switzerland 2015
J. Fischer et al. (Eds.): SDL 2015, LNCS 9369, pp. 91–105, 2015.
DOI: 10.1007/978-3-319-24912-4_8

Based on experiences from teaching, conversations with students and from case studies [4], we have concluded that it is useful to develop a simple metamodel-based language development platform, that attempts to remove some of the complexity of the more popular existing tools, to better support the student in learning the basic principles of computer language handling. It should have a consistent and logical architecture that facilitates language specification, and it should let the student operate on a suitable level of abstraction, and facilitate making and modifying small example languages.

The rest of this article is structured as follows: Sect. 2 covers state of the art in language specification, Sect. 3 covers the design and implementation of *LanguageLab*, and Sect. 4 provides some simple LanguageLab use cases for illustration. Section 5 discusses the results and contributions of the work, and finally Sect. 6 provides a summary.

2   State of the Art in Language Specification

This section covers relevant parts of the state of the art and related work in language specification, with particular emphasis on the meta-model architecture and the language workbench approach.

A description of a modelling language, whether it is a domain specific language (DSL) or a general purpose language, usually involves several different technologies and meta-languages. Traditionally, we are familiar with the distinction between the *syntax* and the *semantics* of a language. The syntax specifies the structure of sentences in the language, while the semantics assign a meaning to the sentences.

In [1], a language definition is said to consist of the following aspects: *abstract Syntax (Structure), Constraints, concrete Syntax (Presentation)* and *Semantics (Behaviour)*. In addition, the aspects Mapping and Extensibility are identified, where the last one is not handled in this article, and mapping is considered a part of Semantics.

Structure defines the constructs of a language and how they are related. This is also known as abstract syntax. Constraints bring additional restrictions on the structure of the language, beyond what is feasible to express in the structure itself.

Presentation defines how instances of the language are represented. This can be the definition of a graphical or textual concrete language syntax.

Behaviour explains the dynamic semantics of the language. This can be a transformation into another language (denotational or translational semantics), or it defines the execution of language instances (operational semantics).

A *language workbench* is a term commonly taken to mean a platform primarily intended for rapid and user friendly development of DSLs, where all aspects of designing the language are supported within the tightly integrated platform, including generation of editors and support for execution or code generation. The term was defined first by Martin Fowler in 2005 in his article "Language

Workbenches: The Killer-App for Domain Specific Languages?" [2], but similar integrated language development platforms existed before that.

There are several language workbenches and workbench-like language development IDEs available. Evolving from compiler-compilers and parser generators like lex and yacc, the first workbenches to appear date at least as far back as 1995 when LISA (based on attribute grammars) was introduced [8].

Among workbenches and workbench-like language development environments should also be mentioned the ASF+SDF Meta-Environment [9], MontiCore, IBM Safari, DLTK (Dynamic Language Tool Kit), Actifsource, Meta Programming System (MPS) [12], MetaEdit+ [10], Rascal (the successor of the ASF+SDF Meta-Environment) [7], Spoofax [6] and Intentional Domain Workbench [5]. There are also several Eclipse plugins that can cooperate to form a language workbench-like environment. While many of these are work in progress, the best of the currently available language workbenches represent a big step forward towards a unified environment that provides the language developer with the high-level tools needed to specify and create complete computer languages.

Language workbenches typically provide specific meta-languages for describing language aspects. Currently, structure, constraints and text syntax are standard, while transformations and execution semantics are still open. Moreover, static semantics issues like typing and identifier resolution are often not handled specifically. All platforms admit that they do not provide a complete set of meta-languages, and they open up for implementation languages like Java to enable complete language description. This is a valid approach for achieving a complete platform, but fails when the interest is in concepts and dedicated meta-languages.

In the OMG four-layer meta-model architecture, every model element on each layer is strictly an instance of a model element of the layer above.

It is common to use meta-models to specify the structure of a language, using existing meta-languages like MOF and Ecore, but they are not expressive enough to handle language aspects like presentation and behaviour.

The approach to the meta-model architecture within the modelling lab at the University of Agder, is based on the premise that all aspects of a language should be defined specifically by using suitable meta-languages on the level above, as described in [11]. We see meta-languages as offering *interfaces* that languages on the level below can use, as shown in Fig. 1.

Thereby, we apply the notion that models can freely be promoted or demoted between levels depending on the intended use, and models in the meta-model architecture are relative to each other based on the relationship between them.

2.1   Introducing the LanguageLab Workbench

In [4], we argue that students of model-driven language design are easily demotivated by complex tools, or too many different tools. There is therefore a need for a student-friendly, transparent and easy to use integrated meta-modelling platform for use in teaching. This platform should allow the student to work on a suitable level of abstraction, avoid unnecessary complexity, and facilitate

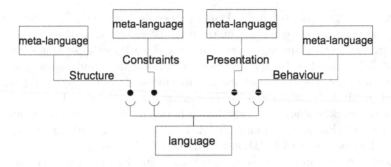

Fig. 1. The architecture used by the modelling lab at University of Agder.

best practices in meta-modelling and language design. Based on experiences from teaching meta-modelling and compiler theory, LanguageLab is designed as a complete environment for experiments with meta-model-based language specification. Its implementation is currently in the state of an evolving prototype that supports the most basic functionality including creation of structure, textual presentation and instantiation semantics.

3   LanguageLab Design and Implementation

The LanguageLab language workbench aims to allow the DSL developer to operate on a suitable level of abstraction for all relevant language aspects, and facilitates making and modifying small languages for use in teaching. In this section, the design and implementation of LanguageLab is described.

3.1   Language Modularity and Instantiation

The most fundamental functionality of the platform is to allow instantiation of modules. When modules are used as languages for defining new modules, they are also called *meta-modules*. A meta-module supports structure, allowing creation of instances based on its instantiation semantics. A suitable presentation can be defined providing an editor that allows for a more user-friendly creation of modules. Then, constraints can be defined on the elements of the module. Finally, a module can have behaviour semantics in terms of transformations or in terms of execution. The definition of meta-modules is done using appropriate meta-meta-modules.

Note that it is also possible to load more than one meta-module for the same language aspect, to provide e.g. different views of the language (usually one presentation meta-module will provide one editor) and/or support for different language features, like e.g. expressions or inheritance.

When a module defining the structure of a language has been developed based on the basic meta-modules, it can be promoted, or "moved up" a level in the meta-modelling hierarchy, by loading it as a meta-module and using its available interface, to offer the structural elements of the language. If a corresponding presentation module for the language has been created, this editor can then be loaded. When a new module (language instance) has been created based on these meta-modules, one may want to execute it. If execution semantics is available (e.g. from a meta-module supporting behaviour), one can again "move up" the created module, and execute it.

Figure 2 shows how a meta-meta-language for structure can be defined using different meta-meta-modules including a version of itself, following the pattern shown in Fig. 1.

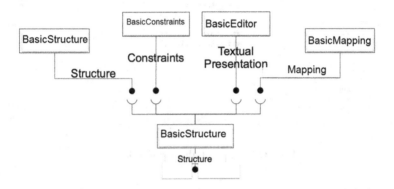

Fig. 2. The LanguageLab architecture used for defining a meta-module.

3.2 LanguageLab User Interface

The two main elements of the Language Lab Graphical User Interface are, from top to bottom:

- **Language Level** contains the loaded meta-modules. Each meta-module exists in a separate tab.
- **Model level** contains the module being developed. The module is an instance of the meta-modules loaded on the language level. The model level always includes the platform view (providing a simple tree structure) of the module being developed. Optionally, it may contain editors in separate tabs, if the loaded meta-modules support it.

In addition, there is an optional *lower interface view*, for displaying the interface of a module in case it is used as a meta-module (see Sect. 4.3).

Presentation. Figure 3 shows the two main parts of the LanguageLab GUI. The upper part is for meta-modules, and in this case it contains a meta-module interface for structure. The lower part is for showing the module being built

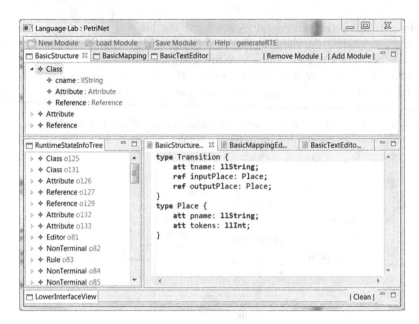

Fig. 3. LanguageLab user interface.

from elements of the loaded meta-module(s). In this case, it is a simple PetriNet language module. In this illustration, the language instance is shown in the built-in system tree view, the so-called runtime state information tree view, on the left side. The `BasicStructure` language meta-module also contains a textual editor (BasicStructureEditor), allowing to display and edit the structure textually.

LanguageLab allows users to switch between different presentation views of a language instance, that are automatically synchronised with the internal representation. Note that the view must be in a consistent state for successful synchronisation to take place.

Behaviour. Modules may contain operations, that will be displayed as buttons in the toolbar when the modules are loaded as meta-modules. For example, the meta-modules in Fig. 4 contain two functions, *genLowerInterface* and *makeSem*.

When executing an operation, its semantics as defined in the corresponding meta-module is used. This is further described in Sect. 4.2. Transformation operations can be defined by using a transformation language meta-module.

Textual code generators can be implemented based on the editor support of LanguageLab, and may be done either as template-based systems where the code generation is one-way, i.e. the generated code is read-only, or it may take the form of a full editor that allows for editing the generated code and have the changes applied to the original language instance.

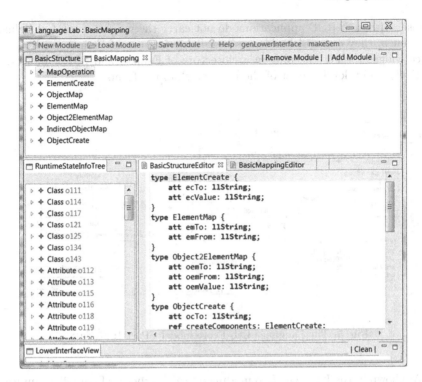

Fig. 4. Combining elements from different meta-modules.

3.3 Module System

It is possible to combine elements from different meta-modules, e.g. for covering different language aspects, as shown in Fig. 4. Here, elements from two different meta-modules are used for defining one module; the `BasicMapping` module is defined using itself as well as `BasicStructure` as meta-modules.

3.4 Implementation

LanguageLab is very abstract and only relying on its available meta-modules. However, at some point all this functionality has to be provided. This is done using the concept of an abstract machine. The LanguageLab platform implements an abstract machine catering for types, objects, operations, and editors. The LanguageLab platform machine is defined using EMF and implemented in Java. The implementation language is hidden to the LanguagLab user.

The starting point for the LanguageLab application is an Eclipse/EMF-based tree-view editor, generated from an Ecore model of the proposed LanguageLab module format. The EMF-based editor plugins were extended with a front-end carrying a full graphical user interface, implemented as a standalone Eclipse RCP application, enabling the language developer to use it independently of

Eclipse. Although RCP applications do not carry the weight of the full Eclipse workbench, they can still build on all available features of Eclipse, such as the JFace widget toolkit, the plug-in architecture of Eclipse, and EMF, allowing a relatively rapid development of the LanguageLab platform.

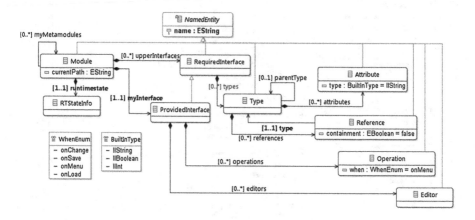

Fig. 5. The Language Lab Ecore model - Part 1: Module.

As shown in the LanguageLab module internal structure Ecore diagram fragment in Fig. 5, the `Module` may contain `RequiredInterfaces` from used meta-modules, and may itself provide a `ProvidedInterface` where the types that are supported by the module are defined. The interface consists of `Types` that can have `Attributes`; supporting basic built-in types: `llBoolean`, `llString`, `llInt`. `Reference` refers to typed objects. If the module provides an interface, it may also contain operations and editors to be used by other modules. The `RTStateInfo` is further described in the `Runtime` part shown in Fig. 6. This part supports instances of `Types` included in the module; `Objects`, `ObjectReferences` and `ObjectAttributes`. The `RTStateInfo` also contains `Notifications` to be used e.g. by constraint modules.

`Operation` elements come in three variants; `CodeOperation` (Java class files), `ConstraintOperation` (for use by constraints meta-modules) and `MapOperation` (used for e.g. instantiation semantics), and grammar-based editors are supported by the type `Editor`.

This implements the architecture described in [11] by allowing a module to both use interfaces from meta-modules as well as offer interfaces for other modules to use. This facilitates not only one module per language aspect, but also other variants such as modules supporting particular language features that can be used as building blocks, as a starting point for creating a partly customised DSL with some stock features.

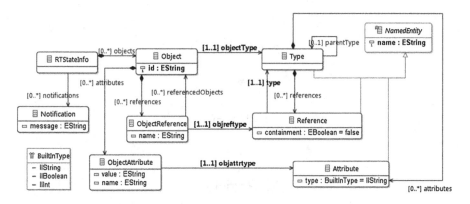

Fig. 6. The Language Lab Ecore model - Part 2: Runtime.

4   LanguageLab in Use

In this section, concrete examples of LanguageLab usage are presented, including how to use it for creating a simple module based on an existing meta-module, how to execute the module, and finally how to create a new meta-module. Figure 7 shows the relation between the different modules and meta-modules described in this section; `BasicStructure` (meta-module for structure), `PetriNet` (a PetriNet meta-module), `MyPetriNet` (an instance of the PetriNet meta-module) and `RT_MyPetriNet` (runtime-instance of MyPetriNet).

4.1   Creating a Module

In this example, we will show how to create a simple module based on an existing meta-module in LanguageLab. The example language is a PetriNet language meta-module. From this meta-module, we will be able to create a PetriNet specification module with places, transitions and arcs.

We start by creating a new module `MyPetriNet`. After a new module is created, meta-modules can be loaded. Note that if we want to use a module as a meta-module, we may load it as a meta-module from the interface menu. For this to be meaningful, the lower interface of the module has to be populated (see Sect. 4.3).

Instances of Place and Transition can be created using the Petri net editor. When an instance is created in the editor, it will show up in the runtime state view as well, as shown in Fig. 8.

We then call the operation `prepareToRun` from the toolbar button to prepare the module for execution, and finally save the module for later use. This operation creates a runtime structure for MyPetriNet as well as execution semantics given as operations init, step, and run.

In Fig. 9, we show how the `prepareToRun` function can be defined by using the BasicMapping meta-module.

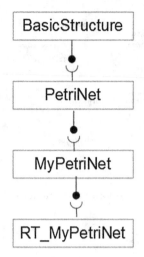

Fig. 7. The (meta-) modules used in this section.

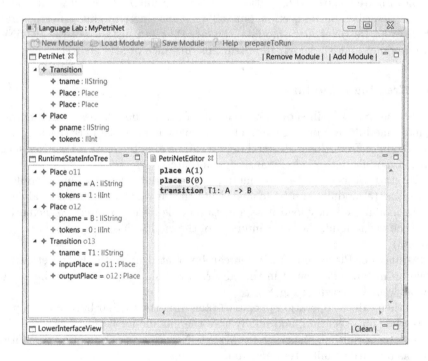

Fig. 8. Creating module elements in the textual editor.

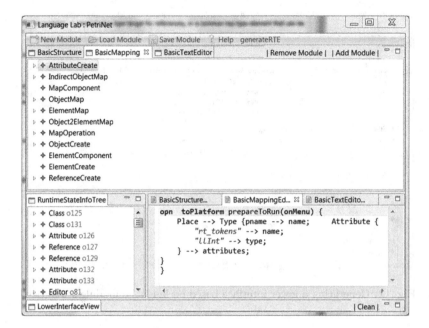

Fig. 9. A runtime element mapping definition for PetriNet.

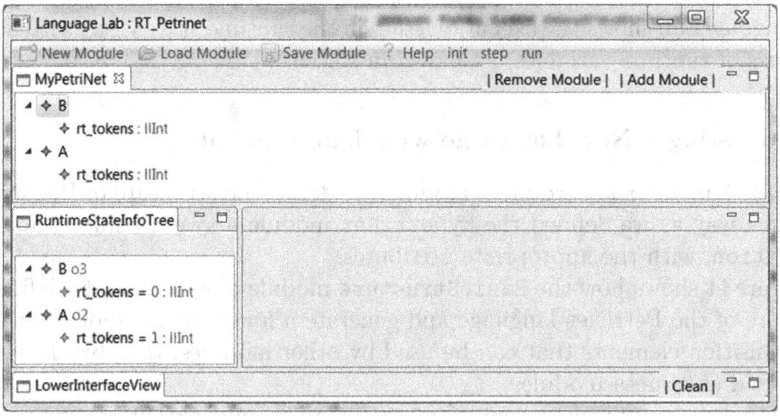

Fig. 10. Runtime view.

Fig. 11. Generating a lower interface based on language module semantics.

4.2 Executing a Module

The execution requires a new module `RT_MyPetriNet` with the MyPetriNet loaded on the language level, i.e. as a meta-module. The runtime variables in the current state are shown in the runtime state view; and in the displayed example, also in a system level text editor. The execution is controlled using the operations `init`, `step` and `run`.

LanguageLab shows the execution state in the runtime state view, with access to values of runtime variables, as shown in Fig. 10.

4.3 Creating a New Language with LanguageLab

Using the `BasicStructure` meta-module, we define the structure of PetriNet in the same way as we defined the `MyPetriNet` module above, adding `Place` and `Transition`, with the appropriate attributes.

Figure 11 shows how the `BasicStructure` module may be used to define the structure of the PetriNet language and generate a lower interface offering place and transition elements that can be used by other modules, thereby allowing it to be used as a meta-module.

Textual or graphical presentations, constraints, and execution or transformation semantics may also be added as needed. For example, Fig. 12 shows the grammar that defines the PetriNet language text editor used in Fig. 8.

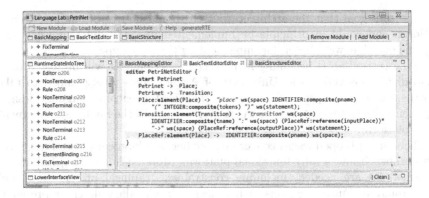

Fig. 12. Specification of the textual editor for the PetriNet language.

5 Discussion

The proposed architecture solves the challenge of consistent and logical handling of all language aspects, and lays a foundation for a fundamental re-thinking of the traditional meta-model architecture. One might initially think that this approach would break interoperability with other tools and technologies in the meta-modelling world, but in practice, the strict levels thinking is not a fundamental property of most of these tools and platforms, but rather an issue that comes up in relation to documentation and explanation of their architecture. Therefore, although variants of the traditional four level architecture of OMG have support from a great selection of language development tools and are very unlikely to be going away soon, the inherent ease of interoperability with any level-based architecture makes the proposed solution very flexible and competitive.

The LanguageLab prototype demonstrates the feasibility of the architecture and shows that the proposed module format and the built-in tree view allows us to create basic language modules and use these for defining language instances. For proving the platform, a complete set of language modules is not needed, rather it is necessary to show the feasibility of using the prototype to make more advanced language modules. The three basic meta-meta-modules BasicStructure, BasicMapping, and BasicEditor are defined using themselves with complete bootstrapping. Comparing the currently implemented features of LanguageLab with existing Language Workbenches may lead to unfavourable results as LanguageLab is still in the early stages of development, particularly when it comes to availability of meta-languages and editors. However, the openness, extensibility and simplicity of the design make it particularly suited for use in teaching.

When it comes to the decisions taken about the implementation of the LanguageLab prototype, one could also have chosen other frameworks to build it on, e.g. MPS, or it could have been developed as a more platform-independent Java application or a web-application. Familiarity with Java, the Eclipse platform and its plug-ins for model-driven language development made a RCP application built on top of an EMF editor a rather clear choice. However, it has been an important goal that the architecture itself should be free of bindings to any platform, and could in principle be implemented in many different ways, not only the one that was chosen for implementing the prototype.

As LanguageLab is becoming increasingly functional, it will be tested on a group of Master-students at University of Agder, where it is planned to take over the role from Eclipse as the platform of choice for teaching language design. Experiences from this test will be taken into account in the further development of the platform.

There are still open issues concerning further development of the Language-Lab workbench into a fully functional platform. More basic LanguageLab meta-meta-modules are needed, including constraints, graphical presentation, and transformation. Future versions of LanguageLab will allow different presentations of a language to support preservation of extra information, elements of the presentation that are also present in some form in other presentations, but not in the structure, as described in [3]. This can be achieved by using a presentation extra-information meta-meta-module. In addition, there are some issues that would benefit from more research, including:

- An improved method of handling language-to-language transformation, e.g. based on common transformation patterns.
- An improved method of handling behaviour for operational semantics, e.g. based on common behaviour patterns in state transitions.

6 Summary

A new meta-model architecture and a language workbench named LanguageLab has been proposed, that facilitates a modular component-based approach to language specification. A prototype implementation of LanguageLab has been developed as a proof of concept. When it comes to implementation of meta-languages, the system is currently bootstrapped with simple modules for structure, textual editing and mapping. Definition of instantiation semantics is also supported by using the mapping module. This way, LanguageLab features the essential aspects of language design.

References

1. Clark, T., Sammut, P., Willams, J.: Applied Metamodeling - A Foundation for Language Driven Development, 3rd edn (2015). arXiv:1505.00149
2. Fowler, M.: Language Workbenches: The Killer-app for Domain Specific Languages? Web (2005). http://www.martinfowler.com/articles/languageWorkbench.html
3. Gjøsæter, T., Prinz, A.: Preserving non-essential information related to the presentation of a language instance. In: Proceedings of NIK 2009 (2009)
4. Gjøsæter, T., Prinz, A.: Teaching model driven language handling. In: ECEASST, vol. 34 (2010)
5. Intentional Developers: Intentional Software. http://intentsoft.com/

6. Kats, L.C.L., Visser, E.: The spoofax language workbench: rules for declarative specification of languages and IDEs. In: 25th Annual ACM SIGPLAN Conference on Object-Oriented Programming. Systems, Languages, and Applications, OOP-SLA 2010, pp. 444–463. ACM, Reno/Tahoe, Nevada (2010)
7. Klint, P., Vinju, J., van der Storm, T.: Rascal - Meta Programming Language. http://www.rascal-mpl.org/
8. Mernik, M., Korbar, N., Žumer, V.: Lisa: a tool for automatic language implementation. ACM SIGPLAN Not. **4**, 71–79 (1995)
9. Meta-Environment Developers: The Meta-Environment Manual (2006). http://www.meta-environment.org/
10. MetaCase Developers: MetaEdit+. Version 4.0. Evaluation Tutorial. Technical report, MetaCase (2005). http://www.metacase.com/support/40/manuals/eval40sr2a4.pdf
11. Mu, L., Gjøsæter, T., Prinz, A., Tveit, M.S.: Specification of modelling languages in a flexible meta-model architecture. In: ECSA Companion Volume. ACM International Conference Proceeding Series, pp. 302–308. ACM (2010)
12. Dmitriev, S.: Language Oriented Programming: The Next Programming Paradigm (2004). http://www.jetbrains.com/mps/docs/Language_Oriented_Programming.pdf

Consistency of Task Trees Generated from Website Usage Traces

Patrick Harms[(⊠)] and Jens Grabowski

Institute of Computer Science, University of Göttingen, Göttingen, Germany
{harms,grabowski}@cs.uni-goettingen.de
http://swe.informatik.uni-goettingen.de

Abstract. Task trees are an established method for modeling the usage of a website as required to accomplish user tasks. They define the necessary actions and the order in which users need to perform them to reach a certain goal. Modeling task trees manually can be a laborious task, especially if a website is rather complex. In previous work, we presented a methodology for automatically generating task trees based on recorded user actions on a website. We did not verify, if the approach generates similar results for different recordings of the same website. Only if this is given, the task trees can be the basis for a subsequent analysis of the usage of a website, e.g., a usability analysis. In this paper, we evaluate our approach in this respect. For this, we generated task trees for different sets of recorded user actions of the same website and compared the resulting task trees. Our results show, that the generated task trees are consistent but that the level of consistency depends on the type of website or the ratio of possible to recorded actions on a website.

Keywords: Usage-based · Task tree generation · Task model analysis

1 Introduction

Task models are a well known way for modeling the functionality of a system and its usage. In addition to others, they define actions users take to utilize a systems functionality supporting a users task as well as the order of actions [19]. Especially, task models are important for the analysis of user behavior [14]. They can be created manually, which is a laborious task causing high effort as many executions variants of a task need to be considered to have complete task models. This can be overcome through generating task models based on recorded user actions. Such task models are much easier created and can aid to understand how users use a system and to detect usability smells [4]. Furthermore, usage-based generated task models are a reliable source of information when considering user-centered system adaptations [3,9]. Here, usage-based generated task models can help a system designer to adapt other system models in means of further tailoring a system to its actual usage. Such adaptations may also be done automatically.

In previous work, we developed a methodology for generating task models based on recorded user actions on websites [5,6]. These models are in fact task

© Springer International Publishing Switzerland 2015
J. Fischer et al. (Eds.): SDL 2015, LNCS 9369, pp. 106–121, 2015.
DOI: 10.1007/978-3-319-24912-4_9

trees, one of several forms of task models. In the previous work, we did not yet evaluate if the generated task trees are consistent, i.e., if they are structurally equal or similar for different recordings of the same website. This consistency is a prerequisite for the representativeness of the generated task trees regarding the usage of the system and also for the validity of the results of any subsequent analysis or system adaptation to be performed based on these task trees [4]. The contribution of this paper is the evaluation of our work described in [5,6] with respect to the consistency of the generated task trees. Hence, we focus on answering the following research question:

RQ: Does the approach described in [5,6] generate the same or similar task trees for different recordings of the same website?

To answer this question, we performed the following analysis: Initially, we recorded users of a web application. Then, we subdivided the recorded data into subsets of equal size. Afterwards, we generated task trees for the subsets using our approach [5,6] and compared the resulting task trees with each other to see if the same or similar task trees are generated for the separate subsets. To the best of our knowledge, there is no similar work done so far by other researchers.

The paper is structured as follows. In Sect. 2, we introduce the terminology used in this paper, the structure of the task trees generated by our approach, as well as the generation approach itself. Then in Sect. 3, we describe how we compare generated task trees. Afterwards, we describe the setup of our case study and its results in Sect. 4. We discuss our results in Sect. 5 and refer to related work in Sect. 6. Finally, we conclude on the results and give a brief outlook on future work in Sect. 7.

2 Task Trees and Trace-Based Task Tree Generation

In this section, we describe the basic concepts and terminology established for the task tree generation in our previous work [5,6] as used and required for this paper. Furthermore, we provide a brief description of the task tree generation process. Our approach starts with recording *actions* of users on a website. Actions are, e.g., clicks on links or entering text into text fields. Then, we post-process these actions to correct platform specific recording issues, e.g., misorderings of recorded actions. Afterwards, we generate task trees based on the actions.

The generated task trees are tree structures describing the order of actions executed by users to accomplish a certain task. The leaf nodes of a task tree are the actions. The root node represents the overall task. The parent nodes including the root node define the order in which their children (other parent nodes or actions) can be executed. The execution order of the children depends on the type of a parent node. Two types of parent nodes are important for this paper: *iteration* and *sequence*. If a parent node is an iteration, it has only one child which is executed several times. If a parent node is a sequence, it has several

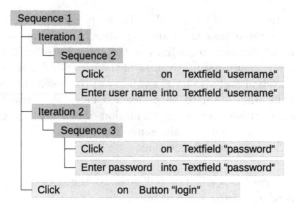

Fig. 1. Example for a task tree of a login process on a website (adapted from [6]).

children, which are executed in their given order. We refer to any node in a task tree, i.e., parent node or action, as *task*. A more formal definition of task models and task trees is given in [19].

An example of a task tree, which could be generated by our approach for a typical login screen on a website, is shown in Fig. 1. The leaf nodes (light grey) are the actions performed by the users like clicking on a user name field. The parent nodes (dark grey) define the order in which the actions were executed. For example, *Sequence 2* defines that first the user clicked on the user name field and then entered text into it. The parent of *Sequence 2*, which is an iteration (*Iteration 1*), defines that *Sequence 2* was repeated several times, i.e., users clicked the text field, entered the user name, clicked the text field again, entered the user name again, and so on.

Our generation process [5,6] creates task trees of the above shown structure through a repeated application of an iteration and sequence detection on a list of recorded actions. Initially, the recorded actions are put into an ordered list of tasks, that we call task list. On this list, we initially perform an iteration detection. If the task list contains several subsequent identical tasks (initially only actions) they are replaced by a new single element in the task list representing an iteration of the repeated tasks. Through this, the task list becomes shorter and in addition to actions also contains iterations. An example for the iteration detection is shown in Fig. 2a and b. Figure 2a is an initial task list containing only recorded actions. For simplification, actions are identified through letters. The order of the action executions by the user is given through the arrows. The initial task list contains two repetitions of Action *b* indicated through the dotted boxes. These are replaced through an iteration having Action *b* as its single child. The result of this replacement is shown in Fig. 2b.

Then, a sequence detection is applied on the task list. For this, we search for sublists in the task list that occur multiple times. The sublist that occurs most often and is the longest is then selected. Each occurrence of the selected sublist in the task list gets replaced by a new single element in the task list representing

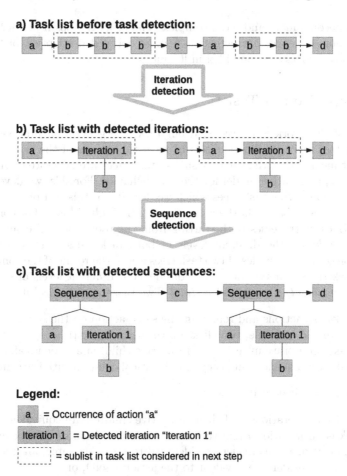

Fig. 2. Example for a task tree generation (adapted from [5,6]).

a sequence. This sequence gets the elements of the selected sublist as its children. Afterwards, the task list contains actions, iterations, and sequences. An example for the sequence detection is shown in Fig. 2b and c. Figure 2b shows a task list in which the sublist (a, *Iteration 1*) occurs twice (indicated through the dotted boxes). This sublist occurs most often in the overall task list and is also the longest sublist occurring that often. Hence, it is replaced through a sequence getting the elements of the sublist as its children. The result of this replacement is shown in Fig. 2c.

Afterwards, the iteration and sequence detection are reapplied alternately. Through this, more and more iterations and sequences are detected and the task list becomes shorter. In subsequent cycles, the iteration detection can also detect iterations of sequences. Furthermore, the sequence detection can detect new sequences having other sequences as their children. Through this, the detected task trees become more and more complex. The process stops if neither further iterations nor sequences are detected. A more detailed description of the task tree generation process is provided in [6] and [5].

3   Comparison of Tasks

The goal of this work is to assess, if our task tree generation process creates consistent task trees on different sets of recorded actions of the same website. Consistent means, that the same or similar task trees are generated. Only then they are a representative model for the user behavior. For this, we developed a heuristic for comparing task trees which we describe in this section.

Our heuristic is based on the comparison of individual tasks. For comparing two task trees, it traverses both starting from the root task and compares the individual tasks on the different levels of both task trees. The result of the comparison of the root nodes of two task trees is also the result of the comparison of both task trees. For two tasks, we consider four different levels of similarity: *identical, equivalent, similar,* and *distinct.* Two tasks are identical if:

- both tasks are actions and represent the same action on the same element of the website (for example, two clicks on the same button),
- both tasks are iterations and their respective children are identical, or
- both tasks are sequences and they have identical children with the same order.

Two tasks are equivalent if:

- both tasks are iterations and their respective children are equivalent,
- one task is an iteration i and the other one is an action or a sequence o and the child $c(i)$ of i is equivalent or identical to o (for example, an iteration of an action is considered equivalent to the action itself), or
- both tasks are sequences and they have identical or equivalent children with the same order.

For determining if two tasks t_1 and t_2 are similar, we create two ordered lists $l(t_1)$ and $l(t_2)$ containing the leaf nodes, i.e., actions, of the respective tasks in the order they would be executed if all iterations of the tasks were executed only once. Two neither identical nor equivalent tasks t_1 and t_2 are similar if

- $l(t_1)$ and $l(t_2)$ contain the same actions in the same order.

Two tasks which are neither identical, nor equivalent, nor similar, are distinct. Based on these definitions, two identical tasks are also equivalent but two equivalent tasks are not necessarily identical. Furthermore, two equivalent tasks are also similar, but two similar tasks are not necessarily equivalent.

Figure 3 shows examples of task trees with identical, equivalent, and similar tasks. For example, *Iteration 1* and *Iteration 3* are identical as they have an identical child (*Click on Text Field 1*). Furthermore, *Iteration 2* is equivalent to *Sequence 2* as its single child, *Sequence 4*, is identical to *Sequence 2*. Finally,

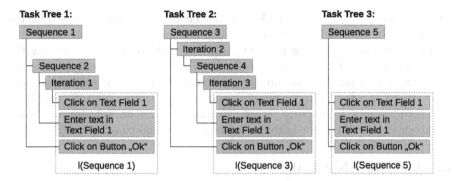

Fig. 3. Example for equivalent (*Task Tree 1* and *Task Tree 3*) and similar tasks (all).

Sequence 1 and *Sequence 3* are equivalent as they both have two children and their first and second child are equivalent (*Sequence 2* and *Iteration 1*) or identical (*Click on Button "Ok"*). As *Sequence 1* and *Sequence 3* are the root nodes, *Task Tree 1* and *Task Tree 2* are equivalent. An example for two similar tasks are *Sequence 3* and *Sequence 5*. *l(Sequence 3)* and *l(Sequence 5)* are indicated through dotted boxes around the leaf nodes of the two tasks. Both lists contain *Click on Text Field 1*, *Enter text in Text Field 1*, and *Click on Button "Ok"* in the same order. Hence, *Sequence 3* and *Sequence 5* are similar. Because these sequences are the root nodes, *Task Tree 2* and *Task Tree 3* are similar. *Task Tree 1* is also similar to *Task Tree 3*.

For comparing two sets of task trees T'_1 and T'_2, we first create subsets $T'_{s1} \subseteq T'_1$ and $T'_{s2} \subseteq T'_2$ of both sets which contain only those task trees having sequences as root nodes. Then, we compare any $t'_1 \in T'_{s1}$ with any $t'_2 \in T'_{s2}$. If we find a t'_1 which is identical, equivalent, or similar to t'_2, we call this a *recall* (similar to the definition of the term as used by Buckland and Gey, 1994 [1]) of t'_1 in T'_2. We do not compare task trees having iterations as root nodes for the following reason. Consider two identical tasks t_1 and t_2, being the root nodes of the task trees $t'_1 \in T'_1$ and $t'_2 \in T'_2$. As t_1 and t_2 are identical, t'_1 is recalled in T'_2. Consider a third task tree $t'_3 \in T'_2$ whose root node is an iteration i_1 of t_2. Due to the comparison rules, t_1 is equivalent to i_1 as t_1 is equivalent or identical to the child of i_1 being t_2. In such a scenario, t'_1 would be recalled twice in T'_2, once through t'_2 and once through t'_3. To prevent this, and also to reduce the number of comparisons, we only compare task trees having sequences as root nodes when comparing two sets of task trees.

4   Case Study

To evaluate the consistency of the generated task trees, we performed a case study. In this case study we recorded actions of users of a website over a long period of time. Then we subdivided the recorded actions into subsets and generated task trees for each of the subsets. Finally, we used our comparison mechanism to check if consistent task trees were generated for the distinct subsets.

The data used for this case study is an extended version of the data used for the case studies in [5,6] including more recorded actions.

The case study including the comparison of task trees was done using the framework AutoQUEST (Automatic Quality Engineering of Event-driven Software) which also provides an implementation of the task tree generation [5,6]. AutoQUEST is a tool suite for quality assurance of event driven software [7]. In addition to others, it supports recording of user actions on websites and based on this diverse methods for usability analysis and usage-based testing.

4.1   Recorded User Actions

Using AutoQUEST, we recorded users of a web-based application portal at our university. This portal is used by bachelor students to apply for the master studies. For this, they submit, e.g., their CV and important graduation certificates. Furthermore it is used by reviewers to assess if the students match required criteria. For the applicants and the reviewers, the portal provides two separate views. The *applicants view* is an assistant like interface guiding the students through the application process. It consists of 107 pages of which 42 are the wizard itself. Most of the other pages are quite similar to the wizard pages as they allow a subsequent edit of the data provided in the wizard. For example, there is a wizard page requesting the applicants name and date of birth, and there is a corresponding page with a similar form allowing to change the name and date of birth. Furthermore, there are pages on the applicants view giving an overview of all provided application data as well as for login and registration. A screen shot of the wizard page requesting for the personal data of an applicant is shown in Fig. 4. The *reviewer view* allows the reviewers to have overviews of all applications, to look at details of individual applications, and to assess the applications. It is more flexible than the applicants view as it has no wizard like structure. It consists of 32 pages of which some, e.g., the login screen, are shared with the applicants view.

Over a period of 15.5 months, we recorded users of the portal performing 1,396,163 actions. As described in our previous work [5], recorded actions were post-processed. This post-processing includes, e.g., dropping of implicit user actions such as changing the keyboard focus to a specific text field. These actions can be dropped, as subsequent actions like entering text into a text field implicitly contain the action that the keyboard focus has been changed to the respective text field. In addition, we performed a reordering of some actions as, due to our recording process, the actions are not always recorded in the order in which they are performed. For example, when leaving a text field using the tabulator key, the recording first records the pressing of the tabulator key and afterwards the preceding entering of a text into the text field although users first entered the text and then pressed the tabulator key.

After the post-processing, the remaining actions based on which the task trees were generated are 807,654 of which 147,458 were executed on the reviewer view and 656,100 on the applicants view. 4,096 actions belonged to test sessions covering both views which we only considered in our evaluation as part of the

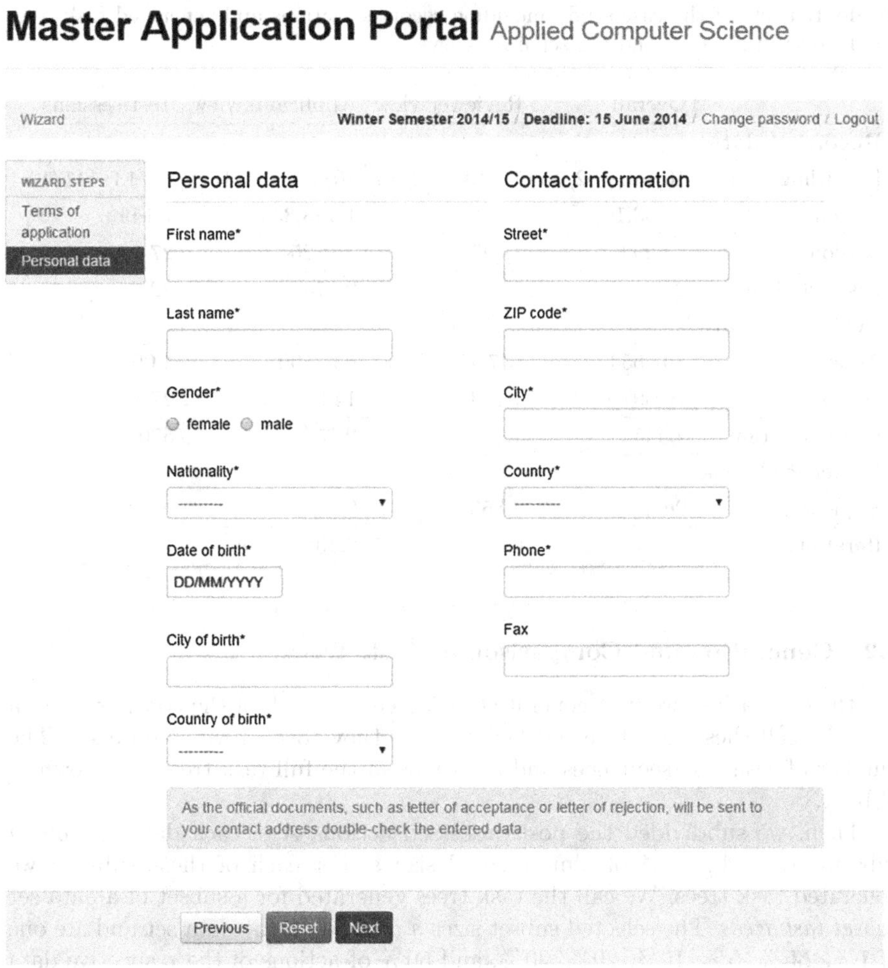

Master Application Portal Applied Computer Science

Wizard   **Winter Semester 2014/15 / Deadline: 15 June 2014** / Change password / Logout

WIZARD STEPS

Terms of
application

Personal data

Personal data

First name*

Last name*

Gender*

○ female ○ male

Nationality*

\---------   ▼

Date of birth*

DD/MM/YYYY

City of birth*

Country of birth*

\---------   ▼

Contact information

Street*

ZIP code*

City*

Country*

\---------   ▼

Phone*

Fax

As the official documents, such as letter of acceptance or letter of rejection, will be sent to
your contact address double-check the entered data

Previous   Reset   Next

Fig. 4. Screenshot of the wizard page requesting for the personal data of an applicant
in the applicants view of the website used for the case study.

whole data set but not on their own. The actions are distributed over 16,397
user sessions, where a session begins with the opening of the website and ends
either with the closing or with a timeout. We did not determine the number
of distinct recorded users as for this non-anonymous data would have to be
recorded to identify them. But we identified different client browser instances
which may give an impression on the number of different users. The number of
client browsers are 2,757 of which 2,575 used only the applicants view and 163
only the reviewer view. More details can be found in Table 1. There, also the
number of distinct available actions per view is listed. Some actions are shared
between both views because the views also have common pages, e.g., the login
screen.

Table 1. Facts of the case study including recorded actions and generated task trees for the overall data set and the separate views.

	Overall	Reviewer view	Applicants view	Test sessions
Recorded data				
Recording period	10/13 – 02/15	11/13 – 02/15	10/13 – 02/15	11/13 – 11/14
Actions	1,396,163	245,680	1,143,334	7,149
Sessions	19,299	1,547	17,725	27
Distinct clients	2,758	162	2,574	22
Post-proc. data				
Actions	807,654	147,458	656,100	4,096
Sessions	16,397	1,463	14,907	27
Distinct actions	4,445	1,740	2,754	570
Generated tasks				
Sequences	26,353	4,855	21,452	–
Iterations	2,821	696	2,139	–

4.2   Generation and Comparison of Task Trees

For the evaluation, we first generated task trees for each of the considered data sets. We call these task tree *full task trees* as they cover a whole data set. The number of resulting sequences and iterations in the full task trees are shown in Table 1.

Then, we subdivided the post-processed actions A of each data set into n subsets $A_1^s \ldots A_n^s \subset A$ of almost equal size s. For each of these subsets, we generated task trees. We call the task trees generated for a subset of a data set *subset task trees*. The selected subset sizes s depend on the data set and are one of 1 %, 2.5 %, 5 %, 10 %, 20 %, 30 %, and 50 % of actions of the respective data set. The subsets with $s \leq 20$ % are disjoint, i.e., no session occurs in more than one subset. Larger subsets share sessions.

The separation of actions into subsets was done by creating subsets of user sessions. This was required to not split user sessions into parts. As the number of actions per session differs, a subset represented by a session subset, may not exactly match the intended subset size. Which sessions were added to a subset was decided randomly. We did not consider all possible permutations of combining the sessions into subsets of almost equal size as these were too many. Hence, our subsequent analysis is only based on a sample of possible subsets. The details for the subsets we considered in our analysis are listed in Table 2. This table also shows how many task trees we generated for the subsets on average. For example, for the reviewer view we created 30 subsets with $s = 1$ % (first row for reviewer view). On average, these subsets consisted of 1,477 actions (standard deviation of 10). The average number of sequences generated for these subsets was 117.

Afterwards, we compared the generated task trees. We performed comparisons of subset task trees with each other, where the subsets were of the same size. In addition, we compared the subset task trees with the full task trees of the respective data set. Table 2 shows how many comparisons of subset task trees were performed either with other subset task trees or with the full task trees of the data set. For example, for the reviewer view, we performed 15 comparisons between the subset task trees with $s = 1\%$ and 10 comparisons of these subset task trees with the full task trees generated for the reviewer data set. A dash in the table indicates, that the corresponding comparisons have not been done. This is due to the large comparison runtime caused by larger subsets.

Table 2. Information on created subsets, generated task trees, and the comparisons done for the data sets.

	Subsets		Comparisons		Actions		Sequences		Iterations	
	size s	count	subset	full	average	dev.	average	dev	average	dev.
Overall	1%	30	15	10	8,076	0	635	34	220	21
	2.5%	30	15	5	21,191	0	1,361	40	389	24
	5%	20	10	-	40,383	3	2,420	49	591	31
	10%	8	5	-	80,765	0	4,246	66	882	54
Reviewer view	1%	30	15	10	1,477	10	117	14	37	9
	2.5%	30	15	10	3,730	201	255	28	67	14
	5%	20	10	10	7,373	40	430	50	99	19
	10%	10	10	5	14,746	2	771	45	163	20
	20%	5	10	5	29,490	0	1,350	47	264	21
	30%	6	5	-	44,237	0	1,871	45	348	21
	50%	10	5	-	72,378	37	2,800	63	467	24
Applicants view	1%	30	15	5	6,561	0	529	21	186	11
	2.5%	30	15	5	16,402	0	1,132	26	331	20
	5%	20	10	5	32,802	3	1,985	30	506	37
	10%	10	10	-	65,610	3	3,447	31	725	17

In general, the comparison of two sets of task trees T_1' and T_2' is time consuming. If T_1' contains n_1 tasks trees to compare and T_2' contains n_2 tasks trees to compare, then $n_1 \times n_2$ comparisons have to be done. In addition, a single comparison of two task trees t_1' and t_2' has to perform several comparisons of the individual tasks of the task trees. In the worst case, each task of t_1' will be compared with one task of t_2'. To be able to efficiently handle that many comparisons, we implemented the comparison in a way so that we can perform individual comparison of sets of task trees with individual starts of AutoQUEST. Through this, we were able to run several comparisons in parallel on different cores of a CPU or on different machines.

After the comparisons were done, we counted the recalls to get a measure for the consistency of the generated task trees. A recall means, that for different subsets, the task tree generation process generates identical, equivalent, or similar task trees. The higher the number of recalls, the more consistent are the task trees. If the task trees have a high consistency, then we consider them as a representative model also for other data sets and, hence, for the usage of a website. This is a prerequisite for a subsequent usability analysis or other usage of the generated task trees.

We considered both, the recalls of all task trees of a subset and the recalls of the *most prominent task trees* of a subset. The most prominent task trees are those covering most of the actions in a subset. To get the most prominent task trees, we determined for all task trees generated for a subset the number of actions they cover. Then, we created sets of task trees with the same amount of covered actions. Afterwards, we joined the sets containing the task trees with the highest coverage until the resulting set contains at least 20 % of the generated task trees. As during this process a set may be joined containing more task trees than required to achieve 20 %, the resulting set can contain more task trees than 20 % of them. But as we performed our comparison on several subsets and, hence, task tree sets, we have similar percentages of task trees to be considered as the most prominent ones.

4.3   Comparison Results

The resulting average recalls of all comparisons mentioned in Table 2 are shown as bar charts in Fig. 5. The upper bar charts represent the average recalls between subset task trees. The lower bar charts show the average recalls of subset task trees in full task trees. Each bar chart shows the recalls in percent (y-axis) for a specific subset size (x-axis). For each subset size, there are two bars. The left refers to the average recalls of all subset task trees. The right shows the average recall of the most prominent tasks (mp) of a subset. The black part of a bar indicates recalls of identical tasks, dark grey recalls of equivalent tasks, and light grey recalls of similar tasks. For example, in the applicants view data set (middle column) the recall of identical task trees (black part of bar) between subset task trees (upper bar chart) with $s = 10\%$ (right bars) was on average 28 % for the most prominent task trees.

The recalls between subset task trees (upper bar charts) for the reviewer view are below 25 % for all subset task trees and below 50 % for the most prominent task trees. For the applicants view, the recalls are higher but still below 35 % for all subset task trees and below 65 % for the most prominent task trees. The recalls in the whole data set are below 32 % for all subset task trees and below 55 % for the most prominent task trees. The recalls of the most prominent task trees are roughly twice as high as the recalls of all subset task trees.

The recalls of subset task trees in the full task trees (lower bar charts) are higher (reviewer view above 60 %, applicants view above 75 %, overall above 75 %). The difference between the recall of most prominent task trees and all task trees is not as high as for the recall between subset task trees, but still the

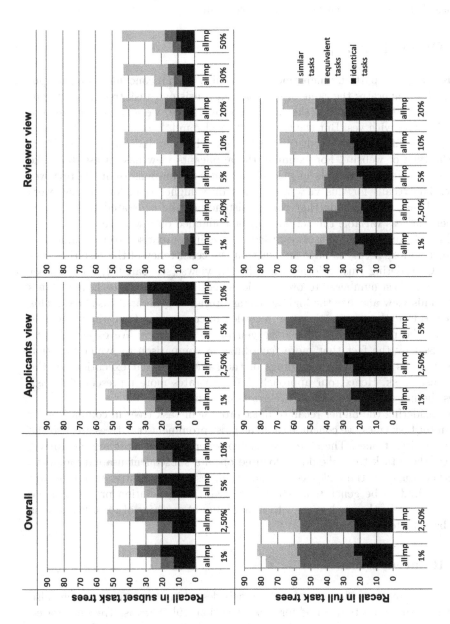

Fig. 5. Average recalls of subset task trees in other subset task trees (upper row) and in full task trees (lower row).

recall of the most prominent task is always higher. The recall between subset task trees increases with increasing subset size. The recall of subset task trees in full task trees decreases with increasing subset size although the recall of identical task trees increases with increasing subset size.

5 Discussion

Considering the partially high amount of recalls, we can conclude that our approach [5,6] generates the same or similar, i.e., consistent, task trees for different sets of recorded actions for the same website. Hence, we answer our research question **RQ** with yes. But the amount of recalls and, hence, the task tree consistency, is different for the distinct data sets. This may indicate a dependency on the type of website. For example, the applicants view has an assistant like structure being less flexible in possible action combinations than the reviewer view. The recalls for this view are significantly higher than for the reviewers view. Hence, we conclude that the consistency of the generated task trees is higher, the less variable the actions can be combined on a website.

In addition, the number of recorded actions in comparison to the number of distinct actions seems to have an effect on the consistency of the resulting task trees. Considering this ratio for the different views (see Table 1), the data set with the highest number of recorded actions per distinct actions is the applicants view. This view also has the highest average recall of generated task trees. This indicates that the more actions are recorded in comparison to distinct available actions, the more consistent are the generated task trees. We expect this to be caused by the fact that more recordings in comparison to available action combinations cause more recordings of the same or similar executions of the same user task. Hence, our approach [5,6] generates more representative task trees the more recorded actions are available as input.

Considering the higher recall of most prominent task trees in comparison to all subset task trees, we conclude that the most prominent task trees are also the most consistent ones. Therefore, we also consider them as most representative. Hence, these task trees should be focused on in a subsequent usability analysis or other usages of the task trees. In addition, less representative task trees are not required to be generated. Hence, the task tree generation process can be stopped if no further task trees with a minimum of coverage of recorded actions can be detected.

6 Related Work

Task trees are a specific form of task models describing task structures but also user goals and objects required for task execution [19]. The task trees generated by our approach [5,6] provide only a task decomposition and a task flow description. They do not provide further information. As the task trees are generated based on recorded user actions of a fully functional website, they can be used for a summative analysis and through this support subsequent design adaptations.

Similar to ours, there are other approaches utilizing tree structures for task modeling. These include TaskMODL [18], Goals, Operators, Methods, and Selection Rules (GOMS) [11], and ConcurTaskTrees [13, 15]. Usually, these models are trimmed to support a certain modeling goal. For example, GOMS models are used to predict the efficiency of an average user performing a task. In addition, there are approaches that focus on detecting tasks in recorded user action, e.g., Automated Website Usability Analysis (AWUSA) [17], ACT-R [10], and Convenient, Rapid, Interactive Tool for Integrating Quick Usability Evaluations CRITIQUE [9]. These approaches usually require labels in the recorded data to indicate which actions represent the execution of a specific task [12]. Furthermore, approaches like Maximal Repeating Patterns (MRPs) provided statistical data about action combinations performed by users [16]. Our approach does not require labeled input data and provides more than just statistical information about user actions.

The utilization of a website by users is similar to a language spoken by users and interpreted by the website. Such a language can be modeled using formal grammars. Task trees are quite similar to these grammars [8]. Therefore, approaches for generating a grammar for examples of a given language, called grammatical inference, could be applicable to generated task trees. But most of these approaches require labeled data [2] which is not required by our approach. To the best of our knowledge, there is no related work that evaluates the task trees generated by our approach or by other approaches. There is work evaluating approaches for grammatical inference. But as grammatical inference requires labeled input data and does not directly result in the generation of task trees, we do not cover it in this section.

7 Conclusion and Outlook

In this paper, we evaluated our approach [5, 6] for usage-based generated task trees. We generated task trees using our method for different data sets of recorded user actions on the same website and compared the resulting task trees with each other. Through this, we evaluated the consistency of the generated task trees for different data sets. Our results show, that the task trees are consistent and representative for the usage of a website. Especially the most prominent tasks can, therefore, be used for a subsequent usability analysis. But, we also observed that the consistency may depend on the number of recorded actions in comparison to the number of available actions on a website as well as on the type of website for which the task trees are generated.

In future work, we will perform further comparison analyses to address these two issues and to determine, if these potential effects need to be considered. We will also perform comparisons of merged task trees [5]. In addition, we will check if our task tree generation process can be adapted in a way that only most prominent tasks are generated. Furthermore, we will implement a different type of comparison between subsets that will determine how many actions belonging to a subset are executions of tasks generated for another subset.

References

1. Buckland, M., Gey, F.: The relationship between recall and precision. J. Am. Soc. Inf. Sci. **45**(1), 12–19 (1994). http://dx.doi.org/10.1002/(SICI)1097--4571(199401)45:1⟨12::AID-ASI2⟩3.0.CO;2-L
2. D'Ulizia, A., Ferri, F., Grifoni, P.: A survey of grammatical inference methods for natural language learning. Artif. Intell. Rev. **36**(1), 1–27 (2011). http://dx.doi.org/10.1007/s10462-010-9199-1
3. Gomez, S., Laidlaw, D.: Modeling task performance for a crowd of users from interaction histories. In: Proceedings of the SIGCHI Conference on Human Factors in Computing Systems, pp. 2465–2468, CHI 2012. ACM, New York, NY, USA (2012). http://doi.acm.org/10.1145/2207676.2208412
4. Harms, P., Grabowski, J.: Usage-based automatic detection of usability smells. In: Sauer, S., Bogdan, C., Forbrig, P., Bernhaupt, R., Winckler, M. (eds.) HCSE 2014. LNCS, vol. 8742, pp. 217–234. Springer, Heidelberg (2014)
5. Harms, P., Herbold, S., Grabowski, J.: Extended trace-based task tree generation. Int. J. Adv. Intell. Syst. **7**(3 and 4), 450–467 (2014)
6. Harms, P., Herbold, S., Grabowski, J.: Trace-based task tree generation. In: Proceedings of the Seventh International Conference on Advances in Computer-Human Interactions (ACHI 2014), XPS - Xpert Publishing Services (2014)
7. Herbold, S., Harms, P.: AutoQUEST - automated quality engineering of event-driven software. In: Software Testing, Verification and Validation Workshops (ICSTW), IEEE (2013)
8. Hilbert, D.M., Redmiles, D.F.: Extracting usability information from user interface events. ACM Comput. Surv. **32**(4), 384–421 (2000). http://doi.acm.org/10.1145/371578.371593
9. Hudson, S.E., John, B.E., Knudsen, K., Byrne, M.D.: A tool for creating predictive performance models from user interface demonstrations. In: Proceedings of the 12th Annual ACM Symposium on User Interface Software and Technology, pp. 93–102. UIST 1999. ACM, New York, NY, USA (1999)
10. John, B.E., Prevas, K., Salvucci, D.D., Koedinger, K.: Predictive human performance modeling made easy. In: Proceedings of the SIGCHI Conference on Human factors in Computing Systems, pp. 455–462, CHI 2004. ACM, New York, NY, USA (2004)
11. Limbourg, Q., Vanderdonckt, J., Michotte, B., Bouillon, L., Florins, M., Trevisan, D.: USIXML: a user interface description language for context-sensitive user interfaces. In: Proceedings of the ACM AVI2004 Workshop, Developing User Interfaces with XML: Advances on User Interface Description Languages, pp. 55–62, Press (2004)
12. Norman, K.L., Panizzi, E.: Levels of automation and user participation in usability testing. Interact. Comput. **18**(2), 246–264 (2006). http://dx.doi.org/10.1016/j.intcom.2005.06.002
13. Paternò, F.: ConcurTaskTrees: an engineered approach to model-based design of interactive systems, pp. 1–18. The Handbook of Analysis for, Human Computer Interaction (1999)
14. Paternò, F.: Model-based tools for pervasive usability. Interact. Comput. **17**(3), 291–315 (2005). Elsevier
15. Paternò, F., Mancini, C., Meniconi, S.: ConcurTaskTrees: a diagrammatic notation for specifying task models. In: Proceedings of the IFIP TC13 International Conference on Human-Computer Interaction, pp. 362–369, INTERACT 1997. Chapman & Hall Ltd, London, UK (1997)

16. Siochi, A.C., Hix, D.: A study of computer-supported user interface evaluation using maximal repeating pattern analysis. In: Proceedings of the SIGCHI Conference on Human Factors in Computing Systems, pp. 301–305, CHI 1991. ACM, New York, USA (1991). http://doi.acm.org/10.1145/108844.108926
17. Tiedtke, T., Mrtin, C., Gerth, N.: AWUSA - a tool for automated website usability analysis. Technical report (2002). http://citeseerx.ist.psu.edu/viewdoc/summary?doi=10.1.1.83.7285
18. Trætteberg, H.: Model-based user unterface design. Information Systems Group, Department of Computer and Information Sciences, Faculty of Information Technology, Mathematics and Electrical Engineering, Norwegian University of Science and Technology (2002)
19. Van Welie, M., Van Der Veer, G.C., Eliëns, A.: An ontology for task world models. In: Proceedings of DSV-IS98, Abingdon (1998). http://citeseerx.ist.psu.edu/viewdoc/summary?doi=10.1.1.13.4415

On the Semantic Transparency of Visual Notations: Experiments with UML

Amine El Kouhen[1](✉), Abdelouahed Gherbi[2], Cédric Dumoulin[3],
and Ferhat Khendek[1]

[1] Faculty of Engineering and Computer Sciences, Concordia University,
Montreal, QC, Canada
{elkouhen,khendek}@encs.concordia.ca
[2] Department of Software and IT Engineering, École de Technologie Supérieure,
Montreal, QC, Canada
abdelouahed.gherbi@etsmtl.ca
[3] University of Lille, CRISTAL CNRS UMR 9189, Cite Scientifique - Batiment M3,
Villeneuve d'ascq, France
cedric.dumoulin@univ-lille1.fr

Abstract. Graphical notations designed by committees in the context
of standardization bodies, like Object Management Group (OMG), are
widely used in the industry and academia. Naive users of these notations
have limited background on visualization, documentation and specification of workflows, data or software systems. Several studies have pointed
out the fact that these notations do not convey any particular semantics and their understanding is not perceptually immediate. As reported
in these studies, this lack of semantic transparency increases the cognitive load to differentiate between concepts, slows down the learning
and comprehension of the language constructs. This paper reports on a
set of experiments that confirm the lack of semantic transparency of the
Unified Modeling Language (UML) as designed by OMG and compares
this standard to alternative solutions where naive users are involved in
the design of the notations to speed-up the learning of these languages
to new users.

Keywords: Visual languages · UML · Semantic transparency · Crowd-
sourcing

1 Introduction

Over the past three decades, visual languages have been gaining in popularity.
Several of these languages, such as the Unified Modeling Language (UML) have
been designed by standardization bodies involving different contributors, such as
language experts, tool vendors, (expert) users, etc. As reported in [28] these languages (that we refer to as committee-designed languages) have been developed
in a bottom-up approach by reusing existing notations and through consensus

© Springer International Publishing Switzerland 2015
J. Fischer et al. (Eds.): SDL 2015, LNCS 9369, pp. 122–137, 2015.
DOI: 10.1007/978-3-319-24912-4_10

among the experts. As in [28,31] we believe that this is not the best approach, especially when the target audience includes naive users.

Several observations on visual languages have been made over time. The current development process strongly emphasizes the domain conceptualization (i.e. building the abstract syntaxes) and often relegates the visual notations (concrete syntaxes) and their semantic transparency as secondary products (byproducts). However, the visual notation is the first contact of the users with the modeling language and its semantic transparency plays a crucial role in its acceptance. The current development process is criticized by research in diagrammatic reasoning, which shows that the form of representations has an equal, if not greater, influence on cognitive effectiveness as their content [23,39]. A major incentive for using visual notations is the widely-held belief that they convey information more effectively than text, especially to novices [4]. Committee-designed visual notations can sometimes be very distant from semantic concepts they represent. As reported in [13,28,29] this lack of semantic transparency increases the cognitive load to differentiate between concepts and slows down both the recognition and the learning of the language constructs. In [9], the authors suggest that the difficulty of understanding many of UML notations *"supports the argument that the UML may be too complex"*. The authors in [13,28,29] evaluated the visual syntax of several committee-designed languages using a set of evidence-based principles for designing cognitively effective visual notations. The analysis reveals some serious flaws in the notation in terms of cognitive effectiveness of these languages, which are defined as the speed, ease and accuracy with which a representation can be processed by the human mind [23].

In this paper, we ask a rather simple question: to design notations that are understandable by users, why not involve them in the notation development process? If involving end-users in the development of software systems (e.g. participatory design [32], user-centred design) is working well, why should this not also be the case for graphical notations? The purpose is not to make modeling languages understandable without learning, but to speed-up the learning and comprehension of the language constructs and reducing misinterpretations due to the notations complexity.

For this purpose we conducted a set of experiments on UML involving end-users. Some of these experiments have been proposed and applied to another language in [5]. The main difference is our comparison between the outcome of these experiments and the standard UML notations. We have also used as input for this comparison a set of notations created by experts in cognitive sciences according to the Physics of Notations theory, which was not the case in [5]. On the other hand, [5] has used the recognition experiment which was not necessary in our process.

Because of space limitations, we selected only a set of visual elements of UML. We believe this set represents a good sample of UML diagrams widely used and easily understandable without deep technical background. For instance, class, statechart and use-case diagrams are the most widely used UML diagrams by non-experts users [38] and are included in this study. The other diagrams, which are created and used only by system designer experts in their domains and without direct impact to other stakeholders are out of the scope of this study.

The goal of this paper is not to redefine the visual syntax of UML but to show the importance of involving end-users in the design of visual notations. We show the importance of involving end-users actively in the notations design process as *co-designers* rather than as passive *consumers*. The broader goal of this paper is to raise awareness about the importance of the semantic transparency in the acceptance of a modeling language, which has historically received little attention.

2   Background and Related Research

One of the main advantages behind the use of modeling languages is their ability to provide to their target users a set of concrete artifacts (visual notations) that can directly express related domain abstractions (concepts) in a concise, complete and unambiguous way [16]. According to [28], visual representations have greater effect on understanding and performance than their content.

Existing approaches for designing visual notations consist of proposing symbols and voting on them (i.e. expert consensus). For example, in UML diagrams, symbols are conventional shapes on which iconic markers are added. However, symbol shapes seem not to convey any particular semantics: there is no explicit rationale to represent a Class as a rectangle, an action as a rounded rectangle and a use case as an ellipse. The differentiation of UML notations is not perceptually immediate, it is purely conventional. According to [37], to have an unambiguous modeling language its symbols should provide cues to their meaning. Semantically direct representations reduce cognitive load: their meaning can be perceived directly or easily. This kind of representations speeds-up concepts recognition, especially for novices [4,27]. According to [5], current visual notation design practice is characterised by:

– An unselfconscious design approach [1]: there are no explicit principles for designing visual notations [30].
– Lack of design rationale [24]: symbols are chosen without any evidence-based decisions or rational justification [19].
– Small forms variations: similar geometrical shapes are used for different purposes [34]. Without self-conscious design principles, the range of symbols is limited by the imagination of the design team [30].
– Lack of involvement of the target audience: notations design decisions are made exclusively by experts, without the involvement of the target audience. For this reason, we propose our experimental process, which uses end-users (target audience) suggestions as inputs into the language design process made by experts.

2.1   Physics of Notations

On the whole, the most complete and referenced work on the assessment of visual notations is probably the Physics of Notations theory [30] of Moody, which is exclusively devoted to the design, evaluation, comparison and improvement of visual notations. In this work, Moody establishes a set of nine principles defined from theory and empirical evidence and obtained from different disciplines such as: cognitive and perceptual psychology, graphic design, communication theory, cartography, etc.

Each of the principles of the Physics of Notations contains: design strategies, which may contribute towards improving visual notations regarding this principle; a different evaluation procedure or metric that can be used to compare different notations, and examples of notations that satisfy or violate the principle. These nine principles are:

1. *Visual Expressiveness*: use the full capacities of visual variables. The seminal work in the graphical communication field is Jacques Bertin's *Semiology of Graphics* [21]. Bertin identified eight elementary visual variables, which can be used to graphically encode information. These are categorized into planar variables (the two spatial dimensions x, y) and retinal variables (features of the retinal image).

   The set of visual variables define a *vocabulary* for graphical communication: a set of atomic building blocks that can be used to construct any graphical representation. Different visual variables are suitable for encoding different types of information (Fig. 1) The choice of visual variables has a major impact on cognitive effectiveness as it affects both speed and accuracy of interpretation [7, 25, 40].

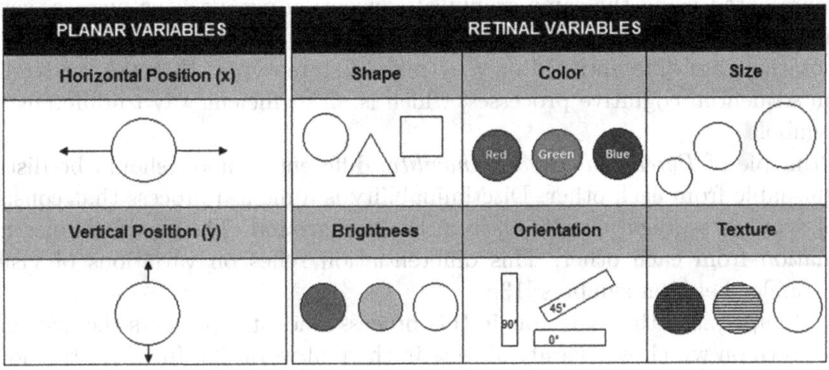

Fig. 1. Visual variables [21]

2. *Semiotic Clarity*: According to [14], there must be a one-to-one correspondence between elements of the language and graphical symbols. The Semiotic Clarity's principle, maximises expressiveness by eliminating the deficit when a domain concept is not represented by any representation and reduces ambiguity by eliminating symbol overload (multiple domain concepts are represented by one representation).

UML visual notation violates the semiotic clarity principle. Many of the diagrams that need to be understandable by everyone (e.g. Structural diagrams) contain high levels of symbol redundancy and symbol overload. For example, of the 33 symbols commonly used on class diagram there are 5 synographs (15 %), 20 homographs (61 %) and 2 symbol excesses (6 %).

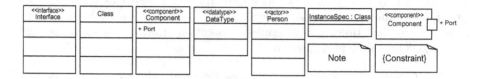

Fig. 2. Zero visual distance between UML notations (homographs)

This assessment was confirmed when we proposed in [10] a framework to specify and reuse visual languages. It turned out that we can reuse up to 71 % of UML notations, which represents a high level of redundancy in this language and thus ambiguity. Symbols are called homographs if they have zero visual distance (i.e. they have identical values for all visual variables) but represent different semantic constructs (Fig. 2). Thus, in UML the majority of graphical conventions used to mean different things. For example, in Class Diagrams, the same graphical symbol can be used to represent objects, classes, interface and attributes. Different types of relationships can also be represented using the same graphical convention e.g. package merges, package imports and dependencies are all represented using dashed arrows. These notations are differentiated only by textual stereotypes. However, text relies on sequential cognitive processes, which is an inefficient way to differentiate symbols.

3. Principle of *Perceptual Discriminability*: different symbols should be distinguishable from each other. Discriminability is a mental process that consists of symbols segregation [36,40] from the background. Then symbols discrimination from each other. This differentiation relies on variations of visual variables between symbols [13]:
   - Shape plays the main role in this process since it represents the first concern on which we classify objects in the real world [2]. In UML, the notations differ on only a single visual variable (shape) and the values chosen are very close together: all shapes are either rectangles or rectangle variants. Given that experimental studies show that rectangles and diamonds are often confused by naive users in Entity/Relation diagrams [33].
   - Some of the symbols have zero visual distance (homographs) and are differentiated by labels or typographical characteristics. It is the case of most of UML links, which have identical shapes but differentiated only by textual stereotypes (Fig. 3). However, according to [28]: text is an inefficient way to differentiate between symbols as it relies on slower cognitive processes.

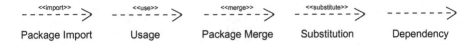

Fig. 3. Symbol overload: UML homographs

- Colour is the most performant and cognitively expressive visual variable. The human visual system can quickly and accurately distinguish between them [40]. However, colours are prohibited in UML: The use of colours is up to tool vendors.

4. Principle of *Semantic Transparency*: using visual representations whose appearances suggest their meaning. We will focus on this principle when we propose our experimental process. We believe that involving target audience into design process may improve this criterion.

5. Principle of *Dual Coding*: enhance diagrams with textual information.

6. Principle of *Complexity Management*: suggest some mechanisms when dealing with notations complexity.

7. Principle of *Cognitive Integration*: suggest explicit mechanisms to support the integration of information from different diagrams.

8. Principle of *Graphic Economy*.

9. Principle of *Cognitive Fit*.

Indeed, these principles have already been used in several works to evaluate and improve other visual committee-designed languages such as i^* [29], Business Process Modeling Notation (BPMN) [13] and UML [28]. In the next section, we reuse the alternative notation proposed by [28], which is based on these nine principles.

3   Experiments on UML Semantic Transparency

This section summarizes a set of related experiments applied to UML Visual Syntax. The experiments and the workflow are shown in Fig. 4. A similar experimental process have been proposed and applied to another language in [5]. In this paper, we reused the Experiments 1, 2, 3 and 4 from [5]. As mentioned earlier, the main difference is our comparison between the outcome of these experiments and the standard UML notations. We also used as input for this comparison, a set of notations created by experts in cognitive sciences according to the Physics of Notations theory , which is not the case in [5]. In [5], authors have used the recognition experiment, which is not the case in our process. As mentioned in the introduction, we limit these experiments to a few elements of UML visual syntax. The purpose is not to redefine the visual syntax of UML but to show the importance of involving end-users into the design decisions made generally by experts.

1. *Symbolization experiment*: naive participants (i.e. with background on Object-Oriented paradigm but without previous knowledge on UML) generated symbols for UML concepts (drawings).

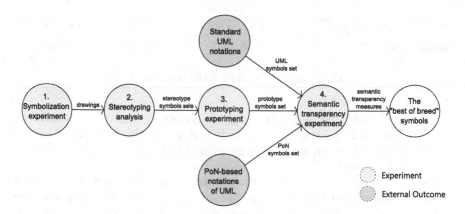

Fig. 4. Experiments Workflow

2. *Stereotyping analysis*: we analysed the results of Experiment 1 and identified the most common symbols produced for each UML concept (stereotype symbols sets).

3. *Prototyping experiment*: other group of naive participants (different from the first one) analysed the drawings produced in Experiment 1 and identified the "best" representations for each UML concept (prototype symbols set).

4. *Semantic transparency experiment*: another group of naive users were asked to infer the meaning of 3 sets of symbols from their appearance alone : Prototypes from Experiment 3 and two external inputs, which are the Standard UML notation and the UML notation based on Physics of Notation Theory (PoN) .

5. *Identify "best of breed" symbols*: based on the results of Experiment 4, we identified the most cognitively effective symbols for each UML concept across all symbol sets.

This experimental workflow combines quantitative and qualitative research methods: Experiments 1, 2, 3 primarily use qualitative methods, while study 4 uses quantitative methods. The used data is primarily in the form of pictures (drawings). The quantitative studies measure the interpretation/recognition accuracy in combination with psychometric scales (for rating the cognitive difficulty of tasks). More detailed data on participants artifacts, samples, results as well as the coded data set and the statistical scripts are available in [11].

3.1   Symbolization Experiment

In this experiment, "naive" participants imagined and drew symbols for UML concepts, a task normally reserved for experts. There were 64 participants in this experiment, all with a background in Object-Oriented concepts. They had no previous knowledge of modeling languages in general or UML in particular: this was a requirement for participation in the study (**inclusion criterion**), to ensure participants were truly naive. UML regular users would not have been suitable participants, due to their technical orientation and knowledge (i.e. the **curse of knowledge** [18]).

Each participant was provided with a two-page questionnaire that consists of a table of constructs (we chose twelve concepts, which are frequently used in software engineering : *Class, Interface, Enumeration, Instance Specification, Component, Signal, Model, Package, Dependency, Merge, Import* and *Substitution*), their definitions, and an empty cell in which participants were instructed to draw the construct.

Participants were asked to draw the constructs in the order in which they appeared. They were instructed to produce drawings that they felt most expressive (conveyed better the meaning of the construct). They were instructed to draw as simple as possible and that the quality of drawings wasn't important: the most important thing was to represent clearly and unambiguously the meaning of the construct.

Table 1. Response rates for symbolization task

UML construct	Non-Responses	Reponse rate
Class	2	96.87 %
Interface	3	95.3 %
Instance spec	4	93.75 %
Enumeration	0	100 %
Component	1	98.44 %
Signal	0	100 %
Model	2	96.87 %
Package	1	98.44 %
Dependency	2	96.87 %
Merge	1	98.44 %
Import	1	98.44 %
Substitution	2	96.87 %
Average	**1.58**	**97.5 %**

The participants produced a total of 749 drawings with a response rate of 97.5 % for a set of twelve UML concepts, which was a high response rate given the known difficulty in *"concretizing"* [22] UML abstract concepts. Instance Specification (6.25 %), Interface (4.68 %), Class (3.13 %) and Model (3.13 %) received the highest number of non-responses, which is more likely to be the case for such abstract concepts. Enumeration, Signal and Package receiving less than 1 % (only 1 non-response out of 64). Table 1 summarizes the response rates.

3.2 Stereotyping Analysis

In this step, we analysed the results of Experiment 1 and identified the most common symbols produced for each UML concept. These defined the **stereotype symbol sets**.

The analysis was conducted by three volunteers. It was done by looking at similarity of drawings. The drawings produced in Experiment 1 were used as input for this experiment. Three copies were made of the drawings to conduct this task independently.

We used the **judges' ranking method** [22], which is an approach for reaching convergence on a set of categories. In the first step, each judge categorized the drawings produced for each concept by sorting them into categories based on their similarity (pattern-matching), following the approach described in [17].

Then, they compared their choices (categories) for each concept and agreed on a common set of categories. Finally, they selected for each concept, a set that consists of a drawing from each category (*the stereotypical category*), resulting in a stereotypical set for each concept (twelve in total).

3.3 Prototyping Experiment

For each evaluated concept, the participants studied the stereotypical sets selected in Experiment 2 and identified the "best" representation. These defined the **prototype symbol set**.

Table 2. Degree of prototypy

Concept	Degree of convergence
Class	24.13 %
Interface	31 %
Instance spec	38 %
Enumeration	72.4 %
Component	44.8 %
Signal	34.5 %
Model	27.6 %
Package	48.3 %
Dependency	51.7 %
Merge	31 %
Import	62 %
Substitution	58.6 %
Average	**43.67 %**

40 naive users participated in this experiment, all undergraduate students in computer science from multiple cultural backgrounds (different universities in

Canada, France, Morocco, Algeria, Indonesia and Jordan). We used a different sample population from Experiment 1 but drawn from the **same** underlying population. It would not have been accurate to use the same participants as in Experiment 1, as their judgements may have been biased by their own drawings.

We conducted this experiment using a form, which consists of a table showing the name and the definition of each concept with the candidate drawings (representatives from each category identified in the stereotyping study). Participants were asked to select the most expressive drawing for each concept (regardless on the aesthetic the drawing). The order of the concepts and the position of the drawings were randomized in the forms to avoid sequence effects.

The output of this experiment was a set of 12 prototypical drawings (one for each evaluated UML concept).

Table 2 shows the Degree of prototypy i.e. percentage of participants who rated the prototype drawing as the best. For all concepts, there was a high level of consensus among judgements of prototyping (43.67 % in average). The highest score was for Enumeration, which achieved more than 72 % agreement, and lowest for Class and Model, which achieved less than 30 % agreement.

3.4   Semantic Transparency Experiment

For this experiment, naive users were asked to infer the meaning of symbols from their appearance alone. The symbols were from one of 3 symbol sets, two designed by experts (the standard UML notation and the notation designed following *Physics of Notations* principles as explained in [28]) and those designed by naive end-users (the prototype symbols set from Experiments 3).

There were 120 participants, all undergraduate students in computer sciences from several universities. As in studies 1 and 3, the participants had no prior knowledge of software modeling languages or UML, so were truly naive.

There were three experimental groups (composed by 40 participants for each of them), corresponding to different levels of input:

1. **Standard** UML notations: official symbols from UML specification (unselfconscious design).
2. UML notations designed according *Physics of Notations* theory (selfconscious design) called **PoN** in Table 3. The details of this notation are available in [28].
3. **Prototype** notations of UML: the best symbols produced by naive users as judged by other naive users.

We conducted this experiment using a multiple-choices questionnaire. One symbol was displayed at the top of each page (representing the **stimulus** [29]) and the complete set of UML constructs and definitions displayed in a table below (representing the possible responses). Participants were asked to choose the construct they thought most likely corresponds to the symbol. In each page, there was one correct response and 11 incorrect responses (distractors). The order in which the stimuli (symbols) were presented (i.e. order of pages) and the order in which the responses (concepts) were listed were randomized to avoid sequence effects.

Participants were instructed to work alone and not share their answers with each other. They were asked to answer each question in order and told to choose one and only one concept for each symbol presented. They were told that they could choose the same concept in response to multiple symbols.

3.5 Identify *Best of Breed* Symbols

Based on the results of steps 4, we identified the most cognitively effective symbols for each UML construct across all symbol sets.

To measure graphical symbols comprehensibility, we used the *hit rates* (i.e. percentage of correct responses). The ISO standard for testing graphical symbols [35] defines 67 % as the hit rate required for acceptance of public information and safety symbols [20]. Only 9 out of 12 symbols across the 3 symbols sets met the ISO required limit for comprehensibility.

Table 3. *"Best of Breed"* symbols

UML Concepts	Experiment 3 : Semantic Transparency			*Best of breed* symbol
	Standard	PoN Notations	Prototype	
Enumeration	30%	45%	77.5%	
Component	22.5%	30%	70%	
Signal	5%	35%	87.5%	
Package	22.5%	20%	87.5%	
Dependency	12.5%	20%	75%	
Merge	27.5%	37.5%	72.5%	
Import	32.5%	42.5%	77.5%	
Group size	40	40	40	
Hit Rate Mean	22%	33%	**71.5%**	

Table 3 shows the best symbols across all symbol sets in terms of hit rates. The *best of breed* symbol set includes 12 symbols from the prototype symbol set and none from the standard UML and PoN symbol sets. The mean hit rate is 71.5 %, which exceeds the ISO threshold for comprehensibility of symbols. For space limitation, we choose to show only symbols, which have met a low level of non-response in Experiment 1, a high degree of prototypy in Experiment 2 and exceed the threshold of 67 % in Experiment 3.

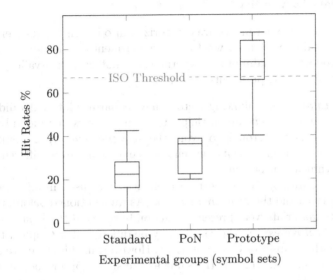

Fig. 5. Differences in hit rate between experimental groups

The differences between groups are visually confirmed by the box and whisker plot in Fig. 5. The *boxes* show confidence intervals for each group mean, while the *whiskers* show minimum and maximum values. The line through the middle of each box represents the median. Figure 5 shows a comparison of semantic transparency results for unselfconscious and self-conscious notation design. We can observe that the prototype symbol set exceeds largely the ISO threshold for comprehensibility of symbols.

Using explicit design principles (self-conscious design) significantly improves semantic transparency (supported by our hypothesis), showing that conscious efforts to improve semantic transparency are likely to be successful. The average hit rate for the *PoN* symbol set was more than 1.5 times that of the standard UML notation, meaning that *PoN* symbols were more than 1.5 times as likely to be correctly interpreted without prior explanation. Moreover, the average hit rate for the *Prototype* symbol set was more than three times that of the standard UML notation and more than twice that of the *PoN* notation, meaning that *Prototype* symbols were by far more expressive and more often interpreted correctly. More detailed results as well as the coded data set and the statistical scripts are available in [11].

In this experiment, our *a priori* hypothesis was confirmed. We find that symbols proposed and chosen by naive users are naturally based on good rules that can be found in theory and empirical approaches. We can thus observe that user-comprehensible notations (Prototype set) have absolutely a better cognitive expressiveness and semantic transparency than the other two symbol sets combined.

3.6 Threats to Validity

The validity of our experiments are categorized into internal and external validity. The internal one refers to whether an experimental condition could be sufficient to support the claim of the experiment or not. External validity refers to the generalization of experiments outcomes [6].

1. *Internal validity.* the following factors may jeopardize internal validity:
   - *Selection of subjects*: all participants in this study were randomly assigned to experimental groups to avoid the *selection bias*. As semantic transparency is culture-specific, we choose participants from different cultural and ethnical background.
   - *Instrumentation*: the same measurements were used in all experimental groups to avoid the *measurement bias*. As we mentioned before, the experiments materials were presented randomly to avoid the *sequence effect*.
   - *Statistical regression*: the results may be different if we applied this study on another subset of UML notations. However, in this study we get 300 % of improvement, which is the same as the study [5] for another modeling language (i^*).
2. *External validity.* the following factors may threaten external validity:
   - To avoid the *expertise bias*, we used naive users in all experiments. We considered computer science students as adequate participants as they must know Object-Oriented concepts to draw them, but we considered only students with no previous knowledge of modeling languages in general or UML specifically to avoid the *knowledge bias* (the curse of knowledge [18]).
   - We used different population samples in the last experiment. It would not have been accurate to use the same participants across the experiments, as their judgements may have been biased by the drawings they produced.
   - Our study evaluated the comprehension of symbols as visual unit rather than complete diagrams, which can represents a threat to this study. Thus the results and their interpretation cannot be generalizable to complete diagrams.
   - We did not consider other principles such as the Principle of Cognitive Fit (ease of drawing of symbols) or the Principle of Graphical Economy (usage of the space), which are important in modeling languages design. For example, the signal symbol may be hard to use when the sender and the receiver are not close in the diagram.
   - In this study, we used hit rates (positive values) as measurements for the semantic transparency. However, Semantic transparency is not a binary

state but a sliding scale (Fig. 6) defined from −1 to +1 : −1 for symbols whose appearance implies an incorrect meaning (semantically perverse) and +1 for symbols whose appearance implies the correct meaning (semantically transparent) [30]. Such kind of measurements need further investigations.

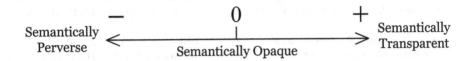

Fig. 6. The semantic transparency and the semantic perversity

4 Discussion and Conclusions

Several works have evaluated the cognitive effectiveness of committee-designed languages, such as UML, BPMN, etc., using theory and empirical evidence from a wide range of fields. The conclusion is that radical improvement is required to improve their cognitive effectiveness. One solution is to involve target end-users as co-designers of these languages rather than as passive consumers as it has been so far. In this paper, we have conducted experiments, for a subset of UML, that have confirmed the importance of involving end-users.

Symbols designed this way increased semantic transparency by almost 300 % compared to the standard UML notation. Reducing misinterpretations by end users could therefore lead to significant cost savings: According to [12,26], design errors are the source of more than half the errors and failure in software development projects [12,15] and are the most costly errors of all, as their post-implementation correction costs 100 times more than correcting them during the design phase [3].

Our experimental approach is an application of the **crowd-sourcing** for UML visual syntax design. This approach also called peer production or collective intelligence [8] enlists a multitude of humans to help solve a problem. One of the advantages of this approach is that it enlarges/expands the range of notations ideas (i.e. beyond the imagination of the language design team), rather than relying exclusively on experts to design notations, one could follow this approach and take into the ideas of the target audience.

Acknowledgements. This work was supported by the internationalization fund of ETS Montreal and the Natural Sciences and Engineering Research Council of Canada (NSERC).

References

1. Alexander, C.: Notes on the Synthesis of Form. Harvard Press, Cambridge (1964)
2. Biederman, I.: Recognition-by-components: a theory of human image understanding. Psychol. Rev. **94**, 115–147 (1987)
3. Boehm, B.W.: Software Engineering Economics. Prentice hall edn, Englewood Cliffs (1981)
4. Britton, C., Jones, S.: The untrained eye: how languages for software specification support understanding in untrained users. Hum.-Comput. Interact. **14**(1), 191–244 (1999)
5. Caire, P., Genon, N., Heymans, P., Moody, D.: Visual notation design 2.0: towards user comprehensible requirements engineering notations. In: 21st IEEE International Requirements Engineering Conference (RE), pp. 115–124 July 2013
6. Campbell, D.T., Stanley, J.C.: Experimental and Quasi-Experimental Designs for Research. Rand McNally College Publishing, Chicago (1963)
7. Cleveland, W.S., McGill, R.: Graphical perception: theory, experimentation, and application to the development of graphical methods. J. Am. Stat. Assoc. **79**(387), 531–554 (1984)
8. Doan, A., Ramakrishnan, R., Halevy, A.Y.: Crowdsourcing Systems on the Worldwide Web. Commun. ACM **54**(4), pp. 86–96 Apr 2011. http://doi.acm.org/10.1145/1924421.1924442
9. Dobing, B., Parsons, J.: How UML is used. Commun. ACM **49**(5), 109–113 (2006)
10. El Kouhen, A.: Spécification d'un Métamodèle pour l'Adaptation des Outils UML. Ph.D. thesis, Université de Lille 1 (2013)
11. El Kouhen, A.: Semantic Transparency Experiment Artifacts. (2014) http://www.lifl.fr/~elkouhen/SemanticTransparencyExperiment/artifacts.zip
12. Endres, A., Rombach, D.: A Handbook of Software and System Engineering: Empirical Observations Laws and Theories. Addison-Wesley, New York (2003)
13. Genon, N., Heymans, P., Amyot, D.: Analysing the cognitive effectiveness of the BPMN 2.0 visual notation. In: Malloy, B., Staab, S., van den Brand, M. (eds.) SLE 2010. LNCS, vol. 6563, pp. 377–396. Springer, Heidelberg (2011)
14. Goodman, N.: Languages of Art: An Approach to a Theory of Symbols. Hackett, Indianapolis (1976)
15. Group, S.: The Chaos Report. (1994). https://www.standishgroup.com/sample_research_files/chaos_report_1994.pdf
16. Guizzardi, G., Pires, L., van Sinderen, M.: Ontology-based evaluation and design of domain-specific visual modeling languages. In: Advances in Information Systems Development, pp. 217–228. Springer, US (2006). http://dx.doi.org/10.1007/978-0-387-36402-5_19
17. Howell, W.C., Fuchs, A.H.: Population stereotypy in code design. Organ. Behav. Hum. Perform. **3**(3), 310–339 (1968)
18. Heath, C., Heath, D.: Made to Stick: Why Some Ideas Take Hold and Others Come Unstuck. Arrow Books, London, England (2008)
19. Hitchman, S.: The details of conceptual modelling notations are important. Commun. Assoc. Inform. Syst. **9**(10), 167–179 (2002)
20. ISO/IEC: 24744: Metamodel for Development Methodologies (2007)
21. Jacques, B.: Semiology of Graphics: Diagrams, Networks, Maps. University of Wisconsin Press, Madison, Wisconsin (1983)
22. Jones, S.: Stereotypy in pictograms of abstract concepts. Ergonomics **26**, 605–611 (1983)

23. Larkin, J.H., Simon, H.A.: Why a diagram is (sometimes) worth ten thousand words. Cogn. Sci. **11**(1), 65–100 (1987)
24. Lee, J.: Design rationale systems: understanding the issues. IEEE Expert **12**(3), 78–85 (1997)
25. Lohse, G.L.: A cognitive model for understanding graphical perception. Hum.-Comput. Interact. **8**(4), 353–388 (1993)
26. Martin, J.: Information Engineering. Prentice hall edn, Englewood Cliffs (1989)
27. Masri, K., Parker, D., Gemino, A.: Using iconic graphics in entity-relationship diagrams. J. Database Manag. **19**(3), 22–41 (2008)
28. Moody, D., van Hillegersberg, J.: Evaluating the visual syntax of UML: an analysis of the cognitive effectiveness of the UML family of diagrams. In: Gašević, D., Lämmel, R., Van Wyk, E. (eds.) SLE 2008. LNCS, vol. 5452, pp. 16–34. Springer, Heidelberg (2009). http://dx.doi.org/10.1007/978-3-642-00434-6_3
29. Moody, D.L., Heymans, P., Matulevicius, R.: An evaluation of i* visual syntax.In: 17th IEEE International Conference on Requirements Engineering (2009)
30. Moody, D.: The physics of notations: toward a scientific basis for constructing visual notations in software engineering. IEEE Trans. Softw. Eng. **35**(6), 756–779 (2009)
31. Morris, S., Spanoudakis, G.: Uml: an evaluation of the visual syntax of thelanguage. In: Proceedings of the 34th Annual Hawaii International Conferenceon System Sciences. IEEE Computer Society, Washington, DC, USA (2001)
32. Muller, M.J., Kuhn, S.: Participatory design. ACM Commun. **36**(6), 24–28 (1993)
33. Nordbotten, J.C., Crosby, M.E.: The effect of graphic style on data model interpretation. Inform. Syst. J. **9**(2), 139–155 (1999)
34. Novick, L.R.: The importance of both diagrammatic conventions and domain-specific knowledge for diagram literacy in science: the hierarchy as an illustrative case. In: Barker-Plummer, D., Cox, R., Swoboda, N. (eds.) Diagrams 2006. LNCS (LNAI), vol. 4045, pp. 1–11. Springer, Heidelberg (2006)
35. Organisation(ISO), I.S.: Graphical symbols - Test methods - Methods for Testing-Comprehensibility (ISO 9186-1). Geneva, Switzerland (2007)
36. Palmer, S., Rock, I.: Rethinking perceptual organization: the role of uniform-connectedness. Psychon. Bull. Rev. **1**(1), 29–55 (1994).http://dx.doi.org/10.3758/BF03200760
37. Petre, M.: Why looking isn't always seeing: readership skills and graphical programming. ACM Commun. **38**, 33–34 (1995)
38. Reggio, G., Leotta, M., Ricca, F.: Who knows/uses what of the UML: a personal opinion survey. In: Dingel, J., Schulte, W., Ramos, I., Abrahão, S., Insfran, E. (eds.) MODELS 2014. LNCS, vol. 8767, pp. 149–165. Springer, Heidelberg (2014)
39. Siau, K.: Informational and computational equivalence in comparing information modelling methods. Database Manag. **15**(1), 73–86 (2004)
40. Winn, W.: An account of how readers search for information in diagrams. Contemp. Educ. Psychol. **18**(2), 162–185 (1993)

Goal Modeling

On the Reuse of Goal Models

Mustafa Berk Duran[1], Gunter Mussbacher[1]([✉]), Nishanth Thimmegowda[2],
and Jörg Kienzle[2]

[1] Department of Electrical and Computer Engineering, McGill University,
Montréal, Canada
berk.duran@mail.mcgill.ca, gunter.mussbacher@mcgill.ca
[2] School of Computer Science, McGill University, Montréal, Canada
nishanth.thimmegowda@mail.mcgill.ca, joerg.kienzle@mcgill.ca

Abstract. The reuse of goal models has received only limited attention
in the goal modeling community and is mostly related to the use of goal
catalogues, which may be imported into the goal model of an application
under development. Two important factors need to be considered when
reusing goal models. First, a key purpose of a goal model is its evaluation
for trade-off analysis, which is often based on propagating the contributions of low-level tasks (representing considered solutions) to high-level
goals as specified in the goal model. Second, goal models are rarely used
in isolation, but are combined with other models that impose additional
constraints on goal model elements, in particular on tasks. For example,
workflow models describe causal relationships of tasks in goal models.
Similarly, feature models describe further constraints on tasks, in terms
of which tasks may be selected at the same time. This paper (i) argues
that reusable goal models must be specified either with real-life measurements (if available) or with relative contributions, (ii) presents a novel
evaluation mechanism that enables the reuse of goal models with relative
contributions, while taking into account additional constraints on tasks
in the goal model expressed with feature models, and (iii) discusses a
proof-of-concept implementation of the novel evaluation mechanism.

Keywords: Reuse · Goal modeling · Feature modeling · GRL · Goal-
oriented Requirement Language · URN · User Requirements Notation ·
Goal evaluation

1 Introduction

Software reuse is a powerful concept due to its potential benefits of increased
productivity, quality, and reliability with faster time-to-market and lower cost.
Reuse has been defined as the process of creating software systems from existing
software artifacts rather than creating them from scratch [15] and as the use of
existing software artifacts in a new context [8]. Consequently, reusable artifacts
must be unaware of the application under development (i.e., they are *generic*),
so that they can be used in many different contexts [19]. Furthermore, reusable

© Springer International Publishing Switzerland 2015
J. Fischer et al. (Eds.): SDL 2015, LNCS 9369, pp. 141–158, 2015.
DOI: 10.1007/978-3-319-24912-4_11

artifacts are assembled into *hierarchies* of reusable artifacts to realize a desired application [3].

The reuse of goal models [9, 13, 23, 24] has received limited attention in the goal modeling community and is mostly confined to the idea of goal catalogues (e.g., security, reliability, etc.) [10], which may be imported as is into the goal model of an application under development. Goal models are typically used to express early requirements, helping to understand stakeholder objectives and any trade-offs among potential solutions for the problem at hand. However, goal models may also be used to better describe a reusable artifact, e.g., the contexts in which the reusable artifact is applicable. Essentially, a goal model is used to express the impacts of the reusable artifact on high-level goals and system qualities, allowing various candidates for reuse to be evaluated. In both usage scenarios for goal models, the reuse of said goal models results - just as for any other reusable artifact - in model hierarchies, supporting trade-off reasoning from small, low-level artifacts to large, system-level artifacts. Even though we motivate the reuse of goal models with the second usage scenario in this paper, our findings are relevant for both usage scenarios, because the composition mechanism for reusable goal models is the same in both usage scenarios.

An important factor to take into account when reusing goal models is that goal models cannot be considered in isolation, because additional constraints on goal model elements (typically tasks) are often expressed in other modeling notations. For example, workflow models may describe causal relationships of tasks, while feature models may describe which tasks may be selected at the same time.

A second factor to consider is the evaluation of goal models for trade-off analysis. Often, goal models employ a propagation-based evaluation mechanism that takes the satisfaction value of a child element and propagates it up to the parent element based on the type and value of the link between the child and parent. A satisfaction value can either be a real-life measurement, a qualitative value, or a quantitative value. Commonly found types of links in goal models are contributions, decompositions, and dependencies. The value of contribution links may be specified by a global or relative value. We investigate, in the context of reuse, these options for satisfaction values as well as these common link types, and conclude that *reusable goal models require real-life measurements (if available) or relative contributions*. In addition, we present a *novel evaluation mechanism that enables the reuse of goal models with relative contributions without additional constraints and with additional constraints expressed by feature models*. We consider feature models in combination with reusable goal models (i.e., a goal model is used to describe the impact of a feature on system qualities), because recent advancements in Concern-Oriented Reuse (CORE) [3] and Software Product Lines [11, 20] use feature and goal modeling in combination.

The remainder of this paper presents background on goal modeling and propagation-based evaluation of goal models in Sect. 2. Section 3 first discusses the implications of the types of satisfaction values and links used in a goal model in the context of reuse, before reaching the conclusion that real-life measurements (if available) or relative contributions should be used. Section 4 explains a novel evaluation mechanism for goal models with relative contributions that enables the reuse of goal models without constraints or in combination with feature models. Section 5 reports on a proof-of-concept implementation of such reusable goal models. Section 6 summarizes related work, while Sect. 7 concludes the paper and states future work.

2   Background on Goal Modeling

While various types of goal models exist, we focus on goal models that are evaluated by propagating satisfaction values of lower-level elements to higher-level elements, as in i^* [24], the Goal-oriented Requirement Language (GRL) [13], or the NFR Framework [9]. We use GRL to illustrate reusable goal models in this paper, but our findings are also applicable to other propagation-based evaluation mechanisms for goal models. GRL is a visual modeling notation for the specification of intentions, business goals, and nonfunctional requirements (NFRs) of multiple stakeholders as well as system qualities. GRL is part of the User Requirements Notation (URN) [4,13], an international requirements engineering standard published by the International Telecommunication Union in the Z.15x series. GRL is based on i^* (in terms of key goal concepts) and the NFR Framework (in terms of evaluating goal models), but allows modeling elements to be more freely combined than i^*.

A GRL *actor* (⬭) represents a stakeholder of a system or the system itself. When representing stakeholders, actors are holders of intentions; they are the active entities in the system or its environment who want goals to be achieved, tasks to be performed, softgoals to be satisfied, and resources to be available. A goal model is a connected graph of *intentional elements* (softgoal, goal, task, resource) that optionally reside within an actor. A goal model shows the high-level business goals and qualities of interest to a stakeholder and the solutions considered for achieving these high-level elements. Goals and qualities are modeled with GRL softgoals and GRL goals. *Softgoals* (⬭) differentiate themselves from *goals* (⬭) in that there is no clear, objective measure of satisfaction for a softgoal, whereas a goal is quantifiable. Therefore, the term *satisficed* is often used to indicate that a softgoal is satisfied and that this satisfaction may be dependent on a stakeholder's point of view. *Tasks* (⬭) represent solutions to goals or softgoals that are considered for a system. In order to be achieved or completed, softgoals, goals, and tasks may require *resources* (□) to be available. Various kinds of *links* connect the elements in a goal graph. AND, XOR, and IOR *decomposition links* (+—) allow an element to be decomposed into sub-elements. *Contribution links* (→) indicate desired impacts of one element on another element, either expressed qualitatively with labels (e.g., + or -) or quantitatively as an integer value between -100 and 100. Finally, *dependency links* (—▶—) model relationships between actors, i.e., one actor depending on another actor for something.

GRL supports reasoning about high-level goals, non-functional requirements, and system qualities, through its evaluation mechanism. GRL shows the impact of often conflicting goals and various proposed candidate solutions to achieve the goals. A GRL *strategy* describes a particular candidate solution by assigning initial qualitative or quantitative satisfaction values to a set of intentional elements in the model, typically leaf nodes in the goal model. The *evaluation mechanism* propagates the initial satisfaction values of goal model elements as specified in a strategy to those of higher-level goal model elements based on the link types connecting the goal model elements. Strategies can therefore be compared with each other to help reach the most appropriate trade-offs among often conflicting goals of stakeholders.

The evaluation mechanism calculates a satisfaction value for each existing node based on its incoming links and the satisfaction values of the node's children, unless the node's satisfaction value is defined directly by the modeler. A satisfaction value can either be in the range of $[-100, 100]$ or $[0, 100]$ (we use the latter range).

If the values in a goal model are specified *qualitatively* (e.g., by labels such as Denied, Weakly Denied, None, Weakly Satisfied, and Satisfied), the evaluation mechanism explicitly defines a mapping that determines (a) which label should be propagated up given a child's satisfaction value, link type, and contribution value (if applicable), and (b) how the propagated labels of a node's children should be combined to yield the qualitative satisfaction value of the node (see Fig. 1a).

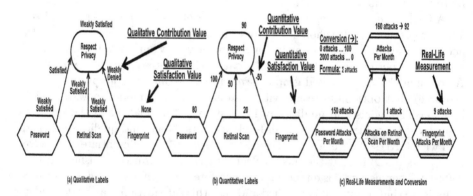

Fig. 1. Qualitative values, quantitative values, and real-life measurements in goal models

If the values in a goal model are specified *quantitatively*, the weighted sum of the children's satisfaction values is propagated across contribution links (e.g., $[(80 \times 100) + (20 \times 50) + (0 \times -50)]/100 = 90$; see Fig. 1b). The result is limited to the allowed range of $[0, 100]$ for satisfaction values. The evaluation of decomposition and dependency links is out of scope for this paper (see [5] for details).

The satisfaction values in a goal model may also be specified by *real-life measurements* with the help of Key Performance Indicators (KPI) (⬡) [13]. In this case, KPIs are propagated upwards based on formulas [21], until the real-life measurement is converted into a goal model satisfaction value based on a conversion function [13] (e.g., the attack KPIs of the children are summed up for the parent as specified by the formula, and the resulting KPI of 160 attacks for the parent is then converted into the goal model value of 92 given a conversion function; see Fig. 1c). A conversion function maps the real-life values onto the allowed [0, 100] range of GRL satisfaction values, enabling the comparison of KPIs measured in different units and other goal model elements. Essentially, the conversion function specifies when a real-life measurement may be considered sufficient (e.g., while a KPI measures waiting time in minutes, the conversion function may specify that 5 min of waiting time fulfills the needs of the application under development instead of some other duration by mapping 5 min to the maximum GRL value of 100, i.e., satisfied).

3 Reuse Scenarios for Goal Models

A goal model may be used to describe why a reusable artifact should be chosen over another candidate artifact, or why a variation offered by a reusable artifact should be chosen over another offered variation. A goal model enables trade-off analysis among these choices by capturing the impact of a choice on high-level goals and system qualities. In this scenario, the goal model is an integral part of the reusable artifact. When a reusable artifact is assembled with a reusing artifact in a reuse hierarchy, the goal model describing the reusable artifact must also be composed with the goal model of the other reusing artifact to enable reasoning about the whole system. Consequently, the goal model is also reused, which is the focus of this paper. Theoretically, a reusable goal model may use any type of satisfaction value and any link type summarized in the previous section. In this section, we argue that this is not the case and that a reusable goal model must use real-life measurements (if available) or otherwise relative contribution values. We refer to the modeler who builds a reusable artifact as the *designer* and the modeler who uses the reusable artifact as the *user*.

Qualitative values: while qualitative values are useful for capturing relationships among choices very early on when not a lot is known about a domain, they are not appropriate for a reusable artifact, because a carefully-built, reusable artifact is well-understood. Qualitative values do not allow nuanced differences among reusable choices to be expressed, and are therefore not the ideal means of expressing impact for reusable goal models. Because qualitative values are typically quite broad (e.g., only two labels - Weakly Satisfied and Satisfied - for positive impacts), a designer may have to classify many different choices the same (e.g., as Weakly Satisfied). This means that the evaluation mechanism cannot differentiate these choices anymore, making it difficult to impossible for the user to determine the most appropriate choice.

Real-life measurements: these measurements are the opposite extreme compared to qualitative values. Concrete, real-life measurements can guarantee consistent assessment and allow for a nuanced description of reusable artifacts. If such measurements are available, then they should be used to describe reusable artifacts (e.g., cost can be straightforwardly measured in \$). However, it may be rather difficult to define appropriate units of measurements for some common high-level goals and system qualities. Security, privacy, and convenience are examples where this is the case. In addition, even if a unit of measurement can be devised, it may be difficult or costly to collect the required data to calculate such measurements. Therefore, an alternative is needed for those cases where the use of real-life measurements is not feasible.

Quantitative values: they are the perfect middle ground as they allow nuanced assessments without the cost of collecting real-life measurements, and hence are the preferred approach when real-life measurements are not feasible. However, there are *two issues* that need to be taken into account before quantitative values can be used for reusable goal models. A designer of a reusable artifact must be able to come up with reasonable quantitative values for the contributions in the reusable goal model to describe well the reusable artifact. Furthermore, a designer must be able to do so without making any assumptions about the application under development, which eventually will use the reusable goal model. As stated earlier, a reusable artifact must not know about application-specific elements - a reusable artifact must be generic!

A designer of a reusable goal model has the choice of either using *global* or *relative* contribution values. Consider the example shown in Fig. 2, which shows a hierarchy with two reusable goal models with global contribution values at the top and the same hierarchy of goals with relative contribution values at the bottom. *Application C* reuses the two goal models. *Reusable Artifact A* describes privacy implications of online security features, while *Reusable Artifact B* describes privacy considerations of famous people interacting with the public. The tasks shown for each reusable artifact represent the reusable solutions offered by the reusable artifact, each with a different impact on privacy captured by the goal model. As *Application C* reuses both artifacts, it undertakes a more thorough assessment of the privacy of famous people, taking some of their online interactions into account.

Issue One: If a designer uses global values, then the implications are that the designer of *Reusable Artifact A* and the designer of *Reusable Artifact B* must agree on rules regarding the assessment of contribution values to ensure consistency across all goal models for a specific quality. If not, then the impact on the quality (e.g., *Privacy*) may be inflated by one reusable artifact compared to the other, which makes it impossible to combine them into a goal model hierarchy for *Privacy*. For example in Fig. 2a, the designers would have to agree that *Password* contributes more (i.e., 100) to *Privacy* than *Disguise* (i.e., 60). In the absence of concrete units of measurements, an agreement is unlikely to be feasible, as both designers would need to be aware of the details of each other's *Privacy* goal models (as well as those of any other reusable artifact impacting *Privacy* built by other designers).

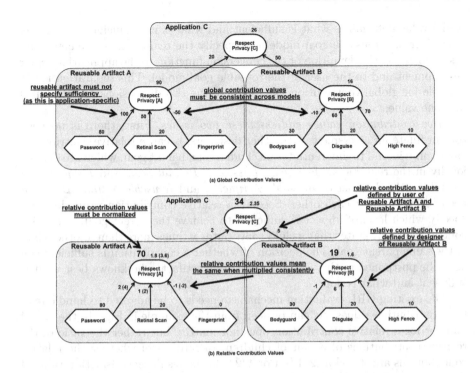

Fig. 2. Global and relative contribution values in reusable goal models

Issue Two: let us examine in more detail the contribution value of *Password* (Satisfied or 100; see Fig. 1a and b, respectively). The contribution value, regardless of whether it is a qualitative or quantitative value, indicates that choosing *Password* is sufficient to achieve the parent goal, i.e., *Privacy*, in this case. If it were not sufficient, then Weakly Satisfied or a value lower than 100 would have to be chosen. However, this decision cannot be made by the designer of the reusable goal model, as it depends on the application context. While the *Password* solution may be perfectly acceptable for one context, it may not be sufficient in another context. A generic reusable goal model cannot state that a particular solution is sufficient, because that would mean the designer of the reusable artifact is able to anticipate each and every use of the reusable artifact. This, however, is not possible without violating the key characteristic of a reusable artifact being generic.

At the heart of this problem is the fact that a contribution value in goal models captures two dimensions: first, it defines the degree of impact on the parent goal, and second, it defines the threshold for what is sufficient to achieve the goal and what is not. In a reusable goal model, the former but not the latter must be specified.

Note that real-life measurements with KPIs do not have this problem, because in that case the two dimensions have already been separated. The real-life measurement captures the degree of impact, while the conversion into a goal model value determines what is sufficient and what is not sufficient. Therefore, a designer of a reusable goal model can specify the real-life measurements and easily postpone the definition of the conversion function to the application under development and to the user of the reusable goal model. This separation is not possible for global contribution values where the two dimensions are combined into one value.

Relative contribution values address these two issues. First, there is no need to coordinate an assessment with other designers, because relative contribution values only intend to differentiate the children of a parent goal, which are defined locally in the reusable artifact (e.g., *Password*, *Retinal Scan*, and *Fingerprint*). Therefore, the designer of *Reusable Artifact A* and *Reusable Artifact B* do not need to know about each other. Second, a relative contribution value does not specify which level of impact is sufficient to achieve the parent goal. A relative contribution only states that a child contributes x times more than another child of the same parent goal. The decision of whether a contribution is sufficient can again be postponed to the user of the reusable artifact, who knows best what is sufficient and what is not.

The existing GRL evaluation mechanism needs to be adapted to handle relative contribution values. As can be seen from the example in Fig. 2b, the actual number for a relative contribution does not matter, but rather the ratio of the relative contributions of a pair of children. Regardless of whether the relative contributions are stated as $2/1/-1$ or $4/2/-2$, the resulting satisfaction value of the parent goal should be the same, because the ratio of the relative contribution values has not changed (see *Reusable Artifact A*). The existing GRL evaluation mechanism, however, calculates two different satisfaction values (1.8 for the first set of relative contribution values and 3.6 for the second). Clearly, the satisfaction value needs to be normalized, as indicated by the larger values next to the *Privacy* goals in Fig. 2b (i.e., 70, 19, and 34), before allowing the satisfaction value to be propagated further. The normalized satisfaction value is calculated by determining the potential maximal and minimal contribution of all children (3 and -1 for *Respect Privacy* [A] and 13 and -1 for *Respect Privacy* [B]), and then mapping this range to the goal model range of [0, 100].

This normalization step also enables reusable goal models to be combined into goal model hierarchies as illustrated in Fig. 2b with the *Respect Privacy* [C] goal in *Application C*. Fundamentally, relative contributions lead to a different way of thinking about reusable goal models, based on two distinct spheres of knowledge. The first sphere of knowledge belongs to the designer of a reusable goal model, who focuses on understanding the impacts of the choices in the reusable goal model and ranking them relatively. The designer is the most qualified person for this ranking, as she is the domain expert for the reusable artifact (e.g., the designer can determine the relative privacy implications of the *Password*, *Retinal Scan*, and *Fingerprint* choices). Each designer of a reusable artifact has her own sphere of knowledge, which is limited to the reusable artifact. The user of a reusable artifact (i.e., the designer of *Application C*) has a different sphere of knowledge, which focuses on the application under development. The user is the most qualified person for this task, because she is the domain expert for the application (i.e., she can determine what the relative contributions are of the *Password/Retinal Scan/Fingerprint* choices versus the *Bodyguard/Disguise/High Fence* choices). The user knows best how these choices are employed in the application and therefore is in the best position to determine the relative contributions of *Respect Privacy* [A] and *Respect Privacy* [B] towards the application-specific *Respect Privacy* [C].

4   Relative Contributions in the Context of Reuse

As motivated in the previous section, reusable goal models must use relative contributions, and to specify them correctly the user of the reusable goal model relies on the fact that the possible maximal/minimal satisfaction values of goal model elements are all the same. To ensure that this is the case, the satisfaction value of each goal model element needs to be normalized. Consequently, each goal model element can be reused by the user. Normalization in GRL means that the possible maximal/minimal satisfaction value for each goal model element is always 100/0. To perform normalization, the actual minimal and maximal satisfaction values of a goal model element need to be determined (e.g., 3 and -1 for *Respect Privacy* [A] in Fig. 2b).

4.1   Reusable Goal Models Without Constraints

If there are no constraints among children of a parent goal model element, the minimal and maximal satisfaction values for a parent p are easily calculated. Let C_i stand for the relative contribution of child i towards the parent p, and S_i stand for the satisfaction value of child i. In that case, the actual maximal and minimal satisfaction values for parent p are:

$$Smax_p = \sum_{C_i > 0} \frac{C_i * S_i}{100} \quad Smin_p = \sum_{C_i < 0} \frac{C_i * S_i}{100}$$

For example, for *Parent A* in Fig. 3, the actual maximal satisfaction value is 7. It is reached when all children that contribute positively, i.e., *Solution 1, 2*, and *5*, are selected, i.e., their satisfaction values S1, S2, and S5 are 100. The minimum is −4, which occurs when all children that contribute negatively are selected (*Solution 3* and *4*). The maximum/minimum is 0 if there are no C_i that are greater/less than 0, because such a maximum/minimum of 0 is always given with all $S_i = 0$.

A scaling factor *SF* and an offset *OF* then ensure that 7 is mapped to 100 and −4 is mapped to 0 (the offset is applied first and then the scaling factor):

$$SF_p = \frac{100}{Smax_p - Smin_p} \quad OF_p = 0 - Smin_p$$

If the actual maximal and minimal satisfaction values for a parent are the same, this means that the selection of its children has no influence on the evaluation of the parent. In this case, $SF = 1$ and $OF = 100 - Smin_p$.

4.2 Reusable Goal Models with Constraints

If there are constraints among the goal model elements, the calculation needs to take them into account. For example, if there is an XOR constraint among all children (i.e., exactly one child's satisfaction value must be greater than 0 and all other ones 0), then the maximum for the parent is the maximal C_i (i.e., 4 for *Parent A*) and the minimum is the minimal C_i (i.e., -3). Because constraints may occur across any branches in the goal model (e.g., between the left and right branch of *Parent C*), the determination of the actual minimal and maximal satisfaction values becomes much more complex. It may be the case that a constraint does not allow both *Parent A* and *Parent B* to be maximized at the same time. As a result, when determining the maximum satisfaction value of *Parent C* it may be necessary to use the next lower maximal satisfaction value for *Parent A* or *Parent B*, until a combination is found that does not violate a constraint. In other words, some S_i in the maximum calculation may not be 100, but less. The same reasoning applies to the minimum calculation, where some S_i could be not 0, but more. The following paragraphs describe an algorithm that calculates the maximum (and by analogy also the minimum) and takes constraints into account.

In the worst case, 2^n combinations have to be examined to find the maximal satisfaction value without a violated constraint, where n stands for the number of nodes with user-defined satisfaction values (i.e., typically the leaf nodes in the reusable goal model). The proposed, novel evaluation algorithm avoids combinatorial explosion with a recursive, top-down approach that uses a lazy calculation of the next highest sum. This reduces the expected calculation time significantly, but the worst case still requires 2^n combinations to be examined. An example calculation for the maximal satisfaction value of *Parent C* is shown in Fig. 3, assuming a list with all possible satisfaction values sorted from highest to lowest for each child of *Parent C* (i.e., *Parent A*, *Solution 8*, and *Parent B*; see left side of Fig. 3). An entry in this list identifies the selection of *Parent C*'s grandchildren and the corresponding normalized satisfaction value for *Parent C*'s child. Each entry does not violate any constraints. In our example, there is only one constraint shown at the top right of Fig. 3 that indicates that *Solution 3* and *Solution 8* cannot be used together.

The algorithm gets the next highest combinations in step I, then calculates the potential maximal satisfaction value for each next highest combination (step II), and checks if any constraints are violated by the best combination (step III). If a constraint is violated, the algorithm goes back to step I. If no constraint is violated, the algorithm has found the maximal satisfaction value for the current parent. The algorithm proceeds by getting the minimal satisfaction value using an analogous approach except that the list of all possible satisfaction values is sorted from lowest to highest instead of from highest to lowest. Once both the maximum and the minimum are known, the algorithm calculates the scaling factor and the offset for the parent (step IV).

For example as illustrated in Fig. 3 for *Parent C*, the combination [1, 1, 1] is examined in step I of the first iteration (i.e., this indicates the combination

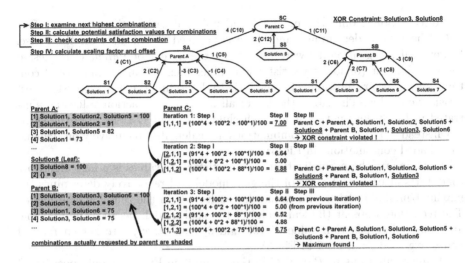

Fig. 3. Normalization of goal model elements (Maximal Satisfaction Value)

with the highest satisfaction value of each of *Parent C*'s children (*Parent A*, *Solution 8*, and *Parent B*, respectively)). The combination results in the potential maximum of 7 (step II of first iteration), but because of the XOR constraint between *Solution 3* and *Solution 8* this result is not valid (step III of first iteration).

Therefore, the next best combinations are examined in step I of the second iteration. These combinations are determined by going to the next best possible satisfaction value for each child in the invalid combination. Because each child's list is sorted from highest to lowest, the next best combinations can only be those where the index of each child is advanced individually by one. Since [1, 1, 1] is invalid according to the first iteration, the combinations [2, 1, 1], [1, 2, 1], and [1, 1, 2] must be examined next. This results in the potential maximums of 6.64, 5.00, and 6.88, respectively, i.e., the third combination [1, 1, 2] is the next best option (step II of second iteration). However, this combination still includes *Solution 3* and *Solution 8* and hence is again invalid (step III of second iteration).

In step I of the third iteration, the next best combinations are again examined (i.e., since [1, 1, 2] is invalid according to the second iteration, [2, 1, 2], [1, 2, 2], and [1, 1, 3] are the next combinations added to the already examined combinations). This results in the new potential maximums of 6.52, 4.88, and 6.75, respectively. Considering the remaining combinations from the second iteration (i.e., [2, 1, 1] with 6.64 and [1, 2, 1] with 5.00), the combination [1, 1, 3] with 6.75 is the next best option (step II of third iteration). This time, the combination is valid as no constraint is violated (step III of third iteration). Therefore, the maximal satisfaction value for *Parent C* is 6.75. Once the minimal satisfaction value has also been found, the scaling factor and the offset can be calculated (step IV).

At that point, only the maximal and minimal satisfaction values of *Parent C* have been determined and there is no need to calculate anything else. However, if the goal model were bigger and the parent of *Parent C* requested the next highest (or lowest) satisfaction value, then the algorithm would continue with further iterations of steps I–III to determine the next highest/lowest satisfaction value. Therefore, the list of all possible satisfaction values as illustrated in Fig. 3 does not exist for each child of *Parent C* right from the start, but instead only the needed combinations are calculated recursively on demand (see shaded combinations in Fig. 3).

In summary, the normalization of the satisfaction values is a lazy algorithm that starts at each root node of the goal model and recursively determines the maximal/minimal satisfaction values for each node in the reusable goal model. The recursion stops at the leaf nodes of the goal model, because the maximal and minimal satisfaction value of 100 and 0, respectively, are known for leaf nodes (e.g., see *Solution 8* in Fig. 3).

The contributions to *Parent C* in the example in Fig. 3 are only positive. If there were a negative contribution, then the algorithm would ask the corresponding child for its minimal value instead of its maximal value when calculating the maximal value for the parent (and vice versa for the minimal value of the parent). Furthermore, for space reasons, only contribution links are discussed here. However, the algorithm works also with decomposition and dependency links without significantly increasing its complexity.

4.3   Reusable Goal Models Combined with Feature Models

While some constraints such as XOR can be modeled with goal models, more sophisticated constraints are typically defined in dedicated models that are used in conjunction with goal models, e.g., feature models. In this context, a *feature model* [14] captures the variations, i.e., features, of a reusable artifact, identifying *features* (□) common to all reuses of the artifact and those that vary from one reuse to the next. Feature models capture *mandatory* parent-child relationships (—•), *optional* parent-child relationships (—○), *alternative (XOR) feature groups*, *OR (IOR) feature groups*, as well as *includes* and *excludes integrity constraints*.

If a feature model is used to define these additional constraints, then step III involves the evaluation of a feature model to determine whether a constraint is violated. This is typically done by converting the feature model and the selected features into a propositional formula, which is then given to a SAT solver, e.g., as provided by the feature modeling tool FAMILIAR [1,12]. A straightforward integration of goal and feature models therefore involves simply replacing the constraint check described in Sect. 4.2 with a check performed by a SAT solver. The constraint check is the only part of the algorithm that needs to be tailored to whatever model is chosen to capture the constraints. The rest of the algorithm, however, stays the same and *constitutes an essential part of reusable goal models*.

The remainder of this section describes an improvement to the above algorithm for performance reasons, because calling the SAT solver is an expensive operation. The SAT solver is best used for cross-tree constraints (i.e., includes/excludes), because many levels of indirections potentially have to be considered, which is difficult to do without converting the feature model into a logic formula. OR and XOR constraints, however, are much easier to handle, because violations can be determined by simply looking at the feature tree, hence reducing the number of evaluations done by the SAT solver. As it turns out, the same lazy, recursive algorithm used for calculating the minimal/maximal satisfaction values in the goal model can also be used to reduce calls to the SAT solver.

When goal and feature models are used in conjunction, the tasks in the goal model are also features in the feature model [18]. In this case, the recursion in the goal model stops at a parent of tasks and hands the tasks over to the recursive algorithm for the feature model to determine their candidate contribution to the maximal/minimal satisfaction of the parent (e.g., in Fig. 3, the children of *Parent A*, i.e., *Solution 1* to *Solution 5*). Note that mandatory features do not need to be included in the goal model, because their contributions are always the same regardless of the selected features.

Since the example in Fig. 3 showed the calculation of a maximal satisfaction value, the following feature model example in Fig. 4 shows the calculation of a minimal contribution of features to their parent.

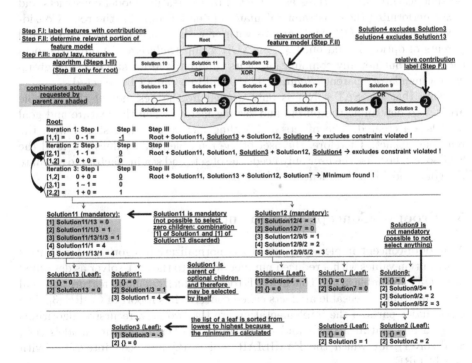

Fig. 4. Contributions in feature model (Minimal Contribution of Parent A's Children)

For each parent, the algorithm starts with labeling the features with their contributions to their goal model parent (step F.I; e.g., the contributions shown for *Parent A* in Fig. 3 are added as labels in Fig. 4). From then on only a portion of the feature model needs to be considered, i.e., the union of the paths from the labeled features to the root feature including any siblings in OR/XOR groups encountered on a path (step F.II), because these paths capture all relevant OR/XOR constraints. The siblings are included, because the selection of a sibling influences the minimal/maximal contribution to the parent in the goal model (e.g., *Solution 13* with contribution 0 may be selected instead of *Solution 1* with contribution 4). The last step F.III uses the same lazy, recursive approach as for reusable goal models (i.e., steps I to III).

Steps I to III are exactly the same, except that the calculation of the potential satisfaction value is now a simplified calculation of the potential contribution value. Because a feature is either selected or not (i.e., S_i is either 100 or 0, respectively [18]), the sum of $C_i * S_i$ divided by 100 reduces itself to the sum of C_i. Even though the labels appear at different levels in the feature model, they can still be added up directly, because they all represent contributions at the same level in the goal model (e.g., option [2] of *Solution 1* adds up 4 and -3 of *Solution 1* and *3*, respectively).

The reduction in calls to the SAT solver is achieved by considering only the possible feature combinations as restricted by the feature model constructs and hence performing the constraint calculation (step III) only for the root. Considered constructs are OR/XOR groups with or without a mandatory parent and parents of optional children. E.g., an XOR group (*Solution 12*) only considers each child, but not any combination of its children, and for an OR/XOR group with a mandatory parent (*Solution 11*), 0 children cannot be selected.

Note that the SAT solver is only needed by the designer of the reusable artifact to determine the offsets and scaling factors when the feature and goal models are created. The offsets and scaling factors are then stored with the reusable artifact. Therefore, the user of the reusable artifact does not need the SAT solver, because the user only needs the offsets and scaling factors to evaluate the goal model based on feature selections.

5   Proof-of-Concept Implementation

A proof-of-concept implementation of the normalization algorithm for relative contribution values with a reduced number of calls to the SAT solver as described in Sect. 4 is available in the TouchCORE tool [2], which combines feature and goal modeling to build reusable artifacts called concerns in support of CORE [3]. The three major parts of the implementation are the two lazy, recursive algorithms for goal and feature models and a constraint checker for feature models (i.e., SAT solver), for which the FAMILIAR tool [1,12] has been integrated with TouchCORE.

To evaluate the performance, we select feature and goal models with a complexity that is comparable to those in reusable concerns we have previously specified such as Authentication, Transaction, and Workflow Engine: 50 features; a goal model with one root goal, a maximum depth of 3, and a total of 6 subgoals. Half of the features were evenly selected from the feature model, and then randomly assigned with a 15 % chance to contribute to each leaf goal with a random relative contribution between 1 and 10, leading to a total of 18 goal model elements. One root goal was chosen because each root goal is evaluated individually. Five different feature models are evaluated (A/C/E/G/I): one where all links are optional links, one with all XOR links, and three with random link types. Five additional feature models (B/D/F/H/J) are derived by adding five random includes/excludes constraints to A/C/E/G/I. We chose to add 5 constraints because this is the maximum we ever encountered in a feature model while building reusable concerns. For the selected feature and goal models, the algorithm without the described improvement takes several minutes or longer to complete.

Table 1 reports the results of the performance evaluation with execution time now in the millisecond range. The results indicate that the algorithm execution time is acceptable for the chosen size of feature and goal models, and hence for realistic models of reusable concerns (note that the reported time is the average of the last 100 out of 110 runs to discount for program startup time). The columns detailing the combinations for the goal and feature model show the combinations requested by a parent as well as all combinations that had to be calculated to determine the requested combinations. The combinations are significantly less than the 2^n possible combinations, giving an indication of the effectiveness of the recursive, lazy normalization algorithm. The figures for

Table 1. Performance Results

	Measurements					
	Execution time (ms)	Calls to SAT solver	Requested combinations		Calculated combinations	
			Goal	Feature	Goal	Feature
A	17.6	14	14	82	14	82
B	40.8	49	49	168	77	207
C	15.6	14	26	146	37	160
D	18.3	15	32	131	43	140
E	15.4	14	14	82	14	82
F	80.6	22	47	160	69	189
G/H	20.5	14	547	185	641	185
I/J	22.4	14	232	163	289	155

A...only optional links in feature model; B...A plus includes/excludes constraints; C/E/G...randomly assigned links in feature model; D/F/H...C/E/G plus includes/excludes constraints;
I...only XOR links in feature model; J...I plus includes/excludes constraints;

the requested/calculated combinations in feature models and the actual calls to the SAT solver give an indication of the reduction in calls to the SAT solver thanks to the recursive, lazy algorithm for feature model. The results for models G/H and I/J are the same because the added constraints are between different XOR features and hence have no effect on execution time and combinations.

6   Related Work

To the best of our knowledge, reusable goal models with a propagation-based evaluation mechanism [5] have received very little attention in the requirements engineering community, mostly based on the notion of a goal catalogue [10]. Goal catalogues, however, are intended to be imported as a monolithic entity into the application goal model, thus advocate a centralized approach with global contribution values and little support for reuse hierarchies, and hence exhibit the disadvantages discussed in Sect. 3. Quality-Based Software Reuse [16] is another approach that is based on goal-oriented modeling, in this case combined with aspect orientation, and explicitly addresses the need to apply reusable artifacts in new contexts. However, this approach suffers from similar problems, as reuse hierarchies are not taken into account. A pattern-based approach in combination with contextual goal modeling [17] has also been suggested, but addresses only qualitative values in goal models.

Often, goal models, quality impact models, or other models of stakeholders are used in addition to feature models in a reuse context, but these approaches primarily focus on the analysis of intentional models to inform the selection of reusable features (e.g., [6,11,22]) and not on how to reuse goal models in a different context. Feature models can also be augmented with feature attributes, which are often used to capture qualities and non-functional requirements [7]. However, contrary to goal models, complex relationships among such attributes are in this case not that easy to express. Concern-Oriented Reuse (CORE) [3] is another reuse paradigm that combines feature and goal modeling. CORE intends - contrary to other approaches - to reuse generic goal models in hierarchies, but a specific technique for composing reusable goal models such as the one proposed in this paper has not yet been defined.

7   Conclusions and Future Work

This paper investigates which kind of values may be used in *reusable goal models* that are evaluated with a propagation-based algorithm. We argue that real-life measurements should be used, and if not available, quantitative values with relative contributions must be used instead.

A reusable goal model with relative contribution values must guarantee to the user of the reusable goal model that the possible maximal/minimal satisfaction values of all goal model elements are the same, i.e., they must be normalized. An improved, propagation-based evaluation algorithm is presented that (i) performs such normalization to the [0,100] range, (ii) is capable of taking constraints on goal model elements into account expressed with goal models or feature models, and (iii) avoids combinatorial explosion with a recursive, top-down approach that uses a lazy calculation of the next best combination. This reduces the expected calculation time significantly, but the worst case still requires 2^n combinations to be examined. The feasibility of the proposed algorithm is shown with performance results of a proof-of-concept implementation using TouchCORE and FAMILIAR.

In future work, we plan to extend the presented algorithm to support constraints on tasks specified by other models (e.g., workflow models) and apply the algorithm to runtime adaptation of an application based on the re-evaluation of goal models.

Acknowledgement. Supported by NSERC Canada Discovery Grants.

References

1. Acher, M., et al.: FAMILIAR: a domain-specific language for large scale management of feature models. Sci. Comput. Program. (SCP) **78**(6), 657–681 (2013). http://dx.doi.org/10.1016/j.scico.2012.12.004
2. Al Abed, W., Bonnet, V., Schöttle, M., Yildirim, E., Alam, O., Kienzle, J.: TouchRAM: a multitouch-enabled tool for aspect-oriented software design. In: Czarnecki, K., Hedin, G. (eds.) SLE 2012. LNCS, vol. 7745, pp. 275–285. Springer, Heidelberg (2013). http://dx.doi.org/10.1007/978-3-642-36089-3_16
3. Alam, O., Kienzle, J., Mussbacher, G.: Concern-oriented software design. In: Moreira, A., Schätz, B., Gray, J., Vallecillo, A., Clarke, P. (eds.) MODELS 2013. LNCS, vol. 8107, pp. 604–621. Springer, Heidelberg (2013). http://dx.doi.org/10.1007/978-3-642-41533-3_37
4. Amyot, D., Mussbacher, G.: User Requirements Notation: the first ten years, the next ten years. J. Softw. (JSW) **6**(5), 747–768 (2011). http://dx.doi.org/10.4304/jsw.6.5.747-768
5. Amyot, D., et al.: Evaluating goal models within the Goal-oriented Requirement Language. Int. J. Intell. Syst. (IJIS) **25**(8), 841–877 (2010). Wiley. http://dx.doi.org/10.1002/int.20433
6. Bagheri, E., Di Noia, T., Ragone, A., Gasevic, D.: Configuring software product line feature models based on stakeholders' soft and hard requirements. In: Bosch, J., Lee, J. (eds.) SPLC 2010. LNCS, vol. 6287, pp. 16–31. Springer, Heidelberg (2010). http://dx.doi.org/10.1007/978-3-642-15579-6_2
7. Benavides, D., Segura, S., Ruiz-Cortés, A.: Automated analysis of feature models 20 years later: a literature review. Inf. Syst. **35**(6), 615–636 (2010). Elsevier. http://dx.doi.org/10.1016/j.is.2010.01.001
8. Braun, C.L.: Nato standard for the development of reusable software components, vol. 1/3 (1994)
9. Chung, L., et al.: Non-functional Requirements in Software Engineering. Kluwer Academic Publishers, Boston (2000)
10. Cysneiros, L.M., Werneck, V.M., Kushniruk, A.: Reusable knowledge for satisficing usability requirements. In: 13th IEEE International Requirements Engineering Conference (RE 2005), pp. 463–464. IEEE CS (2005). http://dx.doi.org/10.1109/RE.2005.60

11. DiVA Project Website - DiVA Reasoning Framework. https://sites.google.com/site/divawebsite/divastudio/diva-reasoning-framework
12. FAMILIAR project website. http://familiar-project.github.io/
13. International Telecommunication Union: Recommendation Z.151 (10/12), User Requirements Notation (URN) - Language definition (2012). http://www.itu.int/rec/T-REC-Z.151/en
14. Kang, K., et al.: Feature-oriented domain analysis (FODA) feasibility study. Technical Report CMU/SEI-90-TR-21, Software Engineering Institute, Carnegie Mellon University (1990)
15. Krueger, C.W.: Software reuse. ACM Comput. Surv. **24**(2), 131–183 (1992). ACM. http://dx.doi.org/10.1145/130844.130856
16. Leite, J.C.S.P., Yu, Y., Liu, L., Yu, E.S.K., Mylopoulos, J.: Quality-based software reuse. In: Pastor, Ó., Falcão e Cunha, J. (eds.) CAiSE 2005. LNCS, vol. 3520, pp. 535–550. Springer, Heidelberg (2005). http://dx.doi.org/10.1007/11431855_37
17. Li, T., Horkoff, J., Mylopoulos, J.: Integrating security patterns with security requirements analysis using contextual goal models. In: Frank, U., Loucopoulos, P., Pastor, Ó., Petrounias, I. (eds.) PoEM 2014. LNBIP, vol. 197, pp. 208–223. Springer, Heidelberg (2014). http://dx.doi.org/10.1007/978-3-662-45501-2_15
18. Liu, Y., et al.: Combined propagation-based reasoning with goal and feature models. In: 4th International Model-Driven Requirements Engineering Workshop (MoDRE 2014), pp. 27–36. IEEE CS (2014). http://dx.doi.org/10.1109/MoDRE.2014.6890823
19. Mussbacher, G., Kienzle, J.: A vision for generic concern-oriented requirements reuse[RE@21]. In: 21st IEEE International Requirements Engineering Conference (RE 2013), pp. 238–249. IEEE CS (2013). http://dx.doi.org/10.1109/RE.2013.6636724
20. Mussbacher, G., et al.: AoURN-based modeling and analysis of software product lines. Softw. Qual. J. (SQJ) **20**(3–4), 645–687 (2011). Springer. http://dx.doi.org/10.1007/s11219-011-9153-8
21. Pourshahid, A., Richards, G., Amyot, D.: Toward a goal-oriented, business intelligence decision-making framework. In: Babin, G., Stanoevska-Slabeva, K., Kropf, P. (eds.) MCETECH 2011. LNBIP, vol. 78, pp. 100–115. Springer, Heidelberg (2011). http://dx.doi.org/10.1007/978-3-642-20862-1_7
22. Than Tun, T., et al.: Relating requirements and feature configurations: a systematic approach. In: SPLC 2009, pp. 201–210. Carnegie Mellon University (2009)
23. van Lamsweerde, A.: Requirements Engineering: From System Goals to UML Models to Software Specifications. Wiley, Chichester (2009)
24. Yu, E.: Modeling strategic relationships for process reengineering. Ph.D. thesis, University of Toronto, Canada (1995)

Adding a Textual Syntax to an Existing Graphical Modeling Language: Experience Report with GRL

Vahdat Abdelzad, Daniel Amyot[✉], and Timothy C. Lethbridge

School of Electrical Engineering and Computer Science,
University of Ottawa, Ottawa, Canada
{v.abdelzad,damyot,Timothy.Lethbridge}@uottawa.ca

Abstract. A modelling language usually has an abstract syntax (e.g., expressed with a metamodel) separate from its concrete syntax. The question explored in this paper is: how easy is it to add a textual concrete syntax to an existing language that offers only a concrete graphical syntax? To answer this question, this paper reports on lessons learned during the creation of a textual syntax (supported by an editor and transformation tool) for the Goal-oriented Requirement Language (GRL), which is part of the User Requirements Notation standard. Our experiment shows that although current technologies help create textual modelling languages efficiently with feature-rich editors, there are important conflicts between the reuse of existing metamodels and the usability of the resulting textual syntax that require attention.

Keywords: Goal-oriented Requirement Language · Graphical modeling language · jUCMNav · Metamodel · Textual syntax · Xtext

1 Introduction

A model is an abstraction of the reality that helps engineers and other users focus on specific aspects of a problem or a system in order to support communication, understanding, analysis, and decision making. Modeling languages often have a graphical and/or a textual representation, called *concrete syntax*. The concepts of a modeling language are often captured with an *abstract syntax*, for example in the form of a grammar or a metamodel [14]. Concrete syntaxes bring understandability, usability, and often visualization to the concepts defined at the abstract level.

Graphical and textual syntaxes both have strengths and limitations [25]. With diagrams, it is often easier to understand non-linear relationships (such as graphs) and appreciate analysis results than with text. On the other hand, textual models are often easier to create and manipulate (e.g., through intelligent editors or simpler copy-pasting). It is also challenging to find appropriate symbols and metaphors in a graphical language in order to assure a suitable cognitive fit for all users. The cognitive effectiveness of notations has been explored

© Springer International Publishing Switzerland 2015
J. Fischer et al. (Eds.): SDL 2015, LNCS 9369, pp. 159–174, 2015.
DOI: 10.1007/978-3-319-24912-4_12

substantially in the past few years, based on frameworks such as Physics of Notations [21], and illustrated on different graphical languages such as for goal modeling [21] and scenario/process modeling [11].

Ideally, modelers should be given the choice of using among the concrete syntaxes that best suit the tasks they have to perform, for example, a textual syntax to create a model and a graphical syntax to communicate the model and visualize analysis results. Several standardized languages already support textual and graphical syntaxes (e.g., [13,15,17]), but often they have been designed to support both from the beginning. In this paper, we are more interested in exploring the challenges related to the *addition* of a textual concrete syntax to an existing language for which only a concrete graphical syntax already exists. This exploration is done through the design of an actual editor-supported textual syntax for the Goal-oriented Requirement Language (GRL), a requirements-level goal modeling language standardized as part of the User Requirements Notation (URN) [3,16]. One challenge here is that the abstract syntax of URN is based on a metamodel oriented towards the graphical representation of its concepts, without consideration for a potential concrete textual syntax.

Section 2 presents work related to modeling language design, together with background on GRL and existing tool support (jUCMNav [4,28]). Section 3 introduces some of the main challenges we have observed when adding a textual syntax to an existing metamodel-based graphical language, together with elements of solutions. Section 4 presents our case study, where we created a grammar for a *Textual GRL* (TGRL), together with an Eclipse-based rich editor and a transformation mechanism that converts TGRL models to URN models readable by jUCMNav. Not all modeling languages are based on metamodels and not all language editors are using Eclipse, but our experience report does involve metamodels and Eclipse technologies. A short discussion of lessons learned is presented in Sect. 5, followed by conclusions and future work in Sect. 6.

2   Background

This section reviews closely-related work on modeling language design and highlights the background concepts on GRL and jUCMNav required to understand the examples of challenges and solutions discussed later in the paper.

2.1   Related Work on Textual and Graphical Languages

Several languages already support textual and graphical syntaxes. Among the languages standardized by the *International Telecommunication Union - Telecommunication Standardization Sector* (ITU-T), common examples include the Specification and Description Language (SDL) [13], Message Sequence Charts (MSC) [15], and the Testing and Test Control Notation (TTCN-3) [17]. All are supported by many tools, some of which allowing modelers to use both syntaxes interchangeably and transparently. TTCN-3 even offers an additional *tabular* concrete syntax [18]. While SDL uses an abstract grammar as abstract syntax, TTCN-3 is based on a metamodel. However, these languages have developed their concrete textual syntax, concrete graphical syntax, and abstract syntax more or less at the same time. With URN and GRL, there are already a metamodel and a graphical syntax that have been in place for many years, so adding a textual syntax is more problematic in that context.

In the Unified Modeling Language (UML) world, several textual syntaxes have been proposed for subsets of UML, often as a means to create models and then visualize them. Cabot as collected a list of such languages and tools [6]. We are not really interested in these technologies as they do not allow modelers to create instances of the UML metamodel, which would have enabled analysis and transformations based on standard UML. These tools have their own internal representations.

In a different and more recent approach, we find *Umple*, a textual language that integrates concepts from UML class/state diagrams and patterns with programming languages such as Java [8]. Umple models are written using human-readable text seamlessly integrated with code. Umple models can also be visualized with the UML notation. This *model-is-the-code* approach helps developers maintain and evolve code as the system matures simply by the fact that both model and code are integrated as aspects of the same system [10]. Still, Umple uses its own metamodel, not UML's.

2.2   Related Work on Enabling Technologies

The *Object Management Group* (OMG) has proposed the *UML Human-Usable Textual Notation* (HUTN), a technology for automatically supporting user-readable concrete syntaxes of models and model instances based on the *MetaObject Facility* (MOF) [23]. One interesting feature of HUTN is that the textual syntax does not need to reflect exactly the structure of the metamodel. Parameters can be used to create *short-hands* and make the syntax more readable and usable. For example [23], one can set:

- The use of a class attribute as the class unique identifier for a given scope;
- The representation of a Boolean or enumerated attribute as a keyword;
- The use of default values for mandatory attributes (making them optional);
- The selection of an alternate name for any model element;
- Alternative representations for associations.

Unfortunately, HUTN is supported only a few tools, including the one proposed by Rose et al. [27], which is part of the Eclipse Epsilon project. HUTN was shown to be complicated to use, and resulting editors have limited capabilities.

Eclipse's *Xtext* [32] is one of the enabling technologies used to produce feature-rich editors for a textual language. Xtext usually takes a language grammar as input and the corresponding metamodel is automatically built in the background. It also allows reusing already-existing metamodels, but then there is no flexibility in the design of the language syntax. In other words, importing metamodels constrains the design of language. Changing the grammar changes the underlying metamodel, which might create some issues with transformations that use such metamodel as a source. In that context, Schmidt et al. [30] proposed a category of refactorings for Xtext that use asymmetric bidirectional model transformations to synchronize the various artifacts of language descriptions, including transformations (based on Xtend [31]).

Other technologies for textual syntax development include EMFText from Heidenreich et al. [12], which generates automatically default syntax from *Eclipse Modeling Framework* (EMF) models, with some possibilities for syntax tailoring before the generation of text editors. Jouault et al. [19] also proposed *Textual Concrete Syntax* (TCS), a generative solution that transforms grammars into editors and tools for model-to-text and text-to-model transformations. Both EMFText and TCS are however far less popular and mature than Xtext, and their development seems to have stopped several years ago.

Finally, as graphical syntaxes often include textual syntaxes for various kinds of expressions, Scheidgen presented techniques to *embed* textual editors into graphical model editors and provided a proof of concept involving Eclipse-based technologies [29]. However, we are more interested here in generating a new textual syntax than in embedding one in a graphical syntax.

2.3   Goal-Oriented Requirement Language (GRL)

The URN standard is composed of two complementary sub-languages: (i) GRL for modeling the intentions of actors and systems, together with their various relationships, and (ii) Use Case Maps (UCM) for modeling causal scenarios and processes superimposed on a structure of components [16]. GRL core concepts include *actors*, *intentional elements* (e.g., goals, softgoals, tasks, resources and beliefs), *links* (decompositions, dependencies, weighted contributions) and *indicators* (Fig. 1). GRL model elements are URN model elements. As such, they can have *metadata* (name-value pairs) and typed *URN links* connecting pair of elements; these concepts are useful to extend and tailor URN to specific domains, in a standard way [3].

Many of the concepts of GRL have a visual representation. In URN, the graphical language metamodel is a pure superset of the abstract syntax metamodel. For example in Fig. 2, an actor reference (ActorRef) is the visual representation of an actor in a GRL graph and hence possesses attributes such as a size, a label, and a position. The actor itself has color-related attributes, which are shared by all its references.

GRL model analysis, whether qualitative (using contribution, satisfaction, and importance values from their respective enumerated types in Fig. 1) or quantitative (using integer values in specific ranges), is done through *strategies*. A strategy provides initial satisfaction values to some of the intentional elements in the GRL model, and an evaluation algorithm propagates this information (through the GRL links) to the other intentional elements and to the actors in order to compute their resulting satisfaction values [3,16]. As it is often difficult to agree on the weights of contribution links in GRL models, the standard also includes *contribution changes* as a mechanism to specify and group (in collection

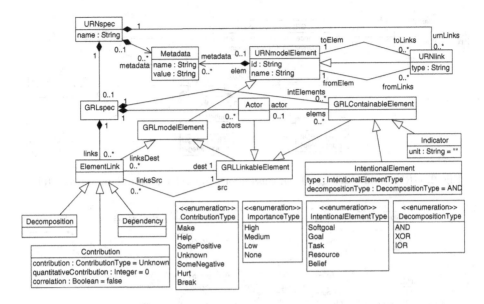

Fig. 1. GRL metamodel: core GRL concepts (adapted from [16])

contexts) a local modification to the weight of a contribution link, which can be applied to a base model before evaluating its strategies. What is important to observe here is that strategies (not shown here) and contribution changes (Fig. 3) do not currently have any concrete syntax, and hence these parts of a model need to be specified through a tool's user interface and tree-structured views, as is currently done in jUCMNav [4].

The absence of a complete graphical syntax and of a textual syntax has already been observed as a "sin" in the design of the GRL language [22]. In addition, the graphical syntax has similar cognitive efficiency weaknesses as those observed for the i^* goal modeling language [21], as GRL's syntax is based in part on the one from i^*.

2.4   jUCMNav Tool

jUCMNav is an open-source Eclipse plugin for URN modeling, analysis, reporting and transformation, developed since 2004. The GRL modeling and analysis part was first provided by Roy et al. [28], and has substantially evolved since then to support new features and newer concepts now found in the standard [16].

Given that jUCMNav was initiated before the first version of URN was standardized in 2008, and given that jUCMNav is also used as a platform for exploring new language concepts that could be integrated into URN in the future (like contribution changes were integrated in the 2012 edition of URN [16]), there are many differences between jUCMNav's metamodel and URN's (see http://bit.ly/1GCbhNa for details). For example, jUCMNav's metamodel uses interface classes (for reusability across its UCM and GRL editors) and packages, there are

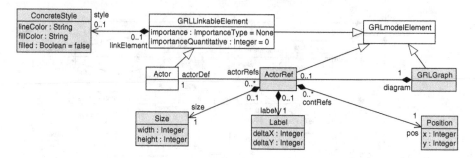

Fig. 2. GRL metamodel: graphical classes for actor references (adapted from [16])

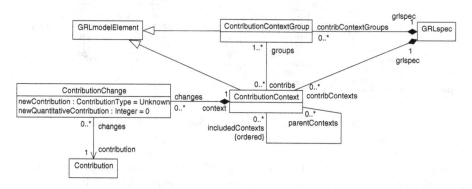

Fig. 3. GRL metamodel: contribution changes, with no graphical syntax [16]

minor mismatches in how indicators and strategies are supported, and there are additional classes to support aspect-oriented modeling. jUCMNav however can import and export models in the Z.151 XML-based interchange format.

3   Challenges Faced When Adding a Textual Syntax

Adding a concrete textual syntax to a metamodel-based language with an existing concrete graphical syntax involves steps in which there are technical and non-technical challenges. The designer of the textual syntax has to define related keywords, build a consistent structure associated with the definitions and assignments, keep the metamodel of the textual language (if any) compatible with the abstract syntax (language metamodel), select the proper technology to implement the textual language, implement a mechanism to apply specific restrictions and rules, and finally develop a mechanism to synchronize the textual and graphical syntax representations.

3.1   Choice of Keywords

Keywords of a textual language have an important role in the usability and adoption of the language. They must be chosen from the domain vocabulary and be close to the language abstract syntax (assuming that the abstract syntax constructs have meaningful names). If the textual keywords are also aligned with the graphical syntax symbols and keywords, then this will also help the adoption of the textual language by already-existing users while also decreasing the learning curve. Balancing this closeness is not an easy task and usually results in tradeoffs. The users of graphical languages work with graphical notations and often names are hidden implicitly in the shape of notations. These hidden names sometimes cannot be expressed by a single word, supposed to be considered as a keyword in the textual syntax. Using the exact graphical or abstract names may potentially result in a bulky language.

During the design of TGRL, we have faced that challenge and we decided to consider three important criteria while defining keywords: (1) be consistent with the abstract syntax in terms of the semantics; (2) favor usability over rigid following of the metamodel; and (3) avoid defining keywords when possible. For example, we defined the keyword decomposedBy for the element link decomposition and did not use a specific keyword for defining evaluation elements for strategies. Note that when discussing usability in a textual modeling language, we do not try to compare it with that of a graphical modeling language (these are separate problems).

In terms of process, we first defined keywords similar to concept names from the abstract syntax. This helped us have a blueprint of the textual language and revealed some challenges, e.g., conflicting keywords or a high number of keywords. We then changed some keywords in order to solve conflicts, modified them to be more human readable, and finally simplified the language by removing unnecessary keywords.

3.2 Structure Consistency

Each defined keyword would have some structure and properties that need to be set during the development of models. The values assigned to properties and their structure should be kept similar, because this promotes language learnability. For this purpose, they are several patterns that can be adapted from either programming or modeling languages. For our language, we adopted a structure inspired from Umple [8,10]. For example, if there are several properties needed to be set, we use the name of the property along with its value. However, if there is only one property, we just assign the value without requiring the property name.

3.3 Alignment of Metamodels

When keywords and structures are defined, the grammar must be implemented. There are two general ways to do this. The first one is to use the already-existing language metamodel and cover it with the definition of the textual language. This approach makes the implementation process straightforward, but there might be situation where the grammar and the metamodel, which becomes a constraint, cannot be aligned properly without greatly affecting usability. The second approach is to let the textual language build its own metamodel, à la Xtext. This approach allows getting the maximum benefits of having a simple and human-readable textual syntax, but it might result in an underlying metamodel that will require the creation of major internal model transformations from instances of the textual metamodel to instance of the abstract syntax metamodel.

We have experienced both approaches and recognized that the first approach results in a textual syntax that is too synthetic, especially if the language abstract syntax was never designed with a potential concrete textual syntax in mind (which is the case for GRL's). Furthermore, the second approach allows having several alternatives for a definition while it is not the case in the first approach. For example, we could design two alternatives ways of defining element links. The first alternative has an independent structure and needs both the link source and the link destination to be specified while the second alternative depends on the location in the source and just needs the destination to be specified. In our case study (next section), we have chosen to adopt the second approach.

3.4   Technology Selection

In order to implement one of the approaches discussed in the previous section, a suitable technology must be selected. As discussed in Sect. 2.2, there are several technologies such as Xtext, EMFText, and TCS that can be used for these purposes. The choice will be largely influenced by how potentially usable a textual syntax (automatically) generated from the abstract syntax can be, by the intended usage of the textual language, and by the required quality of resulting editor tooling.

In our study of TGRL, we have selected Xtext because it is an active project and provides a rich editor for the language. Working with Xtext is simple and fast, but everything has to be based on the Xtext grammar. This prevents developers from improving or "tweaking" the structure of the final metamodel.

Hence, this choice came at the cost of having to transforms Xtext-based models (from TGRL) to the target abstract syntax (in our case, URN's metamodel). In such a context, such transformation can be done with model-to-model transformations (e.g., with Java or specialized languages such as Eclipse's ATL Transformation Language [5]) or with model-to-text transformations targeting serialized models (e.g., again with Java or with enhanced technologies such as Xtend [31] or Acceleo [2]). As we had good experiences using Acceleo in the past, we opted for this path.

3.5   Handling Restrictions and Rules

The implemented syntax comes with restrictions and rules that need to be checked and applied continuously. These rules and restrictions come from two main sources: the abstract syntax (and its static semantics constraints) and the concrete syntax itself. For example, the identifier (ID) could have to follow a specific pattern, or cyclical definitions may need to be prevented. The rules from the abstract syntax are usually clear and already defined, but the ones from the concrete syntax must be specified. Such rules may be used to improve the readability of the concrete syntax (especially if alternative representations are supported) or keep the syntaxes compatible. Part of this validation can be supported automatically by the technology used to implement the language (e.g., Xtext). However, the rest must be implemented manually. For example, checking the validity of a reference is supported by the editor provided by Xtext while checking for duplicates of a link must be implemented manually.

3.6   Synchronizing Textual and Graphical Models

Keeping connections between the textual syntax and the graphical syntax is important in order to fully benefit from the iterative use of both syntaxes by modelers. Generally, there are two ways to do this: *synchronously* and *asynchronously*. In the synchronous case, the transformation is done automatically and both syntaxes are refreshed continuously so as to show a consistent representation (in a way to the model-view-controller pattern). This is the most desirable case but its feasibility depends on the technology employed to develop the concrete syntaxes. If the technology used in either the textual or the graphical syntaxes does not support external synchronization, then this option might be impossible. In the asynchronous case, users work on a concrete syntax and when one needs to have the other representation, the transformation is done explicitly, on demand. This approach is a solution to the cases where the synchronous approach in unfeasible or when synchronization is too costly in terms of speed or memory usage.

In our case study, we used asynchronous transformations because of issues regarding the synchronization with the technology used for graphical syntax (e.g., jUCMNav). So far, we investigated only one transformation (from TGRL to URN), the reverse one being left for future work. As explained in Sect. 3.4, the current transformation is performed through a model-to-text approach implemented with Acceleo, which is a pragmatic implementation of OMG's *MOF Model to Text Language* (MTL) standard. jUCMNav can read the files generated in that way, and its auto-layout mechanism can be used to visualize the models.

4   Case Study: TGRL

4.1   TGRL Concrete Syntax

In this section, we describe a case study involving the design of a concrete textual syntax for GRL (called TGRL) with tool support (editor and automated transformation). Any concrete syntax has general rules that are applied for all keywords and their related structures. In our concrete textual syntax, the general rules are as follows:

- GRL elements are usually defined through keywords using camelCase boundaries (e.g., a softgoal intentional element is represented by a softGoal).
- Model element properties and sub-elements are set inside curly brackets.

- Every definition ends with a semicolon except when a pair of curly brackets is utilized to include properties or sub-elements.
- String values are surrounded by quotation marks.
- Comments are delimited by //.

TGRL model elements have a textual identifier (ID) as well as optional metadata (name-value pairs). Intentional elements (goals, softgoals, tasks and resources) also have qualitative/quantitative importance values (to their containing actor). For example, Fig. 4 shows the TGRL representation of a simple GRL model with three actors, their intentional elements, and various links. This is a common GRL pattern where alternative ways of achieving some system functionality have different impacts on the concerns of stakeholders (such as users and developers). IDs are used as names unless specified otherwise. Qualitative values and quantitative values (between −100 and 100) can be used interchangeably. Lists can be used for definitions and usages (e.g., see the decomposedBy relationship in the example).

As in Umple [8,10], links can be specified inside one element or outside the relevant elements, depending on the modeler's preference. In Fig. 4, one contribution is defined inside the System actor, one is defined in the User actor and targets an element of another actor, and two other contributions are defined outside all actors.

Note that scoping is also used to resolve potential naming issues. For example, in the contribution link inside the System actor, task FirstOption is local but softgoal ReuseComponents is defined elsewhere, and hence must be prefixed by its containing actor (Developer). GRL dependency links are handled in a similar way.

TGRL also supports contribution changes (for which there is no graphical syntax in standard URN, see Fig. 3) and handles advanced constructs such as contribution inclusion and value ranges. For example, Fig. 4 contains a group (SomeOverrides) of two sets of contribution changes that make reference to two contribution links named C1 and C2. The first set (FirstOverride) changes C1 and C2 with new quantitative and qualitative values, respectively. A tool such as jUCMNav will substitute the targeted contributions weights with the new values specified in this contribution set before analyzing any strategy. The second set (SecondOverride) extends the first one (and hence inherits the make value for C2), but now C1 is defined as a range of values that go from −40 to 0 by steps of 10 (i.e., {−40, −30, −20, −10, 0}). In jUCMNav, when such a range is specified, the selected strategy is evaluated iteratively for all the contribution values in that range, leading to sets of resulting evaluations for all intentional elements and actors in the model (which is useful for sensitivity analysis). In TGRL's grammar, it was decided to keep the start, end, and step keywords in order to make the meaning of the values explicit and more easily understandable.

Similarly, TGRL supports groups of evaluation strategies, with strategy inclusion (for reuse), indicator initialization, and value ranges. Again here, TGRL provides a concrete textual syntax for elements that do not have a graphical syntax in URN.

```
grl SDL2015 {
    comment "This is a simple TGRL model"; // Model comment

    actor User {
        // Default name is the ID name, "User" in this case.
        // Goal with specific name and quantitative importance.
        softGoal EasyToUse {name="Have a system that is easy to use";
                            importance = 100;
        }
        indicator LowLearningTime; // Indicator definition
        // Link definition inside the actor, qualitative weight
        LowLearningTime contributesTo EasyToUse {name=C2;help};
    }
    actor Developer {
        softGoal ReuseComponents {importance=100;}
    }
    actor System {
        // Goal with qualitative importance, and OR decomposition type
        goal SomeFunctionality {importance=high; decompositionType=or;}
        task FirstOption {metadata stereotype="SomeValue";}
        task SecondOption {description = "Better alternative";}
        SomeFunctionality decomposedBy FirstOption, SecondOption;
        // Link across actors, quantitative weight
        FirstOption contributesTo Developer.ReuseComponents {75};
    }

    // Links defined outside their actors
    System.FirstOption contributesTo User.EasyToUse {hurt};
    System.SecondOption contributesTo User.EasyToUse {name=C1;60};

    // Contribution overrides
    contributionGroup SomeOverrides includes FirstOverride, SecondOverride;
    contribution FirstOverride {
        C1 = 30; C2 = make;
    }
    contribution SecondOverride extends FirstOverride {
        C1 = {start = -40; end = 0; step = 10;}
    }

    // Strategy examples
    strategy SelectFirst {
        System.FirstOption = satisfied;
        User.LowLearningTime = {unit="minutes"; target=30.0; threshold=60.0;
                                worst=120.0; eval=90.0;}
    }
    strategy SelectSecond extends SelectFirst { // Strategy inclusion!
        System.FirstOption = none; // Overridden
        System.SecondOption = 100; // Added, quantitatively this time
    }
    strategy RangeExample extends SelectFirst {
        System.FirstOption = {start = 10; end = 40; step = 5;}
    }
    strategyGroup MyGroup includes SelectFirst, SelectSecond, RangeExample;

    // URN links
    link mustUse; // Link type definition
    User mustUse System; // Link instance between two actors
}
```

Fig. 4. Simple illustrative TGRL model

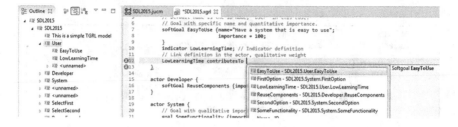

Fig. 5. Overview of the TGRL editor, with content assistance

Note also at the end of Fig. 4 that URN links are also supported. In this example, a link of a user-defined type mustUse connects the User to the System. Again, standard URN does not have a concrete graphical for this element, and jUCMNav relies on dialog boxes for creating such model elements (which are not displayed on the diagrams).

4.2   TGRL Editor and Transformation to jUCMNav

As Xtext was used to implement the TGRL syntax, we were able to get a feature-rich editor for very little effort. The Eclipse-based TGRL editor comes with configurable syntax highlight (as shown in the code in Fig. 4), an outline view, annotation of syntactic errors, content assistance, and code formatting. Figure 5 gives an overview of the editor.

The modeler, using Control-Space, can invoke code completion at any moment. Not only is this available for the keywords found in the grammar, this is also available for references to existing elements. For example, in Fig. 5, several suggestions are provided as potential targets of an incomplete contribution link. This greatly accelerates the coding, and also the learning of the language as one can get suggestions at any step.

The transformation between TGRL models and URN/jUCMNav models serialized in XML was implemented with Acceleo. While designing the TGRL syntax, we were able to make quick iterations from changing the Xtext-based grammar to adapting the Acceleo code and regenerating the editor and executable transformation, often within two minutes. Our transformation does not handle the layout of the generated GRL diagrams, but jUCMNav has several features for creating views of a model and for automatically laying out elements. For example, Fig. 6 shows the GRL model corresponding to the ongoing example, as imported by jUCMNav. The evaluation of the strategy SelectFirst is also shown, using quantitative values, and without any contribution change applied.

5   Discussion

In their original draft proposal for GRL in 2001, Liu and Yu defined a GRL ontology with a graphical syntax, a textual syntax, and an XML interchange format (but without a fully defined abstract syntax) [20]. The textual notation they proposed was cognitively hard to understand and did not cover the advanced

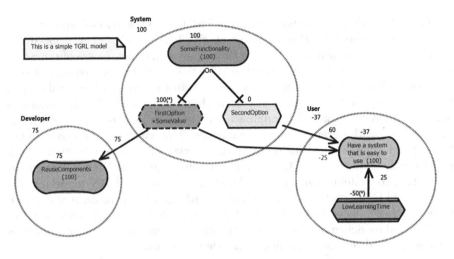

Fig. 6. Sample GRL model imported in jUCMNav, with a strategy evaluated quantitatively

GRL features found in standard URN (e.g., indicators, strategies, quantitative values, metadata, URN links, and contribution changes). We believe that the syntax for GRL should be intuitive, without requiring keywords when the context is clear (e.g., TGRL contribution weights do not require a keyword as they are expected to be provided 99 % of the time). TGRL is the first concrete syntax to cover all of GRL's constructs, and in that sense it goes beyond URN's standard graphical syntax [16].

Rashidi-Tabrizi et al. also proposed and implemented (in jUCMNav) an import mechanism for GRL models and strategies in a *tabular concrete syntax*, as comma-separated value files [26]. This allows people knowledgeable in tools like Excel to create GRL models without having to use jUCMNav, and then use jUCMNav for visualizing and analyzing models (as we do). However, their mechanism is limited to a subset of GRL (e.g., without contribution changes), and targets a very specific type of GRL models for the laws and regulations domain. Hence, their solution is not as generic and exhaustive as TGRL's.

Engelen and Van Den Brand have used two techniques, named *grammarware* and *modelware*, for the integration of textual and graphical modeling languages by implementing a textual surface language as an alternative for activity diagrams in UML [7]. In the grammarware technique, a text-to-text transformation was used while model-to-text, text-to-model, and model-to-model transformations were used in modelware. Their approach enabled them study the benefits and drawbacks of both techniques. Other similar comparisons were done by Gargantini et al. [9]. In our implementation, we utilized a modelware-like approach in which we have a model-to-text transformation used to generate jUCMNav files from TGRL models. However, more importantly, the availability of a GRL graphical editor (jUCMNav) and of a textual editor (TGRL) now enables us to compare both approaches quantitatively and answer usability questions in requirements engineering and system development contexts.

The integration of textual and graphical multi-view domain-specific languages was explored by Pérez Andrés et al. [24], in which they utilized the AToML model transformation tool. In their approach, a metamodel of the whole language must be defined first and then subsets have to be selected for different viewpoints. Then, a viewpoint metamodel is transformed into a textual model, from which a parser is automatically derived and integrated with the generated multi-view environment. This approach can be seen as a bridge between the modelware and the grammarware approaches. This viewpoint approach might be revisited in our context as in fact GRL is a view of URN. If a textual syntax is eventually produced for UCM (the other sub-language of URN), it might be interesting to evaluate whether it is beneficial to support URN models, UCM models, and GRL models (the three views) with standalone tools. It would also be interesting to consider providing different concrete textual syntaxes for GRL, e.g., for goal modeling in general, or with different keywords for specific domains such as law and regulation modeling, as needed in [26].

6   Conclusions and Future Work

In this paper, we have reported on the challenges that exist when trying to add a usable concrete textual syntax to a rich metamodel-based language predominantly oriented towards a concrete graphical syntax. We have discussed several alternatives for addressing challenges related to the choice of keywords, to structure consistency, to the alignment of metamodels, to the selection of suitable language design technologies, to rule handling, and to the synchronization between textual and graphical representations.

Many of these challenges were illustrated based on our case study, where we created a textual syntax for the GRL modeling language called TGRL. In addition to the observations we have made based on our experience, this paper led to the creation of the first textual syntax for an i^*-based goal-modeling language (as far as we know). TGRL also covers GRL fully, even concepts for which there is no standard graphical syntax (e.g., strategies, contribution changes, and URN links). A feature-rich, Xtext-based editor is now available for TGRL, together with a transformation to a URN model serialized in XMI and readable by the jUCMNav tool [1]. The availability of TGRL now enables researchers to compare the efficiency and usability of textual and graphical syntaxes in a goal modeling context, for different tasks and types of users.

In terms of future work, as this paper reports on only one language, it would be important to gather additional experience on other modeling languages, including some that are not based on metamodels. This would help identify common problems and trends across languages of different natures. It would also be interesting to better separate concerns related to language definition and tool integration.

On the TGRL side, further validation of the correctness and usability of this language is needed. One important feature currently missing is the availability of a transformation from jUCMNav to TGRL, which would enable modelers to go back and forth between the two representations. The support for additional well-formedness and semantic rules in the TGRL editor would also represent a good improvement. Another obvious step is the extension of this language to support the whole URN standard, including UCM (where, again, several concepts do not have a graphical syntax [11]). This could even lead to improvements to the URN standard at ITU-T. We also envision opportunities to combine TGRL (for goals) with Umple (for design and implementation) as they provide complementary concepts. Finally, the study of various concrete syntaxes for GRL (or URN), targeting different domains, is also something to explore, especially in terms of cognitive fitness.

Acknowledgement. This work was sponsored in part by the Natural Sciences and Engineering Research Council of Canada (NSERC) through its Discovery grant program.

References

1. Abdelzad, V.: Textual modeling language for GRL (2015). https://github.com/vahdat-ab/TGRL/
2. Acceleo (2015). http://www.eclipse.org/acceleo/
3. Amyot, D., Mussbacher, G.: User requirements notation: the first ten years, the next ten years. J. Softw. (JSW) **6**(5), 747–768 (2011)
4. Amyot, D., Shamsaei, A., Kealey, J., Tremblay, E., Miga, A., Mussbacher, G., Alhaj, M., Tawhid, R., Braun, E., Cartwright, N.: Towards advanced goal model analysis with jUCMNav. In: Castano, S., Vassiliadis, P., Lakshmanan, L.V.S., Lee, M.L. (eds.) ER 2012 Workshops 2012. LNCS, vol. 7518, pp. 201–210. Springer, Heidelberg (2012). http://softwareengineering.ca/jucmnav
5. ATL Transformation Language (2015). https://eclipse.org/atl/
6. Cabot, J.: UML tools - textual notations to define UML models (2009). http://sumo.ly/5Mb. Accessed 6 June 2015
7. Engelen, L., Van Den Brand, M.: Integrating textual and graphical modelling languages. Electron. Notes Theor. Comput. Sci. **253**(7), 105–120 (2010)
8. Forward, A., et al.: Model-driven rapid prototyping with Umple. Softw. Pract. Exper. **42**(7), 781–797 (2012)
9. Gargantini, A., Riccobene, E., Scandurra, P.: Deriving a textual notation from a metamodel: an experience on bridging modelware and grammarware. In: 3M4MDA. CTIT Workshop Proceedings Series WP06-02, pp. 33–48 (2006)
10. Garzón, M., Aljamaan, H.I., Lethbridge, T.C.: Umple: A Framework for Model Driven Development of Object-Oriented Systems. In: SANER 2015, pp. 494–498. IEEE CS (2015)
11. Genon, N., Amyot, D., Heymans, P.: Analysing the cognitive effectiveness of the UCM visual notation. In: Kraemer, F.A., Herrmann, P. (eds.) SAM 2010. LNCS, vol. 6598, pp. 221–240. Springer, Heidelberg (2011)
12. Heidenreich, F., Johannes, J., Karol, S., Seifert, M., Wende, C.: Derivation and refinement of textual syntax for models. In: Paige, R.F., Hartman, A., Rensink, A. (eds.) ECMDA-FA 2009. LNCS, vol. 5562, pp. 114–129. Springer, Heidelberg (2009)
13. International Telecommunication Union: ITU-T Recommendation Z.100 (12/11) - Specification and Description Language - Overview of SDL-2010 (2011). http://www.itu.int/rec/T-REC-Z.100-201112-I

14. International Telecommunication Union: ITU-T Recommendation Z.111 (11/08) - Notations and guidelines for the definition of ITU-T languages (2008). http://www.itu.int/rec/T-REC-Z.111-200811-I
15. International Telecommunication Union: ITU-T Recommendation Z.120 (02/11) - Message Sequence Chart (MSC) (2011). http://www.itu.int/rec/T-REC-Z.120-201102-I
16. International Telecommunication Union: ITU-T Recommendation Z.151 (10/12) - User Requirements Notation (URN) - Language Definition (2012). http://www.itu.int/rec/T-REC-Z.151-201210-I
17. International Telecommunication Union: ITU-T Recommendation Z.161 (11/14) - Testing and Test Control Notation Version 3: TTCN-3 Core Language (2012). http://www.itu.int/rec/T-REC-Z.161-201411-I
18. International Telecommunication Union: ITU-T Recommendation Z.162 (11/07) - Testing and Test Control Notation Version 3: TTCN-3 Tabular Presentation Format (TFT) (2012). http://www.itu.int/rec/T-REC-Z.162-200711-I
19. Jouault, F., Bézivin, J., Kurtev, I.: TCS: a DSL for the specification of textual concrete syntaxes in model engineering. In: GPCE 2006, pp. 249–254. ACM Press (2006)
20. Liu, L., Yu, E.: GRL - goal-oriented requirement language. University of Toronto, Canada (2001). http://www.cs.toronto.edu/km/GRL
21. Moody, D.L., Heymans, P., Matulevičius, R.: Visual syntax does matter: improving the cognitive effectiveness of the i^* visual notation. Requir. Eng. **15**(2), 141–175 (2010)
22. Mussbacher, G., Amyot, D., Heymans, P.: Eight deadly sins of GRL. In: 5th International i^* Workshop (iStar 2011), CEUR-WS, vol. 766, pp. 2–7 (2011)
23. OMG: UML Human-Usable Textual Notation (HUTN). Version 1.0, formal/2004-08-01 (2004). http://www.omg.org/spec/HUTN/1.0/
24. Pérez Andrés, F., de Lara, J., Guerra, E.: Domain specific languages with graphical and textual views. In: Schürr, A., Nagl, M., Zündorf, A. (eds.) AGTIVE 2007. LNCS, vol. 5088, pp. 82–97. Springer, Heidelberg (2008)
25. Petre, M.: Why looking isn't always seeing: readership skills and graphical programming. Commun. ACM **38**(6), 33–44 (1995)
26. Rashidi-Tabrizi, R., Mussbacher, G., Amyot, D.: Transforming legulations into performance models in the context of reasoning for outcome-based compliance. In: RELAW 2013, pp. 34–43. IEEE CS (2013)
27. Rose, L.M., Paige, R.F., Kolovos, D.S., Polack, F.A.C.: Constructing models with the human-usable textual notation. In: Czarnecki, K., Ober, I., Bruel, J.-M., Uhl, A., Völter, M. (eds.) MODELS 2008. LNCS, vol. 5301, pp. 249–263. Springer, Heidelberg (2008)
28. Roy, J.-F., Kealey, J., Amyot, D.: Towards integrated tool support for the user requirements notation. In: Gotzhein, R., Reed, R. (eds.) SAM 2006. LNCS, vol. 4320, pp. 198–215. Springer, Heidelberg (2006)
29. Scheidgen, M.: Textual modelling embedded into graphical modelling. In: Schieferdecker, I., Hartman, A. (eds.) ECMDA-FA 2008. LNCS, vol. 5095, pp. 153–168. Springer, Heidelberg (2008)
30. Schmidt, M., Wider, A., Scheidgen, M., Fischer, J., von Klinski, S.: Refactorings in language development with asymmetric bidirectional model transformations. In: Khendek, F., Toeroe, M., Gherbi, A., Reed, R. (eds.) SDL 2013. LNCS, vol. 7916, pp. 222–238. Springer, Heidelberg (2013)
31. Xtend (2015). http://www.eclipse.org/xtend/
32. Xtext (2015). http://www.eclipse.org/Xtext/

Use-Case Modeling

Generating Software Documentation in Use Case Maps from Filtered Execution Traces

Edna Braun, Daniel Amyot[(✉)], and Timothy C. Lethbridge

School of EECS, University of Ottawa, Ottawa, Canada
{ebraun,damyot,tcl}@eecs.uottawa.ca

Abstract. One of the main issues in software maintenance is the time and effort needed to understand software. Software documentation and models are often incomplete, outdated, or non-existent, in part because of the cost and effort involved in creating and continually updating them. In this paper, we describe an innovative technique for automatically extracting and visualizing software behavioral models from execution traces. Lengthy traces are summarized by filtering out low-level software components via algorithms that utilize static and dynamic data. Eight such algorithms are compared in this paper. The traces are visualized using the Use Case Map (UCM) scenario notation. The resulting UCM diagrams depict the behavioral model of software traces and can be used to document the software. The tool-supported technique is customizable through different filtering algorithms and parameters, enabling the generation of documentation and models at different levels of abstraction.

Keywords: Feature location · Software documentation · Trace summarization · Use Case Map · Utility · Visualization

1 Introduction

Understanding software during maintenance activities is often very difficult due to incomplete, outdated, or non-existent documentation. In the absence of up-to-date documentation, programmers frequently need to extract structural and behavioral information directly from the code. A number of techniques and methods have been developed in order to facilitate program comprehension [7,18,19], and several others, especially focusing on the use of dynamic analysis, are compared in a survey from Cornelissen et al. [8]. Feature location and comprehension approaches [12,14,22,23,26–29] have also been investigated by many researchers, and several others are summarized in a survey by Dit et al. [10].

In this paper, we propose a new approach to extract high-level behavioral models of a software feature by using execution traces. A *feature* is defined as a realized functional requirement of a system that can be triggered by a user, as explained by Eisenbarth et al. [14]. A feature represents a functionality that is defined by requirements and accessible to developers and users [10]. As execution traces are often too lengthy for comprehension, we simplify them by *filtering out*

© Springer International Publishing Switzerland 2015
J. Fischer et al. (Eds.): SDL 2015, LNCS 9369, pp. 177–192, 2015.
DOI: 10.1007/978-3-319-24912-4_13

software components that are too low level to give a high-level picture of the selected feature. We use static information to identify and remove small and simple (or uncomplicated) software components from the trace. We define a *utility method* as any element of a program designed for the convenience of the designer and implementer and intended to be accessed from multiple places within a certain scope of the program. *Utilityhood* is a metric defined as the extent to which a particular method can be considered a utility. Utilityhood is calculated using different combinations of selected dynamic and static variables. Methods with high utilityhood values are detected and removed iteratively. By filtering out utilities, we are left with a much smaller trace. In order to visualize reduced traces, we selected the Use Case Map (UCM) notation [6,17], a standard scenario language used to specify requirements of dynamic systems and explain their emergent behavior. The behavioral model is then displayed as UCM diagrams, which combine structure and sequences of activities. The abstracted diagrams can be used as documentation that summarizes feature behavior. The approach offers parameters that enable the selection of how much information to preserve in the traces (Fig. 1).

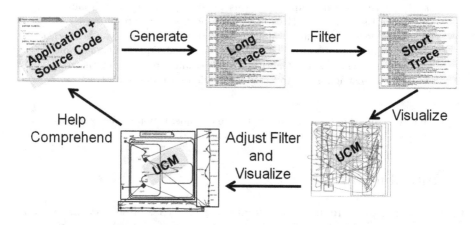

Fig. 1. From source code to traces and behavioral models

Section 2 of this paper gives background on UCM with a mapping from traces, and definitions of static and dynamic metrics used in our approach. Section 3 presents utilityhood functions used by eight algorithms for our comparative analysis. Section 4 highlights our new automated approach (TraceToUCM) for converting execution traces to UCMs. Sections 5 to 7 give an illustrative example, followed by a discussion and conclusions.

2   Mapping and Metrics

This section gives a brief summary of the UCM scenario modeling notation for reverse-engineered behavioral models, with a mapping from execution traces.

Then, it introduces the static and dynamic information used by our utility filtering algorithms.

2.1 Mapping Traces to Use Case Maps

The UCM notation is part of the User Requirements Notation (URN) [2,17], an international standard used for the elicitation, analysis, specification, and validation of requirements. UCM has first been suggested for trace visualization by Amyot et al. in [1].

We chose Use Case Maps to visualize the reduced execution traces because they are a rich requirements-level notation for showing at a glance the various control-flow possibilities in a system. Unlike Message Sequence Charts and UML sequence diagrams, which are often used for trace visualization [27], UCMs abstract from the inter-component communication to focus on the business/feature logic. Using jUCMNav [21], an Eclipse-based tool for URN modeling, analysis and transformations, we are however able to generate sequence diagrams (with synthetic messages) from UCMs, enabling one to visualize the scenarios represented in two different formats.

As in UML activity diagrams, UCMs can integrate many scenarios with operators for looping and forking/joining alternative or concurrent paths. Complex maps can also be decomposed into sub-maps (through stubs, shown as diamonds). Stubs may contain multiple sub-maps, allowing for flexible integration and exploration of scenarios that have overlapping parts. The various scenario elements can be bound to components (shown as rectangles). The latter can have sub-components, enabling structures to be visualized in two dimensions, in a compact way.

Each item in a filtered execution trace is visually communicated using UCM. To translate execution traces to UCM maps, Table 1 provides a mapping from trace elements (in a formalized trace format [4]) to UCM notation elements. This is an extension of a preliminary informal mapping we studied in [15].

2.2 Static Data Metrics

Static analysis examines a program's code to derive properties that hold for all executions [3]. The static analysis is performed without actually executing programs. The relevant static data metrics collected here are the following:

- *Method Lines of Code (MLOC)*: Total number of lines of code inside method bodies, excluding blank lines and comments.
- *Nested Block Depth (NBD)*: The depth of nested code blocks.
- *McCabe Cyclomatic Complexity (McCabe)*: Number of flows through a piece of code [20].

This data is collected via Metrics 1.3.6 [24], an Eclipse plug-in used to gather static data on software (in Java) at the package, class, and method levels.

Table 1. Mapping of trace elements to UCM elements

Trace element	UCM element	Symbol
Package	Shown as a rectangle with thick border.	▢
Class	Shown as a rectangle in another rectangle (Package).	▢
Beginning / End of trace	Start point (circle) / End point (bar) (also used as connectors for linking sub-scenarios to the parent stub)	● ⊣
Method	Method name (shown as a X on a path)	..⌐—✕——...
Block of x or more instructions in the same class/object	Stub (diamond) with the name of the first instruction that is not a constructor. This stub contains a plug-in (another sub-map) showing the sub-sequence with one responsibility per instruction. The number of instructions that are placed in a block is set in the TraceToUCM tool.	..⌐_IN1_◇_OUT1_...
Repeated method	Method name (repetition count between curly brackets)	method {2} ..⌐—✕——...
Order of trace items	Direction of scenario flow (shown as an arrow head). We use the order of trace items in execution traces to dictate the direction of the scenario flow.	... ⟶—— ...

2.3 Dynamic Data Metrics

Dynamic analysis derives properties that hold true for one or more executions by examination of the running program through instrumentation. This can provide useful information about the behavior of programs for the specific input parameters that are entered. We use the Eclipse TPTP tracer and Java profiler [13] to collect execution traces and CPU usage. An execution trace contains the list of each method that was called, in order of calls, and the depth of the call tree. We process the execution trace and derive more detailed information for each of the method calls:

- *Fan-in*: Number of methods that called this method.
- *Fan-out*: Number of methods this method called.
- *UniqueFanin* (array): Unique set of methods that called this method. The length of the array is the fan-in.
- *NumberOfTimesCalledBy* (array): List of all methods that this method has been called by (contains duplicates).
- *UniqueFanout* (array): Unique set of methods that this method called. The length of the array is the fan-out.
- *NumberOfTimesMethodsCalled* (array): List of all methods that this method called (contains duplicates).
- *TotalSegmentPresence*: Total number of trace segments this method was found in, based on Dugerdil and Jossi's approach [11].
- *PercentageOfSegmentsMethodPresentIn*: Percentage of trace segments this method was found in.

- *Depth*: Depth of this method in the call hierarchy.
- *BaseTime*: Time taken to execute the invocation of a method.
- *CumulativeCpuTime*: Amount of CPU time spent in a method accumulated from all invocations.
- *CpuUsageAverage*: Cumulative CPU time divided by the number of calls.

3   Utilityhood Algorithms

We use different combinations of the static and dynamic data we have collected to develop a number of algorithms to calculate utilityhood functions ($U(r)$) for each method r in the execution traces. This selection of functions is based on preliminary experiments involving 18 Java open source systems used to determine the most promising metrics (based on correlations between metrics) from which utilityhood should be computed [4]. Table 2 gives a summary of these utilityhood functions, where N is the number of unique methods in the execution trace, $RelativeMethodSize(r)$ is the size of a method r in relation to other methods in the system, and $TotalNumberOfSegments$ is the total number of segments the execution trace is broken into [4].

- *Algorithm 1*: based on earlier work done in [15]. The higher the number of callers a method has, the more likely that it will be eliminated as a low-level utility class.
- *Algorithm 2*: based on work done by Hamou-Lhadj [16]. In this case, a fan-out is also taken into consideration. If two methods A() and B() have the same number of callers but B() also calls out to other methods, it will rank lower on the utilityhood index.

Table 2. Summary of utilityhood function algorithms

Name	Utilityhood function
Algorithm 1 [15]	$U(r) = \dfrac{UniqueFanin(r)}{N-1}$
Algorithm 2 [16]	$U(r) = \dfrac{UniqueFanin(r)}{N} \times \dfrac{log(\frac{N}{UniqueFanout(r)+1})}{log(N)}$
Algorithm 3	$U(r) = \dfrac{1}{Nbd(r) \times McCabe(r) \times RelativeMethodSize(r)}$
Algorithm 4	$U(r) = \dfrac{fanout(r)}{Nbd(r) \times McCabe(r) \times RelativeMethodSize(r)}$
Algorithm 5 [11]	$U(r) = \dfrac{SegmentPresence(r)}{TotalNumberOfSegments}$
Algorithm 6 [28]	$U(r) = \dfrac{1}{(UniqueFanin(r) \times UniqueFanout(r))^2}$
Algorithm 7	$U(r) = \dfrac{UniqueFanin(r)}{(N-1) \times AverageCallHierarchy \times RelativeMethodSize(r)}$
Algorithm 8	$U(r) = \dfrac{1}{CpuUsageAverage(r) \times McCabe(r) \times RelativeMethodSize(r)}$

– *Algorithm 3*: we use the McCabe value, also known as cyclomatic complexity [20], to measure the number of linearly independent paths through a method. One of the hypotheses we are testing is that methods that are simple are more likely to be utilities than methods that are more complex.
– *Algorithm 4*: we test our hypothesis that smaller methods are more likely to be utilities than larger ones, and therefore methods that are designed to be accessed from multiple places would tend to be small. We use the relative size of a method within the whole system as a measure, instead of an absolute size, to account for differences in programming styles, and the size of the whole system. A method considered large in one software system might be the smallest in another.
– *Algorithm 5*: based on the work of Dugerdil and Jossi [11], who developed trace segmentation and clustering techniques to reverse-engineer software systems. While segmenting the execution trace, they remove classes present in most of the segments of the execution trace. They observe those classes "perform some utility work, not specific to any functional component". We take the trace segmentation part of their methodology and test it here.
– *Algorithm 6*: based on an algorithm developed by Wang et al. [28]. They claim that the static (syntactical) situation of a software program reflects only inaccurately the situation of the dynamic behavior of the system, using factors like actual number and type of procedure calls, as well as size of the actual transferred information. They hypothesize that methods with high fan-in or fan-out values implement the system's main functions, and can be used to infer the subject system's functionality.
– *Algorithm 7*: we look at each method in the execution trace and calculate a value that represents the average call hierarchy, also called average call tree depth. The average call hierarchy is calculated by taking the depth at which each method is called during the run, and then dividing it by the number of different depths from which it is called. For example, if method A() is called through Z() → Y() →A(), which is of depth 3, and also called through Z() →X() → W() → A(), which is of depth 4, then the *AverageCallHierarchy* would be $(3+4)/2 = 3.5$.
– *Algorithm 8*: tests the hypothesis that most complex methods with the highest average processor (CPU) time, and with the most lines of code, are the most important methods and should be used to include in the behavioral model of a feature.

4   Automated Approach

We developed a tool called *TraceToUCM* that takes three required inputs (an execution trace, CPU profiling information, and the metrics discussed in Sect. 2), with optional lists of Java methods to be explicitly included or excluded in the resulting traces, and filtering parameter information (e.g., thresholds for each algorithm). The tool generates automatically a UCM diagram using the mapping shown in Table 1 for each of our filtering algorithms, in addition to other files with intermediate or by-product information (e.g., data tables, statistics, rankings, etc.). We also created an automatic layout function to draw all the UCM diagrams, which helps keep the layout variable consistent between the diagrams obtained from different utility detection algorithms.

The following is a brief summary of the main steps taken by the automatic trace summarization tool, illustrated in Fig. 2.

1. Run the target program and collect the execution trace and CPU information (using TPTP). Use Metrics 1.3.6 [24] for producing the various static metrics.
2. Remove methods explicitly excluded.
3. Remove duplicate loops from the trace (but preserve loop counts).
4. Remove data access methods (`.get*()` or `.set*()` with less than 2 lines of code and a complexity index less than 2).
5. Remove small methods (with fewer than 5 lines of code) and simple methods (that score 2 or less on the complexity index). This is kept as a separate step from the previous one as the notion of "small method" is configurable.
6. Integrate the static data and CPU data for the methods.
7. Calculate utilityhood for all the methods using each of the 8 algorithms.
8. Filter the traces according to each utilityhood result and generate UCMs from the resulting traces.
9. If required, re-iterate to raise or lower the level of abstraction (through the filtering information file).
10. If required, a sequence diagram can also be generated from each UCM diagram via jUCMNav.

5 Illustrative Example

We use an example to demonstrate the approach proposed in this paper. We run one feature of the software, collect the trace, reduce the execution trace and produce UCM behavioral models. We selected a Java application called *Use Case Editor (UCEd)*, version 1.6.2 [25], which is an environment for use-case-based requirements engineering. UCEd contains tools for editing use cases, such as use-case integration and use-case simulation. UCEd has 700 classes, 3284 methods, and 33,004 lines of code. We run the feature "Open a project".

We collected the execution trace and the profiling information while a file was being opened. We also collected static information on the code using Metrics [24]. We then filtered the trace and generated UCM diagrams. Table 3 highlights the size of the trace after each step (in a cumulative way in the top part) and then after each algorithm (independently from one another in the bottom). We can see that before the algorithms are applied to the trace (as alternatives), just by removing repeated loops, access methods, as well as small and simple methods, we have reduced the execution trace from 19,543 to 1987 lines, which already represents a 90 % reduction in size.

The eight UCM diagrams are then generated, one per algorithm. In the first iteration, we actually have set the filter at 40, i.e., the 40 methods ranked as

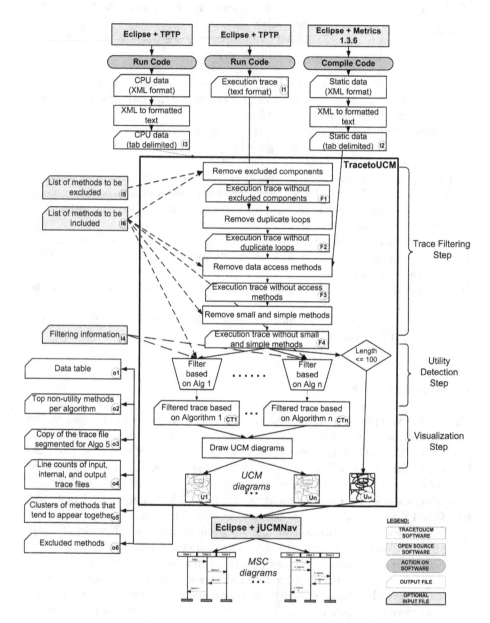

Fig. 2. Overview of the TraceToUCM tool

Table 3. UCEd execution trace line count (top: cumulative; bottom: alternatives)

Trace name	Trace size	Reduction
Uced_Original	19543	0.00 %
Uced_Original_LoopsRemoved	7698	60.61 %
Uced_AccessMethodsRemoved	3088	84.20 %
Uced_Original_SmallSimpleMethodsRemoved	1987	89.83 %
Uced_Algorithm_1	72	99.63 %
Uced_Algorithm_2	73	99.63 %
Uced_Algorithm_3	53	99.73 %
Uced_Algorithm_4	164	99.16 %
Uced_Algorithm_5	29	99.85 %
Uced_Algorithm_6	20	99.90 %
Uced_Algorithm_7	61	99.69 %
Uced_Algorithm_8	99	99.49 %

non-utility would be included in the trace and the UCM diagram. Figure 3 shows the generated UCM diagram based on the top 40 methods ranked according to Algorithm 4. The diagram is cluttered and is hard to follow, but it does show many UCM nested components capturing classes within their packages.

We then raised the level of abstraction a bit higher 1) by using the top 20 methods instead of 40 and 2) by using UCM stubs to hide some of the low-level details in sub-diagrams. Although stubs could in theory be used to preserve the entire trace, enabling analysts to drill down into low-level details, we believe that traces would still be too large for this to be practical with current UCM tools. The result is shown in Fig. 4. This new UCM diagram is much easier to follow than the UCM diagram in Fig. 3, but may miss important information. One can play easily with such levels of abstraction in order to at least generate a diagram that stands a chance of being understandable.

In order to assess which of the algorithms lead to the most understandable and intuitive results for this trace, we showed the corresponding UCM diagrams to two UCEd designers and asked them whether the diagrams contained the main methods used for understanding the "Open a project" feature. Both designers chose the UCM diagrams based on Algorithms 1 and 4, for 20 methods (e.g., the one in Fig. 4).

The UCM models produced by the TraceToUCM tool also contain *scenario definitions*, which allow one to simulate the UCM model and to transform each execution sequence into a sequence diagram. This hence provides a different visualization of the same information. Each UCM component becomes a lifeline in the sequence diagram, but containment relationships are more difficult to understand. Sequence diagrams are also general less compact than UCM diagrams (especially with synthetic messages), but on the other hand UCM diagrams may have more complicated layout issues, possibly with paths crossing each other.

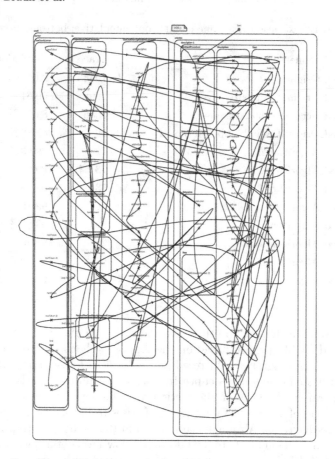

Fig. 3. Use Case Map model derived for the UCEd trace using the top 40 methods (not meant to be read)

6   Discussion and Evaluation

6.1   Additional Experiments

In [4], we also report on the additional evaluation of traces obtained from two other Java projects: jUCMNav (with 94 KLOC, and 3 developers for validation) and Umple (with 79 KLOC, and 4 developers). Again, the developers were asked to determine which UCM diagrams were suitable for understanding specific features. Looking at the scores from the three groups of designers (including UCEd's), Algorithms 2 and 4 generally come ahead of the other algorithms. The algorithms that did better than the others used method size, method complexity and nested block depth metrics. More work needs to be done to fine-tune the combinations of those parameters in the algorithms. Based on answers to a questionnaire, there was agreement among the designers that UCM diagrams were

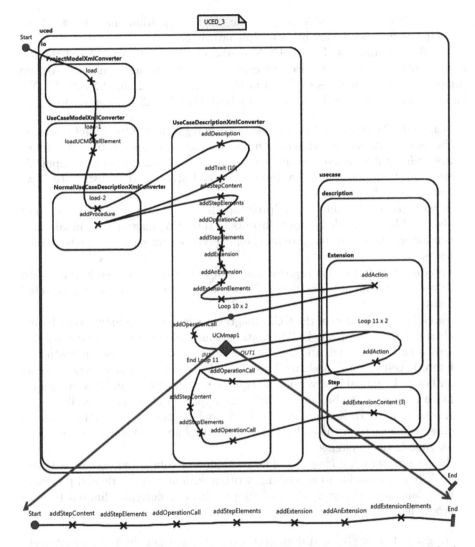

Fig. 4. Use Case Map model derived for the UCEd trace using the top 20 methods, with stubs

suitable to represent execution traces. 7 out of 8 designers agreed (including one who strongly agreed) and one was neutral.

We have also reverse-engineered our own TraceToUCM tool (3.4 KLOC) by producing UCM diagrams for its main feature. These diagrams were presented to 16 students and software engineers who were asked to pick the top three diagrams/algorithms that they felt gave enough information to describe what the program did. The results showed that reduced traces, visualized by using the UCM notation, can be helpful in documenting software. We also learned that it may not be desirable to pick one "best" algorithm since a few of the participants expressed they had multiple favorites.

While designing the TraceToUCM method and tool, we considered the following criteria, which were used to assess 11 other existing dynamic program comprehension approaches explored in [4], including [9,12,16,22,23,28,29]. We look at each criterion and briefly discuss how TraceToUCM measures up.

- *Scalability*: TraceToUCM is scalable because regardless of the target software, the user can focus the behavioral model extraction on one feature at a time.
- *Scalability for trace size*: TraceToUCM can be used regardless of the input file size. UCM supports recursive levels of nested stubs, and by using stubs we can visualize large traces.
- *Visualization*: The auto-layout program that is used by jUCMNav was not always able to provide readable layouts of the UCM diagrams. Manual intervention was necessary to move overlapping component names and intertwined paths.
- *Level of prior knowledge required*: No prior knowledge of the code is required to use this technique. The user only needs to know how to run the selected feature.
- *Validation*: Validation of the UCM diagrams was done with many participants already familiar with the UCM notation, which adds some bias to our results.
- *Usability*: Even though all that the user needs to do is exercise the feature of interest, collect data, and run TraceToUCM, a process that is hence mostly automated, manual intervention is required to untangle larger UCM diagrams. More work needs to be done to make the approach more user-friendly.
- *Intrusive data collection*: TraceToUCM, which builds on TPTP, has an observer effect from the collection of CPU data and is therefore not suitable for time-critical systems.
- *Target programming language*: The technique of comparing execution traces is likely generalizable to all systems written with an object-oriented programming language. However, the tool support itself is currently limited to Java programs.

In general, TraceToUCM does better on average than the 11 other program comprehension techniques exploiting dynamic analysis studied in [4], with some weaknesses in terms of visualization, validation and utility, where some other approaches have at times scored better.

6.2   Threats to Validity

There are some threats to the validity of our approach. We analyze at them with general framework proposed by Wohlin et al. [30], which is used by grouping the factors that limit our ability to draw valid conclusions from empirical experiments into four classes: external, internal, construct and conclusion threats.

External validity is the ability to generalize the observed results to a larger population. Important potential threats include the following: 1) *Participants were not representative*: Use Case Maps are used widely around the University of Ottawa and therefore most of the graduate students were familiar with UCM. This is not the case for all software engineers in general. This may make our results difficult to generalize because the participants were more familiar with them than the average software engineer outside of the University of Ottawa community. 2) *Programs were not representative*: all of the software studies were open source Java systems. Although care was taken to use tools that will work with object-oriented programming languages in general, the methodology needs to be tested with non-open source and non-Java systems.

Internal validity in our context refers to internal correctness of experiment design and to the absence of bias. Four threats have been identified here.

1. Software error: Although care was taken to debug and verify the TraceToUCM tool, it is not a production system and therefore could contain bugs that affect the results of the experiment.
2. The same person, namely the first author, selected the programs to be studied, the algorithms and the subjects who were invited to participate. This possibly introduces bias. However, to partially mitigate bias issues, all the developers of the three systems under study were invited to participate, the small programs were selected from an open source repository (Standard Widget Toolkit examples), and the protocol was reviewed by the university's research ethics board.
3. We used TPTP to collect an execution trace and CPU data in two different runs. Care was taken to make sure the runs are as identical as possible. However, when dealing in milliseconds, one can rarely guarantee trace equality, and therefore it would be best to do the experiment using a tool that can collect all the data in the same run.
4. In the filtering step, useful data may get thrown out by the Small and Simple filter. A good example where this could occur would be a recursive function that is very small. We try to mitigate this threat by keeping the methods with the highest average CPU usage no matter what its size, complexity or method name are. In addition, the inclusion input file (labeled I6 in Fig. 2) can be used to ensure important methods are not filtered out even if they score low by the filters and algorithms.

Construct validity refers to the ability of the experiments to capture the effect being measured. We designed and explored two types of case studies to validate whether behavioral maps of a feature can be extracted from execution traces by filtering out utilities. We tested the use of the behavioral maps for software comprehension (with three open source software applications) and for software documentation (with our own TraceToUCM tool). The first type of case study was constructed incrementally. In the first iteration (published in [15]), we studied one system, TConfig, using one utility detection algorithm and validated the result with its (only) designer. Using lessons learned from the first iteration, we designed the second iteration with five algorithms (four new ones and one from the first iteration) and also compared our algorithms with 3 algorithms found in the literature [12,16,28]. In the first iteration, trace processing and UCM diagram creation were manual, which can potentially add a lot of variability to the quality of the filtered trace and the UCM diagrams. We were able to mitigate this risk by automating the trace processing and UCM diagram generation in the second iteration, making the process repeatable, less error-prone and more user-friendly and efficient. However, we were not able to eliminate the risks entirely as jUCMNav's auto-layout feature does not produce a UCM diagram that is free of overlap and easy to read, and manual intervention was necessary. Therefore, understandability of the UCM diagram may have been hampered by the layout tool.

Conclusion validity is the ability to draw conclusions from statistical tests. The main threat here is that our sample size for real systems is only three, with few designers available for each (as designers with a general and deep understanding of their systems are difficult to access), which prevents statistical significance from being reached. Work needs to be done using larger collections of software systems, where dozens of developers are available.

7   Conclusion and Future Work

This paper contributes TraceToUCM, an environment where different algorithms targeting the filtering of utilities (exploiting dynamic, static, and CPU information) can be implemented for comparison and evaluation. TraceToUCM also supports the visualization of reduced traces with Use Case Maps and sequence diagrams for software feature documentation and comprehension. A comparison of eight filtering algorithms was performed with three real software projects and their designers (who know the systems), and with one additional project where people who did not know the software had to explain and rank generated UCM diagrams. A brief comparison with other related approaches along eight criteria highlighted the benefits, limitations, and overall good potential of TraceToUCM.

Note that this work focused on programs written in Java. Yet, there is much legacy code written in non-Java programming languages. The study needs to be repeated using software from different programming languages and paradigms.

Further characterization of utilities could be done as another future work item. One could investigate how context-dependent utilities are used in different contexts. For example, for the same piece of software, is there one fixed set of utilities? Or do utilities change from one feature to another? Are there differences between utilities of a single trace (or feature), and utilities of many traces (or features)?

The current approach might benefit from a more specific handling of multi-threaded or even distributed applications, where causality needs to be recovered from processes that have potentially different local clocks. At the moment, elements in a trace might come from concurrent threads and hence lead to increased visualization complexity (as UCM responsibilities would alternate between components rather than being shown as concurrent sub-sequences connected with parallel forks) to loops that are not correctly detected (because different iterations might have different orderings resulting from multiple interleaving threads).

Improvements could be inspired from work done by Briand et al. [5] on the reverse engineering of behavior from distributed Java applications.

Acknowledgements. This work was sponsored in part by the Natural Sciences and Engineering Research Council of Canada (NSERC, Discovery grant).

References

1. Amyot, D., Mansurov, N., Mussbacher, G.: Understanding existing software with use case map scenarios. In: Sherratt, E. (ed.) SAM 2002. LNCS, vol. 2599, pp. 124–140. Springer, Heidelberg (2003). http://dx.doi.org/10.1007/3-540-36573-7_9
2. Amyot, D., Mussbacher, G.: User requirements notation: the first ten years, the next ten years. JSW 6(5), 747–768 (2011). http://dx.doi.org/10.4304/jsw.6.5.747-768
3. Ball, T.: The concept of dynamic analysis. In: Wang, J., Lemoine, M. (eds.) ESEC 1999 and ESEC-FSE 1999. LNCS, vol. 1687, p. 216. Springer, Heidelberg (1999). http://dx.doi.org/10.1007/3-540-48166-4_14
4. Braun, E.: Reverse engineering behavioural models by filtering out utilities from execution traces. Ph.D. thesis, University of Ottawa, Canada (2013). http://hdl.handle.net/10393/26093
5. Briand, L., Labiche, Y., Leduc, J.: Toward the reverse engineering of UML sequence diagrams for distributed Java software. IEEE Trans. Softw. Eng. 32(9), 642–663 (2006)
6. Buhr, R.: Use case maps as architectural entities for complex systems. IEEE Trans. Softw. Eng. 24(12), 1131–1155 (1998)
7. Burtscher, M., Ganusov, I., Jackson, S., Ke, J., Ratanaworabhan, P., Sam, N.: The VPC trace-compression algorithms. IEEE Trans. Comput. 54(11), 1329–1344 (2005)
8. Cornelissen, B., Zaidman, A., van Deursen, A., Moonen, L., Koschke, R.: A systematic survey of program comprehension through dynamic analysis. IEEE Trans. Softw. Eng. 35(5), 684–702 (2009)
9. Di Lucca, G., Di Penta, M.: Integrating static and dynamic analysis to improve the comprehension of existing web applications. In: Web Site Evolution 2005, (WSE 2005), Seventh IEEE International Symposium, pp. 87–94, Sept 2005. http://dx.doi.org/10.1109/WSE.2005.8
10. Dit, B., Revelle, M., Gethers, M., Poshyvanyk, D.: Feature location in source code: a Taxonomy and survey. J. Softw. Evol. Process 25(1), 53–95 (2013). http://dx.doi.org/10.1002/smr.567
11. Dugerdil, P., Jossi, S.: Empirical assessment of execution trace segmentation in reverse-engineering. In: ICSOFT 2008, Volume SE/MUSE/GSDCA, pp. 20–27. INSTICC Press (2008)
12. Dugerdil, P., Repond, J.: Automatic generation of abstract views for legacy software comprehension. In: ISEC 2010, pp. 23–32. ACM, New York (2010). http://dx.doi.org/10.1145/1730874.1730881
13. Eclipse Foundation: Eclipse Test and Performance Tools Platform Project (2011). http://www.eclipse.org/tptp/
14. Eisenbarth, T., Koschke, R., Simon, D.: Locating features in source code. IEEE Trans. Softw. Eng. 29(3), 210–224 (2003). TSE.2003.1183929

15. Hamou-Lhadj, A., Braun, E., Amyot, D., Lethbridge, T.: Recovering behavioral design models from execution traces. In: 9th Software Maintenance and Reengineering (CSMR), pp. 112–121, March 2005. http://dx.doi.org/10.1109/CSMR.2005.46
16. Hamou-Lhadj, A.: Techniques to simplify the analysis of execution traces for program comprehension. Ph.D. thesis, University of Ottawa, Canada (2006). http://hdl.handle.net/10393/29296
17. International Telecommunication Union: ITU-T Recommendation Z.151 (10/12) - User Requirements Notation (URN) - Language Definition (2012). http://www.itu.int/rec/T-REC-Z.151-201210-I
18. Lee, H.B., Zorn, B.G.: BIT: a tool for instrumenting Java bytecodes. In: USITS 1997, pp. 7–7. USENIX Association, Berkeley (1997)
19. von Mayrhauser, A., Vans, A.: Program understanding behavior during adaptation of large scale software. In: IWPC 1998, pp. 164–172, Jun 1998. http://dx.doi.org/10.1109/WPC.1998.693345
20. McCabe, T.J.: A complexity measure. IEEE Trans. Softw. Eng. **2**(4), 308–320 (1976)
21. Mussbacher, G., Amyot, D.: Goal and scenario modeling, analysis, and transformation with jUCMNav. In: Software Engineering - Companion Volume, pp. 431–432, May 2009. http://dx.doi.org/10.1109/ICSE-COMPANION.2009.5071047
22. Richner, T., Ducasse, S.: Recovering high-level views of object-oriented applications from static and dynamic information. In: IEEE International Conference on Software Maintenance, pp. 13–22 (1999). http://dx.doi.org/10.1109/ICSM.1999.792487
23. Rilling, J., Seffah, A., Bouthlier, C.: The CONCEPT project - applying source code analysis to reduce information complexity of static and dynamic visualization techniques. In: Visualizing Software for Understanding and Analysis, pp. 90–99 (2002). http://dx.doi.org/10.1109/VISSOF.2002.1019798
24. Sauer, F.: Metrics 1.3.6 (2013). http://metrics.sourceforge.net/
25. Somé, S.S.: Use Case Editor (UCEd) (2007). http://www.site.uottawa.ca/ssome/Use_Case_Editor_UCEd.html
26. Systä, T.: Understanding the behaviour of Java programs. In: WCRE 2000, pp. 214–223. IEEE CS (2000). http://dx.doi.org/10.1109/WCRE.2000.891472
27. Systä, T., Yu, P., Muller, H.: Analyzing Java software by combining metrics and program visualization. In: 4th Software Maintenance and Reengineering Conference, pp. 199–208, Feb 2000. http://dx.doi.org/10.1109/CSMR.2000.827328
28. Wang, Y., Li, Q., Chen, P., Ren, C.: Dynamic fan-in and fan-out metrics for program comprehension. J. Shanghai Univ. (English Edition) **11**(5), 474–479 (2007). http://dx.doi.org/10.1007/s11741-007-0507-2
29. Wilde, N., Scully, M.C.: Software reconnaissance: mapping program features to code. J. Softw. Maintenance Res. Pract. **7**(1), 49–62 (1995)
30. Wohlin, C., Runeson, P., Höst, M., Ohlsson, M.C., Regnell, B., Wesslén, A.: Experimentation in Software Engineering: An Introduction. Kluwer Academic Publishers, Norwell (2000)

Towards the Generation of Tests in the Test Description Language from Use Case Map Models

Patrice Boulet, Daniel Amyot$^{(\boxtimes)}$, and Bernard Stepien

School of EECS, University of Ottawa, Ottawa, Canada
{pboul037,damyot,bernard}@eecs.uottawa.ca

Abstract. The Test Description Language (TDL) is an emerging standard from the European Telecommunications Standards Institute (ETSI) that targets the abstract description of tests for communicating systems and other application domains. TDL is meant to be used as an intermediate format between requirements and executable test cases. This paper explores the automated generation of TDL test descriptions from requirements expressed as Use Case Map (UCM) models. One generation mechanism, which exploits UCM scenario definitions, is prototyped in the jUCMNav tool and illustrated through an example. This transformation enables the exploration of model-based testing where the use of TDL models simplifies the generation of tests in various languages (including the Testing and Test Control Notation – TTCN-3) from UCM requirements. Remaining challenges are also discussed in the paper.

Keywords: Model-based testing · Test Description Language · Tool · Use Case Map

1 Introduction

The *Test Description Language* (TDL) [5–8] is an emerging standard of the European Telecommunications Standards Institute (ETSI) created for documenting and specifying rigorously high-level test purposes and abstract test cases. TDL is mainly intended for communication systems but can also be used in other application domains [16]. TDL can be effective in a *model-based testing* (MBT) context [15] by:

- generating TDL test descriptions from requirements (the subject of this short paper) or from behavioral models, and/or
- generating test cases from TDL in an executable testing language such as the *Testing and Test Control Notation* (TTCN-3) [9] or some scripting language.

TDL can be used by engineers who are not specialized in standard test languages (e.g., TTCN-3), and may hence help reduce their learning curve.

TDL focuses on configurations of test components and the exchange of abstract messages between them and the *System under Test* (SUT). It imports

© Springer International Publishing Switzerland 2015
J. Fischer et al. (Eds.): SDL 2015, LNCS 9369, pp. 193–201, 2015.
DOI: 10.1007/978-3-319-24912-4_14

pro-forma data type definitions and test data or test oracles definitions as templates that can be defined directly in TTCN-3. TDL supports the specification of sequences of test events, including alternate paths and parallelism. TDL is strictly a description language, i.e., it is not meant to be executable as is.

The goal of this paper is to explore the first type of MBT transformation (requirements to TDL), starting with *Use Case Map* (UCM) scenario models as input. The UCM language is part of the *User Requirements Notation* (URN) standard and focuses on causal sequence of responsibilities superimposed on a component structure [10]. UCM is selected here as this is a standard language focusing on a level of abstraction compatible with TDL's. TDL tests generated from UCM models contribute positively and rigorously to system validation at the requirements level.

This paper contributes an automated model-to-model transformation from scenarios (partial orders) extracted from UCM models to TDL test descriptions. This transformation is supported by the jUCMNav modeling environment for URN [11]. Section 2 recalls the process of extracting scenarios from UCM models, and a transformation of UCM scenario elements to TDL elements is highlighted in Sect. 3. A discussion and conclusions then follow in the last two sections.

2   UCM Scenarios

As defined in [1,10], UCM models have maps that contain any number of paths and components. *Paths* express causal sequences starting at *start points* (●) and ending at *end points* (❙), which respectively capture triggering and resulting conditions/events. Along a path, *responsibilities* (✖) describe required activities to fulfill a scenario. Paths can be combined as alternatives with guarded *OR-forks* (⌐) and merged with *OR-joins* (⌐), while *AND-forks* (⊥) and *AND-joins* (⊥) depict concurrency. Loops can be modeled implicitly with OR-joins and OR-forks. Joins and forks may be freely combined. *Waiting places* (●) and *timers* (☺) denote locations on the path where the scenario stops until a condition is satisfied. UCM models can be decomposed using *stubs* (static or dynamic ◌), that contain sub-maps. *Components* (▭) are used to specify the structural aspects of a system. Map elements that reside inside a component are said to be bound to it. Components, which can be of different types (not shown here), can also contain sub-components, recursively.

UCM models can be edited, analyzed and transformed with the jUCMNav tool [11]. One of its main features is a *UCM traversal mechanism* that takes as input a model and a *scenario definition* (start points triggered, and initial values assigned to the model variables used in OR-fork/timer/stub conditions) and produces as output a scenario that contains the UCM elements traversed [12]. Generated scenarios are partial orders containing sequenced and concurrent responsibilities only; all conditions and alternatives have been resolved during the traversal. A scenario can be used to highlight the paths traversed on the visual model itself (e.g., in red or grey). In Fig. 1, we find a model with two maps, five responsibilities, and two highlighted scenarios.

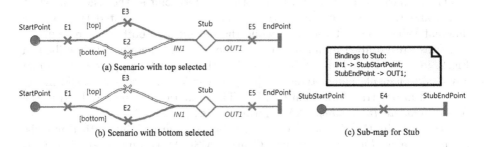

Fig. 1. UCM model with a stub and a plug-in map, with two highlighted scenarios

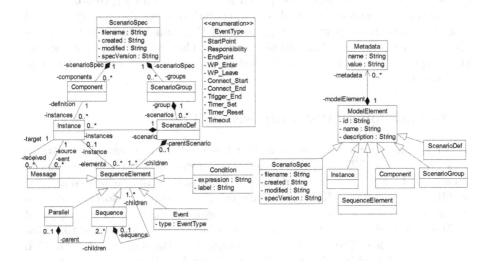

Fig. 2. Metamodel for scenarios generated from UCM models

```
<?xml version="1.0" encoding="ISO-8859-1"?>
<ucmscenarios:ScenarioSpec xmi:version="2.0" xmlns:ucmscenarios="http:///ucmscenarios.ecore" ... >
  <components id="C0" name="Environment" description="The external environment." ... />
  <components id="19" name="POTS : System"/>
  <components id="20" name="User : Actor"/>
  <groups id="21" name="ScenarioGroup5">
    <scenarios id="24" name="Top">
      <instances id="I0" name="Environment" description="The external environment." ... />
      <children xsi:type="ucmscenarios:Sequence">
        <children xsi:type="ucmscenarios:Sequence">
          <children xsi:type="ucmscenarios:Event" id="25" name="StartPoint" ... />
          <children xsi:type="ucmscenarios:Event" id="28" name="E1" type="Responsibility" ... />
          <children xsi:type="ucmscenarios:Condition" id="30" name="top" expression="Path==TOP" ... />
          <children xsi:type="ucmscenarios:Event" id="32" name="E3" type="Responsibility" ... />
          <children xsi:type="ucmscenarios:Event" id="36" name="E4" type="Responsibility" ... />
          <children xsi:type="ucmscenarios:Event" id="40" name="E5" type="Responsibility" ... />
          <children xsi:type="ucmscenarios:Event" id="27" name="EndPoint" type="EndPoint" ... />
        </children>
      </children>
    </scenarios>
```

Fig. 3. Extract of the first scenario from Fig. 1 as an instance of Fig. 2, in XMI

The scenario definitions in Fig. 1 both use StartPoint as the triggering start point, and they both set an internal variable of an enumerated type with a different value: the first uses top, while the second uses bottom. The resulting scenarios are grouped as an instance of the scenario metamodel described in Fig. 2, initially defined in [12] but refined in this paper to support *metadata* on any model element. The metadata objects are carried over from the UCM model and used in our transformation to TDL. The scenarios can be serialized in the *XML Metadata Interchange* (XMI) format (Fig. 3).

Scenarios in this format can further be transformed into other models, for example as Message Sequence Charts (MSCs), as supported by jUCM-Nav [12,14]. They are also ideal for the generation of *test purposes* as they naturally isolate classes of test behavior. The generation of tests from UCM and scenario definitions was already explored for MSCs [3] and for Web-based systems tested via Fitnesse [2]. UCM scenario definitions can also specify pre- and post-conditions and expected end points, and they can extend other scenarios (for managing complex collections of scenarios). They can help analyze and validate requirements, and they can be used as a regression test suite as the UCM model evolves.

3   Generation of Test Purposes in TDL

In our transformation, the scenario model is used as an intermediate format between UCM and TDL (see Fig. 4), and the corresponding traversal mechanism already exists in jUCMNav. We also reuse the message synthesis procedure used by Miga et al. [14] and Kealey and Amyot [12] in their transformations from scenarios to MSCs. The second and new transformation requires a mapping of UCM scenario elements to TDL elements, which is summarized for the main elements in Table 1. TDL's metamodel is available in the standard [5], and TDL models are serializable in XMI too. The resulting TDL descriptions can further be visualized with UML (mainly package and sequence diagrams) with the tool prototype developed by Makedonski et al. [13].

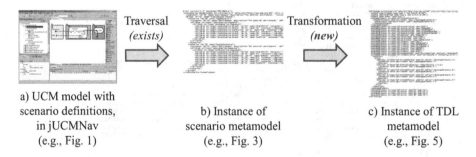

a) UCM model with
scenario definitions,
in jUCMNav
(e.g., Fig. 1)

b) Instance of
scenario metamodel
(e.g., Fig. 3)

c) Instance of TDL
metamodel
(e.g., Fig. 5)

Fig. 4. Flow of transformations from UCM to scenarios to TDL (thumbnails only)

Table 1. Supported mapping from UCM scenarios to TDL

Use case map scenario	TDL
ScenarioDef	*TestDescription* (with *Behaviour* and *Block*)
Component	*ComponentInstance* (with *ComponentType*)
Event of type Responsibility	*ActionReference* (+ *Action, Annotation, AnnotationType*)
Event of type Timer_Set	*TimerStart*
Event of type Timer_Reset	*TimerStop*
Event of type Timeout	*Timeout*
Message	*Interaction* (+ *Connection, GateInstance, GateType*)
Parallel	*ParallelBehavior* (with *Block*)

Mapping UCM Scenarios to TDL: The mapping and the model-to-model transformation from UCM scenario elements (in sans-serif) to TDL elements (in *italic*) is as follows.

UCM scenario ScenarioDef objects are mapped to *TestDescription* objects in TDL. Each scenario is exported to a single file with the name of the ScenarioDef as filename. A TDL "main" *Block* contains all the *Behaviour* of one *TestDescription*.

UCM scenario Component objects are mapped to *ComponentInstance* objects in TDL. The name attribute of a Component is also used to determine the *ComponentType* of the generated *ComponentInstance*. This name must follow the format "ComponentName : ComponentType", where ComponentName is assigned to the *name* of the generated *ComponentInstance* and ComponentType is assigned to its corresponding *ComponentType*'s name.

Responsability objects are mapped to *ActionReference* objects of a certain *Action* . Every *ActionReference* must have a *name* and a *body*, converted in TDL as *AnnotationType* named "STEP" and "PROCEDURE". Each *ActionReference* must be generated with one *Annotation* of each of these two *AnnotationTypes*.

UCM scenario Timer_Set events are mapped to *TimerStart* objects in TDL. A *TimerStart* must have a period that defines the duration of the timer from start to timeout. The *period* is transferred from the Timer_Set to *TimerStart* as a Metadata that must follow this convention: name = "period" value = "timeValue timeUnit" (e.g. "45 seconds"). Timer_Reset events are mapped to *TimerStop* objects, whereas Timeout events are mapped to *Timeout* objects.

Message objects are mapped to *Interactions*. For two *ComponentInstance* to interact, there must be a unique *Connection* between the two, which is created implicitly during the transformation. Furthermore, a *GateInstance* of a certain *GateType* is needed as attribute of each *ComponentInstance* at both ends of a *Connection*. A default *GateType* is used for every *GateInstance* as a scenario Message is synthetic and abstract, and could be refined with metadata.

Parallel objects are mapped to TDL *ParallelBehaviour* objects contained in the "main" *Block*. As the parallel parts are seen as sequences, the transformation generates one child *Block* for each parallel Sequence.

TDL Model Generation: In jUCMNav, a ScenarioSpec object is extracted with a traversal listener from the traversal mechanism and sent to the transformation algorithm that targets TDL. A TDL *Package* is then created as the parent container for other TDL objects. The new jUCMNav plug-in for generating TDL test descriptions, written in Java, consists in an application of the mapping described above. The result is a TDL model (an instance of the TDL metamodel) serialized in the XMI interchange format specified in [7]. This allows further generation of different kinds of representation such as the TDL graphical [6] or code-like textual representations. We have chosen to generate TDL in the exchange format to allow the use of both representations using further transformation tools.

The TDL XMI file consists first in a number components and declarations of elements by default, followed by a block that contains the elements of the topmost sequence of events of the scenarios. The example is Fig. 5 was produced for the top scenario from Fig. 1(a) and Fig. 1(c); note that the traversal mechanism flattens the use of submaps, so resulting scenarios and test descriptions do not have sub-scenarios. Responsibility E1 has the following scenario representation:

```
<children xsi:type="ucmscenarios:Event" id="25"name="E1"
    instance=//@groups.0/@scenarios.0/@instances.0
    type="Responsibility"/>
```

The above is translated into the following TDL element, which is part of a list of elements of a TDL block, as shown in Fig. 5:

```
<behaviour xsi:type="tdl:ActionReference" name="E1"
        action="//@packagedElements.21">
    <annotation value="gEnvironment" key="//@packagedElements.5"/>
</behaviour>
```

4   Discussion and Future Work

We have tested our implementation using several examples from existing and new UCM models of simple telephony examples, with a coverage of all the mappings from Table 1. The transformation plug-in is packaged with jUCMNav version 5.5.0 and above [11]. Documentation, examples, and videos are available online [4]. There is obviously a need to validate this transformation much further, both in terms of technical correctness and usefulness. In particular, we intend to use it in the context of an industrial project from the aerospace domain.

As we would like to eventually explore the generation of TTCN-3 test cases from TDL descriptions generated from UCM models, one issue we are facing is the absence of alternatives in the scenario metamodel (Fig. 2) targeted by jUCMNav's traversal mechanism. There exists a difference between a scenario, which is basically a (partial-order) trace in the UCM model, and a test case that can handle alternate test behavior, e.g., combinations of scenarios. While this principle is correct for forward OR-forks, from a test case point of view, this becomes incorrect when OR-fork branches return to an originating component.

```xml
<?xml version="1.0" encoding="ISO-8859-1"?>
<tdl:Package xmi:version="2.0" xmlns:tdl="http://www.etsi.org/spec/TDL/20130606" name="Top" ... >
  <comment name="Created" body="July 31, 2015 10:30:12 AM EDT"/>
  <comment name="Modified" body="July 31, 2015 10:30:12 AM EDT"/>
  <comment name="Author" body="damyot"/>
  <packagedElements xsi:type="tdl:TestConfiguration">
    <componentInstance name="Environment" type="//@packagedElements.17">
      <gateInstance name="gEnvironment" type="//@packagedElements.6"/>
    </componentInstance>
  </packagedElements>
  <packagedElements xsi:type="tdl:AnnotationType" name="STEP"/>
  <packagedElements xsi:type="tdl:AnnotationType" name="PROCEDURE"/>
  <packagedElements xsi:type="tdl:AnnotationType" name="INSTANCEREF"/>
  <packagedElements xsi:type="tdl:AnnotationType" name="ALTERNINSTANCEREF"/>
  <packagedElements xsi:type="tdl:AnnotationType" name="ACTIONINSTANCEREF"/>
  <packagedElements xsi:type="tdl:GateType" name="DefaultGT"/>
  <packagedElements xsi:type="tdl:VerdictType" name="PASS"/>
  <packagedElements xsi:type="tdl:VerdictType" name="FAIL"/>
  <packagedElements xsi:type="tdl:VerdictType" name="INCONCLUSIVE"/>
  <packagedElements xsi:type="tdl:TimeUnit" name="TICK"/>
  <packagedElements xsi:type="tdl:TimeUnit" name="NANOSECOND"/>
  <packagedElements xsi:type="tdl:TimeUnit" name="MICROSECOND"/>
  <packagedElements xsi:type="tdl:TimeUnit" name="MILLISECOND"/>
  <packagedElements xsi:type="tdl:TimeUnit" name="SECOND"/>
  <packagedElements xsi:type="tdl:TimeUnit" name="MINUTE"/>
  <packagedElements xsi:type="tdl:TimeUnit" name="HOUR"/>
  <packagedElements xsi:type="tdl:ComponentType" name="EnvironmentType" gateType="//@packagedElements.6"/>
  <packagedElements xsi:type="tdl:ComponentType" name="System" gateType="//@packagedElements.6"/>
  <packagedElements xsi:type="tdl:ComponentType" name="Actor" gateType="//@packagedElements.6"/>
  <packagedElements xsi:type="tdl:TestDescription" name="TestTop"
                    testConfiguration="//@packagedElements.0">
    <behaviour>
      <block>
        <behaviour xsi:type="tdl:ActionReference" name="E1" action="//@packagedElements.21">
          <annotation value="gEnvironment" key="//@packagedElements.5"/>
        </behaviour>
        <behaviour xsi:type="tdl:AlternativeBehaviour" name="top\nPath==TOP">
          <annotation value="gEnvironment" key="//@packagedElements.4"/>
        </behaviour>
        <behaviour xsi:type="tdl:ActionReference" name="E3" action="//@packagedElements.22">
          <annotation value="gEnvironment" key="//@packagedElements.5"/>
        </behaviour>
        <behaviour xsi:type="tdl:ActionReference" name="E4" action="//@packagedElements.23">
          <annotation value="gEnvironment" key="//@packagedElements.5"/>
        </behaviour>
        <behaviour xsi:type="tdl:ActionReference" name="E5" action="//@packagedElements.24">
          <annotation value="gEnvironment" key="//@packagedElements.5"/>
        </behaviour>
      </block>
    </behaviour>
  </packagedElements>
  <packagedElements xsi:type="tdl:Action" name="E1" body="E1"/>
  <packagedElements xsi:type="tdl:Action" name="E3" body="E3"/>
  <packagedElements xsi:type="tdl:Action" name="E4" body="E4"/>
  <packagedElements xsi:type="tdl:Action" name="E5" body="E5"/>
</tdl:Package>
```

Fig. 5. Generated TDL model (serialized in XMI) for the scenario in Fig. 3

For the simplified example of a user of a plain old telephone system (POTS) seen as a grey box (Fig. 6), the user shall receive either a connected or a busy signal upon a connection request in a single test case. Here the two separate scenarios

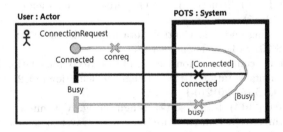

Fig. 6. Alternative responses in a simple UCM model for POTS

connected and *busy* are merged into a single test case containing an alternate behavior. This feature will be addressed in future work.

5   Conclusion

In this paper, we have explored the mapping between scenarios produced from UCM requirements models by the jUCMNav tool and abstract test descriptions in the emerging TDL standard. We provided a free online implementation of this transformation, which also enables visualization of the TDL tests in UML [4,11]. We determined the basic differences between such scenarios and test cases in the handling of alternative paths that result from UCM alternatives. We conclude that the use of scenarios for test case generation is feasible, but requires either a different traversal mechanism with a different scenario metamodel, or post-processing of scenarios to merge those that constitute alternate test behaviors. Further research is also needed on when and how (e.g., with metadata) to introduce concrete data in the generation of executable test cases in TTCN-3.

References

1. Amyot, D., Mussbacher, G.: User requirements notation: the first ten years, the next ten years. J. Softw. (JSW) **6**(5), 747–768 (2011)
2. Amyot, D., Roy, J.-F., Weiss, M.: UCM-driven testing of web applications. In: Prinz, A., Reed, R., Reed, J. (eds.) SDL 2005. LNCS, vol. 3530, pp. 247–264. Springer, Heidelberg (2005)
3. Amyot, D., Weiss, M., Logrippo, L.: UCM-based generation of test purposes. Comput. Netw. **49**(5), 643–660 (2005)
4. Boulet, P.: From UCM Scenarios to Test Description Language (TDL) with jUCM-Nav. Online documentation (2014). http://bit.ly/1GqZ1xy
5. ETSI: Methods for Testing and Specification (MTS); The Test Description Language (TDL); Part 1: Abstract Syntax and Associated Semantics. ES 203 119–1 V1.2.0 (2015)
6. ETSI: Methods for Testing and Specification (MTS); The Test Description Language (TDL); Part 2: Graphical Syntax. ES 203 119–2 V1.1.0 (2015)
7. ETSI: Methods for Testing and Specification (MTS); The Test Description Language (TDL); Part 3: Exchange Format. ES 203 119–3 V1.1.0 (2015)
8. ETSI: Methods for Testing and Specification (MTS); The Test Description Language (TDL); Part 4: Structured Test Objective Specification (Extension). ES 203 119–4 V1.1.0 (2015)
9. ETSI: The Testing and Test Control Notation version 3 - Part 1: TTCN-3 Core Language. ES 201 873–1 version 4.6.1 (2014)
10. International Telecommunication Union: ITU-T Recommendation Z.151 (10/12) - User Requirements Notation (URN) - Language definition (2012). http://www.itu.int/rec/T-REC-Z.151-201210-I
11. jUCMNav 6.0.0 (2014). http://softwareengineering.ca/jucmnav
12. Kealey, J., Amyot, D.: Enhanced use case map traversal semantics. In: Gaudin, E., Najm, E., Reed, R. (eds.) SDL 2007. LNCS, vol. 4745, pp. 133–149. Springer, Heidelberg (2007)

13. Makedonski, P., et al.: Bringing TDL to Users: A Hands-on Tutorial. UCAAT 2014, tutorial (2014). http://bit.ly/1QxlbGp
14. Miga, A., Amyot, D., Bordeleau, F., Cameron, D., Woodside, C.M.: Deriving message sequence charts from use case maps scenario specifications. In: Reed, R., Reed, J. (eds.) SDL 2001. LNCS, vol. 2078, p. 268. Springer, Heidelberg (2001)
15. Schieferdecker, I.: Model-based testing. IEEE Softw. **29**(1), 14–18 (2012)
16. Ulrich, A., et al.: The ETSI Test Description Language TDL and its Application. In: MODELSWARD 2014, pp. 601–608. SciTePress (2014)

Describing Early Security Requirements Using Use Case Maps

Jameleddine Hassine[1]([⊠]) and Abdelwahab Hamou-Lhadj[2]

[1] Department of Information and Computer Science, King Fahd University
of Petroleum and Minerals, Dhahran, Saudi Arabia
jhassine@kfupm.edu.sa
[2] Electrical and Computer Engineering Department, Concordia University,
Montréal, Canada
abdelw@ece.concordia.ca

Abstract. Non-functional requirements (NFR), such as availability, usability, performance, and security are often crucial in producing a satisfactory software product. Therefore, these non-functional requirements should be addressed as early as possible in the software development life cycle. Contrary to other non-functional requirements, such as usability and performance, security concerns are often postponed to the very end of the design process. As a result, security requirements have to be tailored into an existing design, leading to serious design challenges that usually translate into software vulnerabilities. In this paper, we present a novel approach to describe high-level security requirements using the Use Case Maps (UCM) language of the ITU-T User Requirements Notation (URN) standard. The proposed approach is based on a mapping to UCM models of a set of security architectural tactics that describe security design measures in a very general, abstract, and implementation-independent way. The resulting security extensions are described using a metamodel and implemented within the jUCMNav tool. We illustrate our approach using a UCM scenario describing the modification of consultants' pay rates.

Keywords: Goal modeling · Feature modeling · GRL · URN · Goal evaluation

1 Introduction

In the early stages of common development processes, system functionalities are defined in terms of informal requirements and visual descriptions. Scenarios are a well established approach to describe functional requirements, uncovering hidden requirements and trade-offs, as well as validating and verifying requirements. The Use Case Maps (UCM) language, part of the ITU-T User Requirements Notation (URN) standard [14], is a high-level visual scenario-based modeling language that has raised a lot of interest in recent years within the software requirements community. Use Case Maps [14] can be used to capture and integrate functional

© Springer International Publishing Switzerland 2015
J. Fischer et al. (Eds.): SDL 2015, LNCS 9369, pp. 202–217, 2015.
DOI: 10.1007/978-3-319-24912-4_15

requirements in terms of causal scenarios representing behavioral aspects at a high level of abstraction, and to provide the stakeholders with guidance and reasoning about the system-wide architecture and behavior.

Non-functional attributes such as availability, performance, and security are often overlooked during the initial system design. Clements and Northrup [4] have suggested that whether or not a system will be able to exhibit its required quality attributes (NFRs) is largely determined by the selected architecture. Hence, system architecture should address both functional and non-functional requirements.

In order to solve commonly occurring problems in software architecture, architectural patterns were introduced as a well-known reusable solution within a given context [20]. Despite their popularity, architectural patterns suffer from a number of criticisms and deficiencies. One of these weaknesses is that an architectural pattern usually addresses multiple quality attributes at once [18]. To overcome this weakness, the notion of tactics has been proposed by Bass et al. [2] as *architectural building blocks* of architectural patterns, in order to achieve quality attributes, such as availability, safety, and security. As with architectural patterns, architectural tactics emerge from practice through empirical experiments and observations.

It is well-known that software flaws are very expensive when found late in the system development life-cycle. More specifically, security vulnerabilities left in the released software may be catastrophic. Hence, there is a need to consider security from the early stages of the software development process.

The widespread interest in security modeling and analysis techniques, constitutes the major motivation of this paper. We, in particular, focus on the need to incorporate security aspects at the very early stages of system development. This work builds upon and extends our previous work on describing and assessing availability requirements using the Use Case Maps language [6–10] and the Aspect-Oriented Use Case Maps (AoUCM) [11]. This paper serves the following purposes:

- It adopts the security tactics introduced by Bass et al. [3] as a basis for extending the Use Case Maps language with security-related requirements.
- It describes a set of UCM-based security extensions using a metamodel. These extensions are implemented using the jUCMNav tool through metadata mechanism.
- It extends our ongoing research towards the construction of a UCM-based framework for the description and analysis of non-functional requirements in the early stages of system development life-cycle.

The remainder of this paper is organized as follows. The next section provides an overview of system security requirements. In Sect. 3, we present and discuss the proposed UCM-based security annotations. An example of a UCM scenario, describing the modification of consultants pay rates and annotated with security information, is presented in Sect. 5. Section 6 discusses related work, the benefits, and the shortcomings of our proposed approach. Finally, conclusions are drawn in Sect. 7.

2 Security Requirements

In the ITU-T recommendation E.800 [12], the term *'security'* is used in the sense of minimizing the vulnerabilities of assets and resources. An asset is defined as 'anything of value', while a vulnerability is defined as 'any weakness that could be exploited to violate a system or its data'. The ITU-T recommendation X.1051 [13] defines Information Security as security preservation of confidentiality, integrity, and availability of information.

Security can be characterized in terms of confidentiality (e.g., no unauthorized subject can access the content of a message), integrity (e.g., message content cannot be altered), and availability (i.e., system should be available for legitimate use). Other characteristics, such as authentication (e.g., checking the identity of a client), authorization (e.g., checking whether a client might invoke a certain operation), and non-repudiation (which refers to the accountability of the communicating parties), are used to support security [1].

Bass et al. [2] have provided a comprehensive categorization of security tactics) based on whether they address the detection of, the resistance to, and the recovery from attacks. A refined hierarchy of security tactics has been presented later in [3] by adding an additional category of tactics to deal with reacting to attacks and by refining the existing categories. Figure 1 illustrates the four classes of tactics, where the directed arrows show refinement relationships and each element represents an individual tactic:

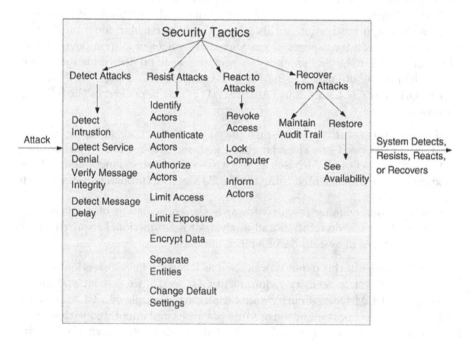

Fig. 1. Security tactics [3]

1. **Detect Attacks** category consists of four tactics:

   – *Detect intrusion* tactic refers to the ability to recognize typical attack patterns trough monitoring and analyzing both user and system/network activities. The detection intrusion tactic can be realized, for example, using a comparison of network traffic (inbound and outbound) or service requests with a set of signatures of known malicious patterns, e.g., TCP flags, payload sizes, source or destination address, port number, etc.
   – *Detect service denial* tactic refers to the ability to detect attempts to make a machine or network resource unavailable (temporarily or indefinitely) to its intended users. It can be realized, for instance, by comparing the pattern/signature of the incoming network traffic with historic profiles of known denial of service attacks.
   – *Verify message integrity* tactic employs techniques such as checksums or hash values to check the integrity of messages, resource files, and configuration files.
   – *Detect message delay* tactic is intended to detect potential man-in-the-middle (MITM) attacks, where the attacker is secretly intercepting and possibly altering the communication between two parties who believe they are directly communicating with each other. This tactic can be realized, for instance, by examining the latency of the exchanged messages.

2. **Resist Attacks** category is divided into eight tactics:
   – *Identify actors* tactic refers to the ability of identifying the source (e.g., user IDs, IP addresses, protocols, etc.) of any external input to the system.
   – *Authenticate actors* tactic ensures that an actor (a user of a computer) is who he claims to be. It can be realized, for instance, by using passwords, digital certificates, and biometric identification.
   – *Authorize actors* tactic ensures that only certain authenticated actors have access to a resource (data or service). It can be realized, for example, by specifying access control mechanisms.
   – *Limit access* tactic aims to limit the access to resources such as network connections, memory, etc. It may be achieved by blocking a host, closing a port, or rejecting a protocol.
   – *Limit exposure* tactic focuses on minimizing the attack surface. It does not proactively prevent attackers from causing harm, but tries to minimize the effect of damage. It may be achieved by having a limited number of access points for resources, data, or services.
   – *Encrypt data* tactic provides extra protection to persistently maintained data beyond that available from authorization. Encryption offers protection (e.g., through VPN or SSL) for passing data over publicly accessible communication links.
   – *Separate entities* tactic ensures the separation of different entities within a system (e.g., different servers attached to different networks). Sensitive data is usually separated from nonsensitive data to reduce the attack possibilities from those who have access to nonsensitive data.

- *Change default settings* tactic forces the user to change default settings, which will prevent attackers from gaining access to the system through settings that are, generally, publicly available.

3. **React to Attacks** category consists of three tactics:
   - *Revoke access* tactic ensures that access to sensitive resources is limited, if an attack is underway.
   - *Lock computer* tactic ensures that a limited access is granted to potentially malicious parties, for example, in case of repeated failed login attempts.
   - *Inform actors* tactic refers to the ability to notify intervening parties in case of an ongoing attack.

4. **Recover from Attacks** tactics are divided into:
   - *Service restoration* tactic ensures the recovery of the system after an attack. It may be realized through redundant hardware. Availability tactics can be deployed to achieve service restoration.
   - *Maintain audit trail* tactic is used to trace the actions of and to identify an attacker.

In this research, we adopt the above security tactics [3] as a basis for extending the Use Case Maps (UCM) language [14] with security annotations. These tactics have been proven in practice for a broad applicability in different industrial domains.

3   Security Modeling in Use Case Maps

UCMs expressed by a simple visual notation allow for an abstract description of scenarios in terms of causal relationships between responsibilities ($\times$, i.e., the steps within a scenario) along paths allocated to a set of components. UCMs help in structuring and integrating scenarios (in a map-like diagram) sequentially, as alternatives (with OR-forks/joins; ⌐/⌐), or concurrently (with AND-forks/joins; ⌐/⌐).

One of the strengths of UCMs resides in their ability to bind responsibilities to architectural components. Several kinds ot UCM components allow system entities ($\square$) to be differentiated from entities of the environment ($\female$). When maps become too complex to be represented as one single UCM, a mechanism for defining and structuring sub-maps becomes necessary. Path details can be hidden in sub-diagrams called plug-in maps, contained in stubs ($\diamond$) on a path. A plug-in map is bound (i.e., connected) to its parent map by binding the in-paths of the stub with start points ($\bullet$) of the plug-in map and by binding the out-paths of the stub to end points ($\blacksquare$) of the plug-in map. For a complete description of the Use Case Maps language, interested readers are referred to the ITU-T standard [14].

The URN standard [14] offers mechanisms in order to support the profiling of the language to a particular domain. One such mechanism is *Metadata*, which are name-value pairs that can be used to tag any URN specification or its model elements, similar to stereotypes in UML. Metadata instances provide modelers with a way to attach user-defined named values to most elements found in a URN specification, hence providing an extensible semantics to URN. A metadata is described using a name (string) and a value (string) of the URN metadata information instance.

In this paper, we propose to implement our security extensions within *jUCM-Nav* [15], the most comprehensive URN tool available to date, using the *metadata* feature. In what follows, we adopt the security tactics introduced by Bass et al. [3] as a basis for extending the Use Case Maps language with security annotations.

3.1 UCM Attack Detection Modeling

The specification of attack detection mechanisms is a key factor in implementing any security strategy. They are modeled and handled at the scenario path level, by associating the type of the deployed detection method with UCM responsibilities along the execution path.

The security requirements of a responsibility can be modeled using two metadata attributes:

1. **SecCategory:** Specifies the security category, if any, that the responsibility is implementing. This attribute may take one of the following four values: *DetectAttacks*, *ResistAttacks*, *ReactAttacks*, and *RecoverAttacks*.
2. **SecTactic:** Denotes the deployed security tactic. This attribute may take one of the seventeen defined tactics. In case the value *DetectAttacks* is selected for the *SecCategory*, one of the following four values: *DetectIntrusion*, *DetectServiceDenial*, *VerifyMessageIntegrity*, and *DetectMessageDelay* may be selected.

A detailed definition of these attributes and their possible values is described as part of the UCM security metamodel in Sect. 4.

Figure 2(a) illustrates a UCM having two parallel (implemented using a UCM AND-fork constructor) responsibilities (i.e., *RespDetectIntrusion* and *RespVerifyIntegrity*) implementing two attack detection tactics (i.e., part of the *DetectAttacks* category), namely, *DetectIntrusion* and *VerifyMessageIntegrity* (see Fig. 2(b)).

Dealing with an attack (e.g., resist, react to, or recover from an attack) after its detection is modeled using failure scenario paths as described in the following sections.

3.2 UCM Attack Resistance, Reaction, and Recovery Modeling

Given the fact that we have adequate detection mechanisms in place to detect potential attacks, a system may be able to resist the ongoing attack. In the case of an unsuccessful resistance, a system may be able to react to the attack. Finally, the system may be compromised (e.g., resources compromised, lost data, etc.). In such a case, the system should be able to recover from the attack.

In the context of Use Case Maps, the realization of the resistance, reaction, and recovery tactics can be assured by:

Component

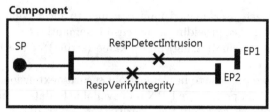

(a) UCM Attack Detection Modeling

RespDetectIntrusion:

Metadata	Name	Value
Advanced	SecCategory	DetectAttacks
	SecTactic	DetectIntrusion

RespVerifyIntegrity:

Metadata	Name	Value
Advanced	SecCategory	DetectAttacks
	SecTactic	VerifyMessageIntegrity

(b) Attack Detection Metadata Attributes

Fig. 2. UCM attack detection modeling

- The definition of metadata attributes, attached to responsibilities, targeting the resistance (i.e., *ResistAttacks*), reaction (i.e., *ReackAttacks*), and recovery (i.e., *RecoverAttacks*) categories. Similarly to the attack detection modeling, the resistance, reaction, and recovery can be modeled using *SecCategory* and *SecTactic* metadata attributes.
- The definition of a hierarchical structure (using UCM static stubs) of cascading failure scenario paths. A failure scenario path starts with a failure start point (**❶**) and a guarding condition (see Fig. 3(a), (c) and (d)). The guard condition can be initialized as part of a scenario definition (i.e., scenario triggering condition) or can be modified as part of a responsibility expression.

Figure 3 illustrates a generic UCM map with a main scenario starting at start point SP1 and executing responsibilities R1 and R2. Responsibility R1 implements the *DetectIntrusion* tactic, part of the *DetectAttacks* category. A successful detection of an intrusion triggers a failure scenario path, by setting the failure guard *R1-AttackDetected* to true. Responsibility *R1* may execute the following code:

```
if (R1_AttDetected)
    R1-AttackDetected := true;
else
    R1-AttackDetected := false;
```

where R1_AttDetected is a Boolean variable that can be initialized as part of a scenario definition.

However, the addition of metadata to responsibilities requires a change to the standard UCM traversal mechanism because a path may have to be stopped at a responsibility and continued at a failure start point.

The execution of the failure path leads to the execution of a plugin embedded in the static stub *R1-ResistReactRecover* (see Fig. 3(c)) starting at start point SP2 and executes responsibility R3 that realizes the *LimitAccess* attack resistance tactic.

An unsuccessful resistance to the intrusion attack would trigger a failure path that starts at failure start point *R3-AttackResistedFailed* and executes the *R3-ReactRecover* stub (see Fig. 3(d) illustrates its corresponding plugin). Responsibility R4 models the *RevokeAccess* tactic, part of the *ReactAttacks* category.

A failure to react to the attack triggers a failure scenario path that executes the *R4-Recover* plugin. Responsibility *R5* implements the *Restore* tactic, part of the *RecoverAttacks* category. The *Restore* tactic is refined using availability tactics (see Fig. 1). In general, availability focuses mainly on redundancy modeling in order to keep the system available. The UCM of Fig. 3(a) illustrates two components C1 and C2 participating in a 1+1 hot redundancy configuration. *C1* is in active role, while *C2* is in standby role. None of these two components is taking part in a voting activity (i.e., Voting : *false*). For a detailed description of the UCM-based availability tactics, interested readers are referred to [7].

Figure 3(e) shows the metadata corresponding to responsibilities R1, R3, R4, R5, and components C1 and C2.

It is worth noting that a system might not implement all categories of tactics (i.e., resist, react, and recover categories). In such a case, the UCM cascading hierarchy may be reduced to one or two levels only. The example in Sect. 5 illustrates such a case.

4   UCM Security-Enabled Metamodel

In this section, we describe our UCM-based security extensions using an abstract grammar metamodel. The concrete grammar metamodel, which includes metaclasses of the graphical layout of UCM elements, is not discussed in this paper since they have no semantic implications.

Figure 4 illustrates an excerpt of the UCM language core abstract metamodel augmented with security and availability concepts. *UCMspec* serves as a container for the UCM specification elements such as *Component* and *Responsibility*. Path-related (e.g., AND-Fork, OR-Fork, etc.) and plugin binding-related concepts are not shown because they do not impact our security and availability extensions.

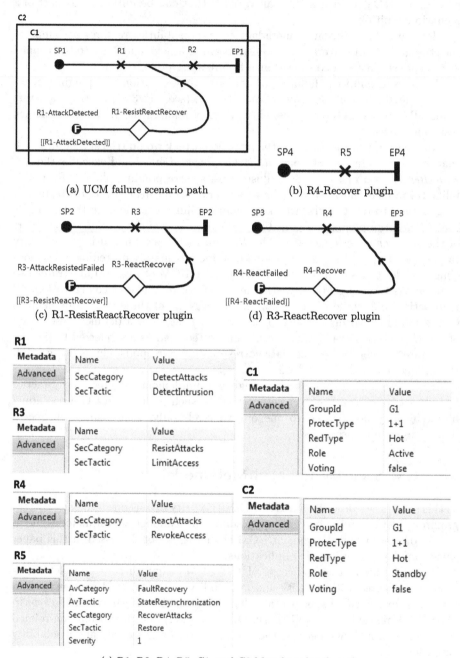

(a) UCM failure scenario path   (b) R4-Recover plugin

(c) R1-ResistReactRecover plugin   (d) R3-ReactRecover plugin

(e) R1, R3, R4, R5, C1, and C2 Metadata Attributes

Fig. 3. UCM modeling of attack resistance, reaction, and recovery

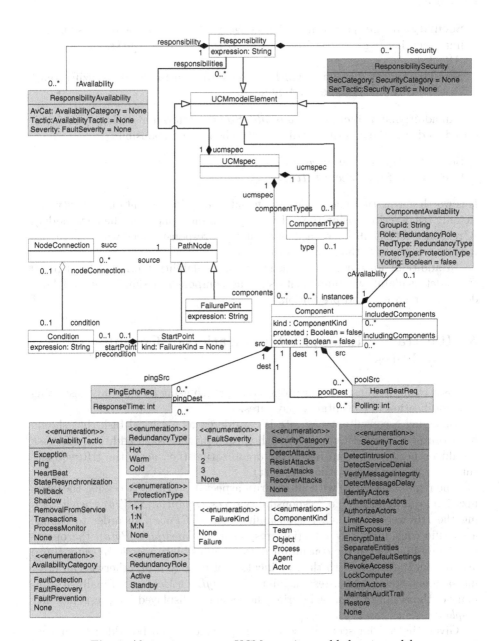

Fig. 4. Abstract grammar: UCM security-enabled metamodel

Two new security-related enumeration metaclasses (shown in dark grey) are introduced:

- **SecurityCategory:** Specifies the category of the tactic a responsibility is implementing (e.g., *DetectAttacks*, *ResistAttacks*, *ReactAttacks*, and *Recover-Attacks*).
- **SecurityTactic:** Specifies which tactic a responsibility is realizing (e.g., *DetectIntrusion*, *AuthenticateActors*, etc.)

An additional metaclass *ResponsibilitySecurity* (shown in dark grey) is introduced to define the security attributes attached to a responsibility:

- **SecCategory** of type *SecurityCategory*.
- **SecTactic** of type *SecurityTactic*.

It is worth noting that one single responsibility may implement one security tactic only (as described using the 0..1 relationship multiplicity in the metamodel). A responsibility shall be refined into multiple responsibilities when there is a need to realize more than one security tactic.

In addition, we reuse the existing set of availability tactics, defined in [7] to model availability requirements such as component redundancy, and fault detection, recovery, and prevention.

5   Illustrative Example: Modification of Consultants' Pay Rates

In this section, we illustrate our proposed approach using a case study describing the modification of consultants' pay rates.

Changing a consultant pay rate is considered as a critical task that should be performed by an HR employee with special privileges. In addition, this task should be performed from inside the organization (i.e., acess the HR web site through the local organization intranet).

The regular scenario (without security aspects), starts by accessing the organization local web page (i.e., responsibility *accessOrganizationWeb*), then accessing the HR web page (i.e., responsibility *accessHRPage*). In order to change a specific consultant pay rate (i.e., responsibility *modifyPayRate*), the operator should first search the consultant data (responsibility *searchConsultantInfo*) and if found proceeds with the modification of his pay rate, otherwise an error message is displayed (i.e., responsibility *DisplayErrorMessage*). Finally, a summary of the actions performed during the session is displayed (i.e., responsibility *displaySessionSummary*).

Given the regular scenario, security requirements can be added by attaching metadata attributes, describing security-related information, to the system responsibilities, and by adding corresponding failure scenario paths.

A potential attacker accessing the HR page from outside the organization (using an intermediate proxy) may result in some delay. The detection of such

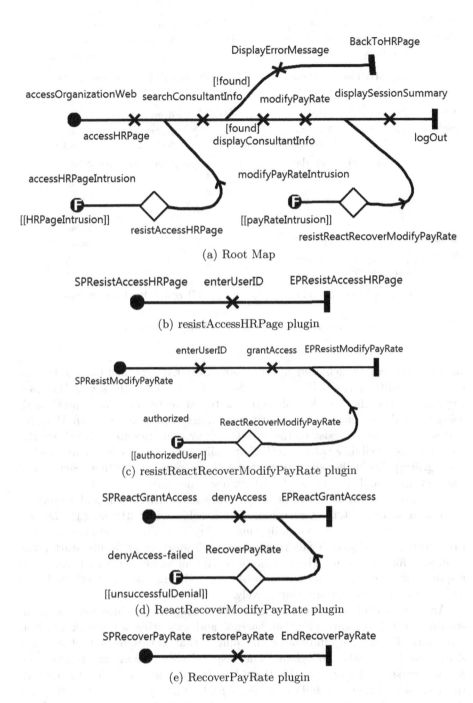

(a) Root Map

(b) resistAccessHRPage plugin

(c) resistReactRecoverModifyPayRate plugin

(d) ReactRecoverModifyPayRate plugin

(e) RecoverPayRate plugin

Fig. 5. Modify consultant pay rate scenario

Metadata	Name	Value
Advanced	SecCategory	DetectAttacks
	SecTactic	DetectMessageDelay

(a) accessHRPage metadata

Metadata	Name	Value
Advanced	SecCategory	DetectAttacks
	SecTactic	DetectIntrusion

(b) modifyPayRate metadata

Metadata	Name	Value
Advanced	SecCategory	ResistAttacks
	SecTactic	AuthenticateActors

(c) enterUserID metadata

Metadata	Name	Value
Advanced	SecCategory	ResistAttacks
	SecTactic	AuthorizeActors

(d) grantAccess metadata

Metadata	Name	Value
Advanced	SecCategory	ReactAttacks
	SecTactic	RevokeAccess

(e) denyAccess metada

Metadata	Name	Value
Advanced	AvCategory	FaultRecovery
	AvTactic	Rollback
	SecCategory	RecoverAttacks
	SecTactic	Restore
	Severity	2

(f) restorePayRate metada

Fig. 6. Responsibilities metadata information

an intrusion can be achieved by attaching *DetectAttacks* metadata attribute to responsibility *accessHRPage* (i.e., *SecTactic = DetectMessageDelay*) (see Fig. 6(a)). Once the attack is detected, a tentative to resist it is performed, using the failure scenario path starting at failure start point *accessHRPageIntrusion*). In order to resist to the attack, the system tries to authenticate the user (i.e., responsibility *enterUserID* that realizes the *AuthenticateActors* tactic, see Fig. 6(c)). No further security related actions are taken (neither reaction nor recovery are modeled), in case the attack resistance fails.

The modification of a consultant pay rate is a critical task and requires a protection against potential intrusions. This is achieved by attaching the *DetectIntrusion* tactic to the responsibility *modifyPayRate*. The detection of a malicious intrusion, triggers a failure scenario path starting at failure start point *modifyPayRateIntrusion*. The resistance to the intrusion is realized using two responsibilities *enterUserID* and *grantAccess* realizing, the *AuthenticateActors* and *AuthorizeActors* tactics, respectively.

An unsuccessful resistance to the intrusion, triggers a failure scenario path, starting at failure start point *authorized* and executing an attack reaction procedure. Figure 5(d), illustrates the plugin that corresponds to the static stub *ReactRecoverModifyPayRate*. The responsibility *denyAccess* realizes the *RevokeAccess* tactic, part of the *ReactAttacks* category. A failure to react to the intrusion, triggers a failure scenario path starting at failure start point *denyAccess-failed* and executes the plugin of the static stub *RecoverPayRate*. Finally, responsibility *restorePayRate* realizes the *Restore* tactic, which also realizes the *Rollback* availability tactic (part of the *FaultRecovery* availability tactic).

6   Discussion

The need to consider security aspects during the early stages of the system development has been recognized by the requirements engineering community. Many techniques and methods have been proposed in the literature [5,16,17,19]. Misuse cases [19], abuse cases [17], and security use cases [5] are security-oriented variants of regular use cases. Unlike regular use cases that describe normal interactions between an application and its users, misuse cases [19] and abuse cases [17] concentrate on interactions between the application and its misusers (i.e., potential attackers) who seek to violate its security requirements. These interactions are harmful to the system, one of the actors, or one of the stakeholders in the system. Security use cases [5] describe countermeasures intended to respond these attacks.

The most closely related work to ours is the one by Karpati et al. [16]. The authors have introduced the notion of *Misuse Case Maps (MUCM)* as a modeling technique that is the anti-behavioral complement to Use Case Maps, which is used to visualize how cyber attacks are performed in an architectural context. Karpati et al. [16] introduced a new set of symbols to visualize potential attack scenarios. These symbols are used to model exploit paths, vulnerable parts (points and responsibilities), misuser actions (using arrows specifying getting/putting/deleting/destroying components), etc. Our approach is different from the one presented in [16] with respect to two points:

- In our work, we view security requirements as assets and services that have to be protected against possible attacks. Hence, our goal is to guard functional behavior against potential threats. This is achieved by attaching security requirements, as metadata attributes, to vulnerable responsibilities. In addition, defense mechanisms are implemented using failure scenario paths. We have used the security tactics to build a secure development approach simpler and faster than methodologies based on threats modeling.
- A UCM describes with precision the functional behavior of a system. However, we don't know precisely how an attacker will break the system security. If such an information is available, the vulnerabilities would have been fixed. In our approach, we specify the types of measures (using the security tactics) that the system should implement in order to detect, resist, react to, and recover from an attack. Once, the threat details are available, they can be integrated within the scenario as functional behavior.

Our proposed approach relies primarily on the security tactics introduced by Bass et al. [3]. One possible threat to the validity of our approach is related to the maturity of these tactics. Indeed, a tactic is considered to be a relatively new design concept that complements the existing architectural and design patterns [18]. However, we believe that these tactics provide a comprehensive coverage of security means, that are general and flexible enough to accommodate various security requirements.

Several attempts have been proposed to revise the set of security tactics initially introduced by Bass et al. [2]. Ryoo et al. [18] have proposed a methodology for revising security tactics hierarchy through derivation, decomposition, and reclassification. However, in order to accommodate the addition of a new tactic or the refinement of an existing one, only minor changes to the UCM security-enabled metamodel are required.

7   Conclusions and Future Work

In this work, we have modeled security requirements at the very early stages of the system development process, before committing to a detailed design. We have extended the Use Case Maps language with security-related features covering the well-known security tactics by Bass et al. [3]. The resulting extensions are described using a metamodel and implemented into the *jUCMNav* tool using the metadata mechanism, allowing for further model refinement and a smooth move towards more detailed design models.

As a future work, we aim at evaluating empirically our approach using real-world case studies. In addition, we plan to conduct a qualitative analysis of the efficiency of the proposed UCM-based security requirements.

Acknowledgment. The authors would like to acknowledge the support provided by the Deanship of Scientific Research at King Fahd University of Petroleum & Minerals (KFUPM) for funding this work through project No. IN131031.

References

1. Avizienis, A., Laprie, J.C., Randell, B., Landwehr, C.: Basic concepts and Taxonomy of dependable and secure computing. IEEE Trans. Dependable Secure Comput. **1**(1), 11–33 (2004)
2. Bass, L., Clements, P., Kazman, R.: Software Architecture in Practice, 2nd edn. Addison-Wesley Longman Publishing Co., Inc, Boston (2003)
3. Bass, L., Clements, P., Kazman, R.: Software Architecture in Practice, 3rd edn. Addison-Wesley Professional, Boston (2012)
4. Clements, P., Northrop, L.: Software architecture: an executive overview. Technical report, CMU/SEI-96-TR-003, Software Engineering Institute, Carnegie Mellon University, Pittsburgh, PA (1996). http://resources.sei.cmu.edu/library/asset-view.cfm?AssetID=12509
5. Firesmith, D.: Security use cases. J. Object Technol. **2**(1), 53–64 (2003). http://dx.doi.org/10.5381/jot.2003.2.3.c6
6. Hassine, J.: Early availability requirements modeling using use case maps. In: Eighth International Conference on Information Technology: New Generations (ITNG), Las Vegas, Nevada, USA, pp. 754–759, April 2011
7. Hassine, J.: Describing and assessing availability requirements in the early stages of system development. Softw. Syst. Model., 1–25 (2013). http://dx.doi.org/10.1007/s10270-013-0382-0

8. Hassine, J., Gherbi, A.: Exploring early availability requirements using use case maps. In: Ober, I., Ober, I. (eds.) SDL 2011. LNCS, vol. 7083, pp. 54–68. Springer, Heidelberg (2011). http://dx.doi.org/10.1007/978-3-642-25264-8_6

9. Hassine, J., Hamou-Lhadj, A.: Towards the generation of AMF configurations from use case maps based availability requirements. In: Khendek, F., Toeroe, M., Gherbi, A., Reed, R. (eds.) SDL 2013. LNCS, vol. 7916, pp. 36–53. Springer, Heidelberg (2013). http://dx.doi.org/10.1007/978-3-642-38911-5_3

10. Hassine, J., Hamou-Lhadj, A.: Toward a UCM-based approach for recovering system availability requirements from execution traces. In: Amyot, D., Fonseca i Casas, P., Mussbacher, G. (eds.) SAM 2014. LNCS, vol. 8769, pp. 48–63. Springer, Heidelberg (2014). http://dx.doi.org/10.1007/978-3-319-11743-0_4

11. Hassine, J., Mussbacher, G., Braun, E., Alhaj, M.: Modeling early availability requirements using aspect-oriented use case maps. In: Khendek, F., Toeroe, M., Gherbi, A., Reed, R. (eds.) SDL 2013. LNCS, vol. 7916, pp. 54–71. Springer, Heidelberg (2013). http://dx.doi.org/10.1007/978-3-642-38911-5_4

12. ITU-T: E.800: Definitions of Terms Related to Quality of Service, September 2008. https://www.itu.int/rec/dologin_pub.asp?lang=e&id=T-REC-E.800-200809-I!!PDF-E&type=items. Accessed 15 June 2015

13. ITU-T: X.1051: Information Technology - Security Techniques - Information Security Management Guidelines for Telecommunications Organizations Based on ISO/IEC 27002, February 2008. https://www.itu.int/rec/dologin_pub.asp?lang=e&id=T-REC-X.1051-200802-I!!PDF-E&type=items. Accessed 15 June 2015

14. ITU-T: Recommendation Z.151 (10/12), User Requirements Notation (URN) Language Definition, Geneva, Switzerland (2012). http://www.itu.int/rec/T-REC-Z.151/en

15. jUCMNav: jUCMNav Project, v6.0.0 (Tool, Documentation, and Meta-model) (2014). http://softwareengineering.ca/jucmnav

16. Karpati, P., Sindre, G., Opdahl, A.L.: Visualizing cyber attacks with misuse case maps. In: Wieringa, R., Persson, A. (eds.) REFSQ 2010. LNCS, vol. 6182, pp. 262–275. Springer, Heidelberg (2010). http://dx.doi.org/10.1007/978-3-642-14192-8_24

17. McDermott, J., Fox, C.: Using abuse case models for security requirements analysis. In: Proceedings of the 15th Annual Computer Security Applications Conference. pp. 55–64. ACSAC '99, IEEE Computer Society, Washington, DC, USA (1999). http://dl.acm.org/citation.cfm?id=784590.784691

18. Ryoo, J., Laplante, P., Kazman, R.: Revising a security tactics hierarchy through decomposition, reclassification, and derivation. In: Software Security and Reliability Companion (SERE-C), IEEE Sixth International Conference (June 2012), pp. 85–91 (2012)

19. Sindre, G., Opdahl, A.: Eliciting security requirements with misuse cases. Requirements Eng. **10**(1), 34–44 (2005). http://dx.doi.org/10.1007/s00766-004-0194-4

20. Taylor, R.N., Medvidovic, N., Dashofy, E.M.: Software Architecture: Foundations, Theory, and Practice. Wiley, New Jersey (2009)

Model-Based Testing

Generating Configurations for System Testing with Common Variability Language

Daisuke Shimbara[1]($^{\boxtimes}$) and Øystein Haugen[2,3]

[1] Research & Development Group, Hitachi, Ltd.,
Yokohama-shi, Kanagawa-ken, Japan
daisuke.shimbara.gk@hitachi.com
[2] Østfold University College, Halden, Norway
[3] SINTEF ICT, Oslo, Norway
Oystein.Haugen@hiof.no

Abstract. Modern systems are composed of many subsystems, so it is necessary to understand how to combine them into complete functional systems. When testing a system that includes hardware, it is important that each selected test configuration delivers maximum information for covering many test cases. We have developed a method and a tool for creating a small set of effective test configurations that is based on a systematic approach to describing and formalizing the functionality of the whole system as well as its component into subsystems using feature models and relational notations between them. We applied our approach to an example point-of-sale checkout system consisting of one server and multiple registers.

Keywords: Feature modeling · System testing · Common Variability Language

1 Introduction

Modern systems are composed of multiple subsystems. These subsystems cannot provide functionality in isolation. They are connected to each other and provide functionality in a coordinated manner. Each subsystem provide a subfunctionality or role, such as server and client, in the system. Subsystems may have been developed as software product line in its own right defined by a variation model. A system may provide multiple subsystems for each role. In many cases, combinations of subsystems are not well defined because of the combination of multiplicity and variation.

We focus on testing a configurable system composed of multiple subsystems with variation. The system testing process is based on the fact that the system is constructed by combining subsystems. The purpose of the whole system is described by the set of system test. Each system test case needs an appropriate configuration of the system to be meaningful. We have to ensure that we find a set of configurations that are sufficient to execute all the system tests.

© Springer International Publishing Switzerland 2015
J. Fischer et al. (Eds.): SDL 2015, LNCS 9369, pp. 221–237, 2015.
DOI: 10.1007/978-3-319-24912-4_16

The theoretical maximum number of configurations is the number of all combinations of the various subsystems. How to combine the subsystems into these various combinations is tacit knowledge that is held by expert developers and not explicitly documented. Therefore, the creation of configurations for system testing requires considerable time resources from busy expert developers. Furthermore, the configurations they suggest may not cover all the test cases since the ability to identify all required configurations normally goes beyond what a human expert can handle. In addition, if the suggested configurations are generated for the respective test cases, the cost of physically changing the system when running the test cases can be huge. What is needed is the smallest set of configurations that cover all test cases.

We have developed a method for generating a small set of configurations that cover all test cases for system testing and a tool implementing this method. The variability of subsystems as well as the variability of the whole system are described by variability models in the form of feature models. We describe the relationships between the variability of the whole system and the those of the subsystems through a dedicated relational notation. The tool provides editors of the variability models and the relational notation with a validation checker. The tool also provides a function for generating configurations from the models. Our method uses the Common Variability Language (CVL) [4] as a feature model and an SMT solver as the configuration generator.

We address following research questions:

RQ1. Can the method generate a small set of configurations that cover all test cases?

RQ2. Can the method elicit and formalize the tacit knowledge needed for combining subsystems?

RQ3. Is the execution time for the generation sufficiently low?

2   Common Variability Language

The CVL is a domain-independent language for specifying and resolving variability. The specifications of CVL are currently being standardized [9]. We use the VSpec model for variability representation and the resolution model for selecting of the variability from the CVL.

2.1   VSpec

The VSpec model has a tree structure and is similar to feature models [7]. The VSpec node types are 'Choice,' 'VClassifier,' 'Variable,' and 'CVSpec' as well as 'Constraints.' A Choice node corresponds to a feature and is shown as a rounded rectangle. A solid line from the parent means that the Choice node is implied by the parent. A dashed line means that is not implied by the parent. A VClassifier node includes an instance multiplicity factor that shows how many instances of it may be created. This node is shown as a rectangle with upper and lower limits. Choice and VClassifier nodes may have a group multiplicity factor to specify how many choices must be selected among its children in the tree. The group multiplicity factor is depicted as a triangle. A Variable node is shown as an ellipse and has a primitive type, e.g., integer. A CVSpec node has a reference to another VSpec structure. In this paper, a CVSpec node is shown as a rounded rectangle with hatching. A VSpec node may have associated constraints which can be described with OCL [10] or Basic Constraint Language (which is defined inside the CVL language itself).

2.2 Resolution

The resolution model has a tree structure that mirrors that of the VSpec model and represents selection of the variations of VSpec. The resolution node types are 'ChoiceResolution,' 'VInstance,' and 'ValueAssignment.' A ChoiceResolution node refers to a Choice node and the decision of 'True' or 'False' for that node. A VInstance node is an instance of a VClassifier node and refer to the VClassifier node. The number of VInstance nodes is limited by the multiplicity defined for the VClassifier node. A ValueAssignment node refers to a Variable node and assigns a specific value. In this paper, we use a table to combine the several resolution models into one view for better understanding.

3   Motivating Example

To show how the tool performs its task, we introduce a running example, a point-of-sale (POS) checkout system composed of one shop server and multiple registers like those typically found in a supermarket.

We assume that there are two teams of developers: the shop server development team and the register development team. Each team discusses and defines the specifications for the products in their portion of the system. The two teams jointly discuss the communication protocol used between the server and registers. Each product has variations and is developed as a product line in its own right.

Figure 1a shows the register variation model defined by the register development team using VSpec. There are four categories of variation: 'Card Reader,' 'Communication Protocol,' 'Currency,' and 'SelfCheckout.' 'Credit Card' and 'Bank Card' are options of Card Reader. The Communication Protocol has two versions: 'Old' and 'New.' New Protocol was introduced because Old Protocol cannot cope with some of the functionalities added after it was defined. Each register can handle only one currency. There are two possible currencies: the Norwegian krone (NOK) and the Japanese yen (JPY). SelfCheckout means that the register is not handled by a clerk but rather customers handle checkout themselves. Table 1a summarizes the variations in the register products. The rows show products of registers, the columns show the nodes of VSpec, and the 'X' means node selection for the product.

Fig. 1. VSpec models

Table 1. Resolution models

(a) Register

Product	Card Reader		Protocol		Currency		Self-
	Credit Card	Bank Card	New	Old	NOK	JPY	Checkout
Reg-Classic-N				X	X		
Reg-Standard-N	X	X		X	X		
Reg-Advance-N	X	X	X		X		
Reg-Self-N	X		X		X		X
Reg-Classic-J				X		X	
Reg-Standard-J	X			X		X	
Reg-Advance-J	X	X	X			X	

(b) Shop server

Product	Transaction			Protocol		Currency	
	Credit	Debit	Banking	New	Old	NOK	JPY
SS-Classic-N	X				X	X	
SS-Debit-N	X	X			X	X	
SS-MiniBank-N	X	X	X	X		X	
SS-Classic-J	X				X		X
SS-Debit-J		X			X		X
SS-Advance-NJ	X	X		X		X	X

The shop server development team defined the shop server variation model shown in Fig. 1b. There are three categories of variations: 'Transaction,' 'Communication Protocol,' and 'Currency.' These are similar to those of the register variation model, but there are significant differences. One difference concerns Transaction. While the register developers consider which kind of card can be read by the register and define Credit and Bank Card variations, the shop server developers consider which kinds of card transaction can be processed by the shop server. They therefore define three options: 'Credit Transaction with Credit Card,' 'Debit Transaction with Bank Card,' and 'Banking Transaction (to withdraw cash) with Bank Card.' Another difference concerns the multiplicity factor for Currency. One register cannot handle multiple currencies because physical cash is stored in the register. The server, on the other hand, can handle multiple currencies because it simply processes information about money. The final difference is that there is no SelfCheckout concept for the shop server. Table 1b summarizes the shop server products.

In industrial system testing processes, test cases are most often described in natural language and are designed without much consideration for how the system needs to be configured. We define the following 5 test cases for our motivating example:

TestCase1. Check that shop server using New Protocol can simultaneously communicate with registers using New protocol and registers using Old Protocol.

TestCase2. Check Banking Transaction.

TestCase3. Check Debit Transaction for NOK.

TestCase4. In a system that can work as Mini Bank, check that Credit Card Transaction works correctly for all registers with Mixed protocol.

TestCase5. In a system that has more than two self lanes, check Credit Card Transaction works correctly.

Our aim is to find the smallest set of configurations that are sufficient to execute all these five test cases. These informal tests need to be formalized into executable test cases. A domain specialist interviews both developer teams to identify the relationships between the two subsystems. From the information obtained, the domain specialist makes explicit the tacit knowledge:

1. All the registers and the shop server in a system must use the same currency.
2. A shop server using New Protocol can communicate with a register using Old Protocol. A register using New Protocol CANNOT communicate with a shop server using Old Protocol.
3. Banking Transactions require New Protocol communication between the register and shop server

A novice engineer trying to create configurations for the test cases would likely suggest invalid configurations. For Test Case 2, a novice may select the SS-MiniBank-N and Reg-Standard-N products because SS-MiniBank-N covers Banking Transaction and Reg-Standard-N covers Bank Card. However, Reg-Standard-N does not use New Protocol, and the tacit knowledge 3 shows New Protocol is required for Banking Transaction. This configuration is thus invalid for Test Case 2.

Our motivating example shows that test cases and associated tacit knowledge must be made explicit and formalized in order to automate the generation of configurations.

4 Proposed Method

As described in the introduction, our proposed method uses CVL as feature model for generating a set of configurations that cover all test cases. Various types of information such as subsystem specifications, system structure, and test cases are needed for the generation, and it is impractical to describe them all together. Therefore, as shown in Fig. 2, we defined three components: the individual subsystems, the connections, and the system.

The method comprises six processes: 1 subsystem feature analysis, 2 structure analysis, 3 system feature analysis, 4 test case formalization, 5 relational analysis, and 6 configuration generation. Processes 1–5 are performed manually, and we have developed a tool to support these processes and validate their results. The process 6 is performed by the tool automatically (Fig. 8).

4.1 Subsystem Feature Analysis

We specify the types of subsystems that compose a system. Register and shop server in our running example are representative subsystems. For each type, the

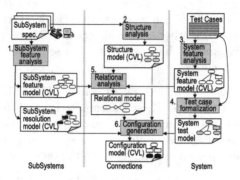

Fig. 2. Overview of proposed method

subsystem developers establish a VSpec model and a resolution model of the subsystem. The developers find these models by using for example the domain analysis method [7]. This process step focuses on each subsystem without any consideration of the whole system.

The VSpec register model is shown in Fig. 1a, and the corresponding resolution model is shown in Table 1a. The Vspec shop server model is shown in Fig. 1b, and the corresponding resolution model is shown in Table 1b.

4.2   Structure Analysis

In the structure analysis process, how the subsystems combine into a system is defined using a VSpec tree as the structure model. In our method the tree can only have three node levels: a root of Choice, VClassifier children of the root, and CVSpec grandchildren under the VClassifier children. The VClassifier level shows how many subsystems under the VClassifier can be contained by the system. The CVSpec refers to the type of subsystem. This process step may cover radically different kinds of subsystems. Figure 3b shows the structure model for the motivating example (Fig. 3a). There is one shop server and one or more registers in the shop system.

Even though our structure model is restricted to three levels, it can describe systems of systems. The CVSpec can refer to any system as a subsystem. If the shop in our motivating example belongs to a supermarket chain and there

(a) Example   (b) Structure model

Fig. 3. POS checkout system

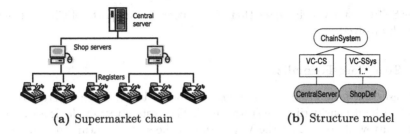

(a) Supermarket chain   (b) Structure model

Fig. 4. System of systems

is a central server that controls the individual shop systems (Fig. 4a), the top level structure model is as shown as Fig. 4b. The ShopDef module refers to the subsystem shown in Fig. 3b.

4.3 System Feature Analysis

A system feature model is used to analyze the variability of the system as a whole. The VSpec is used as the system feature model. The structure model described in the previous process also uses the VSpec for the system. However, the structure model means physical variability that describes which and how many subsystems compose the system. The system feature model describes features from the perspective of the whole system independently of the subsystems. Creation of the system feature model ideally follows the domain analysis method [7] in the same way as the subsystem feature analysis.

Figure 5 shows the result of the system feature analysis for our motivating example. MiniBank means that it is possible to withdraw and deposit money into a bank account in the shop. Selling has three methods of payment. Cash must be supported while Credit and Debit are optional. Protocol has a new third choice, Mixed, meaning the case in which a shop server using New Protocol is connected to at least one register using Old Protocol plus at least one register using New Protocol. This case represents the formalization of tacit knowledge described as 2 in Sect. 3. The tacit knowledge described as 1 is formalized as a multiplicity under Currency and means that the system can handle only one currency. VClassifier VC-Lane indicates the instance multiplicity of queues for registers.

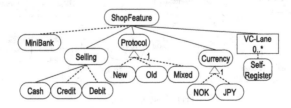

Fig. 5. System feature model

It has SelfRegister which means that the register can support SelfCheckout with
no clerk involved.

4.4 Test Case Formalization

Test cases are formalized as a system test model based on the system feature
model without considering the subsystems. The system test model is a variation
model narrowed down from the VSpec tree of the system feature model, and its
structure is a modified replica of the system feature model. A TestChoice (TC)
is created for each choice in the system feature model. The TC has a decision
property with three values: 'True' (T), 'False' (F), and 'Don'tCare' (*), which is
the default. When a test case is read, the choice implied by the test case is found,
and the decision value is set as 'True' or 'False' for the corresponding TC. The
system test model created for Test Case 1 of motivating example is shown in
Fig. 6a. TC-Mixed is set as 'True,' which corresponds to the choice Mixed in the
system feature model. TC-New and TC-Old are deduced to be 'False' because
of the multiplicity constraint of TC-Protocol when TC-Mixed is 'True.' We do
not bother to add this deduced information to the test model because this will
be sorted out eventually by the tool anyway.

For each VClassifier in the system feature model, the system test model has
a TestVClassifier (TV) node. TV is the multiplicity constraint of VInstance,
which is specified by the subtree of TV. Figure 6b shows the tree for the system

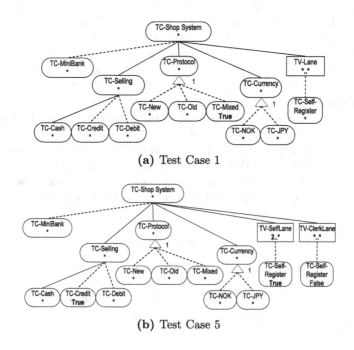

(a) Test Case 1

(b) Test Case 5

Fig. 6. System test models

Table 2. System test models

Test Case	Mini Bank	Transaction		Protocol			Currency		TV-SelfLane
		Credit	Debit	New	Old	Mixed	NOK	JPY	
1	*	*	*	*	*	T	*	*	*..*
2	T	*	*	*	*	*	*	*	*..*
3	*	*	T	*	*	*	T	*	*..*
4	T	T	*	*	*	T	*	*	*..*
5	*	T	*	*	*	*	*	*	2..*

test model for Test Case 5. TV-SelfLane specifies more than two VInstances and the subtree has 'True' for SelfRegister. This model shows that the system for Test Case 5 should have more than two VInstances that have SelfRegister functionality. The test cases are summarized in Table 2. Mandatory or middle position choices are not shown.

4.5 Relational Analysis

With the processes so far, we can describe subsystem feature models, subsystem resolution models, a system structure model, a system feature model, and test case models. Now we need to identify a set of subsystem resolution models as a configuration for each test case model. A subsystem resolution model is narrowed from the subsystem feature model and the test case model is narrowed from the system feature model. Therefore, the relationships between the subsystem feature model and the system feature model are needed. In addition, since a system includes multiple subsystems, the relationships should describe the multiplicity differences. We thus define a notation for the relationships that complement CVL.

The relational notations are defined using BNF:

$$
\begin{aligned}
\langle relation \rangle &::= \langle systemRef \rangle + \\
\langle systemRef \rangle &::= \langle systemVSpec \rangle \, \langle context \rangle ? \, \langle orComp \rangle * \\
\langle context \rangle &::= \langle systemDefRoot \rangle \mid \langle vclassifier \rangle \\
\langle orComp \rangle &::= \langle andComp \rangle + \\
\langle andComp \rangle &::= \langle subsystemChoice \rangle \, \langle vclassifierRef \rangle * \\
\langle vclassifierRef \rangle &::= \langle quantifier \rangle \, \langle vclassifier \rangle \\
\langle quantifier \rangle &::= \text{‘ForAll’} \mid \text{‘Exist’}
\end{aligned}
$$

The terminals of the grammar are given as follows: The $\langle systemVSpec \rangle$ points to a VSpec node in the system feature model, that is the source of the relationship. The $\langle subsystemChoice \rangle$ points to a choice in the subsystem feature model, that is the targets of the relationships. Multiple instances of $\langle subsystemChoice \rangle$ exist for one $\langle systemVSpec \rangle$ and take the disjunctive normal form with compositions of $\langle orComp \rangle$ and $\langle andComp \rangle$. The $\langle systemDefRoot \rangle$

Table 3. Relational model of choice Mixed

< system VSpec >	<context>	OR-AND	<subsystem Choice>	<quantifier>	<vclassifier>
Mixed	ShopDef	◇—✕	New$_{SS}$	ForAll	VC-SS
			New$_R$	Exist	VC-R
			Old$_R$	Exist	VC-R

points to the root node of VSpec in the structure model, and the ⟨*vclassifier*⟩ points to a VClassifier in the structure model or the subsystem feature model.

In the motivating example, Choice Mixed in the system feature model has a ⟨*systemRef*⟩, which is described in Table 3. In this example, the subscripts 'SS' and 'R' mean shop server and register. The OR-AND column shows the disjunctive normal form for multiple ⟨*subsystemChoice*⟩. The Mixed means that the system includes a shop server using New Protocol, registers using New Protocol, and registers using Old Protocol at the same time. This is shown in the ⟨*subsystemChoice*⟩ column.

The ⟨*quantifier*⟩ handles multiplicity. A system includes one shop server and multiple registers, but the simple relation do not cope with multiplicity. We thus introduce ⟨*quantifier*⟩ that specifies 'ForAll' or 'Exist' toward the ⟨*vclassifier*⟩ in the ⟨*vclassifierRef*⟩. Table 3 shows the ⟨*quantifier*⟩ for the choice Mixed. The choice New$_{SS}$ has the 'ForAll' quantifier with VClassifier VC-SS, meaning that all shop servers in the system must have New$_{SS}$. The choice New$_R$ has the 'Exist' quantifier with VClassifier VC-R, meaning that at least one register in the system has New$_R$. Old$_R$ is the same as New$_R$.

The ⟨*quantifier*⟩ in ⟨*vclassifierRef*⟩ are added in accordance with a rule using ⟨*context*⟩. The ⟨*context*⟩ means correspondence between a VClassifier in the system feature model and a VClassifier in the structure model or the subsystem feature model.

We introduce relationships in our motivating example as shown in Fig. 7. Figure 7a depicts the relationship between Mixed in the system feature model and Old in the subsystem feature model for register. Figure 7b depicts the relationship between SelfRegister and SelfCheckout. These figures show extracts from three VSpec trees: (1) the structure model with a focus on register, (2) the subsystem feature model of register, and (3) the system feature model with Mixed and SelfRegister. The ⟨*context*⟩ of the root choice in (3) is set as the root choice in (1). The ⟨*context*⟩ of choice is inherited automatically from the context of the parent node. Because of the inheritance, the ⟨*context*⟩ of choice Mixed in (3) refers to choice ShopDef, and ⟨*subsystemChoice*⟩ points to choice Old in (1). When we virtually connect the trees of (1) and (2) vertically, VClassifier VC-R between ⟨*context*⟩ and ⟨*subsystemChoice*⟩ is identified for ⟨*quantifier*⟩. The Identified VClassifiers are added to the relational model with the 'Exist' or 'ForAll' quantifier. In other words, VClassifier VC-R is the multiplicity difference between choice Old in (1) and choice Mixed in (3).

In contrast, the ⟨*context*⟩ of VClassifier in (3) the system feature model is set manually to a VClassifier in (1) or (2). Figure 7 shows that there is

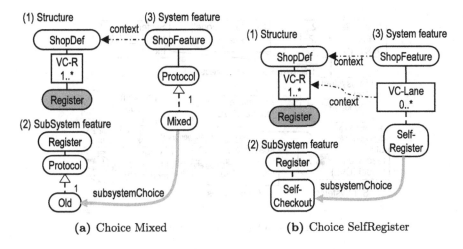

(a) Choice Mixed   (b) Choice SelfRegister

Fig. 7. Context examples

correspondence in the context between VC-Lane and VC-R. This means that the VInstance for VC-Lane needs a VInstance for VC-R. For SelfRegister, there is no ⟨quantifier⟩ because ⟨context⟩ refers to VC-R, and there is no VClassifier between VC-R and choice SelfCheckout.

As another example, NOK in the system feature model has relations with 'ForAll' quantifier to choice NOK of register and shop server. It describes the tacit knowledge 'All the registers and the shop server in a system must use the same currency.' These relational model is used for the selection of subsystems from the system test model in the next process.

4.6   Configuration Generation

A small set of configurations covering all test cases is generated by the tool. The configurations are resolutions of the structure model (Fig. 3b). There are five steps in the full process. The first four steps are shown in Fig. 8 and performed for each test case. Models with dashed lines mean models in the tool. The final step traverses all test cases, and the smallest set of configuration models that satisfy all test cases is selected.

Subsystem Test Model Generation. For each system test model that is created for the system feature model, subsystem test models are generated using the relational model. The system test model for Test Case 1 is shown in Fig. 6a, which depicts a shop server as a subsystem. The decision of choice Mixed in Test Case 1 is 'True,' and the choice Mixed has a relational to choice New in the shop server with the 'ForAll' quantifier (Table 3). Therefore, a subsystem test model for shop server is generated with choice New as 'True,' and the other choices as 'Don'tCare.' On the other hand, there are two relationships for registers with

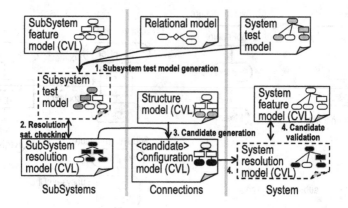

Fig. 8. Configuration generation

the 'Exist' quantifier in the relational model of choice Mixed. These relationships mean that there is at least one register using New Protocol and at least one register using Old Protocol in the system. Therefore, two subsystem test models for register are generated.

Resolutions Satisfiability Checking. In this step, the tool uses an SMT solver to identify the subsystem resolution models for each subsystem test model generated in the previous step. The solver checks the satisfiability of each resolution model for the subsystem test model. For the Test Case 1 of shop server, SS-MiniBank-N and SS-Advance-NJ in Table 1b are suitable because these resolutions have choice New. For registers, the solver identifies resolutions; the results are shown in Table 4.

Table 4. Subsystem resolutions for Test Case 1

Subsystem	Subsystem resolutions
ShopServer with New	SS-MiniBank-N
	SS-Advance-NJ
Register with New	Reg-Advance-N
	Reg-Self-N
	Reg-Advance-J
Register with Old	Reg-Classic-N
	Reg-Standard-N
	Reg-Classic-J
	Reg-Standard-J

Table 5. Generated configuration models

ShopServer	Register	Test Case
SS-MiniBank-N	Reg-Advance-N	1
	Reg-Advance-N	2
	Reg-Standard-N	3
		4
SS-Advance-NJ	Reg-Self-N	1
	Reg-Self-N	5
	Reg-Standard-N	

Candidate Generation. The tool creates all combinations of the resolutions identified in the previous step and creates candidate configuration models for each system test model. As shown in Table 4, Test Case 1 has three subsystem test models, which respectively have 2, 3, and 4 subsystem resolutions. Thus, there are 24 potential combinations.

Our tool checks the validity of the system test model in this step. If the model is invalid, the candidate configurations are not generated for the model, and the tool removes the model. For example, consider a system test model that has both TC-MiniBank and TC-Old. Since there is no shop server with Banking and Old Protocol, the tool cannot create a candidate configuration. This system test model is judged to be invalid, and the tool removes it.

Candidate Validation. Each subsystem test model in Table 4 is independent of the other ones. Therefore, candidate configurations created in the previous step may violate the constraints of the system feature model. The tool creates system resolution models for each candidate configuration and validates the system resolution models with respect to the system feature model.

For example, consider the combination of SS-MiniBank-N, Reg-Advance-N, and Reg-Standard-J from Table 4. Choice NOK in the system resolution is 'False' because the relational model for Choice NOK is defined as all registers should have NOK. Choice JPY in the system resolution is also 'False.' Therefore, the combination violates the currency constraint, i.e., a system must have only one currency. The tool removes this combination from the candidates.

Configuration Set for All Test Cases. At this point, each system test model (Test Cases 1–5) has configuration candidates that can run their own test case. The tool checks whether the configuration candidates can also run other test cases. The tool uses a greedy algorithm and an SMT solver to select the smallest set of candidates that cover all test cases.

In the motivating example, the tool generates two configuration models that together cover all test cases (Table 5). A row in the table shows one configuration, the first column shows the selection of the shop server in the configuration, and the second one shows the selection of the register. The last column shows test cases that can be executed by the configuration.

5 Tool: CT-CVL

We developed 'Configuration Tool with CVL' (CT-CVL[1]) for use with our method. CT-CVL is deployed as eclipse plug-ins. The tool consists of a VSpec editor for subsystem feature models, a resolution editor for subsystem resolution models, a VSpec editor for structure models, a VSpec editor for system feature models, a test model editor, a configuration generator, and a results viewer for the configuration models. Only the configuration generation process (Sect. 4.6)

---

[1] http://modelbased.net/tools/ct-cvl.

is supported as an automatic function by the CT-CVL while the other processes need manual operations on the editors. However, the editors have validation functions with models that are inputted in the other editors.

The CT-CVL tool uses the Eclipse Modeling Framework [15]. The meta-model of CVL is the same as that of the CVL 2 Tool from SINTEF [13]. There-fore, CT-CVL is compatible with the CVL 2 Tool. In addition, we use the Graph-ical Modeling Framework [16] for the VSpec editors. We use CVC4 [1] as the SMT solver for checking suitability and constraints.

6   Discussion

6.1   RQ1: Can the Method Generate a Small Set of Configurations that Cover All Test Cases?

Our tool generates configuration candidates for each test case, and each config-uration candidate is checked for suitability against other test cases. Then, our tool uses an SMT solver to select the smallest set from the configuration can-didates with greedy algorithm. For the motivating example, our tool generated 51 configuration candidates and selected two configurations that covered all test cases (Table 5).

6.2   RQ2: Can the Method Elicit and Formalize the Tacit Knowledge Needed for Combining Subsystems?

Our method treats the subsystems, the system, and the connections between them as separate elements. We can thus analyze the subsystems independently without considering the whole system. For the system, we can formalize test cases written in a natural language as system test models without considering the subsystems. For the connections, we can formalize the tacit knowledge about combinations between subsystems as a structure model and a relational model. The tool can automatically generate configuration models by using these models.

In the motivating example, we assumed that three pieces of tacit knowledge were formalized as models. The five test cases were formalized as system test models, and the tool generated configuration models that covered all test cases.

6.3   RQ3: Is the Execution Time for the Generation Sufficiently Low?

Our method has six processes: five done manually with tool support and one done automatically by the tool. For the motivating example, we spent two hours analyzing the subsystem feature models, system feature model, and relational model by using our tool. The results of the analysis can be reused, so the time for analysis is shorter the second time. A system test model is created for each system testing, and it is not reusable. For the motivating example, it took ten minutes to create a system test model from five test cases in natural language. The ten minutes is sufficiently low.

It took our tool 2 min 56 s to generate configurations for the motivating example on a PC (CPU: Core i3-3217U, 1.8 GHz; Memory: 4 GB; OS: Windows8, 64 bit). During the generation, 474 problems were solved by the SMT solver, each within a few seconds. Most of the time was spent used generating text files for input to the solver.

As an additional experiment, we added five choices to the register, five choices to the shop server, and five choices to the system feature model and connected them with additional relationships that have the 'ForAll' quantifier. These modifications did not require adding a subsystem test model and did not change the number of problems (474) to solve. The tool now spent 3 min 12 s. This means that the size of each problem increased, but it did not affect the time much. In contrast, when we added five extra test cases to this example, it took 9 min 34 s, and there were 1456 problems. An increase in the number of test cases creates more subsystem test models and more combinations of configuration candidates. These combinations generate more problems to solve. Therefore, the time for generation grows exponentially with the number of test cases. The scalability of our process and our configuration generation with respect to an increase in the number of test cases must be investigated further in future projects.

6.4   Threats to Validity

We checked the validity of our method for only the motivating example and a few small examples. Case studies and experiments with actual projects are needed to fully validate our method and tool.

Configuration synthesis may generate a smaller set of configurations. Rather than hoping that a configuration created from Test Case 1 can also satisfy Test Cases 2–5, it would be better to find a combination operator that would combine configurations. Thus, one configuration satisfying Test Case 1 could be combined with one satisfying Test Case 2, and the synthesized configuration would satisfy both cases. If the synthesized candidate has no constraint violations, the set of configurations is smaller. However, configuration synthesis is difficult because the method used for synthesization depends on the structure model. For the motivating example, the system is composed of one shop server and multiple registers. This case is simple, and configuration candidates that have the same shop server can be synthesized from the union of registers. In contrast, if the system is composed of multiple shop servers and multiple registers, we should consider which synthesis of shop servers is suitable, union or intersection.

7   Related Research

As a test suite generation for software product line, Bürdek et al. [2] proposed a method that achieves complete coverage with program variants. Our focus is combinations of variations on a higher abstraction level than Bürdek program variant. As a test design method using feature model, Olimpiew and Gomaa [11] proposed a method that uses a feature model to automatically create a decision table as test specifications. This method reduces the test specifications that cover all use case scenarios. In addition, there are methods that combine a feature model and a pair-wise method and generate feature sets to be tested [5,12]. A test case design method using propositional satisfiability with a feature tree has been proposed [8]. While these methods are similar to ours, they target a single product with many variations. Cohen et al. [3] proposed combinatorial interaction testing for configurable systems. Their model of configurable systems has no expressions for a distinction between a system and subsystems, and the multiplicity of subsystems. Our method focuses on testing for a configurable system composed of multiple configurable subsystems with unique variations.

Hsu and Orso [6] proposed a framework that minimizes the number of test cases by using a modern integer linear programming solver with various criteria. This framework does not support our purpose directly. However, it may be possible to use this framework for our configuration generation process by using feature models as factors or criteria.

A previously proposed method uses product maps to generate configurations [14]. A product map is similar to a resolution model but without a multiplicity descriptions like VClassifier. This method uses only subsystem features, so it cannot describe the necessary tacit knowledge.

8   Conclusion

We focused on generating a small set of system configurations to cover all test cases. To automate this generation, there was a need to establish a method for formalizing informal and tacit knowledge. Overall consistency is assured through relating the holistic view of the test engineer with the local views of the subsystem designers.

For the configuration generation, we have developed a method that uses feature models for these variations with CVL and relational notations for connecting them. We implemented this method as the CT-CVL tool that uses an SMT solver to generate a set of configurations that cover all test cases. The system feature models and subsystem feature models are considered separately. We connect them with relational models. Test cases are analyzed and formalized as system test models. The tool automatically generates a small set of configurations that cover all test cases.

We applied this method to a motivating example of a POS checkout system. All tacit knowledge is described explicitly in the relational models, and all test cases are formalized as system test models. The tool generated two configurations that covered all test cases. This motivating example is a simple example, and the method should be validated for actual projects.

References

1. Barrett, C., Conway, C.L., Deters, M., Hadarean, L., Jovanović, D., King, T., Reynolds, A., Tinelli, C.: CVC4. In: Gopalakrishnan, G., Qadeer, S. (eds.) CAV 2011. LNCS, vol. 6806, pp. 171–177. Springer, Heidelberg (2011)
2. Bürdek, J., Lochau, M., Bauregger, S., Holzer, A., von Rhein, A., Apel, S., Beyer, D.: Facilitating reuse in multi-goal test-suite generation for software product lines. In: Egyed, A., Schaefer, I. (eds.) FASE 2015. LNCS, vol. 9033, pp. 84–99. Springer, Heidelberg (2015)
3. Cohen, M.B., Dwyer, M.B., Shi, J.: Interaction testing of highly-configurable systems in the presence of constraints. In: ISSTA2007, pp. 129–139. ACM (2007). http://doi.acm.org/10.1145/1273463.1273482
4. Haugen, Ø., Wasowski, A., Czarnecki, K.: CVL: common variability language. In: SPLC2013, p. 277. ACM (2013)
5. Hervieu, A., Baudry, B., Gotlieb, A.: Pacogen: automatic generation of pairwise test configurations from feature models. In: ISSRE2011, pp. 120–129. IEEE (2011). doi:10.1109/ISSRE.2011.31
6. Hsu, H.Y., Orso, A.: Mints: a general framework and tool for supporting test-suite minimization. In: ICSE2009, pp. 419–429. IEEE (2009)
7. Kang, K.C., et al.: Feature-oriented domain analysis (FODA) feasibility study. Technical report, Carnegie-Mellon University Software Engineering Institute, November 1990
8. Kitamura, T., Do, N.T.B., Ohsaki, H., Fang, L., Yatabe, S.: Test-case design by feature trees. In: Margaria, T., Steffen, B. (eds.) ISoLA 2012, Part I. LNCS, vol. 7609, pp. 458–473. Springer, Heidelberg (2012)
9. Object Management Group: Common Variability Language (CVL) (2012). http://www.omgwiki.org/variability/lib/exe/fetch.php?id=start&cache=cache&media=cvl-revised-submission.pdf
10. Object Management Group: Object Constraint Language (OCL). Version 2.3.1 (2012). http://www.omg.org/spec/OCL/2.3.1/
11. Olimpiew, E.M., Gomaa, H.: Model-based test design for software product lines. In: SPLC 2008, pp. 173–178 (2008)
12. Oster, S., et al.: Moso-polite: tool support for pairwise and model-based software product line testing. In: VaMoS 2011, pp. 79–82. ACM (2011)
13. Research Group on Model-driven Software Engineering at SINTEF: The CVL 2 Tool (2014). http://modelbased.net/tools/cvl-2-tool/
14. Shimbara, D., et al.: Feature-analysis-based selection method for system configuration for system testing. In: PLEASE2012, pp. 61–64. IEEE, June 2012
15. The Eclipse Foundation: Eclipse Modeling Framework (2007). http://www.eclipse.org/emf/
16. The Eclipse Foundation: Graphical Modeling Framework (2007). http://www.eclipse.org/gmf-tooling/

Model-Based Product Line Testing: Sampling Configurations for Optimal Fault Detection

Hartmut Lackner[(⊠)]

Department of Computer Science, Humboldt-Universität zu Berlin,
Unter den Linden 6, 10099 Berlin, Germany
lackner@informatik.hu-berlin.de

Abstract. Product line (PL) engineering is an emerging methodology for the development of variant-rich systems. As product lines are viable for this purpose, testing them is complicated in contrast to non-variable systems, as there is an increasing amount of possible products due to the number of features. The question of which products should be chosen for testing is still an ongoing challenge.

We present coverage criteria for sampling configurations from reusable test cases. Such criteria are e.g. choosing as many different products as possible so each of the test cases can be executed once. The main contribution is an analysis of the resulting fault detection potential for the presented criteria. The analysis is supported by an example product line and a mutation system for assessing the fault detection capability. From the results of this example, we draw conclusions about the different coverage criteria.

Keywords: Testing · Reusable software · Sampling · Fault detection

1 Introduction

The purpose of testing is to decrease the risk of releasing a faulty product. In variant-rich systems engineering, there are plenty of possible products to build due to combinatorial explosion [15]. Hence, sampling product configurations for the purpose of testing is a major challenge [14]. Structural approaches for sampling products from the variability model have gained attention, since they scale reasonably with the model's size, e.g. t-wise coverage [13]. These methods demonstrated their effectiveness on real world problems such as Eclipse [7] or automotive systems [16]. However, those methods focus on the variability models and neglect the interactions on the behavioral level.

With the advent of product line-centered test design, product configurations can be sampled from the product line's test cases [11]. So far, the only criterion for which sampling was performed is minimizing the amount of configurations. A valid reason for employing this criterion is to minimize the amount of tested products, and subsequently test effort. However, its fault detection capability has not yet been assessed. In particular, research indicates that testing divers products will increase fault detection than rather testing similar products [6].

© Springer International Publishing Switzerland 2015
J. Fischer et al. (Eds.): SDL 2015, LNCS 9369, pp. 238–251, 2015.
DOI: 10.1007/978-3-319-24912-4_17

In this paper, we address the question whether coverage criteria for sampling configurations from test cases affect the fault detection capability of the test cases. We set up our experiment to reuse the same test suite for every sampling, thus we can measure the effects of different sampling criteria in isolation. The fault detection capability is assessed by our product line mutation framework as proposed in [10]. We do expect the fault detection capability to be increased under the following conditions:

(a) Sampling as much configurations as possible.
(b) Sampling large products by means of activated features.
(c) Sampling divers products.

The remainder of the article is structured as follows: Sect. 2 introduces the fundamentals of product line-centered engineering and reusable test cases. Section 3 presents sampling methods and Sect. 4 shows the experimental setup and initial results achieved so far. Section 5 covers related work and finally Sect. 6 concludes the paper.

2   Product Line Testing

2.1   Model-Based Product Line Engineering

Individual customer expectations and the reuse of existing assets in a product's design are two driving factors for the emergence of product line engineering: increasing the number of product features while keeping system engineering costs at a reasonable level. In terms of software engineering, a software product line (SPL) is a set of related software products that share a common core of software assets (commonalities), but can be distinguished (variabilities) [15].

The definition and realization of commonalities and variabilities is the process of domain engineering. Actual products are built during application engineering. Here, products are built by reusing domain artifacts and exploiting the product line variability.

Like many methodologies, PL engineering can be supported by model-based abstractions such as feature models. Feature models offer a way to overcome the aforementioned challenges by facilitating the explicit design of global system variation points [8].

A feature model specifies *valid* product configurations and has a tree structure in which a feature can be decomposed into sub-features. Figure 1 shows an example feature model that is reused later in this paper. A parent feature can have the following relations to its sub-features: (a) *Mandatory*: child feature is required, (b) *Optional*: child feature is optional, (c) *Or*: at least one of the children features must be selected, and (d) *Alternative*: exactly one of the children features must be selected. Furthermore, one may specify additional (cross-tree) constraints between two features A and B: (i) A *requires* B: the selection of A implies the selection of B, and (ii) A *excludes* B: both features A and B must not be selected for the same product.

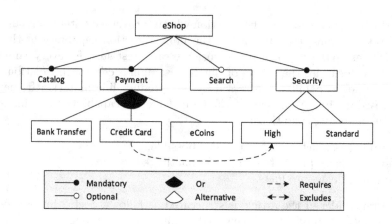

Fig. 1. A feature model for the eShop example.

A feature model (FM) can also be represented as a propositional formula [1]:

$$FM : (F \rightarrow \mathbb{B}) \rightarrow \mathbb{B}$$

where $F = f_1, ..., f_k$ be the set of features belonging to the PL. With this representation a product configuration can easily be validated. The product configuration pc defines which features are part of a product:

$$pc = F \rightarrow \mathbb{B}$$

A product configuration is valid, iff $FM(pc) = true$ holds. We define the set of all valid product configurations specified by the feature model as follows:

$$PC = \{pc : FM \rightarrow \mathbb{B} | FM(pc) = true\}$$

Although a feature model captures the system's variation points in a concise form its elements are only symbols [3]. Their semantics has to be provided by mapping them to models with semantics. Such a mapping can be defined using an explicit mapping model. A mapping model consists of relations from feature model elements to domain model elements. We refer to a PL model as the triple of feature model, mapping model, and domain model. From such a PL model, product models or code can be resolved for a given pc.

Figure 2 depicts the mapping of feature "credit card" to a transition of the payment process. In this case, the domain model is designed in terms of a so called 150% model. A 150% model contains every element that is used in at least one product configuration and, thus, subsumes every possible product [5].

2.2 Reusable Test Cases

Testing a PL faces two major challenges: first, the behavioral test goals must be sufficiently covered and secondly, a meaningful subset of products should be sampled for testing. Model-based testing of product lines allows the application

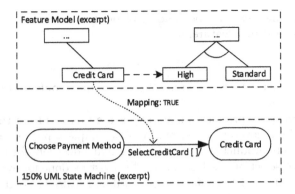

Fig. 2. Mapping of feature Credit Card to a UML transition.

of behavioral coverage criteria as well as the usage of structural coverage criteria like t-wise coverage of features. We distinguish testing processes for PLs into *product-centered* and *product line-centered* testing processes (cf. Fig. 3).

In the first case, a set of configurations is selected by structural criterion for the purpose testing, then corresponding products are resolved from the PL model and tests are designed from the individual product models. In contrast, in the latter process tests are designed from the PL model in the first place. Hence products in a PL share commonalities, PL test cases are not necessarily limited to be applicable to a single product anymore. Instead, a test case is applicable to a set of products of at least one product.

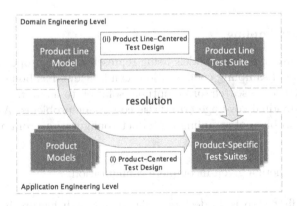

Fig. 3. Product-centered and product line-centered test design.

This is achieved by keeping track of the features that must be selected or deselected for each test case. However, for some features such a decision is unnecessary, if a particular test case is agnostic to said feature. In this case, we mark the feature for this test as *undecided*. Therefore, we introduce *incomplete* product configurations, which extend the concept of product configurations by a third value to be assigned to a feature, here X:

$$pc = F \rightarrow \mathbb{B} \cup X$$

Now, a test designer can create an incomplete product configuration and stores it with the test case.

After test creation, product configurations are sampled from the incomplete configurations by a coverage criterion. We can sample a product configuration from an incomplete product configuration by making decisions for undecided features whether to select or deselect them. This must be done for every undecided feature in every incomplete configuration, until no feature is assigned undecided anymore. From the resulting product configurations, products can be resolved and finally the tests can be executed against their associated product. In the next section, we present coverage criteria for sampling configurations from such reusable test cases.

3   Sampling Configurations from Reusable Test Cases

A main challenge in product line-centered testing, is to sample product configurations from the test cases' incomplete configurations such that every test case can be executed at least once. The products configurations are sampled with the target to maximize the likelihood of detecting faults in the PL during testing. Such sampling of product configurations is facilitated by coverage criteria. In the following, we present novel coverage criteria for sampling product configurations so that each test case can be executed once.

3.1   General Sampling

Due to the nature of feature models being representable as propositional formulas, the problem of sampling configurations can be viewed as boolean satisfiability problem. Hence we search for an optimal solution to a coverage criterion, we present the individual coverage criteria as constraint problems. As a first step, we model the problem of sampling a product configuration from an incomplete configuration:

Problem 1 Complete a given incomplete configuration.

Solution The first step is to declare variables for each feature in F and their domains. The domain varies depending on the feature's assignment:

- $f = true$ then the corresponding variable's domain is $\{1\}$
- $f = undecided$ then the corresponding variable's domain is $\{0, 1\}$
- $f = false$ then the corresponding variable's domain is $\{0\}$

Finally, we define the propositional formula of the feature model as constraints for the variables. A constraint solver is now able to make assignments to undecided features and check its solution for validity against the propositional formula.

The solution of Problem 1 can easily be extended to sample product configurations for all test cases in a test suite.

Problem 2 Complete all incomplete configurations in a test suite with m test cases.

Solution The method to solve problem 1, can be repeated individually for every incomplete configuration in the given test suite. Eventually, all incomplete configurations of the test suite are complete.

3.2 Optimized Sampling

In the following, we define coverage criteria for sampling product configurations from test cases.

Problem 3 Optimize the set of m-test cases for constraints. In particular:

(a) Few/Many configurations not exceeding m,
(b) Small/Large configurations by means of selected features,
(c) Divers configurations,
(d) Combinations thereof.

Solutions

(a) Optimizing the Amount of Configurations. The aim is to select either the few or many products to execute every test case in the given test suite at least once. The optimization problem here is to achieve a maximal or minimal number of product configurations. We model the constraint problem as follows: A product configuration can be interpreted as a binary number b, when we interpret *selected* features as binary value "1" and *deselected* features as "0" respectively. Hence a product configuration pc_n with features $F_n : f_1, ..., f_k$ is interpret as the number:

$$b_n = (f_1 f_2 ... f_{k-1} f_k)_2$$

For a test suite with m test cases, we derive b_n for every product configuration pc_n, where $1 \leq n \leq m$. We collect all b_i in the set Z:

$$Z = \{b_1, b_2, ..., b_{m-1}, b_m\}$$

For receiving a minimal set of concrete configurations we have to minimize the cardinality of Z. Vice versa, we maximize the cardinality of Z, if we want to maximize the number of configurations for testing:

$$\max / \min cost = |Z|$$

In terms of optimization, we refer to the cardinality of Z as costs. The expected costs for the criteria of maximizing or minimizing the amount of configurations are in the range of 1 to the number of test cases m. Where costs of 1 represent that exactly one product configuration was sampled. The upper limit of m, since we require each test case to be assigned to only one product.

(b) Optimizing the Size of all Configurations. We define the size of a configuration as the sum of all *selected* features. For constraint solving, we interpret *selected* as numerical value "1" and *deselected* as "0" respectively. Therefore, we can define the size of a product configuration pc_n as follows:

$$s_n = \sum_{i=1}^{k} f_i$$

When we accumulate sizes of all product configurations, we can optimize towards either a minimal or maximal overall size:

$$\max / \min cost = \sum_{n=1}^{m} s_n$$

Where maximization achieves large product configurations and minimization small product configurations. The costs of the smallest solution is $2 \times m$ for having the root feature and only one other feature enabled (2) and multiply this by the amount of test cases m. The highest cost for solution is $k \times m$, where every feature k is selected in every test case m.

(c) Optimizing the Diversity of Configurations We define diversity over a set of m test cases and k features. First we establish a relation between a single feature i over all configurations. The goal is to have each feature as often selected as deselected, hence we gain most different assignments.

We achieve this by calculating the diversity d_i of each feature $f_{n,i}$, where $1 \leq n \leq m$ and $1 \leq i \leq k$:

$$d_i = \sum_{n=1}^{m} f_{n,i}$$

Next, we calculate the deviation from optimal diversity, which is $m/2$, because we want a feature to be equally often selected and deselected over all n configurations. Subsequently, the deviation of a feature f_i from its optimal diversity is calculated by $|d_i - (m/2)|$. Finally, we achieve maximal diversity by minimizing the sum of all deviations:

$$\min cost = \sum_{i=1}^{k} |d_i - (m/2)|$$

The minimal costs for a solution to this problem is 0 with product configurations being maximally diversified. The highest cost are $(m/2) \times k$, where the same configuration is sampled for every test cases.

We note that this approach does not maximize the amount of sampled product configurations, but their diversity. Inherently, this approach leads to solutions with fewer unique product configurations, if the calculated diversity is higher than for another solutions with more product configurations and less diversity. An approach to increase the amount of product configurations is the combination of the two criteria diversity and maximization of the amount of product configurations.

(d) Combinations In general, all combinations of the previously defined constraints are valid with the exception of:

- few with many product configurations,
- small with large product configurations.

Any other combination is valid, e.g. most with large and divers configurations. For making a preference towards one or more criteria, weights can be added to the costs.

Of course, costs cannot be summed up directly if the optimization targets are opposing, e.g. if large and divers should be combined, the targets are minimization and maximization. In this case, a decision for an overall optimization target must be made (min *or* max) and the costs of the criterion not fitting that target must be inverted. Costs are inverted by subtracting the solution's costs from the expected maximal costs. The result of this subtraction are the inverted costs.

4   Example and Evaluation

In this section, we assess the fault detection capability of an example test suite in respect to sampled configurations. First, we introduce the example and setup, then we present the results.

4.1   Example and Setup

We implemented the coverage criteria as presented in this paper in Java. The constraint solving is supported by JaCoP a constraint programming library [9]. We also implemented an Eclipse plug-in to wrap the code into a GUI interface. Coverage driven sampling from incomplete configuration is now part of the SPLTestBench.

As an example to evaluate the coverage criteria on, we employ our Webshop (eShop) PL. A customer can browse the catalog of items, or if provided, use the search function to do so. Once the customer put items into the cart, he can check-out and may choose from up to three different payment options, depending on the eShop's configuration. The transactions are secured by either a standard or high security protocol. A cross-tree-constraint ensures that credit card payment is only offered if the eShop also implements a high security protocol.

We model the eShop by a feature model, UML state machine model, and a feature mapping for mapping the features onto transitions in the state machine. The feature model, as shown previously, comprises ten features. The state machine model consists of 13 states and 27 transitions, distributed over three sub-machines.

Designing product line-centered tests is facilitated by automated model-based test design as described in [11]. We employ all-transitions coverage as a test selection goal [17]. From the test generator, we receive 13 test cases with incomplete configurations. Five of the incomplete configurations are actually disjunct.

For assessing the fault detection capability of test suites, we proposed a PL mutation framework in [10]. The assessment is independent of the test's creation method, whether being product-centered or product line-centered. For the current experiment, we apply both of the supported types of mutation operators: behavioral operators, which mutate the state machine model, and variability operators, which mutate the feature mapping model.

4.2   Test Assessment for Product Line Tests

Mutation analysis (also mutation testing) [4] is a fault-based testing technique with the intended purpose to assess the quality of tests by introducing faults into a system and measuring the success rate of fault detection.

The process of mutation analysis inserts defects into software by creating multiple versions of the original software, where each created version contains one deviation. Afterwards, existing test cases are used to execute the faulty versions (*mutants*) with the goal to distinguish the faulty ones (*to kill a mutant*) from the original software. The ratio of killed mutants to generated mutants is called *mutation score*. The main goal of the test designer is to maximize the mutation score. A mutation score of 100 % is seldom possible, because some deviations may lead to an unchanged system behavior, i.e. semantically equivalent mutants.

We think that mutation systems for PLs need novel mutation operators and mutation processes. The reason for this is the separation of concerns in model-based PPL engineering, where variability and domain engineering are split into different phases and models. Hence of new modeling languages used in PPL engineering, more *kinds* of errors can be made on the model-level than in non-variable systems engineering. In our case, new errors occur in feature mapping models.

Performing mutation analysis on a PPL differs from conventional mutation systems, since a mutated PL model is not executable per se. Thus, testing cannot be performed until a decision is made towards a set of products for testing. This decision depends on the PL test suite itself, since each test is applicable to just a subset of products.

In Fig. 4, we depict a mutation process for assessing PL test suites, which addresses this issue. Independently from each other, we gain (a) a set of PL model mutants by applying mutation operators to the PL model and identify (b) a set of configurations describing the applicable products for testing. We apply every configuration from (b) to every mutant in (a), which returns a new set of product model mutants. Any mutant structurally equivalent to the original product model is immediately removed and does not participate in the scoring. The model mutants are then derived to product mutants and finally, tests are executed. Our mutation scores are based on the PL model mutants, hence we established bidirectional traceability from any PL model mutant to all its associated product mutants and back again. If a product mutant is killed by a test, we backtrack its original PL model mutant and flag it as killed. The final mutation score is then calculated from the set of killed and the overall number of PL model mutants.

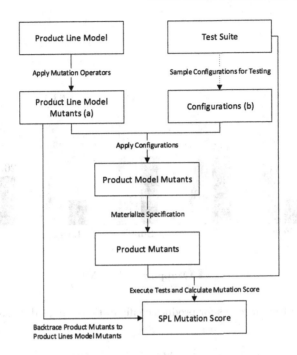

Fig. 4. Mutation Process for PLs

4.3   Results

We performed mutation analysis for the eShop's test suite with different sampling criteria and their combinations. Since the test suite stays the same for all samplings, this procedure assesses the impact of the different sampling criteria on the test suite's fault detection capability. For our first experiment, we assessed the sampling criteria individually: we apply one of the five sampling criteria on the eShop's test suite. In return, we gain a set of PCs (product configurations), where each PC is assigned to one or more test cases of the test suite, but every test case is associated to only one PC. Given the PCs and test cases, the mutation system then creates mutations of the PL model and from these it derives product mutants for every PC and eventually generates code from the models. Finally, the test cases are assessed by executing them against the code and the mutation score is calculated.

The resulting mutation scores for the criteria Few, Many, Small, Large, and Diverse are presented in Fig. 5. Furthermore, the amount of PCs for every criterion we assessed are: 1 (Few), 13 (Many), 4 (Small), 1 (Large), and 7 (Diverse).

In a second experiment, we assessed combinations of sampling criteria. This experiment is conducted with the same procedure as the first. From the twelve possible combinations of sampling criteria, we compare the most extreme combinations:

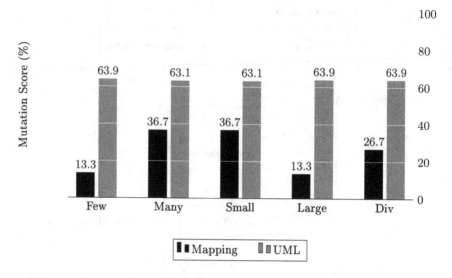

Fig. 5. Mutation scores for product configurations sampled in isolation.

Few+Small+Div, Few+Large+Div, Many+Small+Div, and Many+Large+Div. In Fig. 6, we present this experiment's results of the test assessment. The amount of sampled product configurations for the combination are: 4 (Few+Small+Div), 4 (Few+Large+Div), 10 (Many+Small+Div), and 10 (Many+Large+Div).

4.4   Discussion

As expected, the fault detection capability of the test suite varies with the applied coverage criterion. In particular, the highest fault detection capability of isolated criteria are achieved by maximized amount of products (Many) and - to our surprise - small products (Small). This appeared to be counter-intuitive, since we expected larger products to contain more components and thus be more likely to expose faulty behavior. Instead, large products led to testing too few products for having a positive impact on fault detection. Though Max and Small have the same fault detection capability in this example, Small is much more efficient when it comes to the amount of tested products. For Small only 4 products are selected for testing, for Max 13 products.

The highest scores in the group of combined criteria are achieved by the following two combinations: maximized amount with small and divers products (Max+Small+Div) and by minimized amount with small and divers products (Min+Small+Div). In this case, fault detection efficiency is higher for Min+Small+Div than for Max+Small+Div, since less products are sampled for testing. In general, combined criteria scored equal or lower to the two top scoring isolated criteria Max and Small, but never better.

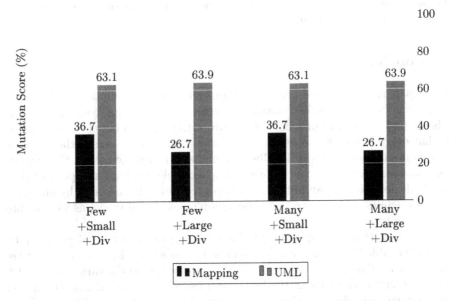

Fig. 6. Mutation scores for product configurations sampled with combined coverage criteria.

Another finding is that the coverage criteria affect the fault detection significantly when the fault is to be found in the variability model. The highest score for detecting faults in the variability model is 2.75 times higher than the lowest score. In contrast, the coverage criterion's impact on the detection of faults in the behavioral model varies by approximately one percent and is thus considerably insignificant.

5   Related Work

Sampling product configurations for testing is an ongoing challenge. Most work is focused on structural coverage criteria for feature models and hence is agnostic to the interactions in behavioral models [13,14]. Still, the test effort is high, since feature interactions are selected for testing where no behavioral interaction is present.

Lochau et al. present incremental test design methods to subsequently test every specified behavior [12]. Here, configurations are sampled as needed to achieve the next test goal. The result is a set of test cases where each is limited to a single product configuration. In contrast, the here presented coverage criteria for sampling configurations rely on reusable test cases.

Similar to the notion of incremental test design Beohar et al. propose spinal test suites [2]. A spinal test suite allows one to test the common features of a PL once and for all, and subsequently, only focus on the specific features when moving from one product configuration to another. This is different from the notion of reusable test cases, where there is no such thing as progressing through product configurations.

6 Conclusion

In this paper, we presented five novel coverage criteria for sampling product configurations from a test suite consisting of reusable test cases. To our knowledge, it is the first assessment of a single test suite with varying product configurations so that every test case can be executed exactly once. We assessed the coverage criteria in isolation and additionally in combination with each other. Our experiment was conducted on an e-commerce shop example, modeled as a product line. The fault detection capability of the eShop's test suite was assessed by mutation analysis. Faults were injected into the eShop's behavioral model as well as into its variability model.

We found that testing many products (Many) or rather small products by means of enabled features (Small) increases the test's fault detection capability in our example. This is particularly true for faults located in the variability model. Fault detection for faults in the behavioral model remained almost equal over all sampling criteria. We also assessed combinations of the defined sampling criteria. The combined criteria scored equal or lower to the two top scoring isolated criteria Many and Small, but never better.

In future, further experiments based on larger examples and industrial case studies are scheduled. This will provide more confidence on the current findings. We also plan to extend the current sampling approach to allow multiple test executions. The reasoning behind this is the following: since all sampled configurations are built anyways, the effort for executing all compatible test cases, rather than only the assigned products, might not be much higher after all. The efficiency of this approach is dependent on the costs for building products in respect to additional the effort for test executions and the setup/tear down phases. Also a comparison and combination with structural coverage criteria, like t-wise, and the criteria presented in this paper is of interest.

References

1. Batory, D.: Feature models, grammars, and propositional formulas. In: Obbink, H., Pohl, K. (eds.) SPLC 2005. LNCS, vol. 3714, pp. 7–20. Springer, Heidelberg (2005)
2. Beohar, H., Mousavi, M.R.: Spinal test suites for software product lines France. In: Proceedings Ninth Workshop on Model-based Testing, MBT 2014, EPTCS, vol. 141, pp. 44–55 (2014)
3. Czarnecki, K., Antkiewicz, M.: Mapping features to models: a template approach based on superimposed variants. In: Glück, R., Lowry, M. (eds.) GPCE 2005. LNCS, vol. 3676, pp. 422–437. Springer, Heidelberg (2005)
4. DeMillo, R.A.: Mutation analysis as a tool for software quality assurance (1980)

5. Grönniger, H., Krahn, H., Pinkernell, C., Rumpe, B.: Modeling variants of automotive systems using views. In: Tagungsband zur Modellierung 2008, Berlin-Adlershof, Deutschland, M"arz 2008, pp. 12–14. LNI, Gesellschaft für Informatik, Bonn (2008)

6. Henard, C., Papadakis, M., Perrouin, G., Klein, J., Le Traon, Y.: Assessing software product line testing via model-based mutation: an application to similarity testing. In: ICSTW 2013: IEEE 6th International Conference On Software Testing, Verification and Validation Workshops 2013, pp. 188–197 (2013)

7. Johansen, M.F., Haugen, Ø., Fleurey, F., Carlson, E., Endresen, J., Wien, T.: A technique for agile and automatic interaction testing for product lines. In: Nielsen, B., Weise, C. (eds.) ICTSS 2012. LNCS, vol. 7641, pp. 39–54. Springer, Heidelberg (2012)

8. Kang, K.C., Cohen, S.G., Hess, J.A., Novak, W.E., Peterson, A.S.: Feature-oriented Domain Analysis (FODA) Feasibility Study (1990)

9. Kuchcinski, K., Szymanek, R.: JaCoP - Java Constraint Programming Solver (2013)

10. Lackner, H., Schmidt, M.: Towards the assessment of software product line tests. In: The 18th International Software Product Line Conference, pp. 62–69 (2014)

11. Lackner, H., Thomas, M., Wartenberg, F., Weißleder, S.: Model-based test design of product lines: raising test design to the product line level. In: ICST 2014: International Conference on Software Testing, Verification, and Validation, pp. 51–60 (2014)

12. Lochau, M., Schaefer, I., Kamischke, J., Lity, S.: Incremental model-based testing of delta-oriented software product lines. In: Brucker, A.D., Julliand, J. (eds.) TAP 2012. LNCS, vol. 7305, pp. 67–82. Springer, Heidelberg (2012)

13. Oster, S., Zorcic, I., Markert, F., Lochau, M.: MoSo-PoLiTe: tool support for pairwise and model-based software product line testing. In: VaMoS 2011, pp. 79–82 (2011)

14. Perrouin, G., Sen, S., Klein, J., Baudry, B., Le Traon, Y.: Automated and scalable t-wise test case generation strategies for software product lines. In: ICST 2010: International Conference on Software Testing, Verification and Validation, pp. 459–468. IEEE Computer Society, IEEE, Los Alamitos, Calif, Piscataway, NJ (2010)

15. Pohl, K., Böckle, G., van der Linden, F.J.: Software Product Line Engineering: Foundations, Principles and Techniques. Springer, New York (2005)

16. Steffens, M., Oster, S., Lochau, M., Fogdal, T.: Industrial evaluation of pairwise SPL testing with MoSo-PoLiTe. In: The Sixth International Workshop, pp. 55–62 (2012)

17. Weißleder, S.: Simulated Satisfaction of coverage criteria on UML state machines. In: ICST 2010: International Conference on Software Testing, Verification and Validation. IEEE Computer Society, IEEE, Los Alamitos, Calif, Piscataway, NJ (2010)

Testing Business Processes Using TTCN-3

Bernard Stepien[(✉)], Kavya Mallur, and Liam Peyton

School of Electrical Engineering and Computer Science,
University of Ottawa, Ottawa, Canada
{bernard,kmall093,lpeyton}@uottawa.ca

Abstract. Business Process Management (BPM) applications in the medical domain pose challenging testing problems that result from parallel execution of test behaviors performed by different actors. Hospitals nowadays function with the principle of pools of personnel. Each pool addresses a specific functionality and each member of the pool can pick any task that is proposed to the pool. The challenge for BPM testing is in the existence of dependencies between actors and the corresponding test description where the stimuli sent to the BPM that is the system under test (SUT) by one actor produces responses that affect a selected number of other actors belonging to a pool. Unit testing of such systems has proven to be of limited efficiency in detecting faults that can be detected only during parallel execution of test components representing actors. We propose an architecture based on the TTCN-3 model of separation of concern and its intensive parallel test component (PTC) concept which provides solutions that are beyond traditional telecommunication systems testing and which have revealed opportunities for improving TTCN-3.

Keywords: Business processes · Testing · TTCN-3 · SOA

1 Introduction

A *business process* [1] is a defined collection of linked structured tasks, activities, and decisions performed together to produce a desired set of results in order to achieve business goals on behalf of the organization. ***Business Process Management*** (BPM) is a generic software system that is driven by explicit process designs to enact and manage operational business processes [18].

Business processes involve collaboration of multiple user roles in parallel activity [5]. For example, a hospital business process may involve many participating actors in the following roles: nurses, doctors, patients. There might exist a dependency between these actors within the parts of the process for a particular instance of the process, for a particular patient (e.g. a doctor will re-assess a patient only after all tests have been completed by different nurses and technicians); or there might be a parallel execution of a task by multiple actors in different parts of the process across many instances of the process for different patients (e.g. many doctors may be assessing and re-assessing different patients at the same time).

© Springer International Publishing Switzerland 2015
J. Fischer et al. (Eds.): SDL 2015, LNCS 9369, pp. 252–267, 2015.
DOI: 10.1007/978-3-319-24912-4_18

BPM development and testing happen in the context of ***Service-Oriented Architecture*** (SOA), a business-centric IT architectural approach that provides agility, flexibility and reusability to respond to changing business requirements [10], and targets delivery of functionalities through loosely coupled services which can be reused to fulfill business processes.

1.1 Hospital's '*Cancer Patient Assessment*' Business Process Case Study

Companies are increasingly taking their business processes online using BPM tools and technologies which allow them to model explicitly the orchestration and interaction of tasks performed by roles (people) and systems (web services) that define a business process, and execute that process as a web application that provides forms for roles to interact with and service interfaces to the underlying SOA.

Figure 1 illustrates a Cancer Patient Assessment Center (CPA) business process model developed using IBM BPM 8.5.5 at a large teaching hospitals in Canada.

The process starts when a referral fax is received. The Cancer Assessment Clerk (CAC) is responsible for opening this fax image and validating the fax. The clerk queries the process database either by putting the Medical Record Number (MRN) or the last name and first name of the patient. The clerk is also responsible for moving the referral to its department, i.e. the clerk can indicate the type of referral (thoracic/colorectal/prostate/other). Depending on the type of referral indicated, the flow is then transferred to thoracic nurse, prostate nurse, colorectal nurse or other registered nurse for review. If the referral is identified to be of colorectal, prostate, or other type, the patient summary is sent to the CAC clerk for printing and the instance ends here. In case of thoracic referral, the flow goes to Awaiting CT if CT scan is needed. Else, the process continues with physician review. The physician reviews the patient information and identifies the tests needed for this patient. The step after physician review is registered nurse (RN) contact where the contact nurse tries to contact the patient and schedules navigation day appointment. After navigation day appointment, the process next moves to clinical triage where the triage nurse is responsible for choosing the ICD codes (International Statistical Classification of Diseases and Related Health Problems) and identifies if the appointment needs to be booked urgently. The referral then moves to consult booking phase where the booking clerk books the available surgeon or respirologist based on the identified status of the patient.

1.2 The Challenges of Testing Business Processes

The research presented here has been performed in collaboration with a large teaching hospital in Canada that is implementing BPM for their process. This allowed us to study a real case and especially fathom the differences between manual testing that was the prevailing testing approach and automated testing.

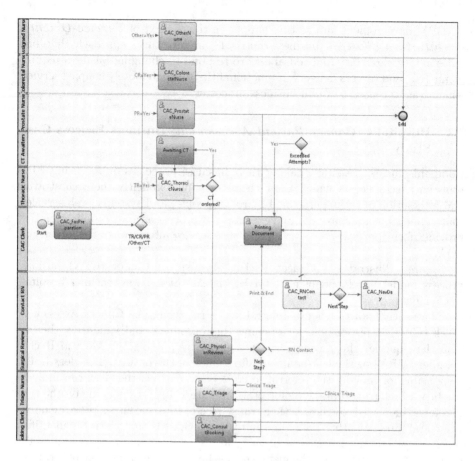

Fig. 1. CPA business process model

Even more interesting was the finding that at least 50 % of test cases failed both for manual testing in the field and automated testing in the lab. After analysis of the detailed logs provided by the test execution tool TTworkbench [17], most of the failures could be attributed to the handling of complex parallel behaviors of actors. Representing the behavior of members of a pool of actors in a hospital is difficult with traditional testing methods, because of the sequential characteristics of programming languages like Junit [16] that make it difficult to represent all the variations that result from the interleaved nature of the behaviors of actors. The use of threads in general purpose languages (GPL) to isolate an actor's behavior is a natural solution but requires complex low level programming to coordinate. The TTCN-3 testing language [6] supports parallel thread directly with considerable high-level constructs that simplify parallel testing [2,3]. The main purpose of this paper was to establish a clear pattern for a TTCN-3 test suite for BPM testing. This pattern can then be used in model based test case generation.

1.3 Limitations of Traditional Business Processes Testing Approaches

Typically, the quality assurance team tests the business process in the same way it would test any other web application. Often, there is ad hoc testing of the system by testers manually interacting with forms in the manner they assume the different roles. Unfortunately, this type of ad hoc testing focuses on testing an application for a single task, from the point of view of a single user whereas the orchestration of tasks across many users and software systems can be quite complex for an online business process. Available tools are not systematically leveraged to verify the complexity of multi-role, multi-server orchestration for BPM [11]. IBM's BPM Testing Asset tool was used to generate the test scripts based on business process model. The testing asset tool generated selenium scripts and offered additional capabilities to identify possible paths in a business process. However this capability was immature and difficult to use. The paths launched by timers were eliminated and in addition, the test script templates had to be manually edited to specify timing constraints. Also, there was no way to coordinate and verify correct roles' behavior when many scenarios were run in parallel.

Unit testing is at first consideration easy to implement with open source tools such as JUnit [9] and various derivatives such as DBUnit or Selenium [13]. However they lead testers to poor designs with little or no re-usability of code as shown in [14] because of lack of separation between behavior and coding/decoding or test oracle verification activities. An excerpt of a Java coded JUnit test of BPM implementation follows:

```java
public void Test1() throws Exception {
    JSONObject bpdArgs = new JSONObject();
    JSONObject results = bpmClient.runBPD(BPD_ID,
            PROCESS_APP_ID, bpdArgs);
    int processId =
            results.getJSONObject("data").getInt("piid");

    results = bpmClient.getInbox();
    JSONObject searchPatientTask = utils.findTask(results,
            processId, "CAC_FaxPreparation");

    Assert.assertNotNull(searchPatientTask);

    int searchPatientTaskId =
            searchPatientTask.getInt("taskId");

    results = bpmClient.startTask(searchPatientTaskId);
    ...
```

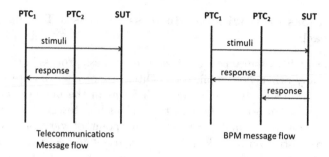

Fig. 2. Differences in parallelism

Handling Parallelism. In Fig. 2, the classic telecommunications testing model supported by TTCN-3, supports for a given test component to send a stimuli and receive one or several responses potentially in interleaved fashions [4,12]. Here the important fact is that it is the same component that sends the simulus that also receives the responses.

However in BPM, because there can be pools of actors for a given role, the stimulus sent by a component such as the submission of a form can result in responses to any component associated to a member of a pool and consists essentially in updating the list of available tasks to be performed. In a hospital environment this is achieved by refreshing the web pages of the actor's browsers. More important is the fact that a task can be executed by only one actor at a time. Thus, this provides opportunities for race conditions and the associated errors they cause.

2   TTCN-3 Model

Testing a BPM could use a classic black box testing approach. However, the BPM itself is composed of at least two nested layers. A Web application is the first layer that a user or a tester interacts with. The web application itself addresses mostly the user interface where users can fill in forms to be submitted and display the results of a form submission. The real logic to be tested resides in the nested layer of the BPM engine itself. The BPM architecture gives us the opportunity to make a choice for the purpose of a test. Faults of such a system can result from any of these two nested layers but moreover, the source of a fault could be hard to distinguish. We have decided to use a grey box approach to focus on the detection of faults of the BPM engine itself, thus ignoring the web application layer entirely. Another consideration is the fact that BPM API produces clearly identifiable results as returned values to a function invocation while web pages contain mostly formatted content where data can only be identified by its value that is changeable and open to interpretation.

2.1   Separation of Concerns

The following section is meant to help non-TTCN-3 experts to understand the differences between the concrete test implementations like JUnit and TTCN-3 and especially show the benefits of abstraction. TTCN-3 was originally designed for testing telecommunication systems. There, codecs are used to format messages to be sent and extract information from formatted messages that are received which are easily separated from protocol behavior. Similarly, the mechanism for communication with a SUT to send and receive messages can also be separated from the protocol behavior. This results in re-usability of codecs and transport layer protocols and moreover renders the test behavior description considerably more readable. While this could be achieved easily with GPL, TTCN-3 provides a clear and re-usable model to do so. In the case of BPM testing, a similar approach to separation of concerns means separating the behaviors of individual actors and roles (a pool of actors) from the actual REST BPM framework APIs. In our case, we found that data typing at the abstract level is an efficient way to drive REST API method invocations as messages sent to the test adapter that in turn uses its data to populate the parameters of REST API method invocations and this rather than TTCN-3 procedure oriented communication possibility. This provides better chances of re-usability compared to mapping REST API to TTCN-3 procedures when using different BPM tools and consequently their corresponding API. In our case this required defining a data type that carries the information of a task to execute by the REST API as follows:

```
type record TaskExecutionRequestType {
  TaskType task
}
```

Where a task is itself represented by the following data type

```
type record TaskType {
  charstring instanceId,
  charstring taskId,
  charstring activityName,
  charstring assignedTo
}
```

A typical actor's test behavior (e.g. the Cancer Assessment Clerk) can be abstracted and isolated into a function as four basic steps of login in, receive a list of tasks to choose from, choose a task to execute, execute the chosen task, get some form to fill in, submit the filled form, receive an updated list of tasks to execute for the next cycle of similar activities. The abstract description of these steps in TTCN-3 is achieved as follows:

```
function cacTest_ClerkBehavior(template BPMloginType
      loginInfo, integer ranking) runs on PTCType {
```

```
...
map(self:bpmPort, system:system_bpmPort);
bpmPort.send(loginInfo);
alt {
  [] bpmPort.receive(cac_fax_preparation_task_t)
       -> value listOfTasks {setverdict(pass);}
  [] bpmPort.receive { setverdict(fail); }
}

updateTaskList();
task := getTask(listOfTasks, "CAC_FaxPreparation",
    ranking);
bpmPort.send(TaskExecutionRequestType: { task  } );
alt {
  [] bpmPort.receive(cac_search_mrn_exec_response_t)
       -> value execResponse {setverdict(pass);}
  [] bpmPort.receive {setverdict(fail); stop;}
}
...
```

In TTCN-3, the keyword *receive* means match the test oracle template indicated as a parameter against data that has been received from the SUT. In the concrete layer test adapter written in the standard XTRI style [8], the abstract task description is passed as an abstract value from which concrete values need to be extracted in order to invoke the necessary REST API methods in a similar way to JUnit testing but in a parametric and thus re-usable way. For example, the above abstract behavior line that sends a task execution request as follows:

```
bpmPort.send(TaskExecutionRequestType: { task  } );
```

will result in the abstract value of the selected task to be executed to be passed on to the concrete layer's test adapter standard method *xtriSend()* as follows:

```
TriStatus xtriSend(final TriComponentId componentId,
TriPortId tsiPortId,  Value sutAddress, Value value){
```

A switching on the actual data type of the abstract value will narrow down the activity as follows:

```
if(value.getType().getName().
    equals("TaskExecutionRequestType")) {
```

A first step consists in extracting the concrete values from the abstract value using standard TTCN-3 API [7], here the actual value of the task Id to be executed:

```
RecordValue taskExecutionValue = (RecordValue) value;
RecordValue taskValue = (RecordValue)
```

```
taskExecutionValue.getField("task");
CharstringValue taskIdValue = (CharstringValue)
    taskValue.getField("taskId");
String taskId = taskIdValue.getString();
int taskIdInt = Integer.parseInt(taskId);
```

Finally, once this concrete data is obtained, the task can be started on the corresponding *bpmClient* instance that is kept in a table with association to the TTCN-3 component Ids (not shown here). This constitutes the actual stimulus to the SUT:

```
JSONObject results = bpmClient.startTask(taskIdInt);
```

The results of the above method invocation are parsed by the codec side of the test adapter and a corresponding abstract object is built and sent to the abstract layer's message queue for matching with a test oracle using the standard *enqueue()* method:

```
xtriEnqueueMsg(tsiPortId, sutAddress, componentId,
    execResponseValue);
```

Race Conditions. One of the major challenges of BPM testing consists in specifying the task that needs to be executed (the stimulus). Tasks have a specific name. However using a task name is actually ambiguous because there may be many tasks with the same name presented to the user as shown for example in Fig. 3. Tasks can only be differentiated with task ids that are the only information used by the REST API to execute a task. These tasks ids are dynamic and generated by the BPM, thus by definition not predictable and not known to the tester at test scripting time. Thus, we need a way to select a task and avoid race condition where two users would pick the same task to execute. We have used two approaches in order to solve this problem. They are described below as part of the discussion on parallelism.

2.2   Handling Parallel Test Components Dependency

The originality of BPM applications testing is in parallelism that is implemented naturally with the TTCN-3 concept of parallel test component (PTC). However, parallelism in BPMs is different because of dependencies among PTCs. There are three kinds of test component dependencies in BPM testing:

  – sequential, parallel and overlapping

Sequential Dependencies. Sequential dependencies result from the mere fact that a given actor needs to wait until another actor upstream performs a given task as shown in Fig. 4. Each actor is represented by a PTC that starts a particular behavior that is appropriate for a given test case. This type of sequencing

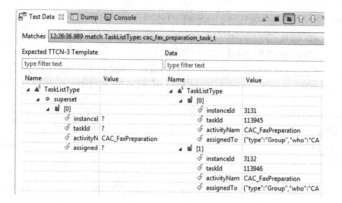

Fig. 3. Race situation

is easy to represent in TTCN-3 by starting the behavior of the dependent PTCs in sequence and moreover forcing the subsequent PTC to wait until the previous PTC completed its behavior using the *component.done* construct that is blocking any further downstream PTC to start its behavior. In the following example, the nurse cannot start working before the clerk has requested a task to be performed by a clerk in the system.

```
testcase clerk_Clerk_Nurse_dependency_test_case()
     runs on MTCType system SystemType {
  var PTCType clerk1 := PTCType.create("clerk1");
  var PTCType nurse1 := PTCType.create("nurse1");

  clerk1.start(clerkBehavior(clerk1_login_t, 1));
  clerk1.done;
  nurse1.start(nurseBehavior(nurse1_login_t, 1));
  nurse1.done;
  setverdict(pass);
}
```

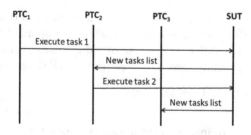

Fig. 4. Sequential dependencies

Parallel Dependencies. Parallel dependencies result from the fact that a given task can be performed by a pool of actors in a hospital environment. For example, tasks to be performed by nurses can be picked by any nurse on duty that is qualified for the specific type of medical treatment that a given case requires. In this case, we use the TTCN-3 PTC *done* keyword for all members of a given pool to let the members of the next dependent pool to start their own behaviors. The following is a full example of seven different pools of two actors each interacting both sequentially and in parallel:

```
testcase cac_scenario_4_2UsersHappyPath()
    runs on MTCType system SystemType {
    ... // PTCs declarations not shown
cacclerk1.start(cac_ClerkBehavior(...,1));
cacclerk2.start(cac_ClerkBehavior(..., 2));
    cacclerk1.done; cacclerk2.done;
thoracinurse1.start(cac_ThoracicNurseBehavior(..., 1));
thoracinurse2.start(cac_ThoracicNurseBehavior(..., 2));
    thoracinurse1.done; thoracinurse2.done;
reviewPhysician1.start(cac_ReviewPhysicianBehavior(...,1));
reviewPhysician2.start(cac_ReviewPhysicianBehavior(...,2));
    reviewPhysician1.done; reviewPhysician2.done;
contactNurse1.start(cac_ContactNurseBehavior(..., 1));
contactNurse2.start(cac_ContactNurseBehavior(..., 2));
    contactNurse1.done; contactNurse2.done;
contactNurse2.start(cac_ContactNurseNavBehavior(..., 1));
contactNurse1.start(cac_ContactNurseNavBehavior(..., 2));
    contactNurse1.done; contactNurse1.done;
triageNurse1.start(cac_TriageNurseNavBehavior(..., 1));
triageNurse2.start(cac_TriageNurseNavBehavior(..., 2));
    triageNurse1.done; triageNurse2.done;
bookingClerk2.start(cac_BookingClerkNavBehavior(..., 1));
bookingClerk1.start(cac_BookingClerkNavBehavior(..., 2));
    bookingClerk2.done; bookingClerk1.done;
setverdict(pass);}
```

Here, the problem to be addressed is to avoid that several actors try to execute the same task on the same patient at the same time. For nurses, this would result in several nurses administering the same medication which of course is highly undesirable and could have life threatening consequences. For surgeons, the case is even more obvious since two surgeons cannot perform the same surgery neither at the same time and neither in sequence. Thus in our test suite, we need to handle the concept of an actors pool based on role. This means that every member of a pool will see all the tasks assigned to the pool until one of its members picks a given task and executes it. In that case, the executed task should no longer be available to the other members of the pool. Here the problem consists in updating the list of tasks that a given member can see and thus choose from. These lists of tasks are obtained in TTCN-3 through the classic stimuli and response paradigm. In our case this occurs when a member logs in to the system. In this case, the member gets a list of tasks to choose from. In other cases, this can also be the result of the execution of a task when several tasks of different kinds are required for a given treatment. Again, the concept of pool here still holds as the various tasks for a given treatment can be performed by different members of the pool. A given actor is not assigned to a particular patient during the lifecycle of a hospitalization. This is a task centric rather than patient centric system. The easy solution to this problem is to verify if the tasks list has not changed in the meantime before picking and executing a task. In the following example we illustrate how to achieve this tasks list update.

The list of tasks is implemented as a PTC variable as follows:

```
type component PTCType {
  port BMPportType bpmPort;
  var template TaskListType listOfTasks;
}
```

First we have a *receive* event that puts the current tasks list in a given state and stores it to the PTC variable *listOfTasks*:

```
bpmPort.send(loginInfo);
alt {
  [] bpmPort.receive(cac_fax_preparation_task_t)
     -> value listOfTasks {...}
}
```

Second, in order to illustrate the fact that another member may have already picked a task during the delay between the previous response and the actual picking and execution of a task, we place a tasks list update mechanism before the actor picks a task from the list of tasks and executes it. Here the function *getTask()* extracts a task with the name "CAC_FaxPreparation" from the list of tasks previously obtained and stored in the PTC variable *listOfTasks* either through the previous state or the updated state. In addition, a ranking mechanism of PTCs allows avoiding racing conditions that would not be caught by this update mechanism.

```
updateTaskList();
task := getTask(listOfTasks, "CAC_FaxPreparation", rank);
bpmPort.send(TaskExecutionRequestType: { task } );
```

The update mechanism consists in a function that tries to receive a new tasks list from the BPM. However, this *receive* statement is blocking by definition. Thus, if no new tasks list has been received, this would block the system unnecessarily. In TTCN-3, the easy way to avoid this situation is to create an alternative with a timer's timeout. The timer can be set to a very small value as its only function is to avoid blocking. If a message has indeed arrived, TTCN-3 will execute the receive statement first and thus eliminate naturally the timeout alternative because of the top down execution attempt of TTCN-3 *alt* constructs.

```
function updateTaskList() runs on PTCType{
  timer waiter;
  waiter.start(0.01);
  alt {
    [] bpmPort.receive(TaskListType:?)
        -> value listOfTasks
      { waiter.stop; setverdict(pass); }
    [] waiter.timeout{}
  }
}
```

However, all of this works in conjunction with activities in the concrete layer's test adapter. Normally, it would be the web application that triggers this update. Thus, we need to simulate this activity by having the test adapter inspect all active BPM clients, check their in boxes and enqueue the updated task lists to the associated PTCs instances. However, we need to tell the test adapter which PTCs belong to which pool. This is achieved via administrative messages between the abstract test case and the test adapter. The test adapter then uses this information to maintain lists of pools and their members. This could be improved by adding the concept of pool to the TTCN-3 language PTC *create* construct such as:

```
nursePTC_1 := PTCType.create("nurse1", "nurses");
```

Overlapping Dependencies. Overlapping dependencies occur when two parallel actors have more than one sequential dependency during the execution of their behaviors. In Fig. 5, user 2 depends on the execution of task T1a and T1b of user 1 before it can execute its own tasks T3a and T3b. further downstream, user 1 depends on user 2's execution of these tasks to be able to perform task T2a and T2b and so on.

This type of configuration can be handled naturally using the same sequencing of PTCs execution as shown for the sequential dependencies case above. The difference is that different behaviors need to be started for the different phases of activity of a given PTC combined with a *ptc.done* statement for each phase. For example, this is the case of a physician that assesses a patient both before and

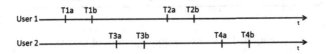

Fig. 5. Overlapping dependencies

after they go into surgery. However, in order to achieve this staggered behavior execution, the PTC needs to be declared with the TTCN-3 *alive* feature as follows:

```
var PTCType contactNurse1 :=
    PTCType.create("contactnurse1") alive;
```

2.3 Maximizing the Benefits of Parallel Test Components Execution

In TTCN-3, parallel test components (PTCs) are implemented by the execution tool as threads. While this concept is very powerful, the only problem is that each thread will attempt to execute its behavior as system resources are available which naturally could mean immediately. The benefits of parallel execution of roles behavior should normally be to verify that any combination of sequencing of test events configuration does not cause the SUT to fail as shown in Fig. 6. Leaving the PTCs to execute their behaviors freely may lead to bad test case coverage. For example, a strict sequence of behaviors where one PTC's behavior executes only after another has completed its execution will be highly unlikely. This problem can be solved by introducing coordination messages to force a BPM to wait until a given state of another PTC has been reached. However, this approach could result in bad coverage too if the tester forgot to address specific interleaving configurations. Also, coordination messages are tedious to manage and are a form of un-flexible hard coding. Instead, we have experimented with the insertion of random delays between test events that combined with repeated executions of the test cases (see Fig. 6) has shown to provide a better test coverage but also truly mimic actors behaviors.

This approach enabled the discovery of faults in the BPM logic as shown for example in Fig. 1 that no one suspected could exist. Such random delays can be implemented using an external function *generateRandomNumber()* to determine the sleep time of a PTC using timers.

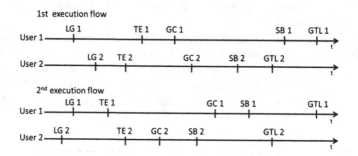

Fig. 6. Effect of random spacing of events

```
function randomDelay() {
  timer delayer;
  var float waitTime := generateRandomNumber() * 2.0;
  delayer.start(waitTime);
  delayer.timeout;
}
```

However, this solution is potentially not optimal as timers can consume system resources. Instead, another solution would be to use the concrete PTC implementation as a thread and its corresponding *sleep()* method. This would require a change in the TTCN-3 execution tool that needs to be addressed by TTCN-3 tool providers.

Also, for BPM testing, random delays between events appeared preferable to coordination messages because coordination messages are static and require duplicating behavior logic. With random delays between test events, the overall behavior as sequences of events remains constant while the execution of events becomes dynamic over time and allows discovering faults resulting from different interleaving of events patterns. Future work would include statistical methods applied to logs that can in turn be used to appraise the resulted test coverage.

2.4 Handling Delayed Responses from the SUT

In the course of testing, we have noticed that sometimes the BPM would respond with unpredictable delays that can be attributed mostly to differences in load. Thus, the list of tasks available to an actor would not be updated as expected. This would result in mismatched test oracles as in the following alternative where a response is not corresponding to the stimulus but instead to an unrelated update of the list of tasks available to a pool:

```
bpmPort.send(click_next_searchPatient_button_t
      (valueof(execResponse.coach), task.taskId));
  alt {
    [] bpmPort.receive(cac_fax_preparation_task_t)
          -> value listOfTasks {setverdict(pass);}
    [] bpmPort.receive {setverdict(fail); }
  }
```

The above *alt* construct can be modified by inserting an alternate receive statement of *TaskListType* data type in second position. This statement however would be combined with a *repeat* construct that enables receiving the expected response later:

```
  [] bpmPort.receive(TaskListType: ?)
        -> value listOfTasks { repeat; }
```

3   Conclusion

Business Process Management applications in the medical domain pose challenging testing problems that result from parallel execution of test behaviors performed by different actors, especially given the practice of creating pools of actors to fulfill particular roles. Addressing such problems using traditional unit testing languages is complex and error prone given the need to coordinate and validate all possible interleaving combinations, as well as dealing with race conditions.

We have proposed an architecture based on the TTCN-3 model of separation of concerns and its intensive parallel test component (PTC) concept to provide solutions to these issues. We successfully used a case study of a Cancer Patient Assessment process to demonstrate the benefits of the proposed approach. In doing so, we used time-based random delays to coordinate interleaving and avoid unintended race conditions in the test framework. This ensured a natural maximization of test coverage. However, this solution is potentially not optimal as our use of timers for random delays can consume system resources. Instead, another solution would be to use the concrete PTC implementation as a thread and its corresponding *sleep()* method. This would require a change in the TTCN-3 execution tool that needs to be addressed by TTCN-3 tool providers.

Acknowledgements. The authors would like to thank Testing Technologies IST GmbH for providing us the necessary tool — *TTworkbench* to carry out this research as well as funding from MITACS.

References

1. Business Process Specification Schema 1.0.1, May 2001 and ebBP, v2.0.4, October 2006
2. Csorba, M.J., Eottevenyi, D., Palugyai, S.: TridentCom: TTCN-3 in testbeds and research infrastructure for the development of networks and communities. In: 3rd International Conference on Experimenting with Dynamic Test Component Deployment (2007)
3. Deiss, T.: TTCN-3 for Large Systems. Nokia Research Centre. http://www.wiley.com/legacy/wileychi/ttcn-3/supp/largesystems.pdf
4. Din, G., Tolea, S., Schieferdecker, I.: Distributed load tests with TTCN-3. In: Uyar, M.Ü., Duale, A.Y., Fecko, M.A. (eds.) TestCom 2006. LNCS, vol. 3964, pp. 177–196. Springer, Heidelberg (2006)
5. Ertugrul, A., Demirors, O.: An exploratory study on role-based collaborative business process modeling approaches. In: S-BPM ONE 2015, New York, NY, USA (2015)
6. ETSI ES 201 873–1: The Testing and Test Control Notation version 3 Part 1: TTCN-3 Core Language, version 4.6.1 (2014)
7. ETSI ES 201 873–6: The Testing and Test Control Notation version 3 Part 6: TTCN-3 Control Interface (TCI), version 4.6.1 (2014)
8. ETSI ES 202 789: The Testing and Test Control Notation version 3; TTCN-3 Language Extentions: Extended TRI, version 1.2.1 (2013)

9. JUnit, Java for Unit Test. http://junit.org/
10. Lee, Y.: An implementation case study: business oriented SOA execution test framework. In: Fifth International Joint Conference on INC, IMS and IDC. IEEE (2009)
11. Mallur, K.: A Quality Assurance Framework for Business Process Management. Masters Dissertation, University of Ottawa (2015)
12. Neukirchen, H.: Taming the raven – testing the random access, visualization and exploration network RAVEN. In: Jónasson, K. (ed.) PARA 2010, Part II. LNCS, vol. 7134, pp. 196–205. Springer, Heidelberg (2012)
13. Selenium. http://www.seleniumhq.org
14. Stepien, B., Peyton, L.: Innovation and evolution in integrated web application testing with TTCN-3. Int. J. Softw. Tools Technol. Transf. **16**(3), 269–283 (2013). doi:10.1007/s10009-013-0278-x. Springer
15. Stepien, B., Xiong, P., Peyton, L.: A systematic approach to web application penetration testing using TTCN-3. In: Babin, G., Stanoevska-Slabeva, K., Kropf, P. (eds.) MCETECH 2011. LNBIP, vol. 78, pp. 1–16. Springer, Heidelberg (2011)
16. Tan, R.P., Edwards, S.H.: Experiences evaluating the effectiveness of JML-JUnit testing. ACM SIGSOFT Softw. Eng. Notes **29**(5), 1–4 (2004)
17. TTworkbench, Testing Technologies GmbH. http://www.testingtech.com/
18. van der Aalst, W.M.P.: Business Process Management Demystified: A Tutorial on Models, Systems and Standards for Workflow Management. In: Desel, J., Reisig, W., Rozenberg, G. (eds.) Lectures on Concurrency and Petri Nets. LNCS, vol. 3098, pp. 1–65. Springer, Heidelberg (2004)

Generating Performance Test Model from Conformance Test Logs

Gusztáv Adamis[1,2], Gábor Kovács[2]([⊠]), and György Réthy[1]

[1] Ericsson Hungary, Irinyi J. u. 4-20, 1117 Budapest, Hungary
{gusztav.adamis,gyorgy.rethy}@ericsson.com
[2] Department of Telecommunications and Media Informatics,
Budapest University of Technology and Economics,
Magyar Tud ósok k ör útja 2, 1117 Budapest, Hungary
{adamis,kovacsg}@tmit.bme.hu

Abstract. In this paper, we present a method that learns a deterministic finite state machine from the conformance test logs of a telecommunication protocol; then that machine is used as test model for performance testing. The learning process is in contrast to most theoretical methods automatic; it applies a sequential pattern mining algorithm on the test logs, and uses a recently proposed metric for finding frequent and significant transition sequences. The method aims to help and speed up test model design, and at the same time it may not provide an exact solution, the equivalence of some states may not be proven. In the paper, we show the results of experiments on random machines, and issues and considerations that arise when the method was applied to 3GGP Telephony Application Server test logs.

Keywords: Test model · Sequential pattern mining · FSM Learning

1 Introduction

Creating test cases for functional testing and traffic scenarios for load testing are complex and manual tasks are carried out possibly independently in different groups of the same enterprise. The tasks themselves require the studying of system documentation, the analysis of SUT traces and lots of discussions with the stakeholders. This requires significant amount of time and resources.

The aim of this paper is to show a method that can help creating test performance test cases from conformance test logs. As functional testing precedes performance testing and functional test cases cover most transitions, logs of test execution can be a starting point for generating a test model. Note that the test logs may contain both valid and invalid behaviour in form of steps of passed and failed functional test cases. As load test tools like TitanSim by Ericsson use FSMs to describe entity behaviour, the test model to be created is expressed in a language describing FSMs. The machine generated may not be complete and may contain inadequately restored transitions, nevertheless, test engineers only

© Springer International Publishing Switzerland 2015
J. Fischer et al. (Eds.): SDL 2015, LNCS 9369, pp. 268–284, 2015.
DOI: 10.1007/978-3-319-24912-4_19

need to complete or refine such machines to be able to start performance testing, human interaction is required only to start the process and after the termination to minimize the output machine.

1.1 Related Work

In the problem of learning an automaton [9], one can supply inputs to a black box implementation machine and observe its outputs. Most existing approaches suppose assume that there exists an oracle, who is able to tell at any time to the learning algorithm whether the machine learnt at the current iteration cycle is equivalent to the black box machine, and if not, provide a distinguishing counter-example. Angluin's pioneering method [2] introduces an observation table that consists of a prefix-closed event sequence, a postfix-closed event sequence and a mapping function that concatenates a prefix, an input event string and a postfix, and decides if the concatenated event sequence can be produced by the machine. The learner algorithm incrementally augments the observation table with the counter-examples provided by the oracle, and maintains its closed and consistent properties. The procedure is terminated when no counter-examples are returned. This algorithm requires the black box machine to have the reliable reset ability. Rives and Schapire proposed an improvement to Angluin's method, their algorithms can find a homing sequence in an unknown automaton [13] that can be used to reset the machine. In [10], Li et al. modify Angluin's method, they modify the observation table such that only input events are considered in the event sequences, and the output of the mapping function are output events. Their second improvement is that instead of using an oracle for teaching they propose to test the system with a test suite generated on the learnt machine by means of a certain test generation strategy, and if a discrepancy is found, then that test case can be considered as the counter-example. This method can be fully automatic, however it includes a test generation and a test execution phase that can be very time consuming. The same authors proposed another improvement in [14], they proposed an algorithm that is able to learn parameterized finite state machines with finite domain input and output parameters, and input guard conditions with a certain set of restrictions. A similar method is introduced in [6] by Howar et al., they incrementally refine the input alphabet with parameters to eliminate nondeterminism in the learnt machine. Hungar et al. propose in their papers to take reactive system specific modeling aspects improving the mapping function into account [7] such as the separation of input and output symbols, not continuing prefixes that have been evaluated positively or negatively, an input event determines the output events, and no input event is applied until all outputs have been determined. In [5], they propose that learning a model of a system developed incrementally should use the previous versions learnt as an input, and improve those models with the new knowledge. Barringer et al. present a framework in [4] that decomposes the machine learnt into parallel components. Algorithms for learning deterministic finite state machines have been reviewed in [3,12]. Though these methods run in polynomial time and learn the exact black box machine, they require too much intervention from an oracle, that is, from one or more engineers.

1.2   Our Contribution

In this paper, we assume that we cannot a directly access the black box implementation machine, however we do have access to test logs of that implementation, and that log contains all input and output events that appear on its interface. This problem is not equivalent to the machine learning problem, however, they share a lot of similarities. In their paper, Rivest and Schapire state that "learning by passively observing the behavior of the unknown machine is apparently infeasible" [13]. Though the complexity of this problem is exponential, the progress in the field of data mining research in the last decade makes a revision possible. In data mining theory, several algorithms have been proposed to find transactions that appear frequently in a specified order in database logs. Such an algorithm is used for finding common behavior patterns of users who browse a web portal, or for finding clinical course patterns based in health-care databases. One of the first sequential pattern mining algorithm is GSP proposed by Srikant and Agrawal [15] which is used in this paper. It is based on the pattern of the famous apriori algorithm [1].

We propose an unsupervised algorithm for reconstructing incompletely specified deterministic finite state machines. The black box machine is not required to have reliable reset. In our approach, GSP is used for building frequent I/O event set sequences incrementally. In each iteration cycle, it tries to append all possible I/O sets to the end of each frequent prefix found so far, and keeps only those new sequences, which occur more frequently in the observation set than a user defined threshold. Then, we build prefix trees from the set of observation sequences, and perform incomplete Mealy machine minimization procedure where we make use of the information extracted from GSP. We assume that the black box machine is the same state partition after each frequent subsequence, if the observable I/O event sets after that subsequence are compatible. The event sequences used are neither prefix, nor postfix closed, hence omitting the front or the tail event from a frequent subsequence, allows the identification of functional dependencies among states, i.e. the next state relations.

As we passively observe the system, we may not learn the unexplored part of the state space of the black box machine, and the reconstructed machine is not reduced, and may not be strongly connected. However, the number of states of the transition system constructed from the observation sequences can be reduced close to the number of the original states. After the termination of our algorithm, pieces of information are available on the compatibility of strongly connected states and not strongly connected states, which can easily be decided with a human eye in front of a visual user interface. Just like most data mining algorithms, GSP is not P-space, however after the identification of the frequent subsequences the rest of the method can run in polynomial time of the size of the I/O alphabet if we take a heuristics on the subsequences into account.

The paper is organized as follows. After a brief overview and the introduction of notations regarding finite state machines, we describe the GSP algorithm in Sect. 2. In Sect. 3, we specialize GSP so that it can detect state partitions, and show how a FSM states and transitions can be reconstructed. Experimental results on random machines and on the 3GGP Telephony Application Server and arising issues are shown in Sects. 4 and 5. Finally, Sect. 6 summarizes the paper.

2 Preliminaries

2.1 Finite State Machines

A Mealy finite state machine is a quintuple $M = (S, I, O, \lambda, \delta)$, where S is the finite and nonempty set of states, I is the finite and nonempty set of input events, O is the finite and nonempty set of output events, and $\delta : S \times I \rightarrow S$ is the next state function, and $\lambda : S \times I \rightarrow O$ is the output function. Both δ and λ can be generalized to accept the input sequence $x = x_1, \ldots, x_k$ such that with the index $j = 1, \ldots, k$ $\delta(s_j, x_j) = s_{j+1}$, and the final state is $\delta(s_1, x) = s_{k+1}$, and $\lambda(s_j, x_j) = y_j$, and the produced output sequence is $\lambda(s, x) = y = y_1, \ldots, y_k$.

The strongly connected property of M means that all states are reachable from all other states, formally $\forall s, s' \in S : \exists x \in I* : \delta(s, x) = s'$.

Machine M is deterministic if $\forall s, s', s'' \in S, i \in I, o, o' \in O : \delta(s, i) = s'$ and $\delta(s, i) = s''$ and $\lambda(s, i) = o$ and $\lambda(s, i) = o'$, then $o = o'$ and $s' = s''$. Machine M is incompletely specified if for a state $s \in S$ and input $i \in I$, $\delta(s, i)$ and $\lambda(s, i)$ are undefined. In this case, we adopt the completeness assumption, and let $\delta(s, i) = s$ and $\lambda(s, i) = \varepsilon$, where ε means the lack of observable output events.

In machine M, states $s, s' \in S$ are equivalent if $\exists i \in I : \delta(s, i) = s'', \lambda(s, i) = o$ and $\delta(s', i) = s''', \lambda(s', i) = o$, where $o \in O$ and $s'', s''' \in S$ are equivalent. If for any $s, s' \in S$ s and s' are not equivalent in M, then M is said to be reduced. States $s, s' \in S$ of the incompletely specified M are said to be compatible, if $\forall i \in I : \exists \delta(s, i)$ and $\exists \delta(s', i)$, then $\lambda(s, i) = o = \lambda(s', i)$ and $\delta(s, i) = s'', \delta(s', i) = s'''$, where $o \in O$ and $s'', s''' \in S$ are compatible.

2.2 GSP

Before introducing the GSP algorithm itself, we define the terms sequential pattern and occurrence.

A sequential pattern is a sequence constructed from the elements of superset Ξ with the concatenation operator, each element of set Ξ is a set of symbols itself. Let $A \in \Xi*$ and $B \in \Xi*$ be two sequences such that $A = X_1, X_2, \ldots, X_k$ and $B = Y_1, Y_2, \ldots, Y_m$ where $X \in \Xi$ is indexed with an integer $1 \ldots k$ and $B \in \Xi$ is indexed with an integer $1 \ldots m$. The sequence A is said to occur in sequence B, if and only if there exists a sequence of integers $1 <= i1 < i2 < \cdots < ik <= m$ such that $X_1 \subseteq Y_{i1}, X_2 \subseteq Y_{i2}, \ldots, X_k \subseteq Y_{ik}$.

The GSP proposed by Srikant and Agrawal [15] can discover such sequential patterns in database transaction sets. A database transaction ($\Xi*$ in the definition above) consists of a sequence of queries (Ξ), which are ordered by their execution timestamps. An element of Ξ is a set itself, which means that a query accesses several attributes of a relation in the database. This algorithm intends to find the sequences of queries that appear in all transactions in the same order. Note that GSP does not require that $ik - i1 = k$, there may be a finite number of Ξ elements inserted in B that are not present in A.

The input of GSP is a set of database transactions, and a threshold value given by the user. The output is a set of $\Xi*$ sequences, which are considered to be frequent, if their occur more frequently than the user defined minimum support threshold would require. The minimum support is a percentage, the number of occurrences divided by the total number of possible sequences.

Algorithm 1. Finding frequent itemsets with GSP

> **input** : $T = \{T_1, T_2, \ldots, T_m\}, T_i \in \Xi*, i = 1 \ldots m; \mu \in [0, 1)$
> /* The input is a set of transactions and a threshold value */
> **output**: $F = \{F_1, F_2, \ldots, F_n\}, F_j \in \Xi*, j = 1 \ldots n$
> /* The output is a set of frequent itemsets */
> 1 data$(i, j, k, F0, FC, F_C)$
>
> /* Initialization */
> 2 $k := 1; F0 = \bigcup_{f=0}^{|\Xi|} T_{if}, T_{if} \in \Xi, i = 1 \ldots m; F = F0;$
> 3 **while true do**
> 4 $\quad FC := \emptyset;$
> 5 $\quad$ **foreach** $i, i = 1..|F|, \text{length}(F_j) = k$ **do**
> 6 $\quad\quad$ **foreach** $j, j = 1..|F|, \text{length}(F_j) = k$ **do**
> 7 $\quad\quad\quad F_C := \text{merge}(F_j, F_i);$
> 8 $\quad\quad\quad$ **if** $\text{occur}(F_C, T) > \mu$ **then** $FC := FC \cup \{F_C\};$
> 9 $\quad\quad$ **end foreach**
> 10 $\quad$ **end foreach**
> 11 $\quad$ **if** $FC = \emptyset$ **then return** $F;$
> 12 $\quad F := F \cup \{FC\};$
> 13 $\quad k := k + 1;$
> 14 **end while**

The GSP algorithm is based on the apriori algorithm, but takes the ordering of sets into account, and instead of growing sets, it merges frequent sequences of the previous iteration if those are the same after removing the head of the one and the tail of the other. This is based on the principle that all subsequences of a frequent sequence are frequent.

The inputs are the set of transactions T, and the minimum support threshold μ. The attribute set used can be derived from T. The output is the frequent itemset F. Three loop variables are used in the body of the algorithm along with the set F that contains attributes derived from T. The set F containing the frequent sequences to be returned that is initialized to $F0$, and the set FC containing the sequences in the current iteration cycle. In the body of the procedure, an infinite loop is formed, where the FC set of current transactions is first initialized to an empty set. Then, each element of the actual output set

F with length k is merged with another element of the same length only if after removing the head transaction of one and the tail transaction of the other the remaining sequence of transactions are the same. In such cases, the resulting candidate sequence is the common sequence appended with in the front with the head transaction and in the back with the tail transaction. Note, that for $k = 2$, the common sequence is empty, so all combinations are generated. Then, it is checked if any element of this newly generated sequence set occurs more frequently in the transaction sets than the μ input threshold, and if it does, that sequence is added to FC. If FC is empty, then the procedure returns the frequent itemset F, otherwise it appends FC to F, increments the maximum length loop variable k, and runs the main loop again.

The complexity of the algorithm is exponential as the worst case number of frequent itemset is $|\Xi|^M$, where M is the cardinality of T_i with the second largest size. Hence, this algorithm does never run in real-time systems, just only in back-offices.

3   Unsupervised FSM Reconstruction

In this paper, we reconstruct the model of an implementation in a black box that is assumed to be originally a deterministic, incompletely specified, strongly connected, reduced Mealy finite state machine. The Mealy machine reconstructed is deterministic, but most probably has neither of the remaining properties. The reconstruction in unsupervised, so the test engineer does not need to have access to the implementation itself, only to conformance test logs, therefore the reconstruction is an automatic process.

In the rest of this section, we propose a way for using GSP to identify frequent event sequences, and show how those can be used to find state partitions of a black box machine in a prefix tree constructed from a large set of observation sequences.

3.1   Initial Considerations

We assume that the observation sequences in the test logs are "long enough", which means practically with an example from telecommunications that they do not terminate immediately when for instance a call set up is completed, just only when the call is already terminated or even beyond that. The rationale behind this assumption is that such long sequences are required for setting up relations between state clusters of the reconstructed machine. Without this, the strongly connected property even for a subset of the state set of the output machine can not be met.

If we have a single sequence that is (however) quasi infinitely long , because of a continuous observation of a system that is in operation, then the sequence is split at random points into a set of sequences such that each one still remains long enough.

It is helpful information, if we can assume that all sequences start from the same state in the black box machine, i.e., there is an initial state, however, this is not a necessary condition. In the case of conformance test logs, we can rely on this property. In general, we allow the observation sequences to start at any time independently from the current state of the black box machine.

The fundamental idea behind our approach is that before and after a frequent sequence the black box machine is in the same state partitions respectively. It is essential to note that the length of frequent sequences has an important role. This assumption only holds if the frequent sequence is "long enough", where this time long enough means that they are assumed to be longer than the longest sequence in the separating family of sequences of the black box machine. As this length information can not be determined at runtime, this must be provided by an oracle before the execution of the algorithm. In general, if we take the completeness assumption into account, the maximum length of separating sequences should be inversely proportional to the size of the I and O sets of the black box machine. Another important note is that the assumption on the state partition before a frequent sequence is weaker than the assumption on the state partition after.

3.2 Specialization of GSP

We specialize GSP for finding frequent subsequences in observation sequences of a black box machine the following way. From the set of observation sequences, we extract the sets I and O. Because of the reactive nature of the Mealy state machines, we can use the input determinism principle of [5], and partition each sequence along input events such that one input event is followed by one output event, or more generally arbitrary number of output events. From these partitions, we construct sets, where each set contains exactly one element from the set input events I and a subset of the output events O, and we add each of these sets to Ξ, which is the set of different I/O behaviors that can be observed. Then, we transform all sequences in T to be $\Xi*$ instead of $(I \cup (O \cup \{\varepsilon\}))*$. Thereafter, let $T = (N, \Xi, E)$ be an input/output transition system. Its graph representation is a directed edge labelled forest with $|T|$ roots and no branches, the kth sequence $X_k = X_{k1}, \ldots, X_{kl}, X_{ki} \in \Xi*$ is mapped such that $(n_{k,i-1}, X_{ki}, n_{k,i}) \in E$, and $n_{k,i-1}, n_{k,i} \in N$, for all $i = 1 \ldots l$.

We reinterpret the input parameter minimum support μ as well, we say that a sequence is supported, if it appears in the execution logs at least a certain number of times, that is, instead of relative occurrence, we use an absolute number for the minimum number of occurrences. We introduce an additional input parameter ν, which represents the minimum length for the frequent subsequences to be returned. This is also an important heuristic parameter that should be set such that it is greater than the length of longest sequence suspected in the separating family of sequences of the black box machine.

As we intend to restore an FSM, when searching for frequent subsequences we must require an exact match between the two Ξ elements compared from the two sequences to be able to talk about the same transition in an FSM. While GSP does not require observed events to be successors, in this case not only the order of Ξ elements has importance, but those must appear strictly one after another in the sequences of T. Hence, we reinterpret the term occurrence as well. Let $A \in \Xi*$ and $B \in \Xi*$ be two sequences such that $A = X_1, X_2, \ldots, X_k$ and $B = Y_1, Y_2, \ldots, Y_m$ where $X \in \Xi$ is indexed with an integer $1 \ldots k$ and $B \in \Xi$ is indexed with an integer $1 \ldots m$. The sequence A is said to occur in sequence B, if and only if there exists a sequence of integers $1 <= i1 < i2 < \cdots < ik <= m$ such that $X_1 = Y_{i1}, X_2 = Y_{i2}, \ldots, X_k = Y_{ik}$ and $ik - i1 = k$.

Algorithm 2. Finding frequent subsequences in observation sequences of a black box FSM

---

    input : $T = \{T_1, T_2, \ldots, T_m\}, T_i \in \Xi*, i = 1 \ldots m; \mu \in \mathbb{N}; \nu \in \mathbb{N}$
    /* The input is a set of observed sequences, minimum occurrence, minimum length */
    output: $F = \{F_1, F_2, \ldots, F_n\}, F_j \in \Xi*, j = 1 \ldots n$
    /* The output is a set of frequent subsequences */

1   data($i, j, k,$ $F0, FC, F_C$)

    /* Initialization */

2   $k := 1; F0 = \bigcup_{f=1}^{|\Xi|} T_{if}, T_{if} \in \Xi, i = 1 \ldots m; F = F0;$

3   **while true do**

4       $FC := \emptyset;$

5   **foreach** $i, i = 1..|F|, \text{length}(F_i) = k$ **do**

6   **foreach** $j, j = 1..|F|, \text{length}(F_j) = k$ **do**

7              $F_C := \text{merge}(F_j, F_i);$

8   **if** $\text{occur}(F_C, T) > \mu$ **then** $FC := FC \cup \{F_C\};$

9   **end foreach**

10   **end foreach**

11   **if** $FC = \emptyset$ **then return** $F, \text{length}(F_j) \geq \nu;$

12     $F := F \cup \{FC\};$

13     $k := k + 1;$

14 **end while**

Algorithm 2 is changed compared to Algorithm 1 at several points. The domain of μ is changed to natural numbers, and an additional integer input parameter ν is introduced. Here, the occur function returns the absolute number of occurrences, instead of relative, it searches for the pattern given as the first parameter in the set of sequences given as the second parameter, and returns the number of times the pattern is found. And finally, only the elements of F with at least ν length are returned in line 11.

The complexity of Algorithm 2 is not changed with the specialization, it is still exponentially proportional to the length of the longest input sequence. The algorithm returns a set of sequences that can be organized into a prefix pyramid. Increasing the minimum support narrows the top of the pyramid, and increasing the minimum length cuts the bottom of the pyramid.

3.3   State Candidate Identification

The inputs of procedure of this subsection are the set of frequent subsequences F, the set of observation sequences T, a user defined threshold τ on the number of prefix trees to be generated, and the user defined value ν is reused. The former user input has significance in improving the confidence of this heuristic approach, and the latter one is used for reducing its complexity. The output of the procedure is a superset Π that is a partition of nodes of transition systems constructed from T, where nodes in each partition are assumed to be in the same state partition of the black box machine.

First, we create prefix trees from the set of sequences T the following way. We select the subsequence $\max_i(\text{occur}(F_i, T)), i = 1, \ldots, |T|$, and cut each $T_j \in T$ after the first occurrence of the F_i subsequence, only if $\text{occur}(F_i, T_j) > 0$. If not present, then T_j is excluded from building the prefix tree. If we know that all sequences in T begin from the initial state of the black box machine, then only one prefix tree is constructed from the beginning of the sequences with cut after an ε sequence. This prefix tree contains all sequences, and one state is exactly identified.

The prefix tree for the cut after the subsequence F_i is a quadruple $PT^{F_i} = (\Sigma^{F_i}, \Theta^{F_i}, \Xi, \sigma_0)$, where Σ^{F_i} is the set of nodes of the tree, $\sigma_0 \in \Sigma^{F_i}$ is the root node of the tree. $\Theta^{F_i} \subseteq \Sigma^{F_i} \times \Xi \times \Sigma^{F_i}$ is the set of edges of the tree labelled with an element of the Ξ set. We define a mapping $\gamma^{F_i} : N \rightarrow \Sigma^{F_i}$ between the nodes of the transition system and the prefix tree. For the case of the cut sequence $T_j \in T$, let $\gamma^{F_i}(n_{j,f}) = \sigma_0$ initially, where f is the position of the cut, and $\forall k = f, \ldots, l$ if $\gamma^{F_1}(n_{j,k}) = \sigma_n$ and $\gamma^{F_1}(n_{j,k+1}) = \sigma_{n+1}$ and $\theta = (\sigma_n, X_{jn}, \sigma_{n+1}) \notin \Theta^{F_i}$, then θ is added to Θ^{F_i}.

After the construction of the prefix tree, for each node of the tree we collect the set of possible next events by applying the labeling function $a : \Sigma^{F_i} \rightarrow \Xi', \Xi' \subseteq \Xi$ that assigns a subset of Ξ to node $\sigma_k \in \Sigma^{F_i}$ such that if there is a sequence $X = X_1, \ldots, X_n, X_i \in \Xi$ and $\forall i < k : \exists(\sigma_i, X_{i+1}, \sigma_{i+1}) \in \Theta^{F_i}$ and $\exists(\sigma_k, X_{k+1}, \sigma_{k+1}) \in \Theta^{F_i}$, then $X_{k+1} \in a(\sigma_k)$.

Let the output of the partitioning with regard to the cut after the F_i frequent subsequence be the set $\Pi^{F_i} = \{\Pi_1^{F_i}, \ldots, \Pi_n^{F_i}\}$, where $\Pi_k^{F_i} \subseteq N$ is a partition of nodes of the T transition system and $\bigcup_k \Pi_k^{F_i} = N$ and $\forall 1 \le k, l \le n : \Pi_k^{F_i} \cap \Pi_l^{F_i} = \emptyset$. The elements of N are partitioned by adopting the definition of compatibility such that $\gamma(n_i) = \sigma_i, \gamma(n_j) = \sigma_j$, where $\sigma_i, \sigma_j \in \Sigma^{F_i}$ are in the same partition $\Pi_k^{F_i}$ if $a(\sigma_i) = a(\sigma_j)$ and $\forall X_k \in a(\sigma_i)$ if $\exists(\sigma_i, X_k, \sigma_i')$ and $\exists(\sigma_j, X_k, \sigma_j')$ and $a(\sigma_i') = a(\sigma_j')$ holds as well. If n_i and n_j are compatible, then they are assumed to be in the same state partition of the black box machine.

If it is known before applying the procedure of this section that all observation sequences start from the same initial state, then the one partitioning without any cut is sufficient. If the initial state of the observation sequences is unknown, then let us repeat the procedure for a certain subset of frequent subsequences $F_i \in F$, where the number of F_i subsequences to be used is provided by the user. If there is a contradiction between any pair of partitions of any cuts such that $\Pi_k^{F_i} \ne \Pi_l^{F_j}$ and $\Pi_k^{F_i} \cap \Pi_l^{F_j} \ne \emptyset$, then both $\Pi_k^{F_i}$ and $\Pi_l^{F_j}$ are atomized into partitions with singleton elements from N. Finally, let the output state partitions be $\Pi = \bigcup_i \Pi^{F_i}$, which means that only those nodes in N are put in the same partitions, which are confirmed to equivalent by all prefix trees independently from the cuts.

If the F_i subsequences are "long enough", then the node partitions contain singleton elements, and we can define the set of states as $S = \Pi$, that is, the set of node partitions are mapped to state set of the black box machine. In general, it is true that the number of states restored this way is greater than the real number of states in the black box.

The space and time complexities of the construction of the prefix tree are proportional to $|T|$ and $L_T = \max_i(\text{length}(T_i))$, while the time cost of cutting the sequences is proportional to L_T and $L_F = \max_j(\text{length}(F_j))$. The complexity of the minimization of an incompletely specified Mealy state machine has been proven to be NP-hard [11], and this can be extended for checking the compatibility of any pairs of nodes of our prefix tree due to the recursion condition on the next nodes. The finite size of the prefix tree puts only an upper bound on the number of conditions on the next nodes to be evaluated, which is worst case $(|I|)^d$, where d is the level of the recursion that cannot be greater than L_T, and in each node of the prefix tree there can be at most $|I|$ next nodes. As a user input ν is available on the suspected length of the longest sequence in the separating family of sequences of the black box machine, it is possible to use that heuristic value to limit the recursion to that level. This means that for each pair of nodes of PT the cost of compatibility check is $(|I|)^\nu$. As $(|T|L_T)^2$ pairs of nodes have to be checked, and checking the equality of two Ξ' sets returned by function a is worst case $(|I| + |O|)^2$, the resulting complexity is $O(|T|L_T|I|^{\nu+2}|O|^2)$.

3.4   Reconstruction of Transitions

The final step of our method reconstructs machine $M^* = (S^*, I, O, \delta^*, \lambda^*)$ from the inputs Π, T and F. The transitions from a state $s^* = \pi$ are determined by $a(\gamma(\pi)) = \Xi' \subseteq \Xi$. According to the definition, $\exists i \in \Xi'$ such that $i \in I$, hence, for each element of Ξ', it is possible to define a $\delta^*(s^*, i)$ and a $\lambda^*(s^*, i)$. The former can be extracted from T, by searching for the edge (n, X_k, n'), where $n \in \pi$ and $i \in X_k$, and then $s'^* = \pi'$ where $n' \in \pi'$. The latter is $\lambda^*(s^*, i) = o$, if $\exists o \in \Xi' : o \in O$, otherwise $\lambda^*(s^*, i) = \varepsilon$ using the completeness assumption.

From each pair $F_i, F_j \in F$, we can construct the $x_1, x_2 \in I*$ input sequences and the $y_1, y_2 \in O*$ output sequences, and if $x_1 = i_{11}, \ldots, i_{1k}$ and $x_2 = i_{21}, i_{11} \ldots, i_{1k}, \ldots$, i.e., x_2 contains x_1 after a one event long prefix, and if σ_1 and σ_2 are two nodes in a prefix tree with the same cut, and there is an edge sequence from σ_1 that is labelled with the sequence F_i and there is an edge sequence from σ_2 that is labelled with the sequence F_j, then in machine M^* there must be a transition between $s_1^* = \pi_1, \sigma_1 \in \pi_1$ and $s_2^* = \pi_2, \sigma_1 \in \pi_1$ with the input i_{21} and the output o_{21}. For example, consider a random machine with four input from a to d, and four output from 0 to 3. If two frequent sequences are $c/0\ c/0\,b/1$, then there is a transition from the state that corresponds to $c/0$ with $b/1$ input and output events to the state that corresponds to $c/0\,b/1$.

Table 1. Observation table for random machine

	a/0	a/1	a/2	b/0	b/1	c/0	c/2	c/3	d/0	d/2
b/1	-	-	c/3 d/2 a/1 b/1	a/0 b/0 c/3 d/2	-	b/0 c/0 b/0 c/0	-	-	-	b/0 c/0
d/0 a/1	-	-	-	a/1 b/0 c/0 d/0	-	a/2 b/0 c/0 d/2	-	-	-	-

The method in the previous paragraph gives trivial dependencies and transitions. As the second stage of reconstruction of transitions, we rely on Angluin's observation table method. As a preliminary step, we associate each $F_i \in F$ with the set of possible next input and output event pairs $a(\Sigma^{F_i}) = \Xi'$ that are observable in the logs. If the set is non-deterministic, i.e. it contains the same input event paired with more than one output events, then the frequent sequence F_i corresponds to a state partition, and ignore that frequent sequence from the rest of the procedure. Then, we construct an observation table so that each row of the table corresponds to a frequent sequence $F_i \in F$, and each column of the table corresponds to a pair of input and output events. Note that we do not create a column for every pair of input and output event, only for the ones that appear in the logs. Then, we each F_i concatenate with each possible follow-up input/output pair, and check for the set of possible pairs of input and output events $a(\Sigma^{F_i.\xi}) = \Xi''$ for each $\xi \in \Xi'$. If there exists $a(\Sigma^{F_j}) = \Xi''$ in the associations, then there is a transition from the state that corresponds to F_i to the state that corresponds to F_j with the input and output ξ. For example, consider the same random machine, and let its observation table be shown in Table 1. Both frequent sequences correspond to a deterministic state partition. There are three transitions from the state that corresponds to $b/1$ to the state that corresponds to $d/0\,a/1$ with both the $b/0$ and the $c/0$ and the $d/2$ events, because both $d/0\,a/1\,b/0$ and $d/0\,a/1\,c/0$ are defined. This also indicates a possible equivalency between the states corresponding to frequent sequences $b/0\,a/1$ and $d/0\,a/1$.

In general, it is possible that the output machine is not strongly connected, and is practically never reduced. The strongly connected property can not be met, if the transition connecting two unconnected subsets of the state set can only be mapped from edges close to the leaf nodes of all prefix trees. This phenomenon is behind the appearance of redundant nodes, if a frequent sequence appears near the end of an observation sequence, then there is insufficient information on the set of possible next events, and that node can not be made compatible with any other nodes, hence a new partition is created.

4   Experiments on Random FSMs

In the small set of experiments shown in this section, a random FSM generator is used for testing the proposed method. Its output is an incompletely specified,

Table 2. Properties of random FSMs and random walk sequences used in the experiments

	$\|S\|$	$\|I\|$	$\|O\|$	Density	$\|T\|$
Machine 1	5	4	4	0.6	30
Machine 2	5	4	4	0.6	100
Machine 3	5	4	4	0.6	200
Machine 4	5	4	4	1.0	30
Machine 5	5	4	4	1.0	100
Machine 6	5	4	4	1.0	200
Machine 7	10	4	4	0.3	30
Machine 8	10	4	4	0.3	200

strongly connected Mealy FSM based on the input parameters number of states, number of inputs, number of outputs and transition density. The transition density is a value in $(0, 1)$, which multiplied by the number of inputs determines the mean number of transitions in a state before the machine is made strongly connected. The observation sequences are generated with a random walk starting from a random state.

In Table 2 below, from the second to the fifth columns represent the numbers of states, input events, output events and density of the black box machine respectively. The sixth column shows the number of traces generated. The length of the random walk sequences is set to $4|S|$ transitions as experience show that it should be at least 3 times the number of states. The value of μ is set to 2, ν is set to 3, and κ is 1, which mean respectively that each subsequence must appear at least twice to be considered to be frequent, each frequent subsequence must contain at least three input events and only one prefix tree is generated. In performance testing, the data flow has little significance, therefore the number of states is selected so that it reflects the number of control states in a telecommunication protocol, which is usually between 5 and 10. The increase of number of the input and output events makes states easier to identify, so the same low number is used in the experiments.

Table 3 shows the evaluation of the restored machines. Its rows correspond to the rows of Table 2. The first column is the number of states of the restored machine before any manual minimization, the second column indicates if the restored machine is strongly connected. The third and fourth columns show the size of the restored state machine, the number of states and the number of transitions. The fifth and sixth columns show the number of errors in the restored and minimized machine. The last two columns show the user time and the memory allocated for the process. The results have been obtained on a PC with 2.4GHz Intel Core i5 processor and 8GB RAM.

The experiments show that if we have long enough observation logs, it is possible to reconstruct the states and transitions of a black box system under

Table 3. Results of a set of experiments on random FSMs and random walk sequences

$|\Pi|$	Connected	States	Transitions	Transition faults	Output faults	Time	Memory
6	Yes	5	17	4	7	2 s	0.5 MB
16	Yes	5	18	1	5	2 s	1.3 MB
15	Yes	5	18	0	0	2 s	3.3 MB
8	Yes	8	22	4	4	2 s	0.5 MB
14	Yes	5	20	0	0	2 s	1.5 MB
21	Yes	5	20	0	0	2 s	2.9 MB
16	No	16	13	12	2	3 s	2.9 MB
33	Yes	10	33	1	0	133 s	6.2 MB

test. The number of states in the output machine increases with the number or length of observation sequences, but remains in all cases close to the order of the number of states in the black box machine. The memory consumption and the time requirement increases heavily as the number of input events grows.

5   Experiment on IMS Telephony Application Server

The test logs analyzed in the experiment are the conformance test logs of an IMS SIP Application Server, a Telephony Application Server (TAS). Altogether 3.3 GB logs of 1051 partly manual test cases have been processed. The manual execution has a significance as that part of the test cases are not optimal, so those may visit parts of the state space that a systematically generated test case would not have done. The TAS implementation can be accesses via multiple interfaces: besides SIP, via HTTP, TCP, UDP, DNS and MSRP (Message Session Relay Protocol). In the level of abstraction we used, we distinguished 83 messages based on the type of the protocol used, and the type field of the payload. Message exchange in the tests was always instantaneous, i.e., there was no delay between a request and a response message. Including timeout triggered interactions in the system under test, 80 different message exchanges (pairs of request and response messages) were observed. The total number of sequences was 16281, the longest one with 829 message exchanges; the average length of sequences was 11.28 message exchanges.

5.1   Frequency Versus Relevance

The method we proposed in Sect. 3 works best when the distribution of the message exchanges in Ξ is uniform. However in the case of test logs, it is skew because of the systematic test case generation. As test engineers use the same sequences of transitions along the edges of a spanning tree to reach a certain state of the state machine, those transitions occur more frequently in the elements of $\Xi*$. This means that spanning tree transitions are frequent, and may suppress a transition traversed only once. Hence we use a recent method proposed in [8], which proposes to use relevance rather than frequency. The transition visited once should have similar relevance value as any spanning tree transition.

The relevance measure ρ is calculated for a prefix $A = X_1, X_2, \ldots, X_k$ where $X_i \in \Xi, i = 1 \ldots k$ and a postfix $B = Y_1, Y_2, \ldots, Y_l$ where $Y_i \in \Xi, i = 1 \ldots l$, and it is associated with the sequence $C = X_1, X_2, \ldots, X_k, Y_1, Y_2, \ldots, Y_l$. Let $f(A, B)$ denote the number of times B appears directly after A in the sequence database. Let $\tilde{F}(A)$ denote the number of sequences A occurs in, and let $\overline{F}(A)$ denote the number of sequences A does not occur in. Let $i(A, B)$ denote the number of times something else than B appears directly after A in the sequence database. Let $|A|$ and $|B|$ denote the lengths of sequences A and B respectively. Then, the relevance of C is calculated as follows

$$\rho(C) = \begin{cases} 0 & \text{if } F(A) = 0 \text{ or } f(A, B) = 0 \\ |A||B|\frac{\overline{F}(A)}{\tilde{F}(A)}\frac{f(A,B)}{i(A,B)} & \text{otherwise} \end{cases} \tag{1}$$

As we use GSP for candidate generation, the new sequence contains only one more transition, i.e., the length of B is always 1. After having calculated the relevance of all C that can be generated from prefix A, we scale relevance values with prefix A into the range $[0, 1]$.

As the test cases in the logs do not always return a pass verdict, the fail verdict can be used to indicate an exclusion with regard to a sequence of message exchanges and a successor message exchange that fails. In such cases the relevance of all prefixes that end directly before the transition that fails concatenated with the transition that fails is set to zero.

5.2   Efficiency of the Method

The experiment was carried on a PC with 2.4 GHz Intel Core i5 processor and 8 GB RAM. The total execution time was 27 hours with a single threaded implementation, the memory requirement was 790 MB. The application identified 61 frequent sequences, of which 15 had a relevance value over 0.1. The state candidate identification process found that these relevant sequences correspond to 10 unique states at the abstraction level defined by the set of messages used, and the states have been found unique and valid with a manual check. The frequent sequences with relevance below 0.1 were mostly found to be loops. Restoring transitions was much easier than in the case of random state machines as most of the interfaces of this TAS implementation define stateless communications and the transitions represent loops around the detected control states.

Nevertheless, we consider this experiment inconclusive because of two reasons. One is the unconvincing separation of data and control portions at the level of input/output message definition, which resulted in the low number of states. Further studies are required for the evaluation of state detection ability of the method. The source of the second problem is the multiple interfaces with stateless protocols, which is addressed in the next subsection.

5.3 State Machine Decomposition

In the experiment above we allowed one interface to be activated "at the same time", it is however possible to give an alternative generalization of GSP for state machine learning. Allowing multiple interfaces leads to race conditions at the composite machine level, but it also allows to reconstruct state machines per interface, which can help us in reducing the number of loop transitions around control states of stateful interfaces.

From Sect. 3.2 on, we have used $A = X_1, X_2, \ldots, X_k$ as the sequence of transitions of the state machine, where each X_i is a pair of an input event and an output event, and the subsequence relation has been defined so that $X_k = Y_{ik}$. GSP is more general than that, it allows X_i to be a set of input/output pairs.

Reconstructing decomposed machines takes place at two levels. For each interface, a state machine can be reconstructed from the sequences that appear on that interface. The second level is the composite machine, for which we propose the following specialization of GSP. Let A and B be defined just like in Sect. 3.2, however let X_k be the set of most recent input/output pairs parsed from the test logs until the second occurrence of an interface, the second event pair on the same interface is not included. Then we can use the original definition of GSP, where A is a subsequence of B, or in other words A occurs in B, if and only if there exists a sequence of integers $1 <= i1 < i2 < \cdots < ik <= m$ such that $X_1 \subseteq Y_{i1}$, $X_2 \subseteq Y_{i2}$, $\ldots$, $X_k \subseteq Y_{ik}$ and $ik - i1 = k$. This way the state of the composite machine can be defined with the total ordering of last activations of parallel interfaces. This further increases the execution cost of machine reconstruction, as instead of equality checks we have to perform subset relation checks.

6 Conclusion

In this paper, we proposed a method that is able to reconstruct the control flow of a protocol as a Mealy finite state machine based on passive observation sequences. The main improvement over existing methods is that engineers are required to touch the system twice, once to start, and at the end to manually correct the machine learnt on a visual user interface, so users do not need to guide the learning process. The main drawbacks are the high time complexity, so this should run overnight, and the fact that a high level of user intuition may be necessary for the minimization process and making the machine strongly connected.

After some small scale experiments on random machines, the experiment on 3GPP TAS shows too that the proposed method is able to reconstruct a valid state machine if the test logs are many and long enough. However, the usability of that state machine strongly depends on the abstraction of the input and output alphabets selected for the learning process. Further studies are required to confirm the correctness of the reconstruction process. Input and output event partitioning, which means the introduction of input and output parameters as in [6,14], seems to be plausible in theory, however must be handled with care based on this industrial experience. Another extension of our approach with significance from the industrial perspective is to take the multiple interfaces of the black box system into account, this further increases the complexity, and requires further research as well.

References

1. Agrawal, R., Srikant, R.: Fast algorithms for mining association rules in large databases. In: Proceedings of the 20th International Conference on Very Large Data Bases, VLDB 1994, pp. 487–499. Morgan Kaufmann Publishers Inc., San Francisco (1994). http://dl.acm.org/citation.cfm?id=645920.672836
2. Angluin, D.: Learning Regular Sets from Queries and Counterexamples. Inf. Comput. **75**(2), 87–106 (1987). http://dx.doi.org/10.1016/0890-5401(87)90052-6
3. Balcázar, J., Díaz, J., Gavaldà, R., Watanabe, O.: Algorithms for learning finite automata from queries: a unified view. In: Du, D.Z., Ko, K.-I. (eds.) Advances in Algorithms, Languages, and Complexity, pp. 53–72. Springer, New York (1997). http://dx.doi.org/10.1007/978-1-4613-3394-4_2
4. Barringer, H., Giannakopoulou, D., Pasareanu, C.S.: Proof rules for automated compositional verification through learning. In: Proceedings of the SAVCBS Workshop, pp. 14–21 (2003). http://citeseerx.ist.psu.edu/viewdoc/summary?doi=10.1.1.3.8668
5. Hagerer, A., Hungar, H.: Model generation by moderated regular extrapolation. In: Kutsche, R.-D., Weber, H. (eds.) FASE 2002. LNCS, vol. 2306, p. 80. Springer, Heidelberg (2002)
6. Howar, F., Steffen, B., Merten, M.: Automata learning with automated alphabet abstraction refinement. In: Jhala, R., Schmidt, D. (eds.) VMCAI 2011. LNCS, vol. 6538, pp. 263–277. Springer, Heidelberg (2011)
7. Hungar, H., Niese, O., Steffen, B.: Domain-specific optimization in automata learning. In: Hunt Jr., W.A., Somenzi, F. (eds.) CAV 2003. LNCS, vol. 2725, pp. 315–327. Springer, Heidelberg (2003)
8. Kardkovács, Z.T., Kovács, G.: Finding sequential patterns with TF-IDF metrics in health-care databases. Acta Universitatis Sapientiae Informatica **6**(2), 287–310 (2015). http://doi.org/10.1515/ausi-2015-0008
9. Lee, D., Yannakakis, M.: Principles and methods of testing finite state machines: a survey. Proc. IEEE **84**(8), 1090–1123 (1996). http://doi.org/10.1109/5.533956
10. Li, K., Groz, R., Shahbaz, M.: Integration testing of components guided by incremental state machine learning. In: TAIC PART, pp. 59–70. IEEE Computer Society (2006). http://dblp.uni-trier.de/db/conf/taicpart/taicpart2006.html#LiGS06
11. Pfleeger, C.: State reduction in incompletely specified finite-state machines. IEEE Trans. Comput. **C-22**(12), 1099–1102 (1973). http://doi.org/10.1109/T-C.1973.223655
12. Prajapati, G.L.: Advances in learning formal languages. In: International MultiConference of Engineers and Computer Scientists, IMECS 2011, pp. 118–126. International Association of Engineers, Hong Kong, 16–18 March 2011. http://www.iaeng.org/publication/IMECS2011/IMECS2011_pp118-126.pdf
13. Rivest, R.L., Schapire, R.E.: Inference of finite automata using homing sequences. In: Proceedings of the Twenty-first Annual ACM Symposium on Theory of Computing, STOC 1989, pp. 411–420. ACM, New York (1989). http://doi.acm.org/10.1145/73007.73047

14. Shahbaz, M., Li, K., Groz, R.: Learning parameterized state machine model for integration testing. In: 31st Annual International Computer Software and Applications Conference, COMPSAC 2007, vol. 2, pp. 755–760, July 2007. http://doi.org/10.1109/COMPSAC.2007.134

15. Srikant, R., Agrawal, R.: Miningsequential patterns: generalizations and performance improvements. In: Apers, P.M.G., Bouzeghoub, M., Gardarin, G. (eds.) EDBT 1996. LNCS, vol. 1057. Springer, Heidelberg (1996). http://dl.acm.org/citation.cfm?id=645337.650382

Author Index

Printed in the United States
By Bookmasters